PALMYRA AFTER ZENOBIA
273–750

An archaeological and historical reappraisal

Emanuele E. Intagliata

OXBOW | books
Oxford & Philadelphia

Published in the United Kingdom in 2018 by
OXBOW BOOKS
The Old Music Hall, 106–108 Cowley Road, Oxford OX4 1JE

and in the United States by
OXBOW BOOKS
1950 Lawrence Road, Havertown, PA 19083

Hardback Edition: ISBN 978-1-78570-942-5
Digital Edition: ISBN 978-1-78570-943-2 (epub)

A CIP record for this book is available from the British Library

Library of Congress Control Number: 2018931550

For a complete list of Oxbow titles, please contact:

UNITED KINGDOM
Oxbow Books
Telephone (01865) 241249, Fax (01865) 794449
Email: oxbow@oxbowbooks.com
www.oxbowbooks.com

UNITED STATES OF AMERICA
Oxbow Books
Telephone (800) 791-9354, Fax (610) 853-9146
Email: queries@casemateacademic.com
www.casemateacademic.com/oxbow

Oxbow Books is part of the Casemate Group

Front cover, *Great Colonnade, Palmyra (Pal.M.A.I.S. photo archive. Courtesy of the Pal.M.A.I.S. archaeological team, Università degli Studi di Milano).*

Contents

Acknowledgements

This book is the result of a Ph.D. conducted at the University of Edinburgh under the supervision of Jim Crow and Andrew Marsham, whose useful advice greatly contributed to shape my research. Enrico Zanini, Antonio Iacobini, Alessandra Guiglia (Centro di Documentazione di Storia dell'Arte Bizantina, Sapienza, Università di Roma), Patrick Michel, and Anne Bielman (Fonds d'Archives Paul Collart, Université de Lausanne) granted me access to their archives and provided me with the necessary equipment to conduct the research *in loco*. The research trips to Lausanne and Rome would not have been possible without the financial support of the School of History, Classics, and Archaeology, University of Edinburgh.

Other people contributed with their ideas to this volume, including Bryan Ward-Perkins, Ine Jacobs, and Eberhard Sauer. Klaus Schnädelbach kindly provided me the results of his topographic work of the site. Further support came from the Pal.M.A.I.S. team (Palmira, Missione Archeologica Italo-Siriana), in particular the director, Maria Teresa Grassi. Izdihar Alodhami, Ahmed Hussien, Teba Tarek, Andrew Marsham, and Jakko Hämeen-Antilla helped me greatly with the translation of Arabic texts; Calum Maciver provided invaluable assistance for the translation of Greek. Patient readers of early drafts of this book were Alessandro Gnasso, Doreen and Anne Intagliata, James Pietro Zanzarelli, Eystein Thanish, Daniel O'Meara, Annamaria Diana, and John Forsyth. Udo Hartmann read the final manuscript and provided very useful scientific advice. My parents shared with me all the joys and sorrows of this research during my Ph.D. and Marta Carlotta Ravizza supported me patiently during the final stage of writing this book. To all of them goes my deepest gratitude.

List of illustrations

Introduction

Dating back to the first serious Western inquiries concerning the site, the history of Palmyra, the 'bride of the desert', is split into two phases with the events of 272–273 at the centre.[1] The first three centuries were a period of prosperity for the city. Palmyra flourished as a crucial caravan centre during the time. Its community was thriving; its art, architecture, and language (Palmyrene, a west Aramaic dialect) are all proofs of the existence of a well-rooted, autonomous identity that was the result of complex cross-cultural interrelations between the East and the West. Most of the archaeological remains still visible today in Palmyra are the direct expression of this culturally mixed community and it is mainly to these remains that the city owes its fame. As a matter of fact, the grandeur and splendour of the unique architecture that developed between the 1st and the 3rd centuries was the first criterion behind the choice of Palmyra as a UNESCO World Heritage Site (UNESCO [n.d.]). The commercial prosperity of the settlement ceased abruptly after the attempt at usurpation by Zenobia and the reaction of the Roman emperor Aurelian (270–275) who marched to the city and put an end to the ambitions of the queen in 272. Written sources report how Palmyra was utterly destroyed (or at least suffered considerable damage) after Aurelian repressed a second revolt in 273 (Zos., *Hist. Nov.* 1.61; *HA Aurelianus* 31.5–9).

As early as the first travels by Europeans to the city, Palmyra has been associated with the Zenobian struggles for independence against oppressive Imperial authority and the monumental archaeological remains from Roman times. Aided by the position of the settlement at the fringe of the desert, these factors have contributed to the creation of a romantic and picturesque image of this ruined city in which the less impressive post-Roman remains have rarely found space. Indeed, a generalised story of decline, greatly inflated by neoclassical scholars and travellers, has dominated the theory used in secondary literature to describe the fate of this settlement following the collapse of the Palmyrene power.

The poor attention granted to Late Antique and Early Islamic Palmyra by the secondary literature, however, does not do justice to the importance of the city in this period. Despite having lost its commercial position in the east–west caravan trade, Palmyra maintained a strategic role throughout Late Antiquity as a stronghold along the eastern borderlands, hosting one legion in the 4th century and one of the two *duces* of *Phoenicia Libanensis* in the first half of the 6th century. In the Early Islamic period, the city remained the political centre of the powerful Banū Kalb and played a pivotal role in supporting the caliphate until the collapse of the Umayyad dynasty. After this event, Palmyra became a minor settlement, experiencing a process of major shrinkage that ended with the creation of a village within the *temenos* of the Sanctuary of Bēl.

The aim of this book is to propose an account of the history of the city during this 'dark age', from the second Palmyrene revolt until the end of Umayyad rule (273–750). For the sake of convenience, the period between 273 and 634, which also includes the short Persian occupation of Syria (613–628), is here considered 'Late Antiquity'. 'Early Islamic period' will indicate the time span between the Muslim conquest of the city (634) and the end of the Umayyad dynasty (750). In ʿAbbāsid time, life in the settlement seems to have continued, albeit in a much reduced way, roughly until the mid-9th century. However, little evidence is left to account for the history of the city during this period and, for this reason, this will mostly be excluded from this study. Before sketching an account of the city's post-Roman history (Chapter 7), a number of research themes or specific items of evidence for which enough material is available to work with are explored in each chapter. These are: Palmyra's hinterland (Chapter 1), post-Classical urbanism (Chapter 2), Palmyrene society through the lens of archaeological evidence from private residential buildings (Chapter 3), religious life (Chapter 4), the military (Chapter 5), and the city's defences (Chapter 6). This is believed to be indispensable in order to present for the first time the totality of the scattered data available in a single, consistent contribution, revise old theories, and propose new. A concluding chapter (Chapter 8) will compare the archaeological evidence from Palmyra with that of other Late Antique sites in the Near East to look at the city through a much wider perspective. An appendix collates the written sources in translation used in the main text.

Framing the research. Secondary literature on Late Antique and Early Islamic Palmyra

This contribution stands at the end of a long history of studies dating back to the first Western expeditions to the site in the late 17th century. The literature on Palmyra prior to 1960 commonly pays particular attention to the events of the late 3rd century. By contrast, the post-Roman phase is often regarded as an uneventful time of decline that is only partially halted by the urban renovation under Justinian reported by Procopius (*Aed*., 2.11.10–12), Malalas (*Chr*., 17.2), and Theophanes (*Chr*., 1.174). A small group of writers, among whom are Halley (1695) and Seller (1705), makes the beginning of this decline coincide with the 'wars of the Saracen Empire' (Halley 1695, 167). This theory frequently appears in the first studies of the site, which see in the conquest of the city by Khālid b. al-Walīd the victory of Islam over Christianity; it is also common in some of the works written in the 1930s and 1940s, possibly under the influence of Pirenne's theory (e.g., Puchstein 1932, 17).

The majority of the writers, however, associated the decline of the city with the Aurelianic disruptions of 272–273. The causes behind the formation of such a theory are many and include the apparent lack of inscriptions after this date, as well as the claims of decline by Procopius. Wood can be said to have been the initiator of this trend. This scholar believes that the fate of the city after Diocletian's reign became rather obscure, stating that, well before the Justinianic renovations, Palmyra had already '... lost its liberty, trade, property and inhabitants ...' (Wood 1753, 20). In a paragraph tellingly entitled 'why the decay of Palmyra was so quick' he claims that the main cause of Palmyra's decline was the abrupt halt of commerce, which had been the main source of subsistence for the city in Roman times (Wood 1753, 20). Similarly, in his seminal work, Gibbon argues that, after the military operations led by Aurelian, 'the seat of commerce, of arts and of Zenobia, gradually sunk into an obscure town, a trifling fortress, and at length a miserable village' (Gibbon 1831, 117). In line with Wood's finding, the events relating to the fall of Zenobia are here clearly seen as the main causes of a sudden transition from a phase of prosperity to one of decay. The words of Woods and Gibbon seem to have inspired the works of contemporary and later travellers to the city, as suggested by the colourful account by Wright written in 1895. Having devoted five chapters to a description of Zenobia's rise and fall, Wright continues his narration by discussing the 'decadence of Palmyra' in a period when '... the meteor-like glory of Tadmur became a thing of the past ...' (Wright 1895, 169; similarly, Maudrel and Shaw 1758, 302). The prevalence of decline in the common theory resulted in the gradual construction of a scholarly 'barrier' that prevented the development of systematic studies devoted to the Late Antique and Early Islamic phases.

In their assessment of the development of Palmyra during its latest phases, these pre-20th century works show two main limitations. The first is a complete lack of reference to Arabic written sources. The work of Grimme, published in Latin in 1886, stands distinctively apart from this trend. The volume, entitled *Palmyrae sive Tadmur urbis fata quae fuerint tempore muslimico*, presents a short history of the city after 273, deliberately omitting the Roman period. Upon examining Arabic sources, Grimme reaches the conclusion that Palmyra was somehow prosperous in the Early Islamic period and was relegated to a minor city only after the end of the Umayyad rule, when the capital was transferred from Damascus to Baghdad (Grimme 1886, 20). Despite having introduced new elements of discussion, however, the work does not seem to have imparted new directions for the ensuing studies.

A second limitation of the early literature is the almost complete lack of any reference to archaeological material, as systematic excavation would not start before the beginning of the 20th century. Two important milestones in the archaeological exploration of Palmyra are the German surveys directed by Wiegand between 1902 and 1917 and the excavations of Gabriel in the 1920s, sponsored by the Académie des Inscriptions et Belle-Lettres (Gabriel 1926; Wiegand 1932a). Although most of the efforts of these scholars were concerned with the monumental remains from Roman times, their works also present information on later buildings. Gabriel's article, for example, shows the plan of two churches in the northwest quarter and goes farther in suggesting that one of them (Church IV) was the cathedral of the city constructed as early as the first half of the 4th century. Yet, the scholar does not express his views on the putative decline of the city. Puchstein (1932, 17), a member of the German expedition directed by Wiegand, believes that the city experienced important urban transformations in Late Antiquity and proposed that its collapse coincided with the coming of Islam.

The 1930s marked a new surge of interest in Late Antique Palmyra. The clearance of the village set within the *temenos* of the Sanctuary of Bēl early in that decade and the dismantling of a mosque installed within its *cella* made it possible to study the architecture of this religious compound for the first time (Dussaud 1930; 1931; Mouterde 1930). The last private residential buildings 'de l'époque ottomane' that surrounded the sanctuary were only dismantled in 1964 (Bounni and Saliby 1965, 121). In their volume dedicated to the sanctuary, Amy, Seyrig and Will (1975, 157–60) document the presence of paintings on the eastern wall of the temple featuring Jesus among saints and suggest the *cella* was converted into a church in the 5th century. The epigraphic surveys published by Cantineau from the beginning of the decade had greatly contributed to the discussion by revealing the existence of significant amounts of evidence, such as the inscription commemorating the construction of the Baths of Diocletian in the city centre by the governor of *Phoenicia Libanenis*, Sossianus Hierocles (*Inv.* 6, 7, n. 2 = *IGLS* 17.1, 112–14, n. 100). It was indeed this inscription that inclined Seyrig to think that '*on à généralement pris trop à la lettre les rapports sur la destruction de Palmyre par Aurélien. En réalité, la depopulation ne fut pas immédiate …*' (Seyrig 1931, 323), an idea taken to an extreme by Cantineau who, a few years later, would write '*d'abord à la fin de l'époque romaine et à l'époque byzantine, Palmyre est restée ce quelle était avant 272, c'est a dire une grande ville*' (Cantineau 1934, 6). The same author, in his *Le dialecte arabe de Palmyre*, prefers not to take any position on the supposed Early Islamic decline of the city, presumably being split between the current Pirenne debate and the work of Grimme, the latter referenced in his volume (Cantineau 1934, 7). In contrast to Late Antique orientated studies, those on Islamic Palmyra of the first half of the 20th century were limited to a very small number of contributions on four medieval Arabic inscriptions (Huart 1929; Sauvaget 1931) and the ramparts (Seyrig 1950).

Despite this, the idea of a post-273 decline and abandonment of Palmyra remained virtually unaltered and interest in the topic gradually diminished. In Starcky's general work on Palmyra, published in the series *Orient Ancient Illustré*, the narration of the post-Zenobian phase of the city is dismissed in a short epilogue (Starcky 1952, 66–8). The 1951 publication of *La Palmyrene du Nord-Ouest* by Schlumberger represents another emblematic example of this tendency. The work discusses the results of the fieldwork conducted in 1934–1935 in 18 sites in the city's hinterland. The writer conclusively states that '*… les époques posterieures á la chute de Palmyre n'ont laissé ells-mêmes que de tres faibles traces… La fin brutale de la grandeur de Palmyre marque certainement aussi la fin de la prospérité de notre région*' (Schlumberger 1951, 133).

The year 1959 marked the beginning of the excavations of the Camp of Diocletian by the Polish team directed by Michałowski and new attention being paid to the latest phases of occupation of the city (Michałowski 1960a). Michałowski and his team documented systematically for the first time the superimposition of modest 'Byzantine' and 'Arab' dwellings in a monumental setting, indirectly claiming the necessity for more exhaustive archaeological investigation not focussed solely on the impressive architecture of Roman times. The scholar seems to have been reluctant to express any judgement on the Late Antique and Early Islamic phases of the city in his reports. Yet, only a few years later, he would give expression to his ideas by dismissing the post-Diocletianic history of the city as 'purely local' (Michałowski 1970, 8). This newly born attention to the post-Roman remains is evident from reading the reports of the excavation of the Sanctuary of Baalshamīn by Collart and his team. The work mostly focusses on the Roman phase of the religious compound, but it does not omit to describe, albeit succinctly, later remains (Collart and Vicari 1969, 84–6). In particular, it concentrates on several structures occupying the temple and its northern courtyard (regarded respectively as a church and private residential buildings).

By the mid-1960s, the mass of archaeological data collected was already impressive. Four intramural churches were known: two churches in the northwest quarter, one church installed in the temple of the Sanctuary of Bēl, and the supposed church in the Sanctuary of Baalshamīn. The excavations of the Camp of Diocletian, the Great Colonnade (Bounni and Saliby 1965), the cemetery in the garden of the Archaeological Museum (al-As'ad 1967; 1968; al-As'ad and Ruprechtsberger 1987, 137–46), and the Sanctuaries of Baalshamīn and Nabū (Bounni 1990; 2004 Bounni *et al.* 1992) uncovered later structures on top of Roman remains and funerary inscriptions that were indisputable proof of a continuous occupation of the site throughout Late Antiquity and the Early Islamic period. At that time, the conclusion advanced by van Berchem (1954) on a Diocletianic chronology of the ramparts of Palmyra had already been universally accepted by the scholarly community. The position of most scholars on the total destruction of Palmyra in 273 is summarised in an article by Will, published in 1966. Having gathered the archaeological data at his disposal, the writer would conclude that '*que Palmyre ait été réduit dès la fin du IIIe siècle au rang d'une simple bourge paraît aujourd'hui tout á fait insoutenable, bien que la chose s'imprime encore á l'occasion. La ville connut une survie plus ou moins honorable jusque dans les premiers temps de la conquête arabe*' (Will 1966, 1411; 1983, 81).

This conclusion would remain substantially unaltered throughout the following decade. In discussing the chronology of the ramparts in 1975, Crouch (1975a, 41) would argue that, 'we must remember that to us the sack of Palmyra by Aurelian's troop was a traumatic event from which the city never recovered, but to the people of the time, it may have been an important but not final event.' The archaeological investigations that followed essentially confirmed this stance. After the excavation of the *Via Praetoria* and the *Principia* of the Camp of Diocletian, the Polish team in 1974 started the work in the Sanctuary of Allāth. The fieldwork ended in 1979 and resulted not only in a better understanding of the religious compound itself, but also in the defining the chronological evolution of its phases of destruction and abandonment at the end of the 4th century. This was believed to have been the result of the anti-pagan measures of Theodosius and the visit of Maternus Cynegius to the city (Gąssowska 1982). By the end of the 1970s, it was thus commonly accepted that the Aurelianic events had not marked the beginning of a phase of abandonment. Excavations had helped define the changed role of Palmyra in Late Antiquity from a caravan city to a military fortress (e.g., Grabar *et al.* 1978, 5), rectifying the information provided by ancient textual sources, whose truthfulness had by then been undermined through archaeological investigations.

If the 1960s and 1970s saw a gradual surge of interest in the city's Late Antique phase, the following two decades marked the beginning of a new, positive attitude towards Early Islamic remains. This was triggered by an important discovery in the heart of the ancient city. In 1977, the Syrian authorities under the direction of A. and M. Taha, started clearing up the westernmost section of the Great Colonnade (Section C). The excavations, which were part of a larger project conducted by the Syrian authorities from the late 1950s in the city centre (Bounni 1967; 1971; 1995), lasted until 1984 and resulted in the unearthing of 47 small rooms in the carriageway of the street. The remains attracted the attention of the Polish team that carried out several soundings in 1985–1986 and dated the structures to between the late 7th and the first half of the 8th centuries (al-As῾ad and Stępniowski 1989). The uncovering of the Umayyad *Sūq* contributed to fitting the settlement into ongoing scholarly debate from which it had been previously excluded. The existence of the *sūq* was considered evidence in support of the theories postulated by Sauvaget around 50 years previously on the disintegration of the Classical city plan in Islamic times and first applied to Latakia (Sauvaget 1934) and then to Aleppo (Sauvaget 1941).

From the early 1980s, archaeological investigations of the site intensified significantly. Excavations have been conducted by international archaeological teams in tandem with the Directorate-General of Antiquities and Museums (DGAM). In the mid-1980s, the Syro-Polish team, which had always shown interest in the post-Roman phase of the city, started the investigations of the northwest quarter under the direction of Gawlikowski. This area, which beyond Gabriel's work, had remained almost totally unexplored in the past, disclosed, *inter alia*, two more churches with their dependencies and a large block house. The Syro-Polish excavations also contributed greatly to shedding more light on the two ecclesiastical buildings identified by Gabriel at the beginning of the century. If building activities on the churches seemed to have been mainly concentrated in the 6th century, the house appeared to have been occupied from Roman times up to the Early Islamic period (overviews in Gawlikowski 1997a; 2001; see Chapter 3). A survey conducted by Majcherek in 2005 within the city walls resulted in the identification of three more churches along the Great Colonnade, which were tentatively dated to the reign of Justinian (Majcherek 2005). More recently, a Syro-Italian team operated in the southwest quarter, between 2007 and 2010. Having surveyed the whole area, the team directed its efforts to the excavation of the so-called Peristyle Building, the original phase of which has been dated to between the end of the 2nd and the beginning of the 3rd century (Grassi 2009a; 2009b; 2010; 2011; 2012; Grassi and al-As῾ad 2013). Nonetheless the structure had apparently undergone considerable later restorations, among them being the subdivision of large rooms into smaller units and the blocking of passageways and the intercolumnia of the peristyle of the courtyard.

Investigations by the Syro-French team in 2001–2005 in the Suburban Market has also shown that the occupation of the northwest quarter continued well into the Early Islamic period. The building, possibly a *macellum* in Roman times, underwent substantial later alterations, including the monumentalisation of the entrance gate, the installation of dwellings in the western wing, and the formation of a cemetery in the eastern wing. Archaeological investigations were also conducted in two nearby U-shaped towers flanking the 'Dura Gate' [A305] further north (Delplace 2006–2007; 2013). Not far from the Syro-French group's work area, the Syro-Swiss team directed by Genequand has identified a mosque installed in a former *caesareum*, immediately next to the Umayyad *Sūq* (Genequand 2008a; 2009a, 189; 2010; 2011; 2012, 52–66; 2013). Previous surveys by Genequand (2012; see Chapter 2) in the hinterland of Palmyra, mostly focussed on the study of aristocratic Umayyad residences, suggest that Schlumberger's theory on the collapse of the broader Palmyrene region after the Zenobian collapse must also be revised. This conclusion seems to be supported by recent surveys in the northwest region of Palmyra carried out by a Syro-Norwegian team (Meyer 2008; 2009; 2011; 2013).

A significant contribution to the understanding of post-Roman Palmyra comes not only from reports of excavations, numerous but quite often preliminary in their nature, but also from a new approach to the research already in motion in the 1980s and continuing nowadays (e.g., al-As῾ad and Ruprechtsberger 1987; Genequand 2012, 25–67), which aims to re-analyse and re-interpret evidence already brought to light. The three pioneering works of Kowalski can be considered as emblematic of this tendency. In 1994, Kowalski presented the unpublished results of the excavation the *Praetorium* of the Camp of Diocletian, which was unearthed during the 1975–1976 excavation of the Sanctuary of Allāth. A 1996 article in *Damaszener Mitteilungen* revised the conclusions reached by Collart and Vicari in 1969, rejecting the hypothesis that the Late Antique remains to be found within the temple of the Sanctuary of Baalshamīn are those of an early 5th century church. In 1997, Kowalski published in *Studia Palmyreńskie* his oft-quoted 'Late Roman Palmyra in literature and epigraphy', which is the first systematic attempt at a history of the city after 273; the article combines the analysis of written sources and epigraphic material, and has, inevitably, inspired the research methodology of this book.

The evidence in use and its limits

Despite sharing a similar methodological approach, this book distances itself from the work of Kowalski by stressing the significance of the evidence of the archaeological record, the abundance of which cannot be ignored when drawing up a history of Palmyra in Late Antiquity and the Early Islamic period. Specifically, archaeological evidence is here analysed within a broad geographical focus, in order to understand whether the situation in Palmyra differs from or resembles other contemporary urban centres. The interpretation of the three main data sets considered in this book – that is to say, archaeology, ancient written sources, and epigraphy – is generally, however, blurred by an extensive array of problems, whose existence should be stressed from the very beginning of this inquiry.

Archaeology

The archaeological record, which has been discussed briefly in the previous section, will be presented in more detail in the course of the book. For the time being, it suffices to say that the majority of the evidence is normally to be found in the form of brief mentions scattered through more extensive interim reports in journals or conference proceedings. The mass of archaeological data is unbalanced, as some areas or buildings are better studied than others. The absence of evidence, therefore, does not necessarily betray phases of decline or abandonment of certain sectors of the site; rather, in most cases, this reflects a patchy and incomplete state of research. A large amount of the archaeological evidence is from the Camp of Diocletian and the northwest quarter, investigated, as seen, since the late 1950s; other areas have undergone less intense archaeological investigations – either because they are occupied by modern constructions, for example the area of the oasis, or because they have only recently attracted the attention of the scholarly community, for example, the southwest quarter. 'Love for the original' might also explain the lack of data from certain areas; earlier excavations might have compromised our knowledge of the development of certain buildings by removing evidence to reach pre-273 phases.

The nature of the evidence, which most of the time consists of unattractive walls made of reused architectural elements within more pretentious Roman buildings, have often failed to fascinate the archaeologist. Consequent problems may arise in the interpretation of published plans in which, for example, boundaries between buildings are not traced clearly or certain phenomena, such as the blocking of passageways, have not been considered worthy of being documented. As far as the chronology is concerned, it is important to stress the high degree of uncertainty surrounding some of the evidence, which, especially for old reports, has often been given only broad chronological labels ('Byzantine', 'Late Antique', 'Islamic', or 'Arabic'). Indeed, not infrequently the main criterion for dating a building is based on fragile associations with written sources. Stratigraphic sequences are very sporadically provided. Typological studies on bulk material, such as pottery or glass, are lacking. If scientific dating analyses (e.g., radiocarbon dating) have been conducted, these have never been published.

For the purpose of this book, some gaps in the documentation of a number of published archaeological features have had to be patched with unpublished data – archival material, in particular. The most significant data presented is from the Centro di Documentazione di Storia dell'Arte Bizantina at Sapienza, Università di Roma. The archive at Rome holds an impressive amount of photographs taken by de' Maffei and his team in Palmyra during two field-surveys conducted in 1987 and 1990. The main target of these shots was the circuit wall of Palmyra. The documentary importance of this archival material should not be underestimated. The photographs taken by de' Maffei show the urban circuit as it was before the recent restorations conducted by the Syrian authorities greatly affected the legibility of the structure of the wall.

Written sources

Written sources constitute a welcome addition to the archaeological data set (see Appendix). The nature of these for Late Antiquity is most varied. Religion is a component of the city's history that is overall better represented than others. Michael the Syrian (*Chr.*, 3.453; 7.2; 9.13; 11.3), 1126–1199, and the *Chronicle of Zuqnin* (3.19), dating from the last quarter of the 8th century, are most valuable informants in Syriac, providing a handful of names of some of the bishops in charge from the Council of Nicaea (325) up until the early 9th century. A colophon in a manuscript held at the British Museum (mid-6th century), written at a monastery near Palmyra, complete the corpus of the already translated Syriac texts mentioning this site (Wright 1872, 2.468, n. 585). Additional information on bishops' names and, more generically, the importance of Palmyra as a Christian centre compared to other settlements, can be obtained from the *Notitia Antiochena* (Honigmann 1925, 75), compiled by the patriarch Anastasius (d. 570), and the information gathered in 18th century works, namely those of Le Quien (1740, 2, 845) and Mansi (1762, 921).

As far as administrative documents are concerned, there is very little left on which to speculate. The *Notitia Dignitatum* (22.30), late 4th century, reports that the city was the base of the commander of the *Legio I Illyricorum*; it also informs about the existence of auxiliary Palmyrene forces (*Not. Dig., Or.*, 7.34; 31.49). The city is further mentioned in the lists of Hierocles (*Synec.*, 717.1–8), early 6th century, George of Cyprus (*Descr. Orb. Rom.*, 984–996), early 7th century, and Stephanus of Byzantium (*Ethnika*, Π 6), 6th century. The vignette representing Palmyra in the *Tabula Peutingeriana* (seg. 10–11), a 4th century *itinerarium pictum*, elevates this settlement to the status of an important stop along the way to Damascus, overall confirming the general impression presented by these administrative documents.

Besides these, more descriptive accounts also exist. Although they certainly provide invaluable insights on the history of the city, they should be taken with reservations, as sometimes they do not match the information from other sources or the archaeological record and, in most cases, they are late informants of the events narrated. The author of the *Historia Augusta, Vita Aureliani* (31.5–9), probably written shortly after the death of Theodosius, and Zosimus' *Historia Nova* (1.60–1), early 6th century, provide accounts of the reconquest of the city by Aurelian in 273, but contain considerable discrepancies. The 5th century is represented only by several mentions in a passage of the *Dialogue of John Chrysostom* (*Pall., Dial. John Chris.*, 20.35–8), composed in *c.* 408 by Palladius of Galatia (*c.* 363–431) and the anonymous *Life of Alexander the Akoimētes* (*Alex. Akoim.*, 35), late 5th to early 6th century. The former reports the exile in Palmyra of Cyriacus; the mention of Palmyra lying 'eight milestones from Emesa' (modern Homs, *c.* 145km from Palmyra, as the crow flies) suggests that the writer, like probably most of those listed here, had never visited the settlement. The passage in the *Life of Alexander the Akoimētes* provides a pitiless account of the state of its inhabitants, who are almost at the point of starvation.

The Justinianic renovation of the city is recounted by Procopius (*Aed.*, 2.11, 10–12), 6th century, Malalas (*Chr.*, 17.2), *c.* 491–578, and Theophanes (*Chr.*, 1.174), 759/760–818. Procopius' general tendency to glorify the conduct of the emperor is well-known and should, thus, put the reader on guard (Cameron 1985, 12–13). Indeed, some of the information in his writings does not match with that in the works of the contemporary Malalas and of the later Theophanes, who follows the latter. Sources mentioning events of the early 7th century are not frequent. Two Arabic writers, Ḥamza al-Iṣfahānī (*Tā'rīkh*, 121), *c.* 893–961, and Abū al-Fidā' (*Taqwīm al-buldān*, 128–30), 1273–1332, report the city to be under the rule of al-Ayham b. Jabala. The account of the life of St Anastasius (*Anas. Per.,* 1.102–4, 129–30), composed in the early 630s, also mentions Palmyra, claiming that this is the site by which the relics of the holy man passed on their way to Jerusalem and where they performed a miracle healing a young blind man.

Nothing is left that documents the short Persian occupation of the city, while the Umayyad history of the site is, overall, well-discussed by Arabic written sources. The bulk of ancient authors writing on the Early Islamic fate of Palmyra comprise historians, biographers, geographers, and poets, none of whom is contemporary with the events narrated. The conquest of the city by Khālid b. al-Walīd in 634 appears to be a most popular episode. Al-Wāqidī (*al-Maghāzī,* 1.44), 747/748–822, and Ibn A'tham al-Kūfī (*Kitāb*, 1.140–2), 8th to 9th century, provide the longest accounts of the conquest; conversely, al-Balādhurī (*Futūḥ*, 111–12), author of a renowned account of the Islamic conquest of the Levant based on earlier sources, d. *c.* 892, and al-Ṭabarī (*Tā'rīkh*, 4.2109), 839–923, who wrote a monumental history from creation until 915, discuss the event only marginally. Among other authors mentioning the episode are al-'Uṣfurī (*Tā'rīkh*, 1.103), d. 854, al-Ya'qūbī (*Tā'rīkh*, 2.134), 9th century, Ibn al-Faqīh (*Mukhtaṣar*, 125), 9th century, Ibn 'Asākir (*Tā'rīkh*, 2.80), d. 1175–1176, and Yāqūt (*Mu'jam,* 1.832), 1179–1229.

Besides the account of its capture, the history of Palmyra in Umayyad times as reported by Arabic written sources rests mainly on the involvement of the city on two major historical events. The first is the prelude to the battle of Marj Rāhiṭ (684), reported by al-Ṭabarī (*Tā'rīkh*, 7.482), Ibn 'Asākir (*Tā'rīkh*, 55.261), and Ibn al-Athīr (*al-Kāmil*, 4.125), 1160–1233; the long-term political implications of this battle, which consist of inter-tribal conflicts between the defeated Qays (mostly Banū 'Āmir and Banū Sulaym) and the Yemenites (Banū Kalb), are recounted by al-Iṣfahānī (*al-Aghānī*, 17.112–13; 22.120–1), 897–967, in two episodes. The second is the revolt led by Thābit b. Nu'aym against Marwān b. Muḥammad (745) known, *inter alia*, also through the pen of al-Hamadānī, 10th century, and which concluded with the alleged demolition of Palmyra's urban circuit (al-Ṭabarī, *Tā'rīkh*, 9.1892–3; 1895–1896; Ibn 'Asākir, *Tā'rīkh*, 17.326; 19.80; Ibn al-Faqīh, *Mukhtaṣar*, 110; Yāqūt, *Mu'jam*, 1.829; al-Hamadānī, *al-Iklīl*, 124).

The city is further mentioned briefly in other episodes, including a clash between al-Ḍaḥḥāk b. Qays and Ḥujr b. 'Adī al-Kindī, which occurred in or near the city during the first *fitna* (656–661) (al-Ṭabarī, *Tā'rīkh*, 6.3447; Ibn al-Athīr, *al-Kāmil*, 3.317), the decision of the caliph al-Walīd b. Yazīd (r. 743–744) to seek refuge at al-Bakhrā', rather than at other fortified places (including Palmyra) in order to escape from the usurper Yazīd b. al-Walīd, and his death, recounted also by Agapius (*Kitāb*, 511–512), 10th century (see al-Ṭabarī, *Tā'rīkh*, 9.1796; al-'Uṣfurī, *Tā'rīkh*, 2.548; Ibn 'Asākir, *Tā'rīkh*, 63.337–338, 345). Little is left by non-Arabic writers. Theophanes (*Chr.*, 1.422), who writes in Greek, mentions the fight between Sulaymān b. Hishām and the caliph Marwān b. Muḥammad, and Sulaymān's escape to Persia via Palmyra; the clash is further reported by the anonymous writer of the *Chronicle of 1234*, composed in the second quarter of the 13th century in Syriac (*Chron.* 1234, 321–2). As far as the later descriptions of Palmyra are concerned, the most detailed can be found in the works of geographers such as al-Muqaddasī (*Aḥsan*, 158–60), 10th century, al-Mas'ūdī (*Murūj*, 1.190; 4.77–8), *c.* 893–956, and al-Dimashqī (*Kitāb*, 39), d. 1327; the work of Ṣafī al-Dīn, d. 1338, *Marāṣid al-iṭṭilāʿ ʿalā asmāʾ al-amkina wa-al-biqāʿ*, in which Palmyra is mentioned (1.200), is a digest of Yāqūt's *Kitāb Muʿjam al-Buldān* (Gilliot 2005, 288).

Overall, it is wise to approach written sources with caution. The majority of ancient authors reporting on the fate of the city before the Muslim conquest have very likely never visited the settlement. Not infrequently, pieces of information given by contemporary written sources appear to contradict each other and in certain cases these are even altered in order to exalt and glorify the conduct of the emperor. The religious dimension is often much stressed; the history of Late Antique Palmyra, as seen through the lens of written sources, is mostly a Christian history and leaves little space for other religious minorities, which, however, existed and have left archaeological evidence. Written sources on Early Islamic Palmyra are mostly distinguished by the extreme repetitiveness of information that is characteristic of the historiographical approach of the time. Starting from common grounds, however, authors may provide different versions of the same episode or include additional information, the truthfulness of which should be taken with reservations. Certain episodes seem to have been more popular than others, such as for example the conquest of the city in 634. As the history of Palmyra through Arabic written sources is written from the point of view of the conquerors, some of the information might be biased to exalt the actions of the Muslims over the Romans. In any case, in both Late Antique and Islamic written sources, a fictional element seems to be very much present; sorting out truth from fiction is a thorny issue that can be attempted, not without difficulty, by setting written sources alongside the archaeological evidence.

Epigraphy

Late Antique and Early Islamic stone inscriptions are sporadic compared to their Roman counterparts. In the latest published catalogue by Yon, the dated Late Antique inscriptions from the city amounts to 35 out of a total of 260 (*IGLS* 17.1, 495–496). The comparative decline of inscriptions is associated with a change in the epigraphic habit and is not informative of a deterioration of the city's fortune (Genequand 2012, 25). A total of 54 stone inscriptions have been gathered for this book. These mostly include the inscriptions collated in the contribution by Yon, and a few more from the city itself and other nearby sites. With two exceptions (*Inv.* 9, 51, n. 39; *Ins. Jud. Or.* 3, *Syr.*, 75–6, n. 48), all are of Late Antique date. When the chronology is not provided in their texts, inscriptions are normally datable by the century. Their nature is varied. Most, however, fall within the funerary sphere; the quality of these is generally not particularly high, often consisting of letters poorly aligned and carved. A number of inscriptions commemorating the construction or reconstruction of specific buildings also exist. Religious dedications are less common before the flourishing of Christianity, but became more frequent later, mostly in the form of graffiti.

As far as the script is concerned, the last Aramaic stone inscription known from the city is dated 279–280 (al-Asʿad and Gawlikowski 1986–1987, 167–8, n. 8; *contra IGLS* 17.1, 96, n. 81 [179/180]; inscr. n. 7 in al-Asʿad and Gawlikowski 1986–1987, 167 = *IGLS* 17.1, 95, n. 80 might also be of the same date: Hartmann 2016, 66, n. 70). Bilingual inscriptions also disappear from the record after this date (but see *IGLS* 17.1, 114, n. 100). The few Latin inscriptions, such as the one commemorating the construction of the Camp of Diocletian (*IGLS* 17.1, 132–3, n. 121), are normally official in nature. One published graffito is in Arabic (*Inv.* 9, 51, n. 39), while five are in Hebrew script (*Ins. Jud. Or.* 3, *Syr.*, 70–6, n. 44–8). All the rest, from the one celebrating the 'building' (but more probably a rebuilding) of the Baths of Diocletian (*IGLS* 17.1,112–114, n. 100), to the graffiti made by devout Christian passers-by along the Great Colonnade (e.g., *IGLS* 17.1, 117, n. 105), are in Greek script.

A great deal of insight can be gathered from inscriptions on pottery, a potential source of information that has been surprisingly underrated by modern scholarship. Their importance should not be underestimated, as suggested by the recent epigraphic discoveries in the Peristyle Building: a Syriac inscription mentioning the personal name Daniel, which would prove that the script remained in use in the city well into Late Antiquity (Grassi *et al.* 2015, 32–3). With just very few exceptions (e.g. Lehner 1932, 107, n. 1; Michałowski 1964a, 184, fig. 214; Grassi *et al.* 2015, 32–3), the inscriptions on pottery published so far come mainly from the Sanctuary of Baalshamīn (Dunant 1975b). Most are in Greek and painted in red or black on transport containers. In most cases, inscriptions on pottery bear simply one or more personal names, possibly of the owner(s) or the producer(s) of the goods contained in the vessel, often preceded or followed by simple crosses or other Christian symbols, such as the eight-spoked wheel (Fig. 43); leaving aside one case (Dunant 1971, 125, n. 28), the occupations of these individuals are not specified in the surviving texts. *Ostraka* providing lists of names (debtors or creditors), inscriptions in Arabic (Dunant 1975b, 121, n. 5),and liturgical inscriptions on bread stamps, remain exceptional occurrences (Michałowski 1964a, 184, fig. 214).

Note

1 Dates are all AD unless specified otherwise. Designations of archaeological features in square brackets provided in the text adhere to the conventions set by Schnädelbach (2010). Except for major sites (e.g., Sirmium, Apamea) ancient place names are given in italics. Transliteration from the Arabic follows the standards of the *Encyclopaedia of Islam*, 3rd ed., with the exception of names of major sites or cities (e.g., Damascus, Homs).

Chapter 1

The Palmyrene

Palmyra was more than an urban area enclosed by a city wall. It also encompassed an extensive hinterland composed by a varied mosaic of smaller settlements, farmsteads, monasteries, forts, and residences of the aristocratic élite and the members of the ruling dynasty. The political, economic, and cultural relation between these and Palmyra must have been vibrant, influencing the history of the site to an extent that is very difficult to investigate in depth with the data at hand. In fact, compared with the evidence brought to light in Palmyra itself, the archaeology of the Palmyrene is still at its infancy. A work devoted to gather the Late Antique and Early Islamic evidence from the Palmyrene, with special focus on the diffused phenomenon of the Umayyad aristocratic residences, has been conducted recently (Genequand 2012). Yet, a brief overview of the archaeology of this region remains indispensable in order to set the city in context.

Palmyra's hinterland

The geography of the *regio Palmyrena* is marked by the presence of two groups of mountains, the Palmyrenides, originating to the west from the anti-Lebanon mountains. At the point where Palmyra is situated, the two groups counterpose and slope gently, thus creating a more easily accessible pass. Each group of the Palmyrenides includes a multitude of different mountain chains divided by steep valleys (Genequand 2012, 9–11). Separating the northern from the southern Palmyrenides is al-Daww, which is an oblong 8000m^2 plain, stretching from the region of Ḥuwwārīn for some 180km. The water flowing into this plain from the surrounding mountains infiltrates rapidly into the soil, feeding the springs of the region (Sanlaville and Traboulsi 1996, 29–30). At the deepest point of the Palmyrene depression (364m a.s.l.), to the southeast of the city, is a vast, 330km^2 salt flat, Ṣabkhat al-Mūḥ, which has benefited the local economy since antiquity (Teixidor 1984, 78–80). No major natural barriers occur to the east of Palmyra until the Euphrates River, which is 240km to the east, as the crow flies (Fig. 1). A plan of the city, with key places and buildings referred to in text, is provided in Figure 2. Figures 3 and 4 show the state of the ruins in 1932 (Autumn) and 1931 respectively.

The administrative limits of the territory under the jurisdiction of Palmyra in Roman times were influenced by the rough geography of the region. Boundary markers help draw two exact limits. One was set at Khirbat al-Bil'ās, to the northwest. Here, two inscriptions commemorate the re-establishment of a pre-existing boundary under Trajan and Antoninus; this had been originally set by Creticus Silanus in 11–17 (Schlumberger 1939a, 61–3). At this point, the *regio Palmyrena* may have adjoined either the territory under the jurisdiction of Antioch (Seyrig 1959, 190, n. 2), or that of Apamea (Balty and Balty 1977, 118). A third boundary marker found at Qaṣr al-Ḥayr al-Gharbī '*inter Hadrianos Palmyrenos et Hemesenos*' set a further limit to the southwest (Schlumberger 1939a, 63–4). The Palmyrenides might have worked as convenient natural boundaries to the north and south of the plain of al-Daww. To the east and southwest of the city no boundary markers are known, but it is very likely that the territory of Palmyra extended to the Euphrates River (Gawlikowski 1983d, 58; recently, Smith 2013, 4). So defined, the territory of Palmyra in Roman times was situated in the province of *Syria* and, with Septimius Severus, *Syria Phoenice*.

Our knowledge of the territory of Palmyra in Late Antiquity is more blurred than that of the Roman period, as no boundary markers are known for this period. It is likely that the mountainous geography of the region helped maintain the administrative boundaries already existing, with the exception, perhaps, of the area comprised between the city and the river Euphrates; this might have experienced a re-shuffle after the fall of Zenobia in the late 3rd century and the following period of political instability of the local nomadic component. At the time, Palmyra and its surroundings were situated in the province of *Phoenicia Libanensis* (Proc., *Aed.*, 6.1.1; 2.11.10; Hier., *Synec.*, 717.1–8; Georg. Cypr., *Descr. Orb. Rom.*, 984–96; *ACO* 2.5.46). Similar uncertainty shrouds our knowledge of the administrative boundaries of the Palmyrene territory

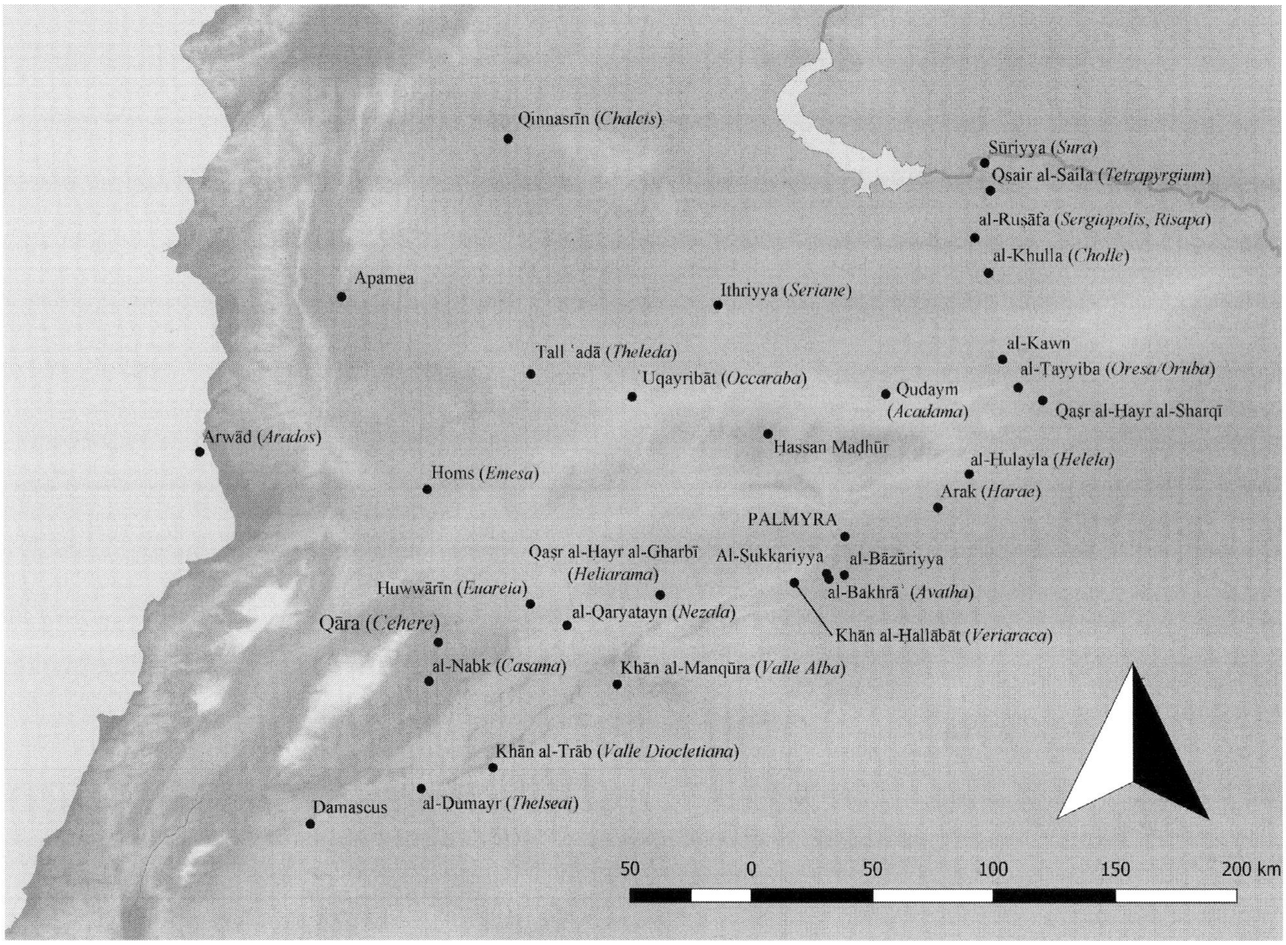

Figure 1. Main sites mentioned in the text (image: author).

in the Early Islamic period, as epigraphic evidence on this regard is non-existent. The general political geography of the time, however, is known. After the Islamic takeover, the provincial system at the base of the Byzantine administration underwent significant changes. During the caliphate of ʿUmar b. al-Khaṭṭāb (634–644), the province of *al-Shām* was created. This was split into four administrative and military districts called *ajnād* (sing. *jund*); Palmyra, and perhaps the territory formerly under its jurisdiction, became part of the *jund* of Homs, ancient Emesa (al-Muqaddasī, *Aḥsan*, 158–9).

A city 'built in a neighbourless region by men of former times'? Remarks on the regional road system, and evidence for travel and commerce

The liminal location of Palmyra and the Palmyrene as well as their remoteness are often emphasised in ancient written sources. Malalas (*Chr.*, 17.2) stresses the city's frontier location, while Theophanes (*Chr.*, 1.174) reports that Palmyra is situated 'on the inner *limes*' (εἰς τὸ λιμιτὸν τὸ ἐσώτερον). The passage of Theophanes has been the cause of confusion among modern historians and archaeologists. Starting from the influential work of Mouterde and Poidebard at the beginning of the last century, the word ἐσώτερον, usually rendered as 'inner' in translation, has often been used by scholars to support the existence of a frontier system consisting of two lines of defence: an 'inner', located around Qinnasrīn (*Chalcis*) and an 'outer' one running from Sūriyya (*Sura*) to Damascus via Palmyra (Mouterde and Poidebard 1945; however, this theory was discredited a long time ago, Liebeschuetz 1977, 487–8; more recently, Tate 1996; for an extended bibliography see, Konrad 1999, 392, n. 2). The translation of ἐσώτερον as 'inner' cannot be applied to our case study since if one has to follow Mouterde and Poidebard's model, Palmyra would be located on the 'outer' line. It is, therefore, likely that by using this term, Theophanes wanted simply to stress Palmyra's remote location at the fringe of the empire (Liebeschuetz 1977, 488). The idea of Palmyra as a settlement in an undefined, isolated, and faraway land had certainly developed earlier. In his *De Aedificiis,* Procopius (*Aed.*, 2.11.10) had already described the city as 'built in a neighbourless region by men of former times' (ἐν χώρα μὲν πεποιημένη τοῖς πάλαι ἀνθρώποις ἀγείτονι, tr. Dewing 1961, 177), and had taken

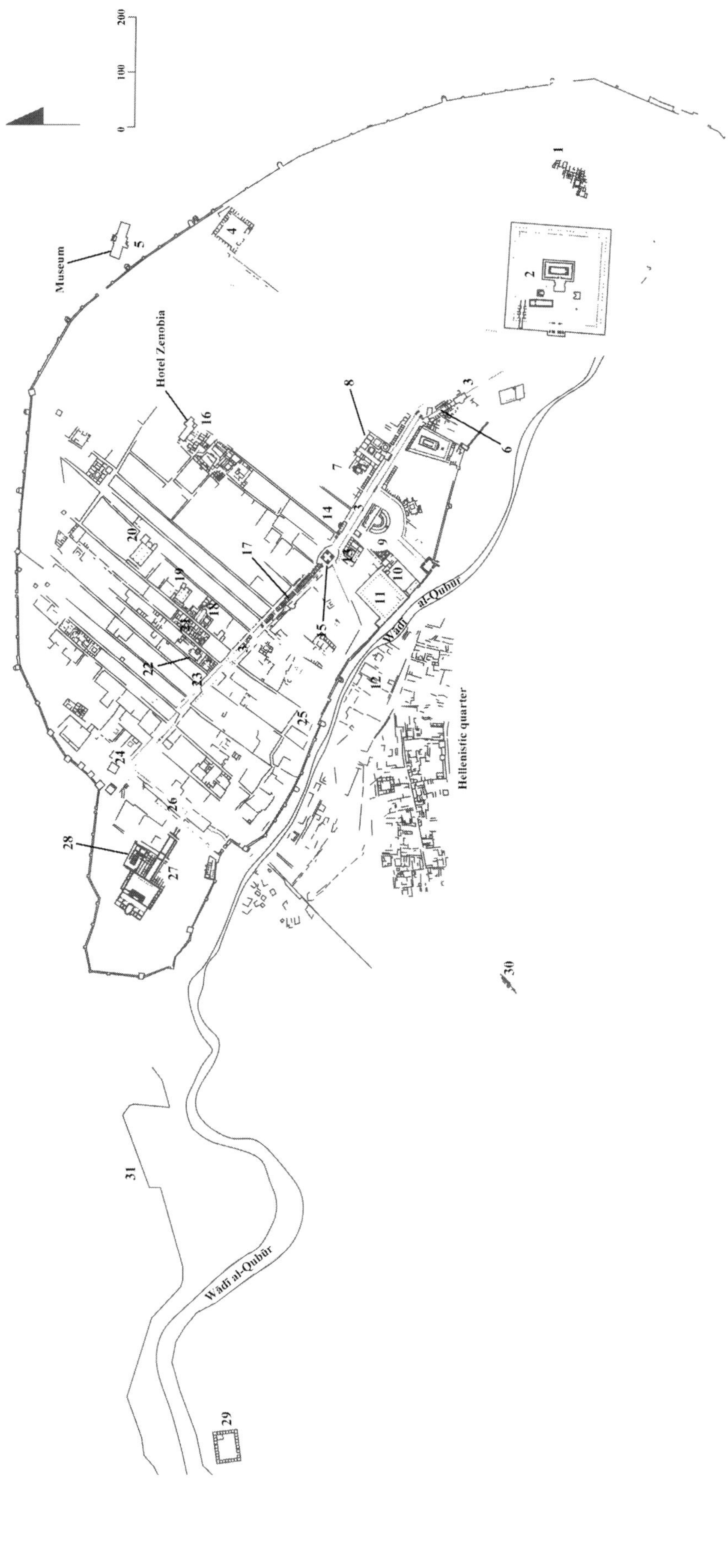

Figure 2. Plan of Palmyra. 1. Houses of Achilles and Cassiopea; 2. Sanctuary of Bēl; 3. Great Colonnade; 4. Suburban Market; 5. Byzantine Cemetery; 6. Buildings encroaching Section A of the Great Colonnade; 7. Church; 8. Baths of Diocletian; 9. Theatre; 10. Annexe of the Agora; 11. Agora; 12. Sanctuary of Arṣū; 13. Congregational Mosque; 14. Church; 15. Tetrapylon; *16. Sanctuary of Baalshamīn; 17. Umayyad* Sūq; *18. Church II; 19. Church III; 20. Church IV; 21. House F; 22. Church I; 23. Bellerophon Hall; 24. Church; 25. Peristyle Building; 26. Transverse Colonnade; 27. Camp of Diocletian; 28. Sanctuary of Allāth; 29. Building [Q281]; 30. Efqa spring; 31. Western Acqueduct (redrawn after Schnädelbach 2010).*

Figure 3. Aerial photograph of Palmyra taken looking southwest (Poidebard 1934, pl. 67).

the Justinianic renovations of the settlement as proof of the ability of the Imperial authority to reach even the most remote location in the empire with its tentacles (Proc., *Aed.*, 5.1.1). The perception of Palmyra that emerges from an attentive reading of the written sources is, therefore, that of a city standing in isolation in the Syrian steppe.

It is legitimate to ask, however, whether this idea reflects the stereotypical perception that the above writers had of the settlements along the eastern frontier, rather than reality. As a matter of fact, information from the *Tabula Peutingeriana,* complemented with the archaeological record, suggests that the city did not sit in remote isolation, but was fully integrated in the road network of the time. The *Tabula Peutingeriana* (*seg.* 10–11, Fig. 5) shows two roads departing from the city. One heads northeast, circumventing the Jabal Abū Rujmayn to the east, to reach *Sura* (Sūriyya). It would have passed via *Harae* (Arāk), *Oresa*/*Oruba* (al-Ṭayyiba), *Cholle* (al-Khulla), and *Sergiopolis* (al-Ruṣāfa – *Risapa* in the *Tabula Peutingeriana*). The second would have led to Apamea via *Centum Putea*, *Occaraba* (ʿUqayribāt), and *Theleda* (Tall ʿadā). The document also reveals a third road, starting not far from Palmyra to reach Damascus via *Heliarama* (Qaṣr al-Ḥayr al-Gharbī), *Nezala* (al-Qaryatayn), *Danova*, *Cehere,* (Qāra), *Casama,* (al-Nabk), and *ad Medera*.

Other major roads are not documented in the *Tabula*, but are known from aerial and ground surveys that were conducted mainly at the beginning of the last century. A second connection to Damascus, known in French literature as the 'route des khāns', followed the eastern slopes of Jabal al-Niqniqiyya, Jabal al-Ruwāq, and Jabal Haymūr. Its course was policed by a number of military installations, on which more will be said below. The section of this road from *Thelseai* (al-Ḍumayr) to Palmyra and the detour to *Avatha* (al-Bakhrāʾ) is known on Tetrarchic milestones with the name of *Strata Diocletiana* (Bauzou 1993; 2000). Another major track connected Palmyra with Emesa (Homs), passing through the plain of al-Daww. Its existence is confirmed by numerous Diocletianic milestones found along its course (see below, p. 21). The incorrect statement of Palladius (*Dial. John Chris.*, 20.35–8), who refers to Palmyra as a city situated 'eight milestones from Emesa', suggests that the road was still functional in the early 5th century. In addition, the body of St Anastasius might have travelled in this road on his way to Jerusalem via *Arados* (Arwād) in 630 (*Anas. Per.,* 1.102–4). A connection existed also between

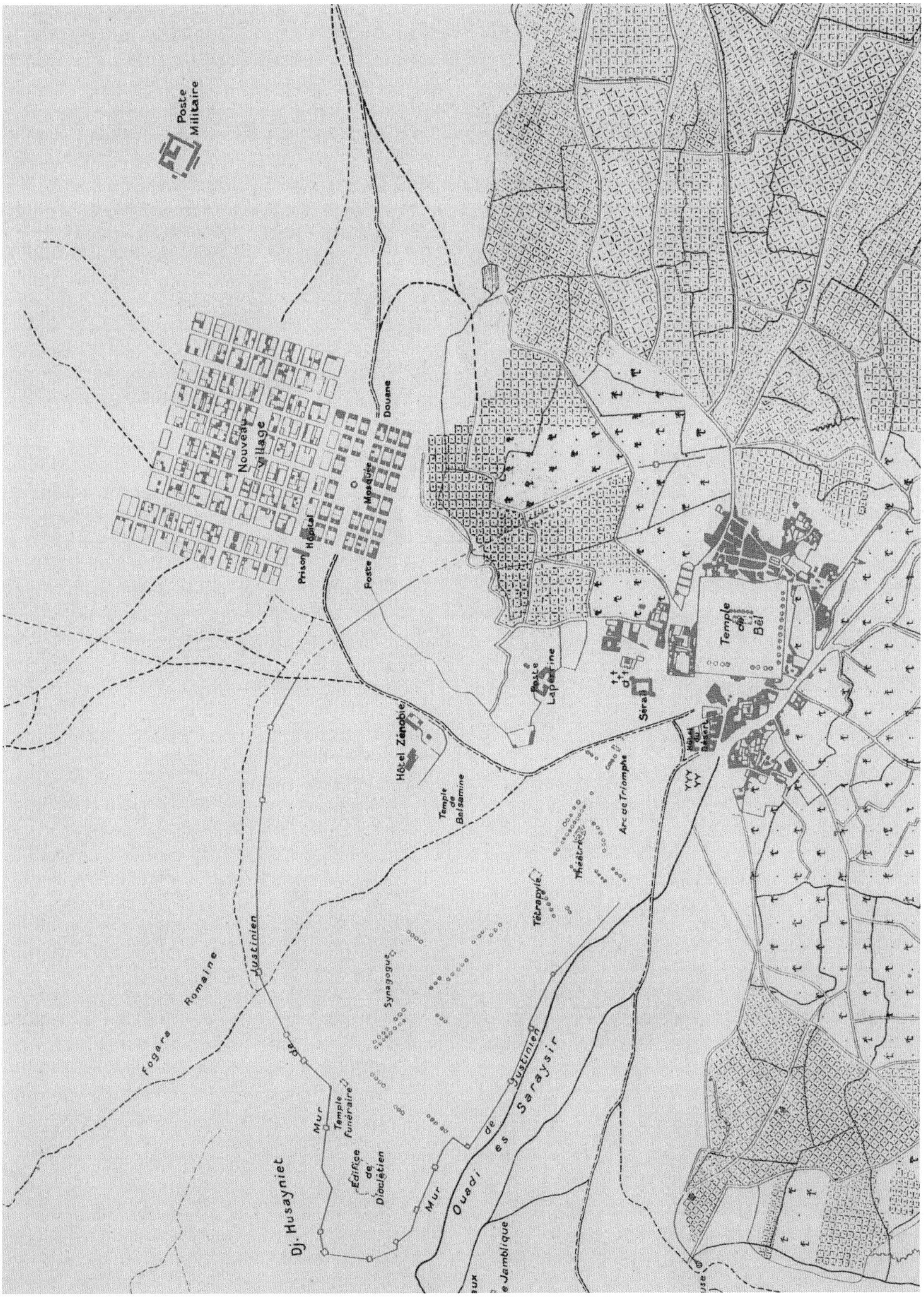

Figure 4. The state of the ruins of Palmyra in 1931, Bureau Topographique des Troupes Françaises du Levant (detail; scale 1:10,000. Courtesy of the National Library of Scotland).

Palmyra and *Acadama* (Qudaym) – the site of a garrison of *Equites Sagittarii* (*Not. Dig., Or.*, 33.12, 21) via Jabal Abū Rujmayn. From there, it was possible to reach *Seriane* (Ithriyya) to the northwest, or *Oresa/Oruba* (al-Ṭayyiba) to the east (Mouterde and Poidebard 1945, 109–15; Fig. 6).

Unlike the relative abundance of pieces of evidence for Late Antiquity, there are no written or epigraphic sources to shed light on the status of the road network in the Palmyrene in the Early Islamic period. It is now believed that the new political geography of the Umayyad period

Figure 5. Tabula Peutingeriana, seg. *10–11 (courtesy of the Austrian National Library).*

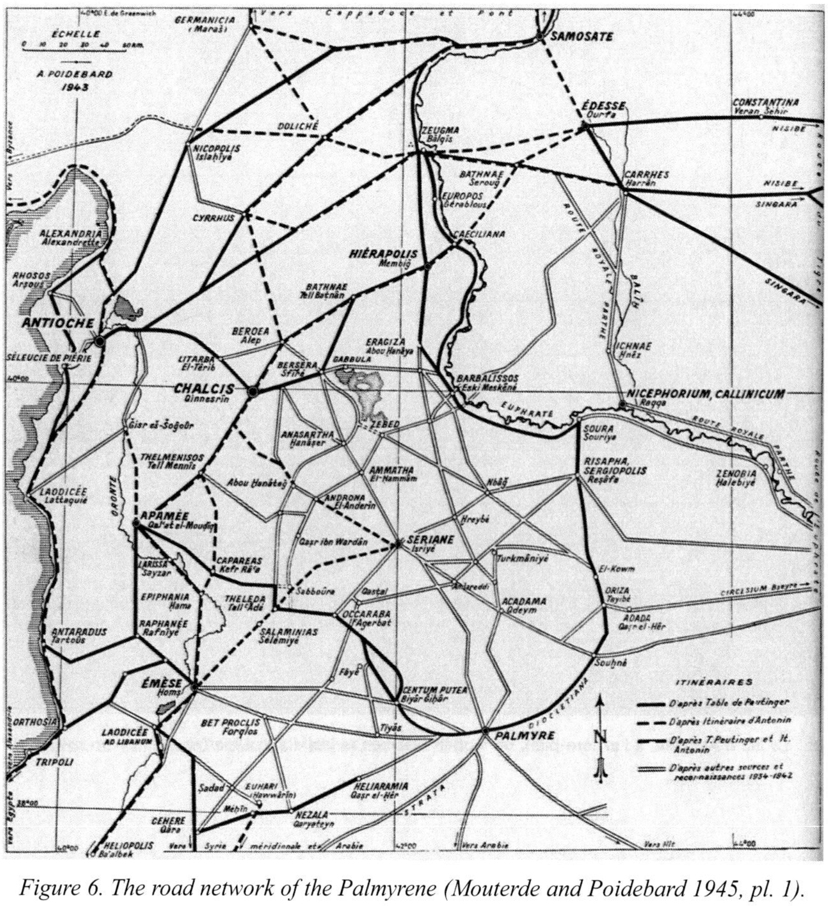

Figure 6. The road network of the Palmyrene (Mouterde and Poidebard 1945, pl. 1).

encouraged the flourishing of trade routes, marking in most cases the end of an insular economy and the reinforcement of long-distance trade networks (Bessard 2013). Due to its location, Palmyra might have benefited from such traffic. In all likelihood, the pre-existing road system would have been of functional use in the Early Islamic period. In addition, the major track leading to Iraq would have been re-established (or reinforced), assuring trade connections with regions on the left bank of the Euphrates.

Blurred evidence of travels through the Palmyrene in Late Antiquity and the Early Islamic period exist. The only inscription recording the presence of Palmyrenes outside Palmyra is a funerary graffito found in the Tombs of the Prophets at Jerusalem, which mentions a certain 'Anamos, *clibanarius teriius* (?) of Palmyra' (Ἄναμος κλιβανάρι(ο)ς [τρίτος?] Παλμύρας – Clermont-Ganneau 1899, 364–7). The soldier (or his body) reached his final resting place passing by Damascus either via Emesa or via the more direct 'route des khāns'. Written sources are only slightly more informative. At the end of the 4th–beginning of the 5th century, Alexander the Akoimētes and his followers are recorded to have stopped for three years in a fort, either at *Oresa/Oruba* (al-Ṭayyiba) or *Sergiopolis* (al-Ruṣāfa), and then to have moved southward to Palmyra, very likely following the *via militaris* described above (*Alex. Akoim.*, 35; Gatier 1995, 452). Finally, the monks translating the remains of St Anastasius from Dastagerd to Jerusalem in 630, travelled through Palmyra to *Arados* (Arwād) presumably through Emesa. From there, he and his companions reached Tyre by sea (*Anas. Per.*, 1.102–4).

In the Early Islamic period, a number of sources mention the journey of Sulaymān b. Hishām with Ibrāhīm b. al-Walīd from Palmyra to the residence of Marwān b. Muḥammad (r. 744–50), near Ḥarrān, to pledge allegiance to the caliph (al-Ṭabarī, *Tāʾrīkh*, 9.1892; Ibn ʿAsākir, *Tāʾrīkh*, 15.83). However, they provide little clue on the route undertaken by the traveller. Similarly, Theophanes (*Chr.*, 1.422) recounts that after being defeated by Marwān, Sulaymān 'escaped first to Palmyra then to Persia' (tr. Hoyland 2011, 258). Analogous generic accounts are not out of the ordinary in Early Islamic written sources. In accounting the life of Dhuʾāla b. al-Aṣbagh b. Dhuʾāla al-Kalbī, Ibn ʿAsākir (*Tāʾrīkh*, 17.326) reports that his three sons, Dhuʾāla, Ḥamza and Furāfiṣa threw off allegiance to the caliph and moved from Palmyra to Homs. It is reasonable to assume that the pre-existing road through al-Daww connecting Palmyra to Homs was used by the travellers. Only sporadically, ancient sources provide detailed clues. In accounting the siege of Palmyra by Marwān, for example, al-Ṭabarī (*Tāʾrīkh*, 9.1895–6) recounts that the caliph and his army camped at Qasṭal 'in the territory of Homs adjacent to that of Palmyra, the distance between them being three days march' (tr. Williams 1985, 7–8). One could conclude, then, that the capillary regional road network in Late Antiquity and the Early Islamic period assured strong links between Palmyra and its hinterland. Palmyra must have served as a regional road hub. The need to construct and restore Palmyra's city gates in Late Antiquity betrays the importance attached to this role (see below, p. 96).

To test the effectiveness of this regional road system, it suffices to look at coin distribution. The most substantial collections of published coins from Palmyra come from the Sanctuary of Baalshamīn and the excavations of the Polish team in the Camp of Diocletian and the northwest quarter. The selection of coins in the final report of the excavations of the Sanctuary of Baalshamīn is poorly informative. Among the coins dated from 293 to the early 7th century with recognisable mint marks, two were issued at Nicomedia, two at Alexandria, two at Antioch, one at Constantinople, and one possibly at Trier (Dunant 1975a, 108–9). The collection of coins recently published by the Polish team add much data to this corpus. Out of 151 issues dated to the period under discussion, roughly half are from Antioch (41) and Constantinople (31). The rest are from a diverse range of mints, including Heraclea (4), Cyzicus (14), Nicomedia (6), Alexandria (6), Siscia (3), Thessaloniki (6), Sirmium (1), Rome (5), Arles (1), and perhaps Carthage (1) (Krzyżanowska 2014, 40–51, 55–60, 65). The 37 Late Antique issues of the coin hoard found in the Sanctuary of Allāth include the mint marks of Antioch (16), Thessaloniki (3), Constantinople (2), Heraclea (2), Alexandria (2), and Nicomedia (1) (Krzyżanowska 2014, 52–5). Overall, the data from the Polish numismatic corpus suggest that most of the coins reaching Palmyra in the 4th century were minted at Antioch. Yet, other mints are sporadically attested; these are mostly from the Levant and the eastern Mediterranean. Issues dated to the 5th century remain under-represented. In the 6th century, most of the coins are from Constantinople, the mint mark of which started to appear in Palmyra as early as the second half of the 4th century (Krzyżanowska 2014, 68).

Byzantine coins remained in circulation even after the monetary reform of ʿAbd al-Malik (r. 685–705) in 694. The majority of these were minted in Constantinople. Out of 25 coins dated from the reign of Heraclius (610–641) to that of Constans II (641–668) found during the excavations of the Polish team, only three (from Thessaloniki, Nicomedia, and perhaps Ravenna) are not from the Byzantine capital (Krzyżanowska 2014, 58–60). In the so-called 'Byzantine hoard' found in 1960 in the Camp of Diocletian, all the 27 gold coins dated between the reigns of the emperors Phocas (602–610) and Constans II bear the mintmark CONOB, that is Costantinople (Skowronek in Krzyżanowska 2014, 60–4). Yet, the question remains if the hoard was actually collected at Palmyra or at some place else before finally being buried. This seems to be certainly true for the so-called 'Sasanian hoard', which was partly assembled at Dārābgird from the Persian occupation of Syria until the late 7th century.

The number of Sasanian and Arab-Sasanian mint marks represented in this hoard amounts to 40 (Gawlikowski 2014, 118–20). The hoard also includes a selection of 35 Arab-Sasanian *dirhams* struck between 663 and 695, mostly at Fārs (Gawlikowski 2014, 114–18). As for post-reform coins, we are aware only of three issues with no mint marks found during the excavations of the Sanctuary of Baalshamīn and generically attributed to the 8th century (Dunant 1975a, 110, n. 36–8). To these it is possible to add 28 more issues (generally identified as 'monnaies Arabes' in Collart's notebook), which have been found during the excavations of the Sanctuary of Baalshamīn. These have never been published (*Notebook* 1966b, inv. n. 45, 58, 63, 66–8, 71–3, 81–2, 84, 89, 92–3, 95, 98, 104, 112–13, 115, 120, 132, 194, 199–200, 207, 211). The Polish corpus reports only four 'imitations Arabes', again with no mint marks and undated (Krzyżanowska 2014, 66).

Small finds from Palmyra, the origin of which is possible to track, would provide us with a better picture of the city's interactions with other urban centres; yet, these have only sporadically been published. An exception to this trend is represented by a liturgical bread stamp found in the area of the *Forum* of the Camp of Diocletian and dated to the 6th or 7th century. The stamp bears an inscription surrounding a circle in which stands a cross with flaring ends on top of a pedestal (Michałowski 1964a, 184 fig. 214). The specimen from Palmyra matches the iconography, inscription, and size of another stamp now at the Byzantine Museum of Athens; this seems to suggest that the two were produced in the same (still unidentified) workshop (Galavaris 1970, 121–2) and that Palmyra was reached by supply routes of liturgical commodities that served also other major cities in the empire.

As for imported bulk finds, such as pottery and glass, the evidence in Palmyra and the Palmyrene is even sparser; works on this kind of evidence have been particularly rare and often devoted to well-preserved or decorated specimens (see Intagliata 2014, 649, on pottery; Romagnolo 2012, 601 n. 5, on glass). In the 1960s publication of the results of the Polish fieldwork in the Camp of Diocletian, for example, the excavators reported the discovery of two fragments of a dish decorated with a female figure painted on its inner surface. The fragments are reported to have been found in the *Groma*, to be 6th or 7th century in date and to come possibly from Antioch (Michałowski 1960a, 212). More recently, systematic ceramic studies have been conducted and published on the material brought to light from the Peristyle Building. A preliminary analysis of the Brittle Ware from this compound has shown that, although most of this iron-rich, thin-walled cooking ware might have been produced in Palmyra itself or its surroundings, some belonged to two regional groups (Group IV, which dominated the markets of Late Antique Apamea, and Group V, produced outside Syria) that were not local. The chronology of most of the ceramic material from the Peristyle Building, which generally belongs to 5th–8th century contexts, needs, however, still to be narrowed down (Cerutti 2014, with further bibliography).

Even less is known about bulk finds from the Palmyrene. In discussing the material evidence for Roman and Late Antique trade at Qaṣr al-Ḥayr al-Sharqī, Genequand (2012, 194) recently stressed the occurrence of fine ware and transport containers from western Syria, Asia Minor, Africa, and Gaul. The results of the surface collection at Umm al-Tlal indicate that most of the pottery found was produced locally, although several imports are attested. These include fragments of LRA 1 and LRA 3 amphorae from, respectively, northeastern Mediterranean and western Asia Minor (Majcherek and Taha 2004, 232–3).

Proof of the economic vitality of Palmyra in Umayyad times is the construction of a *sūq* in the westernmost stretch of the Great Colonnade (Section C), on which more will be said below (see p. 25). The publication of the excavation of the Umayyad *Sūq* does not clarify which goods were traded in its shops. However, the material evidence from Qaṣr al-Ḥayr al-Sharqī remains informative on this regard. Among the sporadic material proving long-range trade are transport containers from Palestine, pottery from central or northern Jordan, the Ḥawrān, and the valley of the Euphrates, steatite vessels likely to be from the Ḥijāz, ivory, foodstuff from western Syria, and timber (from pine and poplar trees) not of local origin. Most of the artefacts found, however, were of local or regional production, with most of the imports, including Brittle Ware, coming from northern Syria (Genequand 2012, 195; Genequand *et al.* 2010, 210–11).

Evidence from written sources and the archaeological record, therefore, suggests that Palmyra was easily reachable by people and goods in Late Antiquity, undermining the stereotype of a city located in a 'neighbourless region'. The existence of a capillary road system must have played a crucial role to prevent the isolation of the Palmyrene. Admittedly, too little has been brought to light, studied, and published to reach an understanding of the inter-regional trade at the time. So far, it seems that northern Syrian goods prevailed in the market over longer distance imports throughout Late Antiquity. The coming of Islam and the consequent reshuffle of the political geography likely resulted in a decline of goods from the Mediterranean regions and an increased demand for Levantine imports (Genequand 2012, 195).

The human occupation of the Palmyrene: the state of the evidence[1]

Late Antiquity

Forts

At the fringe of the Roman Empire, the Palmyrene developed first and foremost as a militarised borderland.

A generalised process of strenghtening of the frontier under Diocletian saw the creation of a defensive system constituted, in some cases, by forts built *ex nihilo* (yet see e.g. Umm al-Tlal; Majcherek and Taha 2004). Smaller military installations, such as signalling towers, must have been constructed as well, but evidence for these remain particularly problematic (e.g., at Qaṣr al-Ḥayr al-Gharbī: Kennedy and Riley 1990, 217–19; Fowden 2004, 179; Genequand 2006b, 70–1, 72–4; on the process of strengthening of the eastern frontier see, Isaac 1990, 162–71; Lewin 2002; 2011). The backbone of this system, which experienced modifications during the 4th century, consisted of auxiliary troops, mostly *alae* and *cohortes* but also *equites*, i.e. élite mounted units hired locally (Southern and Dixon 1996, 30). Four legions were also deployed: two were allocated to *Phoenicia*, at Palmyra (*Legio I Illyricorum*) and *Danaba* (*Legio III Gallica*) and two to *Syria* at *Sura* (*Legio XVI Flavia Firma*) and *Oresa/Oruba* (*Legio IV Scythica*) (*Not. Dig., Or.*, 33.23; 33.28; 32.30–1). Soldiers were deployed along a *via militaris*, discussed above, stretching from Sūriyya to Damascus via Palmyra and defended by numerous military installations. The section from Sūriyya to Palmyra (less than 200km in length) included the forts of *Tetrapyrgium* (Qṣair al-Saila), *Risapa* (al-Ruṣāfa), *Cholle* (al-Khulla), *Oresa/Oruba* (al-Ṭayyiba), and *Harae* (Arāk). The section from Palmyra to Damascus, the so-called 'route des khāns', comprised, *inter alia*, the forts of *Avatha* (al-Bakhrāʾ), *Veriaraca* (Khān al-Ḥallābāt), *Valle Alba* (Khān al-Manqūra), *Valle Diocletiana* (Khān al-Turāb), and *Thelseai* (al-Ḍumayr).

A pragmatic approach to building characterise these military compounds. Most of these forts are of modest size, between 0.16ha and 0.32ha, and develop with simple geometrical plans, squares or rectangles, normally defended by projecting corner towers of different size and shape. The plan of *Veriaraca*, which stands 31km to the south of Palmyra and was the base of an auxiliary unit (the *Ala Nova Diocletiana* mentioned in *Not. Dig. Or.* 32.34), is a 47m square, the 0.27ha of which are limited by a double wall defended by irregular semi-circular corner towers; *Carneia/Cunna* (Khān al-Qaṭṭār) stands to the southwest of *Veriaraca*, of which shares basically the same plan, being, however, smaller in size (a 41m square, 0.17ha; Kennedy and Riley 1990, 203–4). Yet, deviations from this pattern occur. The walls of the 28 × 30m *tetrapyrgium* at *Helela* (al-Ḥulayla), 48km to the northwest of Palmyra seem not to have been defended by any towers (Kennedy and Riley 1990, 155). Like other forts of similar size, it was the base of an auxiliary unit, the *Cohors I Gotthorum* (*Not. Dig. Or.* 33.32).

Forts of larger size are not common. Leaving aside their dimensions, they seem to share some general characteristics with smaller military installations, such as the simple geometrical plans and the corner towers. Interval towers (normally U-shaped) in these cases, however, become a priority in order to provide necessary extra enfilading fire to protect their long walls. The fort at Khān al-Manqūra (*Valle Alba*), base of the *Cohors I Iulia Lectorum* (*Not. Dig., Or.* 32.42), has a simple, 90m square plan (0.81ha) with interval U-shaped towers that occur between fan-shaped corner towers either in isolation or in pairs (Kennedy and Riley 1990, 181–3). The plan of the fort at al-Bakhrāʾ is a 152 × 98.50m rectangle protected by fan-shaped corner towers and, again, interval U-shaped towers (Fig. 7). The interior of the fort still preserves the outlines of the walls of some structures; among them, there is probably the *Praetorium*, the threshold of its main access remaining *in situ* in front of the main gate of the fort (Genequand 2003a, 34–6; 2004a, 229–34; 2004b, 89–92; 2004c, 14–15; 2012, 73–9). The compound is known in written sources and epigraphic record to have been the base of a garrison of *Equites Promoti Indigenae* (*Not. Dig., Or.* 32.22; Bauzou 1993, 47–9). Among the forts of large size, the Camp of Diocletian in Palmyra seems to stand significantly apart from the others both for its dimensions and its architectural monumentality, which is unrivalled along the eastern frontier, as it will be discussed in more detail in a separate chapter (see below, pp. 71–82). The need to provide Palmyra with a major garrison, the *Legio I Illyricorum* mentioned in *Not. Dig., Or.*, 32.30, appears reasonable after a closer look is taken at the geographical morphology of the region and its Late Antique road network; had Palmyra capitulated, the flat, even terrain of the plain of al-Daww would have provided an enemy with an inviting marching track to Emesa, the capital and hearth of *Phoenicia Libanensis*.

The fate of most of these forts in later times is unknown, as archaeological investigations are lacking. It is generally believed that small forts were left abandoned by their garrisons perhaps as early as the 4th century, following a policy that gradually left the defence of this sector of the frontier to local nomadic tribes (Bauzou 2000, 90–1). Yet, archaeological evidence from other fortified installations along the eastern frontier, such as *Tetrapyrgium* (Qṣair al-Saila), which shows evidence of occupation until 580, should put us on guard on this (Konrad 2001, 100). In some of these forts, the nature of the occupation changed completely, as the civilian component (represented by attached *vici* or *canabae*) developed over the military one. This transformed the forts into small settlements, towns, or even cities of a certain administrative, political, and religious importance during the 5th and 6th centuries. Much later, as seen below, a number of these forts underwent different transformations, being converted into aristocratic residences in the Umayyad period.

Settlements

The transformation of forts into civilian settlement is mostly known at sites that had garrisoned élite mounted

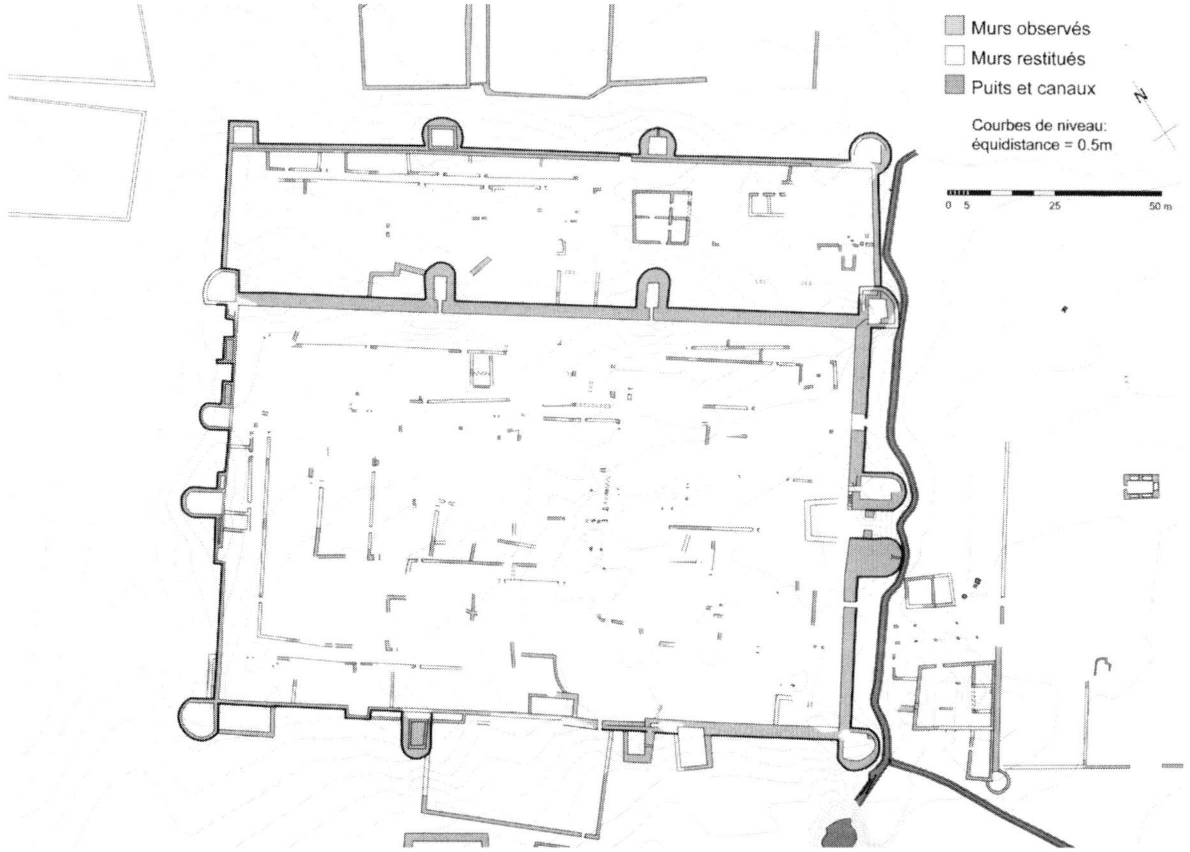

Figure 7. Al-Bakhrā' (Genequand 2012, 75, fig. 46).

units (*equites*). A good case study is represented by *Euareia* (Ḥuwwārīn), which is known through the *Notitia Dignitatum* (*Or*., 32.19) to have been the base of a garrison of *Equites Scutari Illyriciani*. Although the Roman fort has never been located with certainty, there is extensive evidence that proves the civilian occupation of the site during Late Antiquity. The settlement was a bishopric at least since the 5th century. In the 6th century, it was connected with the figure of Magnus the Syrian, a high official with a long history of service for the empire. Five churches are known from this site, one of which standing out from the others for having a central quadrilobate plan and a rich decoration, including painted walls and mosaics (see Zanini 1996; Khoury 2005, with further bibliography). Archaeology seem to confirm this pattern also at *Avatha* (al-Bakhrā'). Among the evidence that might be associated with a Late Antique phase are a number of repairs of the wall of the former fort, including perhaps the addition of new interval towers (either rectangular or U-shaped), a small opening, and a double-faced wall (Genequand 2004a, 232; 2012, 73–9). A church was also identified 10–20m to the east of the southeastern corner tower of the Tetrarchic fort. The church is characterised by a basilical plan with a tripartite sanctuary, the back wall of it being horizontal (Genequand 2004a, 236; 2004b, 94–6; 2004c, 17; 2012, 83–5).

As for settlements not connected with earlier military installations, evidence in the Palmyrene is frustratingly scanty. The surveys conducted by Schlumberger in the 1930s found evidence for Roman villages in the mountains to the northwest of Palmyra. Specifically, Schlumberger counted two small forts in Jabal al-Abyaḍ, and one fort and 15 settlements in Jabal al-Sha'ar. He then concluded that these villages were mostly devoted to husbandry and horse- or camel-breeding (Schlumberger 1951, 133). The settlements normally include walled enclosures, well-built shrines, and modest private residential buildings of various sizes that are structured around a major square inner courtyard. The chronology of these settlements was set to the first three centuries of the first millennium, mostly based on data from epigraphy, numismatic, sculpture, and architecture; only well-preserved pottery specimens were published, but no chronology for these was provided.

The only dated sculptural Late Antique piece of evidence published by Schlumberger are three stuc fragments from a building (Édifice B) at Ḥassan Maḍhūr. The fragments are decorated with vegetal motifs and were believed by Schlumberger to date back to the 5th or 6th centuries. Édifice

B, the nature of which remains unclear, consists of a central room, where the fragments were discovered, surrounded on three sides by a corridor. Three rooms complete the compound to the east and west, and at one of the extremities of the corridor. The building stands at the northeastern end of an extensive settlement, including at least one shrine and a number of buildings with courtyards (Schlumberger 1951, 27–9, 69). If the Late Antique chronology of the stuc fragments is taken as valid, it is difficult to believe that Édifice B would have stood in complete isolation after 272; rather, it is more reasonable to assume that the village remained somehow occupied, to an extent which unfortunately is unknown. The numismatic record is certainly not informative on this regard. Of the coins described in the volume, only three are post-272 in date, but none is from this site. Indeed, two were found at Khirbat Samrīn and one at Khirbat Laqṭīr. On the basis of the description provided by Schlumberger (1951, 61 n. 47 b; 63 n. 9), they can be dated between the late 3rd and the first half of the 4th century (see Krzyżanowska 2014, 43–4, with references for *comparanda* in *RIC* 7).

The results of the recent surveys conducted by a joint Syro-Norwegian team, which have been published in preliminary form, have shed doubts on the general conclusions reached by Schlumberger concerning the nature and chronology of the settlements (Meyer 2008; 2009; 2011; 2013). The investigations, which extended to Jabal al-Sha'ar, Jabal al-Abyaḍ, Jabal al-Marāḥ, and Jabal Abū Rujmayn, identified many new settlements, all at short distances between each other (3–5km). Hard evidence for Late Antique and Early Islamic occupation were found in the form of coins and bulk finds in almost all the sites under investigation (Meyer 2013, 276; 2016, 90). The high density of sites and the evidence found for water management has led to the conclusion that the economy of these villages might have been based on agriculture, perhaps mixed with animal husbandry (Meyer 2013, 275–6). As for the three Roman buildings interpreted by Schlumberger as military compounds, at least one (Rasm al-Sha'ar) has characteristic features that show more similarities to Umayyad élite residences rather than Roman forts (Genequand 2012, 184–6).

Other settlements in the Palmyrene are less known. In discussing the evidence for Late Antique settlements, Genequand (2012, 33, 189–91) reported the existence of two sites at al-Naḍīmī, in Jabal al-Bishrī, and al-Kulaybiyya, 30km west of Palmyra, at al-Daww. The former presents 4th to 5th century houses in mudbrick and *arcosolia* type burials. At al-Kulaybiyya, richly adorned Late Antique baths were excavated by the DGAM (Directorate-General of Antiquities and Museums). The baths, which underwent later alterations, consist of three hot rooms, one of which is apsed, and a large changing room. The decorative apparatus of the building is particularly rich and includes stucs and mosaics.

Overall, despite the lack of archaeological evidence, it seems reasonable to conclude that Palmyra served as the prime market for settlements located in its hinterland (Genequand 2012, 36). Not only the local inhabitants, but also the soldiers garrisoned in the city, must have been seen as a high lucrative source for merchants willing to gain profit from the sale of certain products, from everyday goods such as foodstuff and clothes, to more luxurious imports. The importance of the military component of the city for the economy of the Palmyrene should not be underestimated, considering the high number of soldiers that were quartered in Palmyra in Late Antiquity, and especially in the 4th and 6th centuries.

Isolated farmsteads

Isolated farmsteads, known in written sources as *aulē* (αὐλή) or *monagria* (μοναγρία) (Decker 2009, 44–8), would have also profited from their vicinity with Palmyra for trading their goods. Two of these have been identified at al-Sukkariyya and al-Bāzūriyya, both 20km to the south of Palmyra and dated to the 6th century (Fig. 8). At al-Sukkariyya, an imposing tower, still well preserved up to three floors, marks visibly the site. The tower adjoins a rectangular enclosure accessed through a well-built tower gate on its northern side (Genequand 2003a, 38–43; 2012, 33). Inside the enclosure are a number of rectangular rooms situated against the wall; along its eastern side the presence of reused columns suggests the existence of a roof supported by arcades. A second rectangular enclosure adjoins the first to the northwest and is in turn adjoined by a third enclosure toward the same direction. Reused Roman building material is abundantly attested in the compound, especially in the first enclosure. A *qanāt* was also identified 1km to the west of the site running for further 2km westward.

The site of al-Bāzūriyya consists of three major compounds (Wiegand 1932b, 10–12; Poidebard 1934, 55; Genequand 2003a, 38–43; 2012, 33). Al-Bāzūriyya 1 and 2 include two main enclosures accessed by an imposing tower gate. At al-Bāzūriyya 1 a large tower is also preserved, making this compound more similar to that at al-Sukkariyya; yet, this differs from the latter for the addition of two projecting U-shaped buttress towers along the northern wall of the enclosure. Both the compounds at al-Bāzūriyya 1 and 2 present rooms against their inner wall and are adjoined to the north by two larger walled enclosures. Al-Bāzūriyya 3 is located further to the east and basically shows the same main features. In all three cases, a room covered by a roof supported by arcades would have been located inside the main enclosure, immediately to the left of the entrance.

Monasteries

The religious geography of the Palmyrene in Late Antiquity remains to be fully explored. Undoubtedly, Palmyra must have played an important role as a centre of aggregation for the Christian community in central Syria and as a mean of its diffusion. The first written piece of evidence attesting the

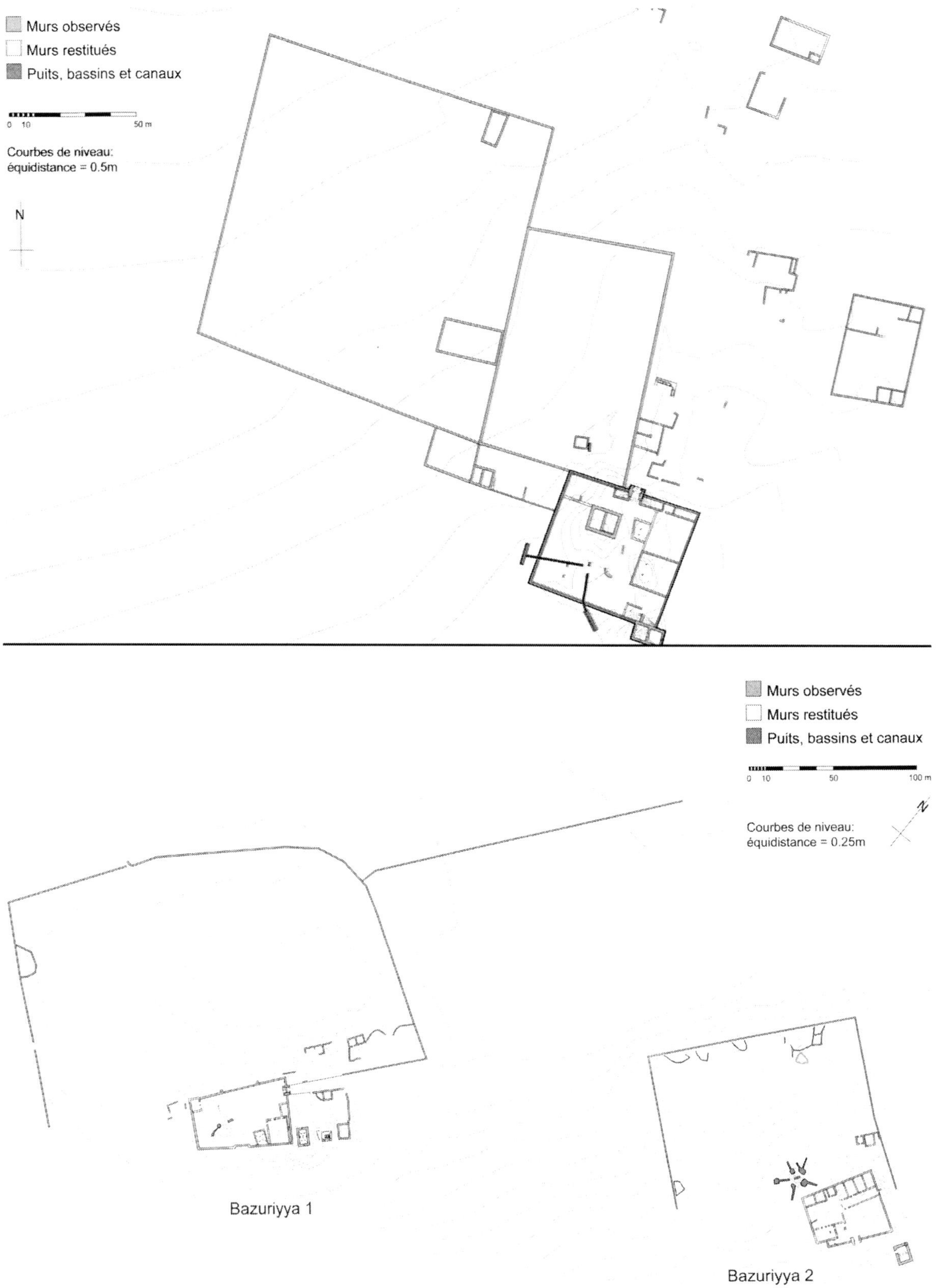

Figure 8. Al-Sukkariyya and al-Bāzūriyya (Genequand 2012, 34, fig. 16; 35, fig. 18).

presence of a bishop in the city goes back to the Council of Nicaea, in 325 (Mich. Syr., *Chr.*, 7.2). Evidence for monasticism in its surroundings are not earlier than the 6th century. The monastery of NṬP DZGL is reported in a colophon of a Syriac manuscript to be situated in the territory of Palmyra in the first half of the 6th century; yet, its exact location remains unknown (Wright 1872, 2. 468, n. 585; Millar 2013, 24–5). Similarly, a Syriac inscription mentions the refortification of a monastery on Jabal al-Bil ʿās under the care of the stonecutter Abraham, in the Seleudic year 886 (574/575).The findspot of the inscription is reported to have been '*au lieu dit par les Bédouins et par les gens de 'Aguerbat "la maison de l'Arménien"*' (Mouterde 1942–1943, 86). More evidence is left on the Late Antique monastery at Qaṣr al-Ḥayr al-Gharbī. The main indications of its existence are four Greek inscriptions (named A to D) published by Schlumberger in 1939. Two of them (A and C) commemorate the erection of a door 'at the time of the God's beloved Sergius' and the restoration of the monastery by a certain John; inscription B mentions the phylarch and *patricius* Arethas, the Jafnid prince al-Ḥārith b. Jabala (529–569); inscription D is an acclamation to the same Arethas and provide the date 870 (559) of the Seleucid era (Schlumberger 1939b; 1986, 26–8 = *IGLS* 5, n. 2553, A–D; see discussion in Genequand 2006b, 69–70). A recent re-analysis of the archaeological evidence from this site conducted by Genequand (2006b, 69–77) would suggest that the monastery consisted of a rectangular or squared enclosure, the original size of which is unknown as the compound was mostly destroyed to make space for a caliphal residence. The enclosure was delimited by a wall against which, on the inside, were room units. In plan, its exterior course was broken by trapezoidal, small towers. A larger (12.8 × 16m) rectangular tower, still preserved up to 16m, was placed along its south side. The evidence from Qaṣr al-Ḥayr al-Gharbī has tentatively been associated with the monastery named *Haliuram* and listed among others in a letter of the archimandrites sent to Jacob Baradaeus (Chabot 1907–1933, 1.233; 2.155), and with the *Heliaramia* of the *Tabula Peutingeriana* (*seg.* 10).

Early Islamic period

Settlements

Our knowledge of the settlement pattern in the Palmyrene becomes more blurred in the Umayyad period. As seen above, the research conducted by the Syro-Norwegian team in the mountains to the north of Palmyra have found Early Islamic evidence in most of the sites analysed. In addition to these, other settlements have sporadically been investigated. Surface collection conducted at the fort of *Acadama* (Qudaym) and al-Naḍīmī have found pottery that strikingly resembles that collected in the Établissement Nord at Qaṣr al-Ḥayr al-Sharqī (Genequand 2012, 192). Only excavations will clarify whether this evidence is proof of a continuity in occupation throughout Late Antiquity and the Early Islamic period. *Euareia* (Ḥuwwārīn), which, as seen above, was occupied in Late Antiquity, is reported to have been visited by the caliph Yazīd b. Mu ʿāwiya, who died and was buried there in 683 (Genequand 2012, 189). Yet, no Early Islamic evidence has been uncovered thus far on the site. Given the state of the research, the relationship between Palmyra and these settlements remains unknown.

Aristocratic residences

The construction of residences for the aristocratic élite or the members of the ruling dynasty was a common phenomenon in the Umayyad Palmyrene. From the outside, these buildings recall an architectural tradition that is characteristic of earlier Roman forts, being provided with outer walls 'defended' by projecting semi-circular interval towers and three-quarter-of-a-circle corner towers. Yet, the defensive limit of these walls, which are normally not particularly thick, and the rich decoration of these compounds shed doubts on a purely military purpose of these installations and betray a different function. Umayyad élite buildings do not generally stand in complete isolation, but are part of extensive sites including industrial and agricultural installations. In most cases, houses were constructed in the immediate surroundings, making these sites look like proper settlements with a detached aristocratic residential building. Aristocratic residences in the Umayyad Palmyrene have recently been the subject of a detailed work by Genequand (2012). In the light of the summary nature of this chapter of the book, it suffices to reconsider here briefly three main case studies, namely Qaṣr al-Ḥayr al-Sharqī, Qaṣr al-Ḥayr al-Gharbī, and al-Bakhrāʾ. Other remains safely identifiable as aristocratic residences in the Palmyrene do exist and include those at Qudaym (Mouterde and Poidebard 1945, 111–13, 120–25; Genequand 2002, 26–7; 2003a, 50–2; 2004c, 11–12; 2012, 174–80), Rasm al-Sha ʿar (Schlumberger 1951, 44–6, 107; Genequand 2004c, 18; 2012, 184–6), and Qaṣr al-Ṣwāb (Poidebard 1934, 112–14; Genequand 2004c, 27; 2012, 186–7). Uncertainty still exists for the sites of al-Baṣīrī (Genequand 2003a, 52–5; 2004c, 22–4) and al-Kulaybiyya (Musil 1928, 134–5; Sauvaget 1967, 29, on these see also the summary descriptions in Genequand 2012, 187–9).

Qaṣr al-Ḥayr al-Sharqī is certainly the best known of these sites, also thanks to its relatively long history of studies (Fig. 9). The first explorations were carried out by Gabriel (1927) as early as the 1920s. The excavations led by Grabar in the 1960s and the early 1970s resulted in the publication of a first monograph (Grabar *et al.* 1978) and the most recent work on the site was carried out by a Syro-Swiss archaeological team (Genequand 2005a; 2005c; 2012, 95–159). Qaṣr al-Ḥayr al-Sharqī is situated 110km to the northeast of Palmyra and consists of a number of archaeological features scattered in an area of over 1000ha, the most prominent of which are two large enclosures,

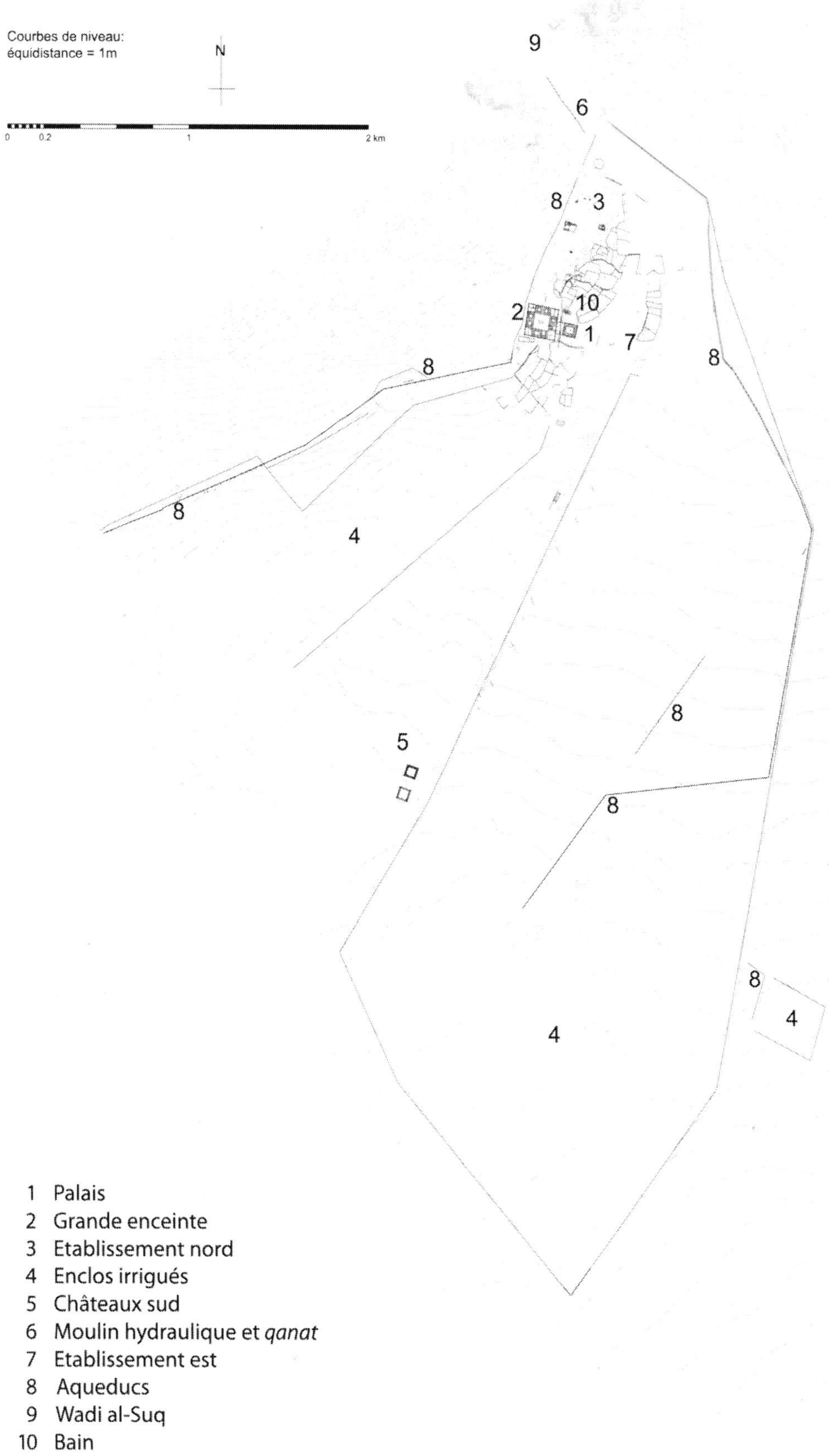

Figure 9. Qaṣr al-Ḥayr al-Sharqī (Genequand 2012, 96, fig. 71).

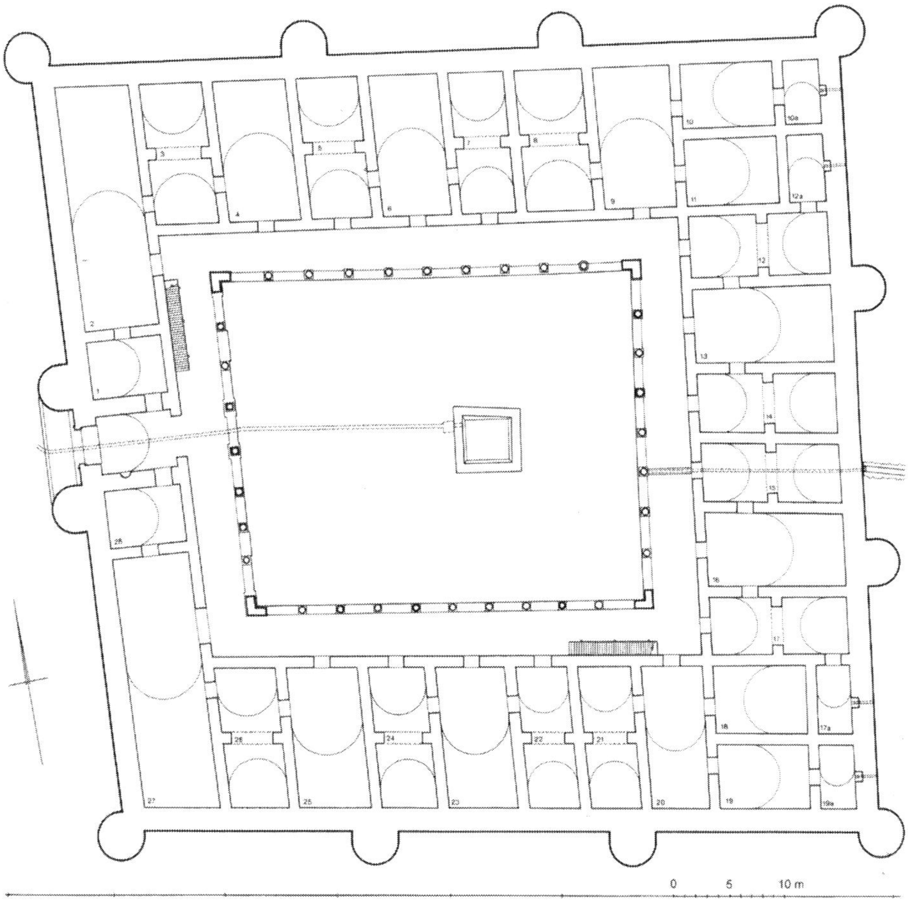

Figure 10. Qaṣr al-Ḥayr al-Sharqī, small enclosure (Grabar et al. *1978, 2, 89, fig. 6d).*

known as the Small and Large Enclosures. The Small Enclosure has a square plan (*c*. 70m per side) delimited by a still well-preserved stone wall broken at regular intervals by projecting semi-circular towers and three-quarter-of-a-circle corner towers (Grabar *et al.* 1978, 15–39; Genequand 2003a, 46; 2004c, 7; 2005c, 22; 2006c, 23–4; 2008b, 262; 2012, 97–9, Fig. 10). The interior develops around a large porticoed courtyard. To the north, east, and west, rooms are arranged into 16 apartments (*buyūt*, sing. *bayt*) on two floors; each *bayt* includes a large vestibule communicating with four or five room units. The western side of the compound, which includes the only entrance gate, was arranged differently, with two long and narrow rooms occupying most of its length. Outside the enclosure, immediately to the north, were detached baths (Grabar *et al.* 1978, 90–7; Genequand 2004c, 8; 2005c, 22; 2008b, 264; 2012, 106).To the opposite side of this compound is the Large Enclosure (167m per side, Fig. 11). The stone wall delimiting its surface recalls that already described, with the exception of its gates, which are four, one along each side (Grabar *et al.* 1978, 40–89; Genequand 2004c, 8; 2005c, 22; 2006c, 24; 2008b, 262–4; 2012, 99–106). Again, the interior develops around a large porticoed courtyard. This is surrounded by 12 separate areas, each consisting of a central courtyard and surrounding clusters of rooms; considerable variations occur from one area to the other. To the eastern side was a large olive oil production facility (Grabar *et al.* 1978, 51–4; Genequand 2012, 322), and a congregational mosque with a hypostyle hall (Grabar *et al.* 1978, 46–51; Genequand 2003a, 44–5; 2004b, 86; 2012, 102). On one of the pillars of the latter was an inscription, now lost, commemorating the construction of a *madīna* by the caliph Hishām b. ʿAbd al-Malik (r. 724–743) in 728–729 (Rousseau 1899, 146–54; Clermont-Ganneau 1900, 285–93; Genequand 2005c, 22; 2008b, 270–1; 2012, 154–7). Next to the mosque and along the southern side of the Large Enclosure is the so-called Unit 6, the function of which has given rise to some dispute. Grabar believed it to be the *dār al-imāra*, or palace of the government (Grabar *et al.* 1978, 70–71); Genequand (2012, 104–5) prefers to consider it as a residential unit.

It is now believed that the Small Enclosure functioned as a palace for members of the ruling dynasty or the caliph himself (Northedge 1994, 235–6; Genequand 2005c, 22; 2012, 97; *contra* Grabar *et al.* 1978, 32). The Large Enclosure would have accommodated members of the aristocratic élite and would have included buildings to assure

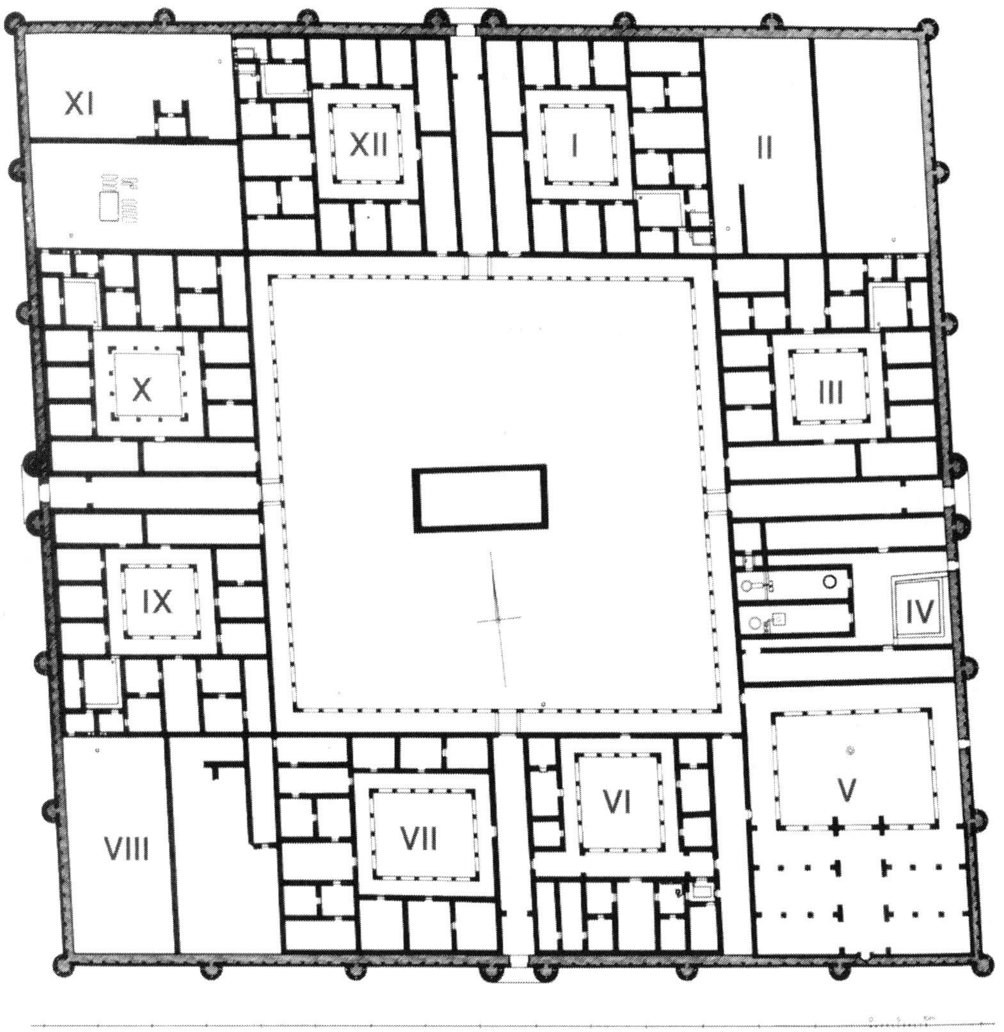

Figure 11. Qaṣr al-Ḥayr al-Sharqī, large enclosure (Grabar et al. *1978, 2, 101, fig. 23d).*

services to its community, such as a mosque (Genequand 2012, 106, 158). Soundings conducted in these compounds and architectural analyses of their curtain walls would suggest that these were occupied from the first half of the 8th century until the early 10th century. A major change in the nature of the occupation, which became more pragmatic and functional, has been noted for the 9th century (Genequand 2003b, 87–94; 2004b, 71–7; Genequand *et al.* 2006, 183–8; Genequand and al-As῾ad 2006–2007, 191–2; Genequand 2012, 106, 152). At a certain point in the history of the site, perhaps in the 12th or 13th century, the space between the two enclosures was occupied by a mosque and a necropolis (Grabar *et al.* 1978, 76, 84, 108; Genequand 2003a, 45–6; 2003b, 72–87; 2004b, 84–5; 2004–2005; 2005c, 26–7; 2008b, 269).

Surrounding the enclosures are a number of other compounds, some of them residential in nature; their existence justifies in full the adoption of the term *madīna* in the foundation inscription of Hishām b. ῾Abd al-Malik found in the mosque (Genequand 2008b, 271–2; 2012, 157–8). To the north are a cluster of buildings (Établissements Nord) built in mud brick on top of stone foundations; of these, four modest houses have partially or entirely been excavated (Genequand 2005b; 2006c, 25–7; 2008b, 264–7; 2009a, 185–8; 2012, 106–30 (summary description); Genequand *et al.* 2006, 163–75; 2007, 126–30, 135–44; 2008, 143–67; 2010, 181–210; Genequand and al-As῾ad 2006–2007, 180–5; Genequand and Studer 2011, 59–79). They seem to have been variously occupied between the early 8th and the mid-9th century. A fifth residence (Bâtiment E), an aristocratic dwelling, stands out from the others for its rich decorative apparatus, its general plan and the rich set of imported goods that it has yielded. It is believed to have been built earlier than the palace and to have remained occupied throughout the 8th century. More clusters of modest houses have also been found in the site immediately to the east and south of the two enclosures (Établissements Est and Sud), but have never been excavated (Genequand 2012, 137–42).

Besides houses, buildings of different function have also been identified at Qaṣr al-Ḥayr al-Sharqī. Some 2.5km to the south of the palace, the Châteaux Sud consists of two opposite enclosures. From the exterior these recall the architecture already described for the Small and Large Enclosures, being delimited by a mud brick wall broken at regular intervals by semi-circular towers and with four three-quarter-of-a-circle corner towers. The inner layout of the northernmost enclosure, which is the best preserved, however, suggests a different function. This consists of two rows of 4 × 4m inter-connecting rooms developed around a large, open courtyard. Such an arrangement conforms more to a stable or a depôt, rather than a residential building (Grabar *et al.* 1978, 103; Genequand 2003a, 47–50; 2004b, 78–84; 2005c, 24; 2006c, 25; 2008b, 266–7; 2012, 142–9; Genequand and al-As'ad 2006–2007, 185–7).

The site of Qaṣr al-Ḥayr al-Sharqī was associated with walled agricultural enclosures, two of which, to the southwest and southeast of the Small and Large Enclosures, encompassed large surface areas, respectively of 160ha and 745ha. The largest of these was delimited by a 14.46km wall with stone foundations and upper part of mud brick. It was broken by five monumental gates and presented at regular intervals semi-circular projecting towers placed alternately on both sides (Grabar *et al.* 1978, 98–103; Genequand 2004b, 86–8; 2004c, 8; 2005c, 22; 2008b, 268–9; 2012, 151, 304–8). The second enclosure was also delimited by a long, 5.065km wall with stone foundation and upper part in mud brick. This remains uncompleted to the southwest (Genequand 2005b, 145; 2008b, 268–9; 2012, 151, 308). Irrigation for the cultivations in these enclosures was assured by a complex system of water distribution (Grabar *et al.* 1978, 101–2; Genequand 2004b, 87–8; 2005b, 145; 2005c, 22; 2008b, 268; 2012, 151, 252–4, 296; 2009b, 160–1; Genequand *et al.* 2006, 179–83. Genequand and al-As'ad 2006–2007, 187–90). This was mostly alimented by a long, 280m dam situated to the north of the site, at the outlet of a *wādī* (the Wādī al-Sūq). Two aqueducts starting at the opposite extremities of this dam brought water to these two enclosures. By contrast, water for the Small and Large Enclosures, the baths, and the houses of the aristocracy was supplied through a different distribution system starting at the two sulphureous springs of al-Kwam and Umm al-Tlal. A 27km long *qanāt* collected the water from these springs into a large reservoir located immediately to the north of the site. Some 2km to the north of the enclosures, a watermill would have benefited from the flow of water of the *qanāt* to work (Genequand 2008b, 268; 2012, 151–2, 340–4; Genequand *et al.* 2006, 175–9; Genequand and al-As'ad 2006–2007, 190–1; Genequand *et al.* 2007, 131–5).

A second well-known case study of aristocratic residence in the Palmyrene is the complex at Qaṣr al-Ḥayr al-Gharbī, located 100km to the southwest of Palmyra. Like its eastern counterpart, Qaṣr al-Ḥayr al-Gharbī develops inorganically across a large area of *c.* 200ha. A large enclosure with a square plan (*c.* 70m per side), which, as seen above, develops on the site of a pre-existing monastery, dominates the site (Schlumberger 1939b, 224–38; 1986, 9–14; Genequand 2012, 162–6, Fig. 12). The compound shares a number of similarities with the palace at Qaṣr al-Ḥayr al-Sharqī, including a wall, this time in mud brick, broken regularly by semi-circular interval towers and three-quarter-of-a-circle corner towers, a single entrance gate provided with flanking towers, and an inner layout developing around a central porticoed courtyard surrounded by separate apartments. The decorative apparatus of the complex stands out for its richness. Stucs are represented in large quantities with vegetal and figurative motifs on decorative panels, columns, friezes, and lintels; high and low reliefs, life-sized statuary and other architectural elements (such as *claustra* for windows) complete the repertory. Well-represented are also wall-paintings, either figurative or geometrical, while less is known of other types of decoration, such as wall mosaics or painted woodwork, which survive in a poor state of preservation (Schlumberger 1939b, 324–32; 1946–1948; 1986, 14–16, 21–3; Genequand 2012, 166–9).

To the north of the palace, 30m from the so-called 'Byzantine tower', were detached baths (Schlumberger 1939b, 213–23; 1986, 6–9; Genequand 2012, 170) and, to the northwest, a *khān*, possibly in use as a storage facility or as a stable (Schlumberger 1939b, 209–13; Genequand 2012, 170–3). On the lintel of the gate of the latter is an inscription commemorating the construction of the building in 727 by the caliph Hishām b. 'Abd al-Malik (Combe *et al.* 1931, 23, n. 27; Genequand 2012, 170). Starting from the first work on the site by Schlumberger (1939b, 332), the dating provided by the inscription of the *khān* has generally been considered valid for the site in its entirety. This conclusion seems to be corroborated by the plan of the palace, which shows, as seen above, striking similarities with that of Qaṣr al-Ḥayr al-Sharqī. Although no stratigraphic data of the excavation exist, it is likely that the palace experienced a main occupation in Umayyad times, perhaps until the early 9th century, when it was abandoned; a later, 12th to 14th century occupation is attested in the form of a modest fortlet placed at the foot of the Late Antique tower. This occupied also part of the northern wing of the palace (Genequand 2012, 163–6).

Among the two agricultural enclosures of the site, the Jardin, *c.* 46ha in size and 2km to the northwest of the palace, is certainly the best known (Schlumberger 1939b, 205–7; 1986, 4–5; Genequand 2012, 308). This was delimited by a wall with stone foundations and upper part in mud brick. The wall was provided by small semi-circular towers placed alternately on both sides at regular intervals and two monumental gates. Water reached the Jardin through three aqueducts connected with an ingenious catchment system, known as the 'Barrage du Jardin'. The Barrage, which

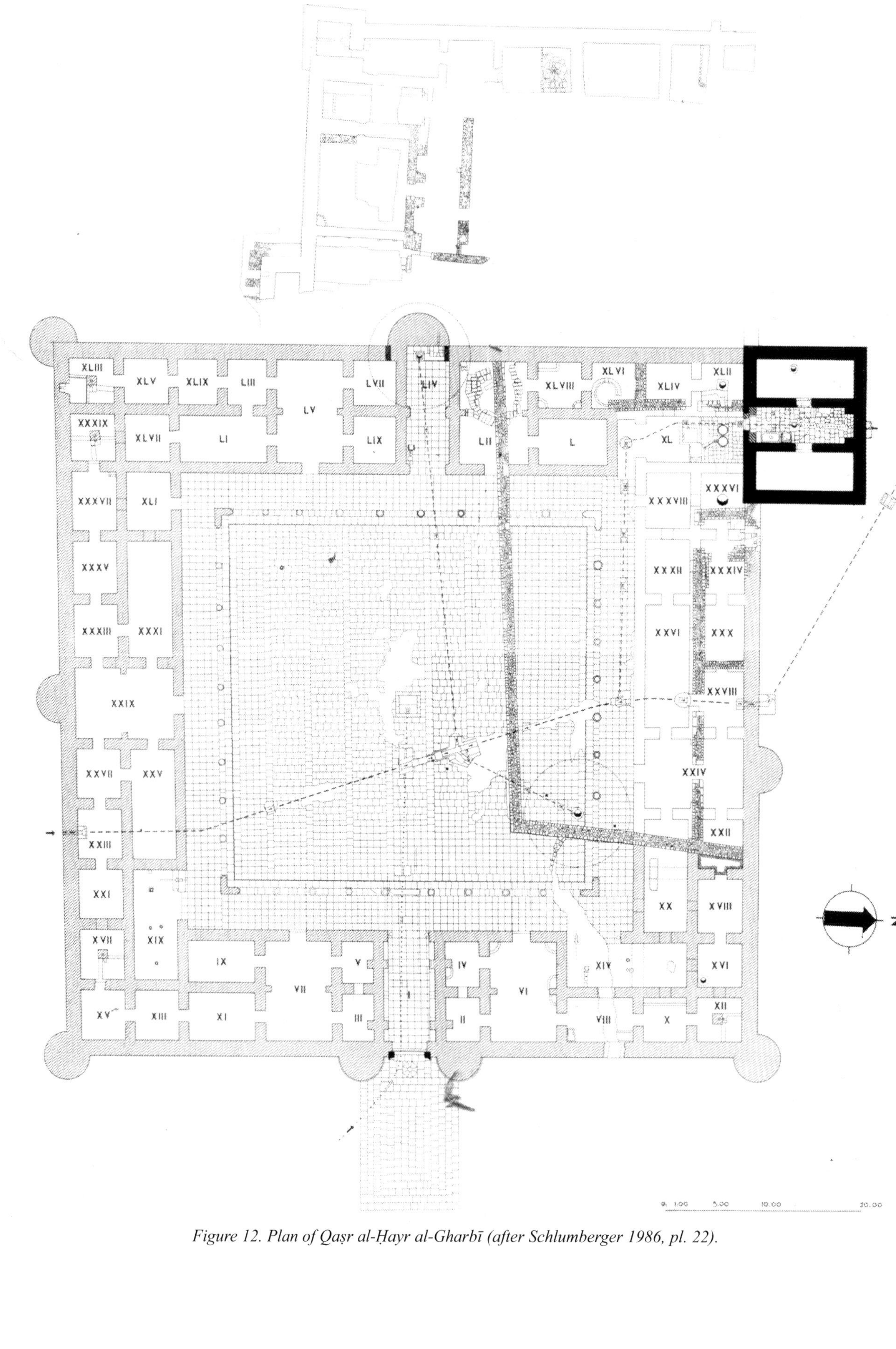

Figure 12. Plan of Qaṣr al-Ḥayr al-Gharbī (after Schlumberger 1986, pl. 22).

is located to the southeast of the agricultural enclosure, consists of a stone wall supported by semi-circular buttresses placed at regular intervals. The wall delimits an area in the shape of a lozenge ending with a semi-circle to the northwest (Schlumberger 1939b, 208–9; 1986, 5; Genequand 2012, 173–4; 258–9). The artificial basin thus formed was used for agricultural as well as recreational purposes (Genequand 2012, 259). Extra water collected by the dam of Ḥarbaqa, which was located 16.5km from the enclosure, would have reached the site by means of an aqueduct (Schlumberger 1939b, 200–4; 1986, 2–3; Genequand 2003a, 58–9; 2006b, 66–9; 2012, 173, 255–7, 289–90; 2009b, 160–6). At about 500m from the Jardin was a watermill, of similar construction and chronology of that at Qaṣr al-Ḥayr al-Sharqī (Schlumberger 1939b, 204–3; 1986, 4; Genequand 2012, 345–8).

A third aristocratic residence is known to be situated at al-Bakhrāʾ (Fig. 7). Evidence of its existence is found in written sources. In discussing the episode of the death of al-Walīd b. Yazīd at al-Bakhrāʾ, al-Ṭabarī (*Taʾrīkh* 2.1795–807) mentions the existence in this site of a village, a military encampment, and the castle or fortress (*qaṣr* or *ḥiṣn*) of Nuʿmān b. Bashīr, where the caliph would, in vain, look for refuge. From an archaeological perspective, the transformation of the ancient Tetrarchic fort into a settlement in Late Antiquity has already been discussed briefly above. In the Umayyad period, the site was further transformed. A rectangular enclosure (156.30 × 35.30m) was added against the northeastern wall of the fort. Its wall tries to mimic the architecture of the pre-existing military installation, being broken by roughly semi-circular (not U-shaped) interval towers. However, the northern corner tower is quadrangular, while the southern tower is a three-quarter-of-a-circle construction. The access to this newly added enclosure was first via a doorway next to one of the towers. Later, this entrance was blocked and accessing the compound became possible only via the Tetrarchic fort (Genequand 2003a, 36–7; 2004a, 234–6; 2004b, 93–4; 2004c, 15–16; 2012, 79–3). The addition to the fort has tentatively been identified as the *qaṣr*/*ḥiṣn* described by al-Ṭabarī (Genequand 2012, 93).

Further Early Islamic remains are found outside this enclosure. A mosque was constructed to the southeast of the fort and adjoining the church. Although there is no hard evidence to prove any chronology, an Umayyad dating remains plausible, given the occupational history of the site (Genequand 2003a, 37–8; 2004a, 236–8; 2004b, 94–6; 2004c, 17–18; 2012, 85–8). The mosque consists of a 24 × 13.50m large hypostyle hall divided into four aisles and a central nave. To the southwest, south, and east of the fort and its extensions are about 30 buildings. These have been interpreted as private residential buildings; their chronology (either Late Antique or Early Islamic) remains uncertain (Genequand 2004a, 238; 2012, 88–9). Similar incertitude on dating surrounds two necropoleis and a number of funerary monuments and burials scattered around the site (Genequand 2004a, 239; 2012, 89–90).

The construction of aristocratic residences in this region seems not to have been a prerogative of the Palmyrene. As a matter of fact, this was widespread across *Bilād al-Shām*. The function of these compounds were many. An economic component is certainly to be considered. Out of 38 of such sites in the Levant, 22 present installations for agriculture or husbandry (Genequand 2012, 369). The construction of such extended sites proves, transversally, that the Palmyrene, although marginal was a territory in which agricultural exploitation was possible by means of controlled water catchment and distribution systems. The archaeological remains confirms a good level of soil exploitation, making the problem of agriculture in the Palmyrene a false myth (Genequand 2012, 361–2; see also, Genequand 2012, 16, for a summary discussion; Debaine and Jaubert 2006, and Meyer 2008, 121–2, with extended bibliography on the deterioration of the steppe; Geyer 2002, 41–2, and Geyer and Rousset 2001, 114 on the fluctuations in the recent Holocene and their impact on the agriculture). Perhaps more important, the ambitious building programs of the first half of the 7th century in the Palmyrene betrays the shift towards new policies that accorded increasing importance to the countryside. Sites such as Qaṣr al-Ḥayr al-Sharqī and Qaṣr al-Ḥayr al-Gharbī served as clear manifestations of power and as places of interaction between the ruling dynasty and the local nomadic tribes (Genequand 2012, 379–96). In the Palmyrene, the latter were mostly represented by the Banū Kalb, who played a major role in supporting the caliphate in Damascus.

Conclusions

Although the Palmyrene remained a frontier territory in Late Antiquity rather distant from the centre of power, it was certainly not as isolated and remote as written sources tend to report. Roads allowed the moving of people and goods across the region. The human occupation of the Palmyrene translates in the presence of forts, villages, isolated farmsteads and monasteries. The widespread occurrence of forts is informative of the military function played by the Palmyrene in the late 3rd–4th centuries. Besides these, which in some cases were transformed into settlements, were proper villages and isolated farmstead that would certainly have benefited from the market of Palmyra to sell their goods. As an early bishopric, the city must have functioned as a centre of aggregation for the Christian communities living in surrounding areas, as well as a centre of diffusion of Christianity in the countryside. Yet, the Christian geography of the Palmyrene remains particularly blurry. We are only aware of three monasteries in the territory of Palmyra, one of which of unknown location.

Nothing is known on the Palmyrene under the short time span of the Persian occupation, while more evidence survives for the Early Islamic period. The military role of the region remained of prime importance during Late Antiquity, but ceased to be a necessity after the Islamic conquest. The collapse of the Roman frontier system meant that the Palmyrene was not any longer a frontier territory and Palmyra lost its military function. The pre-existing regional road system was likely maintained, while the east–west communications were strengthened. Evidence for travel and commerce is sporadic, but for the time being confirms the occurrence of imported goods from a number of sources, including Jordan, the valley of the Euphrates, and northern Syria. Little is known on settlement patterns. By contrast, much information is left on the new phenomenon of the construction of aristocratic residence. The building of opulent compounds for the caliph and his entourage reflects a shift of attention toward the countryside, which was justified, *inter alia*, by the necessity to interact directly with the tribes of central Syria.

Note

1 Like similar sections in this book, the following overview is not intended to be exhaustive; rather, it aims to provide essential information on a selection of archaeological pieces of evidence. For more details, the reader is invited to consult the original reports of the excavations written by the archaeological teams and referenced in the text.

Chapter 2

A changing townscape

In the aftermath of the Aurelianic events, Palmyra revived as a new city. Its legal status was maintained, at least in the short term, but the dynamics of urban living changed dramatically. The pre-existing topography of Roman times, its roads, temples, and public compounds were progressively devoured by the advance of privatisation. Residential buildings started occupying public places and the aesthetic of Roman times was replaced by a tendency toward pragmatism. A broader look at the regional context in which these changes occurred suggests that Palmyra's post-Classical urbanism is in line with that of other contemporary cities in the Near East and beyond. In itself, then, this transformation reflects the adaptability of this city to the administrative, cultural, and political changes of its time.

Palmyra: *polis*, *colonia*, *phrourion*, and *madīna*

Many sources, among whom are Alexander the Akoimetēs (*Alex. Akoim.*, 35), Malalas (*Chr.*, 17.2), Procopius (*Aed.*, 2.11.10–12; 5.1.1), Theophanes (*Chr.*, 1.174), and the author of the account of the miracle of St. Anastasius (*Anas. Per.*, 1.129–30), have a tendency to apply the generic term *polis* (πόλις – lit. 'city') to Palmyra, with the result that it is often difficult to discern whether this is used to define a particular juridical status. A number of inscriptions from Diocletianic milestones found in the road from Homs to Palmyra refer to the latter with the technical term *colonia* (*CIL* 3. 6049 = 6727.4 = Thomsen 1917, 26, n. 39; *CIS* 2.3971, note = Thomsen 1917, 27, n. 47; *CIL* 3.14177[4], 1–2 = Thomsen 1917, 27, n. 45a; Poidebard 1934, 200 n. 1; *cf.* Hartmann 2001, 59). This implies that the 272–273 events did not alter the status of Palmyra, which must have maintained its juridical privileges in the immediate Aurelianic aftermath.

A number of administrative and ecclesiastical sources implicitly recognise Palmyra's importance as a major settlement at the time, but do not make use of any qualitative term to label it. Two 6th century writers, Hierocles (*Synec.*, 717.1–8) and George of Cyprus (*Desc. Orb. Rom.*, 984–96), include Palmyra in an administrative list of cities in *Phoenicia Libanensis*. Works of an ecclesiastical nature record the presence of bishops in Palmyra since the first half of the 4th century. The *Notitia Antiochena* lists the cities according to their importance in specific dioceses. Palmyra appears in third place, after *Heliopolis* (Ba'albak) and *Abila* (Quwayliba) under the jurisdiction of Damascus (Honigmann 1925, 75; Vailhé 1907, 145). In the *Tabula Peutingeriana* (*seg.* 10–11, see Fig. 5), Palmyra is represented in a vignette with two pointed roof towers provided with two large gateways and connected by a wall. The vignette appears frequently in the document, occurring 435 times out of 559; although its exact meaning is obscure, it certainly identifies places of well-known administrative, political, religious, and military importance (Talbert 2010, 119, 121). Indeed, it is noteworthy that, in the same section of the document, identical vignettes are used to represent Homs and Damascus.

Only two authors, Palladius (*Dial. John Chris.*, 20.35–8) and Stephanus of Byzantium (*Ethnika*, Π 6), who reports what written by the undated historian Uranios, stress the military nature of the city by referring to Palmyra as a *phrourion* (φρούριον). To Procopius (*De Aed.*, 2.5.9), this term is the equivalent of the Latin *castellum*. *Phrouria* differ from large fortified settlements mainly because of their modest size. The author of the *De Re Strategica* reports that these were outposts located along the frontiers to guard against potential enemy assaults. He informs us that 'the men in the garrison should not have their wives and children with them', but that 'if a fort is extremely strong … then there is no reason why the men cannot have their families reside there with them' (*De Re Strategica*, 9; tr. Dennis 1985, 29; de' Maffei 1990, 136, n. 4). The term is, however, particularly problematic as it sometimes happens that a city is labelled either *polis* or *phrourion* by different authors (Haldon 1999, 11). Brandes (1989, 31–5) has also observed that the meaning of the term *kastron* (κάστρον), which is not dissimilar from that of *phrourion*, tends to be equated by written sources with that of *polis* in the 6th and 7th centuries.

In Early Islamic written sources the Greek name of the city, 'Palmyra', was replaced by the early Semitic 'Tadmur', which, however, had not completely been abandoned in Late Antiquity. A Syriac codex from a monastery said to be near Palmyra and dated to the mid-6th century, names the city TWDMR (Wright 1872, 2.468–9, n. 585; Millar 2013, 23). If Greek sources refer to Palmyra in a number of ways, the Arabic sources are characterised by the use of a single term, *madīna* (مدينة – lit. 'city'). The list of authors who use this term for Palmyra is long, and includes Agapius (*Kitāb*, 511–12), Ibn al-Faqīh (*Mukhtaṣar*, 110), al-Iṣfahānī (*al-Aghānī*, 17.112–13), Ibn Aʿtham al-Kūfī (*Kitāb*, 1.140–2), al-Masʿūdī (*Murūj*, 1.190; 4.77–8), Ṣafī al-Dīn (*Marāṣid*, 1.200), al-Ṭabarī (*Tāʾrīkh*, 9.1895–6), al-Wāqidī (*al-Maghāzī*, 1.44), and Yāqūt (*Muʿjam*, 1.832). Several works indirectly inform us that the city retained the special status of a fortified place due to its extant city wall. An example is found in al-Ṭabarī (*Tāʾrīkh*, 9.1796; see also Ibn ʿAsākir, *Tāʾrīkh*, 63.337–8): al-Abrash Saʿīd b. al-Walīd al-Kalbī mentions Palmyra to al-Walīd b. Yazīd, whose caliphate was usurped by Yazīd b. al-Walīd (r. 744), among other 'fortified places' of refuge.

Size and limits of the settlement

While the Roman Palmyra had included a considerable area that embraced not only the space within the inner ramparts, but also the so-called Hellenistic quarter south of Wādī al-Qubūr (Schmidt-Colinet, al-Asʿad, and al-Asʿad 2013, with further bibliography), the Late Antique and Early Islamic city was significantly smaller in size (Figs 2–3). The bulk of the post-Roman archaeological evidence has been brought to light in an area situated between the Camp of Diocletian to the west, the Suburban Market to the north, the Peristyle Building to the south, and the Sanctuary of Bēl to the east. The northeast, east, and southeast areas of the ancient city are nowadays occupied by modern orchards and gardens and have never been systematically explored, but presumably even in these sectors urbanisation extended to the urban circuit. Therefore, the physical limit of the urban area in post-Roman times was imposed by the inner city wall (Hammad 2010, 45–54).

Late Antique and Early Islamic evidence outside this limit is attested, albeit in a reduced way. To the north of the city wall, in the gardens of the modern archaeological museum, was the most extended cemetery of the settlement (al-Asʿad 1967; 1968; al-Asʿad and Ruprechtsberger 1987, 137–46). This has yielded Late Antique and Early Islamic material, among it being funerary slabs with carved Christian crosses and Arabic inscriptions (never fully published). Funerary inscriptions from the Valley of the Tombs show that this necropolis still served its original function at least until the 4th century (*IGLS* 17.1, 334–5, 346, n. 435, 451–3). The southwest necropolis was similarly frequented at the time (Ingholt 1932, 16–17; 1935, 106–8; *IGLS* 17.1, 394, n. 527). The Hellenistic Quarter does not seem to have completely been abandoned as the Sanctuary of Arṣū was likely frequented in the immediate Aurelianic aftermath (al-Asʿad and Gawlikowski 1986–1987, 167–8). Building [Q281], located just 1 km to the east of the Camp of Diocletian, on the right bank of Wādī al-Qubūr, was also probably abandoned after the Zenobian collapse. Evidence for post-273 temporary occupation, the chronology of which has proved to be difficult to pinpoint, is attested, however, in the form of scattered bones of cows, sheep, and goats; in a second stage, a lime kiln was installed in the open courtyard (Byliński 1995, 227, 229–30).

The reduction in size of Palmyra was the principal result of the Aurelianic disruptions. The fact that the city did not expand to its former Roman urban limit in Late Antiquity should not be considered in itself proof of the stagnated vitality of the settlement. The occupation of urban areas of small sizes embraced by city walls is a common phenomenon in Late Antiquity (Liebeschuetz 1992, 10–11; Zanini 2003, 214–15). The walled area of a Syrian *polis* such as *Chalcis* (Qinnasrīn), for example, would not have exceeded 80ha (Mango 2011, 95, 97, table 1). If the city wall of Palmyra is taken as the physical limit of the post-Roman settlement, its inhabitable surface would have reached some 127ha, making of the settlement one of the largest cities in Syria. This figure is, however, a rough estimate and should be treated with caution. Indeed, not all of the area embraced by the city wall in Palmyra seems to have been built up, and there is evidence of buildings abandoned for up to two centuries in Late Antiquity, only to be re-occupied thereafter (e.g., the northwest quarter, Żuchowska 2006, 447).

Street network

There is little data to track the evolution of urbanistic features like squares or decorative monuments in post-Roman Palmyra. Yet, something can still be said on the Late Antique and Early Islamic street network. As this mostly originates from the Roman period, to achieve a good understanding of its development it is first necessary to look back at the topography of earlier times. In the 3rd century, the area of Palmyra encompassed by the inner city wall developed around two main topographic features. The easternmost is the Sanctuary of Bēl, which served as the religious hub of the city. It consisted of a monumental temple founded in 32 and a later 205 × 205m *temenos* (Amy *et al.* 1975). The second is an imposing colonnaded street, the Great Colonnade, stretching for about 1.2km from the Sanctuary of Bēl to the Funerary Temple 173d [=E102], to the west; epigraphic evidence seems to suggest that the thoroughfare was constructed in different phases starting from prior to 158 and continuing throughout the 3rd century (Barański 1995; Saliou 1996; Tabaczec 2001, 17–41). Secondary streets of different orientation and size, led from the Great Colonnade to the city's outskirts (Tabaczek 2001, 17–41). These assured circulation within the residential areas in the southwest and northwest quarters of the city, as well as providing access to major public compounds such as the *Agora*, the Sanctuary of Nabū, and the Sanctuary of Baalshamīn. Several of them, such as the Transverse Colonnade leading from the Funerary Temple 173d to the Damascus Gate or that connecting the Theatre with the Theatre Gate, had large carriageways and were even porticoed. Roman Palmyra had never experienced a Classical urban plan with a *cardo*, a *decumanus*, and a regular grid of streets crossing at right-angles (Frézouls 1976a, 192; Dentzer 2000, 159). The Great Colonnade cannot be considered the *decumanus* of the city, since it was developed in three sections that were constructed at different times and with different orientations. Nor is there a unique and regular street pattern (Frézouls 1976a, 196–8; recently Hammad 2010, 39). This form of urbanism finds its best parallel in the oriental urban planning tradition characteristic of cities such as Assur or Hattusa, rather than in those created anew by Romans (Frézouls 1976a, 199, n. 21; see also, Yon 2001, esp. 181). In this light, the installation of the Great Colonnade, which found its origin in Hellenistic times (Bejor 1999), can be read as an attempt to find a compromise between two architectonical traditions (Frézouls 1976a, 199).

Very few changes were introduced to the Roman street grid in Late Antiquity. The Great Colonnade was certainly maintained as the main thoroughfare of the city (Figs 13 and 14). This is hardly surprising, given the similar prominent

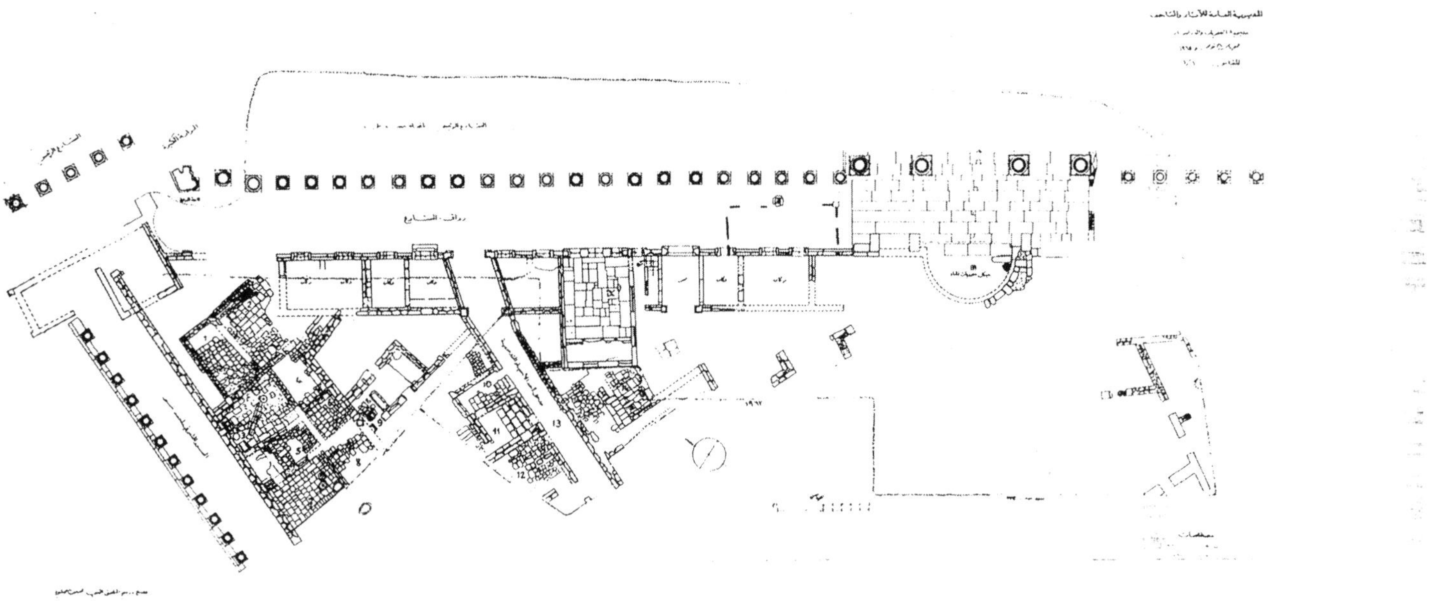

Figure 13. Great Colonnade, Section A (Saliby 1966, 236, pl. 1).

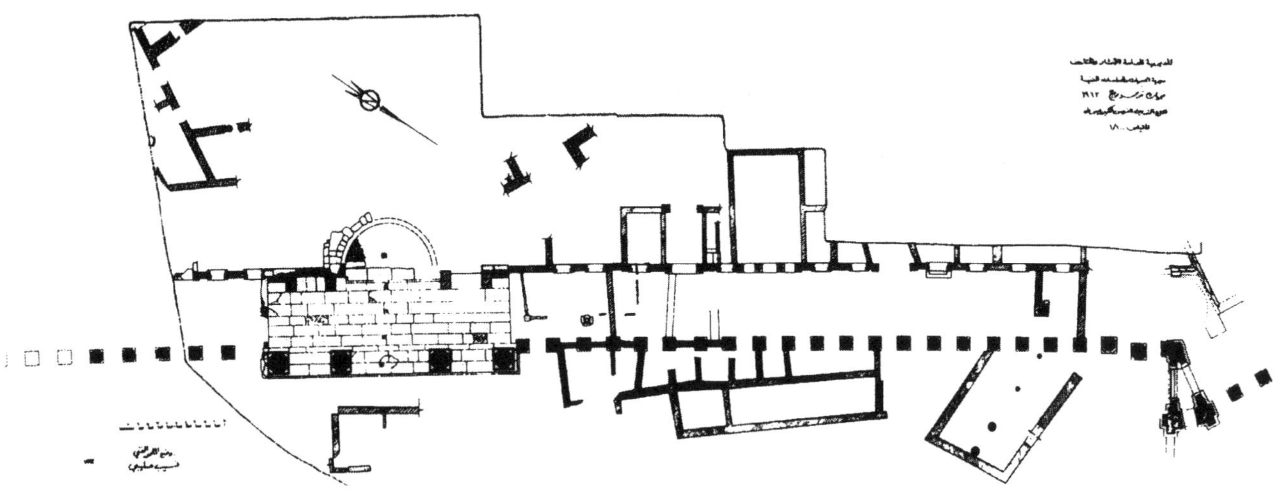

Figure 14. Great Colonnade, Section A (Saliby 1966, 236, pl. 2).

role of this topographical feature in other contemporary urban centres (Jacobs 2013, 112–20). Problems arise in approaching the secondary literature dedicated to the Great Colonnade (Bounni and Saliby 1965, 124–6; Bounni 1967, 43–4; Ostratz 1969; al-As῾ad and Stępniowski 1989; Saliby 1996; Żuchowska 2000; 2003), as most of the post-Roman structures located along its course are dated with difficulty. Three modest churches (or chapels?) have been identified along the Great Colonnade (see Fig. 2). They lie 15m north of the Baths of Diocletian, next to a pre-existing *nymphaeum* near the *Tetrapylon*, and against the northern wall of the Funerary Temple 173c [=A201] (Majcherek 2005), as to sanctify with their presence the whole length of the thoroughfare. In addition, Church I, despite being located some 50m to the north of the Great Colonnade, had one of its entrances opening onto this road axis through a long and narrow stone-paved passage (Żuchowska 2006, 448–50). One should not exclude that the Great Colonnade was in use as processional road in Late Antiquity. Occasional Christian graffiti made by passers-by and dated roughly to the 4th or 5th century demonstrate that this street remained a heavily trafficked artery. Two of these are located on its westernmost section and are genuine expressions of faith – Εἷς θεός. Ζοή ('One god. Long life') and Κύριε ('Lord') (*IGLS* 17.1, 117, 118, n. 105, 107); a third, on a column of the easternmost stretch, is an invocation to God to help a certain Antonius –+ Κ(ύρι)ε β(οη)θῶν +. Ἀντώνιος. [.]ΠΑΥΤΑ [- - -] ('+ Oh Lord helping + Antonios ? [- - -]') (*IGLS* 17.1, 118, n. 106; tr. rev. Kowalski 1997, 57).

Safely-dated evidence for commercial activities along this road axis in this period is scanty but does confirm that the Great Colonnade maintained also its original role as a commercial hub. The excavation of a shop in the southern portico of the western section of the Great Colonnade has yielded evidence of occupation from the 270s until the Early Islamic period (al-As῾ad and Stępniowski 1989, 211; see also, Gawlikowski 1997c, 348). The finds include an Aurelianic coin at the bottom of the sounding, a badly preserved copper coin dated roughly to the 6th–beginning of the 7th century (layer III, lying on top of a mortared floor), Umayyad (layer II, lying on top of a mortared floor) and ῾Abbāsid pottery (layer I, lying on top of stamped clay). Furthermore, new shops were constructed (or refurbished) in the second half of the 4th century in the portico of Insula E (Section C) (Żuchowska 2006, 445).

Other streets gained a new role and prominence in this period. The so-called 'Church Street' represents an informative example. Running from the Great Colonnade northward, this unpaved street would have assured north–south public circulation in the northwest quarter in Roman times. In Late Antiquity, its importance to the Christian community increased as three churches opened onto it. The *Atrium* of Church III, which was likely built together with the church in the 5th century, extended with its flagging onto its carriageway, but did not block its traffic (Gawlikowski 2002, 261–3; see Figs 36, 39). According to the excavators, the street might have been the property of the Church when the *Atrium* was constructed. Only later was it returned to the public as the *Atrium* was transformed into a porch by blocking the *intercolumnia* of its eastern portico (Gawlikowski 2002, 263). Further north, a flagged, squared area (4.75 × 4.85m), limited by four columns at its corners, would have marked the entrance of a *martyrion* (Gawlikowski 2002, 264). The circulation of a parallel street to the west of Church Street was completely blocked by the construction of the apse and *pastophoria* of Church IV.

The appropriation of public streets by the ecclesiastical authority is not a prerogative of Palmyra. At Jerash, the construction of the *Propylaea* Church in the two courtyards of the Temple of Artemis blocked the access to one of the bridges on the river Chrysorhoas connecting the east and west parts of the city in the second half of the 6th century (Brenk 2003, 22). Similarly, at Apamea the construction of the *Atrium* Church and the Cathedral complex hampered the traffic flow by blocking two secondary streets (Balty and Napolene-Lemaire 1969, 27). However, the encroachment of streets in Late Antique Palmyra remains a rather unusual phenomenon, as generally buildings develop within the limits imposed by the pre-existing blocks. A complete blocking by private residential buildings is recorded in the street adjoining the Sanctuary of Baalshamīn to the west. Collart believed this to have occurred in the early 4th century; this conclusion, however, has to be taken with reservation as the structures are located much higher than those of the Roman level (Intagliata 2017a). This suggests a protracted abandonment of the compound between the Roman frequentation of the street and their construction, which might have occurred even in the Early Islamic period.

Evidence for streets laid anew in post-Roman Palmyra is particularly scanty, and includes three sinuous streets within the northern courtyard of the Sanctuary of Baalshamīn and the *Via Praetoria* in the Camp of Diocletian (Fig. 15). The pre-existing Roman grid was generally kept functional through continuous maintenance. An inscription dated to 328 refers to the re-roofing of a portico with eight columns in the westernmost section of the Great Colonnade by a certain Flavius Diogenes, son of Uranios, while curator of the city (ἐν τῇ ἑαυτοῦ λογιστίᾳ) (*IGLS* 17.1, 114–15, n. 101; on this see below, p. 98). The carriageway of this section underwent maintenance interventions from the early 4th until the late 6th century and the street floor of the Roman period, which was made of a layer of limestone gravel, was renewed on several occasions (Żuchowska 2000, 187; *cf.* Żuchowska 2003, 293; Puchstein 1932, 21–30 for similar evidence in Section B of the Great Colonnade). The excavation of a section of an adjacent street to the north of the Suburban Market has shown that this road axis underwent two important renovations in Late Antiquity, one of these being

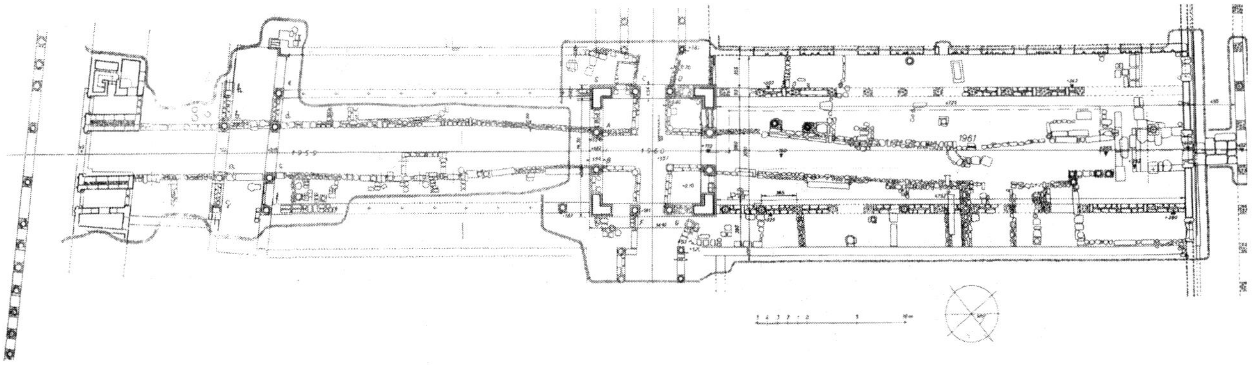

Figure 15. Via Praetoria, *Camp of Diocletian (Michałowski 1962, annex 2; 1963a, annex 1).*

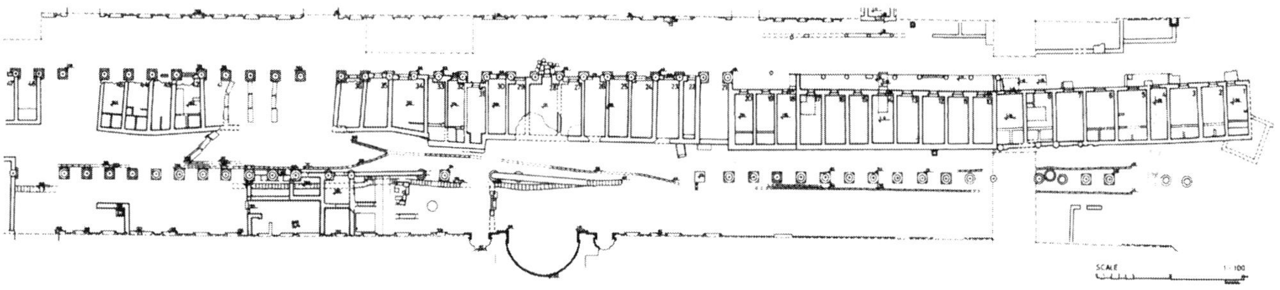

Figure 16. The Umayyad Sūq *(al-As'ad and Stępniowsky 1989, pl. 1. With permission of the German Archaeological Institute).*

the laying of a new flagging over an older one (Delplace 2006–2007, 102).

In the Early Islamic period, even if enchroachment drastically changed the appearance of the pre-existing Roman street pattern, it presumably did not dramatically affect public circulation. As was the case in other cities of the Levant, and as required by Muslim jurists, enough room was usually left to allow people and pack-animals to pass without impediment (Kennedy 1985, 26, citing Bulliet 1975). This occurred, for example, in the *Via Praetoria* of the Camp of Diocletian, which lost its military function in the Early Islamic period, as well as in the west section of the Great Colonnade. The latter not only remained the main axis of the settlement but maintained (and probably increased) its commercial role. Along its westernmost section, a *sūq* was installed between the end of the 7th and the beginning of the 8th century (Fig. 16). What is left of the compound after the excavations of the Polish team and the Syrian authorities is a row of 47 shops located in the middle of the carriageway for a preserved length of *c.* 170m. All the shops open toward the north and are clustered in smaller groups, reflecting the development of the compound in different phases of construction. The *sūq* was built with reused architectural material. The quality of its building techniques differs considerably across the whole compound: ten shops are paved with floors of flagstone, while the others have their surfaces either plastered or provided with a 'dirt floor of hard stamped clay' (al-As'ad and Stępniowski 1989, 209). In all likelihood, the walls of these shops were plastered too. The installation of the *sūq* hindered, but did not completely obstacle, the flow of traffic. Passage was assured through two lanes flanking the longest sides of the new market. The two lanes communicated through the row of shops thanks to a number of transversal passageways. Soundings conducted in the compound were able to clarify the chronological development of the building. As discussed, the pre-existing shops located along this section of the Great Colonnade have been proven to be functioning when the *sūq* was in operation. The excavations revealed that the compound remained active throughout the Umayyad period and was abandoned under the 'Abbāsids (al-As'ad and Stępniowski 1989, 210–11).

Water sources and water supply systems

Ancient Palmyra was blessed by numerous springs in its vicinity. The best known of these is the sulphureous Efqa, on the eastern slope of Jabal al-Munṭār. The spring fits awkwardly in the topography of the Roman, Late Antique, and Early Islamic city (Yon 2009, 97); it is likely that the water from Efqa was mostly used to feed the gardens of the oasis rather than the settlement. As a matter of fact, no traces of water installations have been found close to the entrance of the spring (Juchniewicz and Żuchowska 2012, 63). The Efqa spring has been the object of much scholarly interest; a number of altars devoted to the Anonymous God have been discovered at the entrance of the grotto (Gawlikowski 1974, n. 106–27) and cultual buildings have been unearthed during the construction of the Hotel Meridien (Parlasca 1996; Benbaali 2005). Ṣafī al-Dīn (*Marāṣid*, 1.200) and, much later, Ibn al-Shiḥna (*al-Durr al-Muntakhab*, 275–6, 15th–16th centuries), may have referred to its water course when accounting for the existence of a 'river' exploited to irrigate the orchards of the medieval village in the Sanctuary of Bēl. Within the city wall, a more modest spring in the Camp of Diocletian would have provided water for soldiers quartered in this military compound (see below, p. 75). In addition to this, a third spring (or springs; the 'Serail source') was reported by Carle (1923, 156–60) to be situated to the northwest of the Sanctuary of Bēl and connected with the water from Efqa (see also, Crouch 1975b, 156–7; Juchniewicz and Żuchowska 2012, 61). Other springs are located further outside the city. The spring at Abū al-Fawāris is 10km to the west of Palmyra (Barański 1997, 7; Juchniewicz and Żuchowska 2012, 63). Carle (1923, 155–6) visited the site in the early 20th century and described its intake in detail. The spot is marked by the presence of a monument, likely composed of a single free-standing column, of which a number of architectural elements and two limestone fragments of a statue of Heracles remain still visible on the ground (Bounni and al-As῾ad 1982, 135; Starcky and Gawlikowski 1985, 22; Barański 1997, 15; Hauser 2012, 216–17, n. 43). A vaulted underground conduit with graffiti in Palmyrene was found at the source of Biyar al-῾Amī (Carle 1923, 156; Starcky 1952, 82; Crouch 1975b, 166; Juchniewicz and Żuchowska 2012, 64; Hauser 2012, 216). Finally, a 'southwest spring' is mentioned by Tourtechot (1735, 341) and reported to be located 'between Palmyra and the village of Sedat' (Crouch 1975b, 166; Juchniewicz and Żuchowska 2012, 63). The epigraphic record confirms the existence of diverse springs in the city and its surroundings. The Tax Law of Palmyra, which dates back to 137, mentions two springs 'in the city' (*CIS*2.3913 = Matthews 1984, 177). Similarly, a milestone reports the distance from *Veriaraca* 'to the springs of Palmyra' under the Tetrarchs (the reading '… *a Palmyrae (f) on/tibus Beriarac/m. XVI*' is by Bauzou (1993, 45 = *AE* 1996, 483, n. 1606); *contra CIL* 3.14177$_4$ = Thomsen 1917, 27, n. 45, a2: '… *a Palmyra euntibus Beriarac m(ilia) [p(assuum)] XVI*').

Water from springs located *extra muros* reached the city through a complex system of aqueducts that included two main water lines, namely one from the spring at Abū al-Fawāris and the other from Biyar al-῾Amī. The water from the spring of Abū al-Fawāris was conveyed to Palmyra via the so-called Western Aqueduct. This would have entered the city through the section of the inner urban circuit surrounding the Camp of Diocletian (next to tower [A106]). Its course outside the city wall is visible to some extent on the ground and through satellite imagery. It crosses the Valley of the Tombs from east to west and runs parallel with Jabal al-Abyaḍ to the north and Wādī al-Qubūr to the south. Further west, it passes above a wall which is commonly regarded as belonging to the Roman ramparts of the city later destroyed by Aurelian (Gawlikowski 1975a, 46). The aqueduct runs underground for about 5km and then becomes visible closer to the city (Crouch 1975b, 162). Like all the water installations in Palmyra, the chronology of this aqueduct is still not clear. Investigations carried out by Barański suggest that it was constructed as early as second half of the 2nd century (Barański 1997, 15; *cf.* Meyza 1985, 32–3; Juchniewicz and Żuchowska 2012, 66; Hauser 2012, 216–17). Nonetheless, it experienced later restorations. Large sections of its course show traces of substantial repairs, often made with reused architecture. These include raising the level of the aqueduct and strengthening the original structure with cobblestone and mortar. In several places, the original conduit was integrally replaced by a new one (Barański 1997, 12–13). The latest, datable maintenance interventions are dated to the 8th century, when a post-reform coin was mortared in a section of the structure (Barański 1997, 13). A further water line, the 'Northern Aqueduct', would have brought water from the spring at Biyar al-῾Amī. This would have passed the city wall through tower [A222], which has been recently identified as the *castellum aquae* of the water system (Juchniewicz, al-As῾ad, and al-Hariri 2010, 56; Juchniewicz and Żuchowska 2012, 68; 2013, 345). The chronology of this aqueduct remains, however, to be clarified. The conduit said by Tourtechot to have brought water into the city from the southwest is no more visible (Tourtechot 1735, 341), and the date of construction of this water line remains, therefore, unknown. The conclusions reached by Crouch (1975b, 176), according to whom the aqueduct is dated to Hellenistic or Justinianic times because Tourtechot mentions the presence of Greek inscriptions in his report, rests on a very fragile ground.

Having reached the city wall, the water from Abū al-Fawāris was distributed to the city through a system of pipes that would have started from the Camp of Diocletian. From the 'Water Gate' (located between the Temple Tomb 86 [=D301] and the northernmost shop along the western side of the Transverse Colonnade), a major water line would have run along the Great Colonnade. Throughout Late Antiquity and the Early Islamic period, this underwent considerable restorations, from small repairs to the complete replacement of old pipelines with new ones. The chronology of these interventions remain obscure and still await to be fully investigated. It has been proposed that its mid-4th century pipes were replaced in Justinianic times by a stone conduit laid at street level, consisting of rectangular stone blocks, semi-circular in section, with a 0.24m passage pierced in them to allow the flow of water. This conclusion is mostly based on a passage of Procopius, in which it is reported that the emperor restored the water supply in Palmyra (Juchniewicz and Żuchowska 2012, 67; on the 4th century pipes: Żuchowska 2003, 291–4). By contrast, Barański (1997, 11) believes that, after the stone conduit broke or silted up, it was replaced in Justinianic times by a new pipeline (Type G). More pipes are believed to have been laid in Umayyad times, but were destroyed after a disastrous earthquake and then replaced in the ʿAbbāsid era (al-Asʿad and Stępniowski 1989, 209–10; Juchniewicz and Żuchowska 2012, 70). Water coming from the source at Biyār al-ʿAmī was distributed through a secondary line whose traces have been found in 'Diogenes street' (two pipes in contexts dated to the 5th–6th century), and between Church IV and the city wall (a stone channel) (Żuchowska 2000, 189, fig. 2; Juchniewicz and Żuchowska 2012, 68, 71). The structures within the city associated with the Northern Aqueduct are believed to have been in use well into the Early Islamic period (Juchniewicz and Żuchowska 2012, 71).

From the city's main conduits, the water was distributed through a system of minor pipes, whose pattern is still mostly unknown. It is reasonable to assume, however, that these smaller water lines would have followed the course of the streets. Traces of terracotta pipes and water conduits have been found in the *Agora*, in a private residential building, 100m to the east of the modern Archaeological Museum, in the Northwest Quarter, in the *Praetorium* of the Camp of Diocletian, and in the Sanctuary of Baalshamīn (Seyrig 1940, 238–9; Barański 1997, 11; Kowalski 1994, 58; Gawlikowski 1994, 139; 1998, 199; 2000, 256; 2002, 269; Collart and Vicari 1969, 18; pl. 55, 91–6; 57, 4, 6). Water from these pipes was usually conveyed into small cisterns or, as in the case of Churches II and III (Gawlikowski 2000, 257), larger water tanks.

Another way of supplying water was through *qanawāt* (sing. *qanāt*), sloping tunnels provided with ventilation shafts at regular intervals used to collect water drained from the permeable rock. The dating of these structures is unknown, but they seem to have been in use at least until Carle's visit to the site in the early 20th century (Carle 1923, 154–5; Crouch 1975b, 169, n. 43). Two of them are still clearly visible in satellite imagery. One crosses the city from southwest to northeast, following a straight line from the area of the Camp of Diocletian to the *Tetrapylon*. Crouch associates this *qanāt* with the water line of the Western Aqueduct, but recent discoveries suggest that the two conduits were supplied separately (Crouch 1975b, 162; Barański 1997, 8). A second *qanāt* enters the city from the north (tower [A217]), to end about 200m to the south of the Dura Gate (Crouch 1975b, 169–70).

An alternative way of procuring water at Palmyra consisted in exploiting the region's rich underground aquifers by digging wells. This was relatively easy in ancient time, as the water table was not deeper than 5m. Since then, however, underground aquifers have considerably been reduced. In the early 1990s, the water table was at around 15m below the ground (Gawlikowski 1992a, 71; Benbabaali 2005, on recent water exploitation at Palmyra). This reduction was mostly caused by a major exploitation of water carried out in the 1950s, which coincided with the introduction of motor-pumps in the oasis. The distribution pattern of wells in the city is still mostly unknown and so is their chronology. Recently, Juchniewicz and Żuchowska have praiseworthily attempted the recording of this kind of evidence in a distribution map that, however, remains preliminary in nature (Juchniewicz and Żuchowska 2012, 71, fig. 15; 2013, 342–3, fig. 1). A number of examples can be cited to provide a hint of the extent of this practice. The Polish excavations of the House F in the northwest quarter resulted in the uncovering of five wells, 4.30– 8m in depth, some of which dated to the post-Roman phase of the building (Gawlikowski 1991a, 88 (loc. 13, 4.5m deep; loc. 22, 8m deep); Gawlikowski 1992a, 71 (loc. 18, about 5m deep); Gawlikowski 1994, 139 (loc. 33, depth not specified); Gawlikowski 1996, 143 (loc. not specified, 5m and 5.50m deep); Gawlikowski 2007, 90). The house was not reached by the urban pipe system (Gawlikowski 2007, 90). Other wells in the same quarter have been uncovered in the latest level of occupation of Churches II and III (Gawlikowski 1992a, 75; 2002, 259; 2003, 282), and in the so-called Eastern Building (Room G 3.9. Gawlikowski, 2000, 256). Post-Roman wells in private residential buildings were also excavated in the structures invading the *Via Praetoria* of the Camp of Diocletian. In the latest phase of occupation of the northern area of the Sanctuary of Baalshamīn, two wells were discovered. One, square in plan, was found in the northeast corner of Courtyard Q in Building B. It was delimited by four narrow blocks but was not excavated. The second is located in the courtyard of Bâtiment Nord, next to the so-called 'Arab Fountain', a rectangular monolithic basin pierced in one of its extremities (*Notebook* 1956a, 20 September). Its main features were recorded by Collart in his notebook in 1966 (Fig. 17). It has an opening of 0.55–0.57m and stands out from the ground for about 1m; the visible section is composed of one course of four narrow blocks arranged in a square on top of a 0.3m high second course of smaller stones. The original depth is said to have been 2m (*Notebook* 1966a, 6–7 April).

There is evidence to suggest, therefore, that the Roman water supply system in Palmyra remained functional in Late Antiquity and in the Early Islamic period, thanks to continuous maintenance. Aqueducts were repaired when necessary and new terracotta or stone pipes were laid to replace the older ones. This is hardly surprising; maintenance of pre-existing supply systems was considered a necessity by civic administrations and regulated by law in Late Antiquity

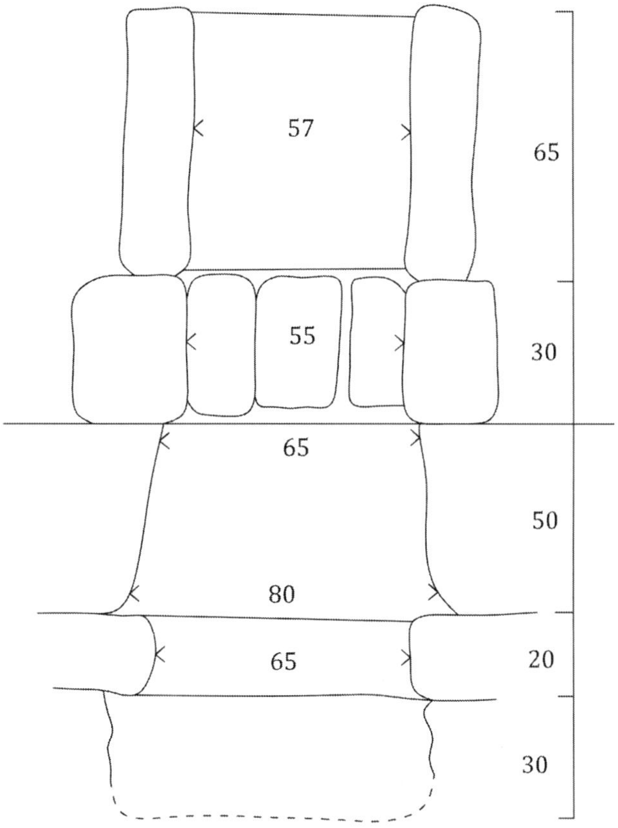

Figure 17. Well in the Portique Rhodien of the Bâtiment Nord, Sanctuary of Baalshamīn, as sketched by Collart in 1966 (redrawn by the author after Notebook *1966a, 7 April).*

(Saradi 2006, 343–9). Additional water for private or public use could be obtained through the excavation of wells and the exploitation of the rich underground aquifers. The evidence collected so far remains, however, scanty and new excavations and targeted research are needed to clarify the development of the water supply system of the city.

Large-scale urban changes: the formation of new specialised quarters

The transformation of Palmyra into a fortress city, the advent of Christianity, and the coming of Muslim settlers contributed considerably to the reshaping of the settlement's townscape. New specialised quarters were created that partially or completely obliterated pre-existing buildings. The details of these transformations will be discussed in depth in the relevant chapters of this book, but for the time being it is necessary to reflect on the significance of these large-scale urban changes in a much wider perspective. As in modern urban centres, extensive areas were destroyed or renovated to serve other purposes through great building enterprises. The continuous metamorphosis of the city throughout Late Antiquity and the Early Islamic period is in itself proof of the vitality and dynamism of the settlement, which was transformed to meet the needs of a changing urban community.

In Late Antiquity, the religious hub of the Roman city moved from the Sanctuary of Bēl to the northwest quarter. Here, a veritable ecclesiastical quarter comprising a number of churches and their dependencies arose in a former residential area in the 5th and 6th centuries. Dated to the end of the 3rd or early 4th century is the installation of the legionary fortress, the Camp of Diocletian. Pre-existing religious, residential, and productive areas were razed to the ground on this occasion, and only the Sanctuary of Allāth was spared from destruction. The Camp of Diocletian remained isolated from the civilian settlement by a 2nd century row of three lines of rooms following a north–south orientation, flanking the Transverse Colonnade to the west. Whether this was conceived as a proper boundary for the civilians is difficult to establish. Access might have been granted to reach the Sanctuary of Allāth, whose temple was eventually pillaged and abandoned at the end of the 4th century.

The arrival of a new Muslim community in the city made necessary the construction of a new religious focus that would have co-existed with the Christian one in the northwest quarter. A congregational mosque was built in a pre-existing *caesareum* between the Theatre and the *Tetrapylon*, and near the Umayyad *Sūq*. Industrial installations were set in proximity to the new urban centre. These have been identified in the Camp of Diocletian, the Baths of Diocletian, and the *Agora* (Michałowski 1964a, 53; Bounni 1995, 18; Bounni and Saliby 1968, 101; Genequand 2012, 49–50); with the exception of the structures in the Camp of Diocletian, the chronology of which is still uncertain, the items of evidence from the two other compounds have never been systematically published. As already noted by Genequand, the construction of a mosque in the city centre and in the vicinity of a market is a '*constant archéologique*', as seen in renovated urban centres such as Jerash or al-Ruṣāfa, as well as in new foundations such as ʿAnjar or Amman. The renovations undertaken in Palmyra in the Early Islamic period, thus, fit perfectly into a contemporary wider pattern of urban transformations (Genequand 2012, 64).

Small-scale urban changes: the transformation 'from *polis* to *medina*'

Besides the creation of new specialised quarters, other more modest urban changes have further contributed to transforming Palmyra's post-Classical townscape. Although of a much smaller scale, these too reflect the existence of a dynamic urban community. In modern literature, these changes, which are paralleled in numerous other sites in the Levant, have often been regarded as the reflection of a deeper process of urban metamorphosis, better known in Kennedy's words as the transformation 'from *polis* to *medina*' (Kennedy 1985), which marked the emergence of a new approach to architecture and urban living. This is characterised by the abandonment of the ostentatious monumentality of the Roman period and a tendency toward pragmatism, which is exemplified by the privatisation of public space and the consequent disintegration of the pre-existing street pattern. Modern scholars have had their share of debate over the terminology to be adopted for this process, 'decline' (Ward-Perkins 1996; 2005; Liebeschuetz 2001a) or 'transformation' (Cameron 1993; Whittow 1990; Haldon 2000), and its chronology, which is now believed to coincide with the second half of the 6th century (Liebeschuetz 2001b; Cameron 2003; Saradi 2006, 13–45; Jacobs 2013, 1–3). Given the incomplete state of the published data, it is impossible to track with accuracy the development of this process in Palmyra. However, if it is true that the process becomes apparent in the city only in the Umayyad period (Gawlikowski 2009, 90), there is evidence to suggest that it started even earlier. Several of its constitutive phenomena were triggered by the events of 272–273. Other, such as the gradual narrowing of streets, began only much later. It is worth summarising these changes in this section, with an eye to comparative examples, even if a number of them have already been discussed while others will be investigated in more detail in the ensuing chapters.

The privatisation of public areas, either open-air spaces or buildings, is an important constituent of this urban process (Saradi 1998; 2006, 186–210; Jacobs 2009; 2013, 622–35). The gradual occupation and consequent narrowing of streets by private residential buildings and new public compounds has already been discussed above. Strictly related to this, is the appropriation of public structures by private individuals and their transformation into residential buildings or areas for commerce and industry. The first dated example of a re-occupation for residential purposes in Palmyra is the *Praetorium* of the Camp of Diocletian, which was installed within the *temenos* of the dismissed Sanctuary of Allāth as early as the end of the 4th or the beginning of the 5th century (Fig. 18). This is admittedly an ambiguous case study; the *Praetorium* is in itself a residential structure, but of an official nature, as it hosted the commander of the fortress. The Sanctuary of Baalshamīn underwent a similar process of expropriation as private residential buildings were erected within its northern courtyard (Intagliata 2017a). Structures of a similar function have been uncovered around the *cella* of the Sanctuary of Nabū (Bounni *et al.* 1992, pl. 8, fig. 12; see Fig. 21), while in the Baths of Diocletian and the *Agora*

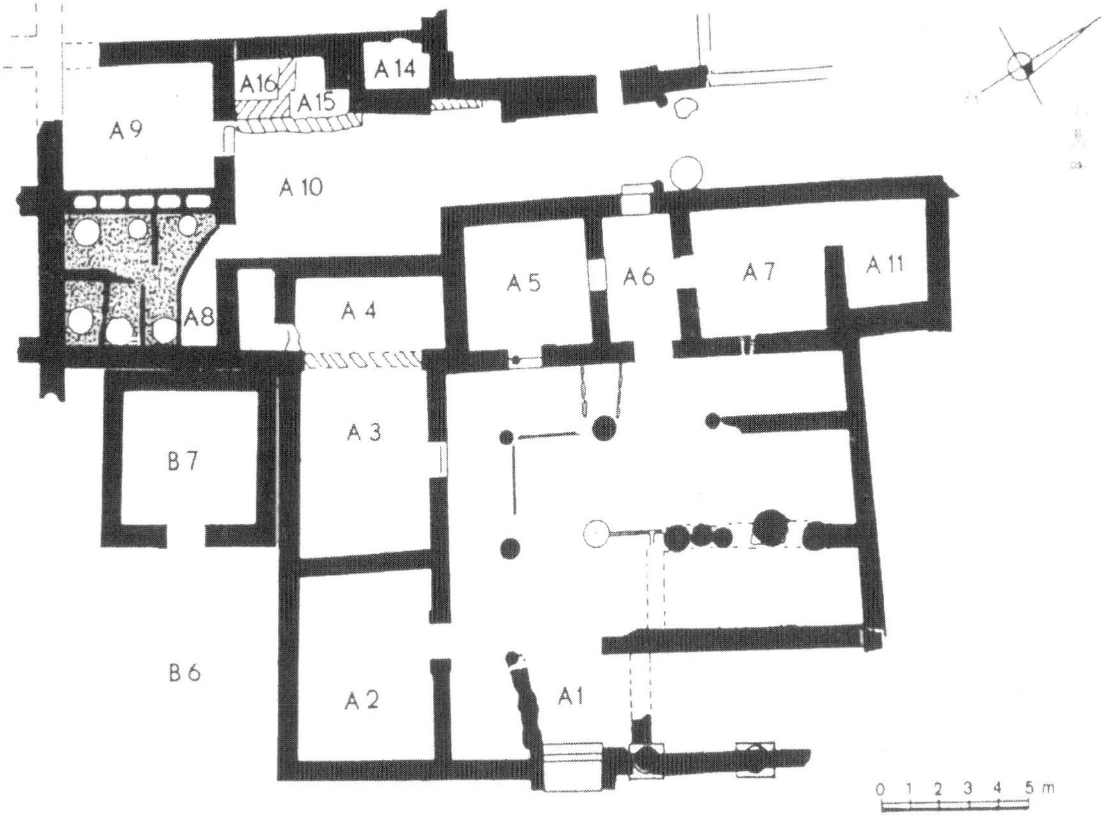

Figure 18. Camp of Diocletian, Praetorium, *final stage of occupation (Kowalski 1994, pl. 28).*

industrial facilities were constructed in the Early Islamic period (Genequand 2012, 55).

The phenomenon of private expropriation of public buildings is widespread across the empire and well documented also in written sources. Joshua the Stylite (*Chr.*, 29), to cite an oft-quoted example, reports that in 497 at Edessa the governor of Osrhoene cleared the main colonnaded street of the booths erected over time by artisans and shopkeepers. The practice was not limited to dwellings of poor squatters, but also included houses of the urban élite (Baldini Lippolis 2007, 200; Saradi 2006, 187). Representative examples can be found at Carthage, where the 5th century Maison du Triconque extended with its *trichora* hall into the nearby *cardo*, Ptolemais, and Philippi (Ben Abed-Ben Khader 1999, 54–74; Ward-Perkins *et al.* 1986; Baldini Lippolis 2001, 203–5). Imperial authorities had always condemned this trend and often attempted to stop it by issuing laws *ad hoc* (Claude 1969, 52–8; Saliou 1994, 267; Baldini Lippolis 2007). Despite these efforts, however, the privatisation of civic properties would remain a typical urban feature of Late Antique cities. With the legislative changes brought about by the Islamic conquest, the process witnessed an acceleration. Expanding the inhabitable surface of the house to the detriment of the streets was the norm among the Late Antique aristocratic élite at Apamea (Balty 1984, 34). The practice remained common in the Early Islamic period, as evidence from the Maison aux Pilastres demonstrates (Gisler and Huwiler 1984, 91). At Pella, in Jordan, the construction of new residential buildings in the Umayyad period in Areas III and IV blocked the public circulation of a nearby street (MacNicoll *et al.* 1982, 106). Encroachment included the occupation of public space with commercial and industrial installations. An example is represented by the Umayyad Potters' Complex uncovered in the dismissed North Theatre at Jerash (Schaefer and Falkner 1986). The Umayyad mosque of this city, which narrows a section of the South *decumanus,* is believed to be contemporary with about 30 shops located along the *Tetrakioinion*, the *cardo*, and the South *decumanus* (Simpson 2008).

Another well-known phenomenon associated with this process, and one particularly visible in Palmyra, is the transformation of the inner arrangement of the Roman *domus*. This is not easily datable and finds its most representative examples in the Peristyle Building in the southwest quarter (see Fig. 24) and in the House F (see Fig. 23) excavated by the Syro-Polish team in the northwest quarter. Typical features are the subdivision of the building into smaller units through the blocking of passageways, the walling up of the *intercolumnia* of the peristyle of courtyards, and the installation of partition walls. This phenomenon seems to go along with the setting up of productive and storage installations. As will be discussed in more detail in the next chapter, the presence of these transformations in the archaeological record contributes to a great extent to reach a better understanding of the urban community in post-Roman Palmyra.

Modern scholarship generally associates this phenomenon with a generalised process of impoverishment of the aristocratic élite (*curiales*), largely completed by the end of the 6th century. Although a number of houses, such as those at Apamea, maintained their monumental appearance throughout the period and were still inhabited by members of the urban upper classes, others were taken over by squatters, who partitioned them to accommodate more families and transformed them into all-encompassing, self-sufficient units (Ellis 1988, 567; Saradi 1998). Papyrological evidence suggests that, in some cases, houses were still owned by the aristocratic élite, but became subdivided into smaller apartments and rented out to poor dwellers to generate profit (Saradi 1998; Ward-Perkins *et al.* 1986, 111–26). A representative case study of this widespread practice is the Palace of the *Dux* at Apollonia, in Cyrenaica (Ellis 1985). In other cases, productive facilities were set in luxurious residential buildings for lucrative investment. In the House of the Bronzes at Sardis, for example, dyeing installations were added next to the still-functional *triclinium* of the house (Hanfmann 1959, 27).

Christianisation contributed in at least three ways to the development of Palmyra's post-classical urbanism. First, it was directly responsible for the closure, destruction, and conversion of pre-existing sanctuaries, a diffused phenomenon probably triggered by the anti-pagan measures undertaken by Theodosius I at the end of the 4th century (Fowden 1978; Cameron 2011, 59–92; Saradi 2006, 355–84; Jacobs 2013, 285–307). Temples were normally left abandoned, becoming visible ruined reminders of the city's pagan past. Indeed, the complete demolition and removal of such compounds would have required substantial financial means to be completed (Walmsley 1996, 139). The Sanctuary of Allāth had its temple deserted after its violent pillaging at the end of the 4th century (Gąssowska 1982). New buildings mushroomed within their limits, as others took advantage of the newly available space. In just one safe case – the Sanctuary of Bēl, the temple was transformed into a church. Similar dynamics might have interested the Sanctuary of Nabū; although there is no evidence to conclude that the temple was destroyed, it was certainly left abandoned and buildings were constructed in its surroundings, as seen above, within the precinct of the sanctuary (Bounni *et al.* 1992, pl. 8, fig. 12; Bounni 2004, 6; see Fig. 21).

A second consequence brought about by the Christianisation of Palmyra was the construction of churches. At least eight *intra muros* churches have been identified in the settlement. This phenomenon follows a well-established pattern in Late Antique cities that reflects a shift in the balance of civic power, now in the hands of bishops. These, together with other local notables, gradually replaced the role of *curiales* (Rapp 2004; Liebeschuetz 2001a, 104–68), and diverted the financial resources, both from private individuals and Imperial funds, to the construction of ecclesiastical buildings (Spieser 1986, 54; Saradi 2008, 317). Small- and medium-sized cities were gradually enriched with chapels, churches and *martyria*, whose religious activity exceeded the real demands of the population (Cameron 1993, 165).

The third consequence was the formation of cemeteries within the city walls. Human remains have been uncovered in the northwest quarter (Gawlikowski 1999, 192–4) and the Suburban Market (Delplace 2006–2007, 107; see Fig. 25). In Roman times, the practice of *intra muro* burials had always been condemned in the empire as early as the promulgation of the Twelve Tables (Dagron 1977, 12). Christianity was at the origin of a re-evaluation of death which was triggered by the permission to move the relics of the first martyrs in city centres under Theodosius in 381 (Dagron 1977, 11–19; Cantino Wataghin 1999; Saradi 2008, 321).

The most emblematic phenomenon associated with this new way of urban living remains, however, the adoption of reused material (*spolia*) in the construction of new buildings. Although the use of *spolia* does not qualify as a change in the urban topography, it marked dramatically the post-Roman buildings in Palmyra and, therefore, fully deserves to be considered among the small-scale changes that the settlement experienced in Late Antiquity and the Early Islamic period. Archaeological literature is now extremely rich in contributions devoted to this phenomenon (Deichmann 1976; Brenk 1987; Vaes 1989; Alchermes 1994; Saradi 1997; Elsner 2000; Coates-Stephens 2003; Baldini Lippolis 2005, 219–24). The values that reused sculpture and architecture acquired when inserted into newly constructed buildings were many, and sometimes went beyond the practical need of acquiring low-cost building material. The widespread adoption of reused architecture had frequently been the object of Imperial legislation, which had often tried to prevent or limit its use in order to preserve the cities' *decorum* (Baldini Lippolis 2007, 219–24). In Palmyra, the practice started at least as early as the end of the 3rd–beginning of the 4th century; the first safely dated occurrences are in the Camp of Diocletian and the Baths of Diocletian (293–303). In some cases, one can note a tendency for reused building material to be found in the foundations of walls and in places not easily visible to the naked eye. A statue of Ḥaggāth dated to the beginning of the 3rd century and a votive altar bearing an inscription from 239–240 were found, for example, in the foundations of the *Groma* in the Camp of Diocletian, together with other sculptures and architectural elements (Michałowski 1962, 15). In other cases, reused materials were adopted in visible parts of buildings for decorative purposes. The portico entrance of the Baths of Diocletian makes use of four reused columns, the original position of which is unknown, made of red granite from Aswān (Dodge 1988, 223 – on the Baths of Diocletian, see more below, p. 33). The builders must have recognised the rarity of this material and, therefore, decided to include them in the most visible part of the building. The phenomenon is also attested to in an ecclesiastical context. The aisle of Church I was provided with benches made of reused architecture plastered into the floor and walls (Gawlikowski 1990a, 43; Fig. 33). The nave of Church II was divided from the aisles by two rows of four reused columns made with local white limestone and granite, 0.5–0.6m in diameter (Gawlikowski 1998, 200–1). In the Early Islamic period, the phenomenon did not come to an end. The Umayyad *Sūq* can be taken as representative of this practice. Different ways of adopting reused material have been noted in this compound. In the easternmost section of the complex between shops 10 and 17 (which is believed to be the most ancient), only a single, evident case of reuse, a drum of a fluted column, has been reported, although it is likely that there might be more. In other sections (Rooms 18–20 and the western wing of the complex), reused architecture is particularly abundant 'giving an impression of hasty and sloppy work' (al-As῾ad and Stępniowski 1989, 208).

The phenomenon of *spolia* should not necessarily be seen as an indicator of a declined civic life or as proof of a state of complete ruin of the city in Late Antiquity and the Early Islamic period. At Jerash, churches were constructed which extensively adopted *spolia*. Yet, this city undoubtedly remained a flourishing Christian centre throughout the 5th and 6th centuries (Kraelig 1938, 66–7). Its Christian community thrived and was capable of large-scale building enterprises, as the evidence from the the city centre suggests. Unlike the new foundations, Late Antique Jerash and Palmyra developed upon pre-existing settlements. It must simply have seemed sensible and consistent to their inhabitants to re-use building material from earlier structures, instead of procuring new material at considerable expense.

Conclusions

Following the dramatic events of 272–273, Palmyra was not abandoned but experienced a shift in its functions. From a caravan stop, the city was transformed into a stronghold along the eastern frontier. It shrank to almost half its original size, yet, its importance was maintained. Indeed, beside its newly acquired military role, Palmyra retained a large civilian community. Written sources refer to Palmyra as a city throughout the period under discussion, implicitly recognising its prominence among other settlements in Syria. An analysis of the city's topography has shown that Late Antique and Early Islamic Palmyra tended to maintain the pre-existing Roman street grid. Despite this element of continuity, there is evidence of changes in the function of certain urban areas, suggesting the existence of a lively urban community.

The way people lived in Palmyra also changed abruptly after the Aurelianic disruptions. Classical urbanism was replaced by a form of urban living that tended to avoid the monumentality typical of the Roman period, and, instead, inclined toward pragmatism. This is manifested through a number of new phenomena that started as early as the 4th century and underwent a drastic acceleration in the Early Islamic period. The coming of Islam did result in a major reshaping of the city, but the way in which this was achieved was through previously-known urban phenomena. In other words, the process 'from *polis* to *medina*' was already in motion in Late Antiquity. Palmyra's post-Classical form of urbanism is, therefore, not an exception to the wider pattern which developed throughout the period under discussion in all the cities of the Near East and beyond. Its constitutive phenomena were a response of the Palmyrene community, not only to local events, but also to large-scale social, religious, and administrative changes.

Chapter 3

Society and housing

The community of Palmyra was animated by a high degree of social dynamism. Soldiers, merchants, and members of the élite and the Church were some of the groups coexisting in the city and whose presence is now only faintly visible through written sources and the epigraphic record. Archaeological remains cannot be as helpful to pinpoint the social stratification of the time, but they are certainly useful to explore wider patterns of changes within the urban society. In this respect, housing represents an important marker of social transformation. Late Antique and Early Islamic houses differ considerably from their Roman counterparts, suggesting a drastic shift of the social composition of the Palmyrene community after the end of the 3rd century. This is represented by a general process of fragmentation of the habitable space, as well as the occurrence of small-scale changes that transformed the residential building into a multi-functional compound. A comparison between the changes in housing occurring in Palmyra with those from a number of other contemporary urban sites in the Near East and beyond, suggests that these transformations are not the results of the particular historical development of Palmyra, but that they fit perfectly into a much wider narrative.

Late Antique and Early Islamic Palmyrene society: facing the lack of evidence

The first obstacle to face when dealing with a social history of post-Roman Palmyra is the relative lack of written sources and inscriptions. We are aware of only two individuals that held prominent titles in the civic administration and must likely have enjoyed a high social status. These are a λογιστής, in the first half of the 4th century, and an ἔκδικος, in the second half of the 5th century (*IGLS* 17.1, 114–15, 375–6, n. 101, 496). With the exception of the restoration of the 'Basilica of Arṣū' (279–280, see below, p. 98), no more acts of religious euergetism by the local aristocracy are attested in the epigraphic record. The reduction in the practice of local euergetism proved by inscriptions is a widespread pattern in 4th century Levant already noted in other large sites where the aristocracy was still thriving (Lewin 2001; Yon 2001, 181). As a consequence, it cannot be considered in itself as direct proof of a generalised decline or the collapse of the urban aristocracy. Although any theories on Palmyrene society in the period under discussion based solely on written sources and epigraphic evidence remains, therefore, necessarily conjectural, it is safe to conclude that an élite playing a leading role in the civic administration must have existed, together with a lively merchant group. Soldiers, a social category that was famously eager to spend their time and rich wages in taverns, markets, and brothels, must have added a certain social and economic dynamism to the community.

Archaeology helps add more data to the discussion. Very little is known on places of social convergence in Palmyra, as the fate of Roman social hubs in Late Antiquity, such as the *Agora* and the Theatre, remains obscure. Kowalski's reinterpretation of the church in the Sanctuary of Baalshamīn as an *andrōn* (ἀνδρών – Kowalski 1996), if taken as valid, would suggest the existence in Palmyra of organised aristocratic groups. A meeting hall similar to the those in the villages of northern Syria, was also identified by Collart (1969, 85) in Building A, in the same compound. Certainly more inclusive was the complex of the Baths of Diocletian (Διοκλητιανὸν βαλανῖον), said by a bilingual inscription to have been built by Sossianus Hierocles, governor (*praeses*) of *Phoenicia Libanensis*, at the end of the 3rd–early 4th century (*IGLS* 17.1, 112–114, n. 100). Despite what is reported in this inscription, the compound, which is located opposite the area between the Theatre and the Sanctuary of Nabū, was probably the result of the renovation of a pre-existing building (a 'palace'?) and was not constructed *ex nihilo* (Hartmann 2001, 202–3; Fellmann 1987). The baths were excavated by the Syrian authorities, but the results of these investigations have never been the object of systematic publications (Ostratz 1969, 114–15; Bounni 1971, 122–3; Bounni and al-As'ad 1982, 215–30; Fellmann 1987; Fournet, 2009a; 2009b). It was accessed via a monumental porticoed entrance, discussed above (see p. 31), directly from the main thoroughfare of the city and included a vast cold bath (*frigidarium*), a pool (*natatio*), and a modest warm/hot sector (*tepidarium/caldarium*). The complex makes use of large quantity of reused marble material, which is still visible on site in rich decorated floors of *opus sectile* (Dodge 1988, 218–23; Wielgosz 2013, 320–1). The construction of the baths by the governor of Syria, who was the same person responsible for the building of the Camp of Diocletian, hides a military involvement in this operation and leads to believe that the compound might have been used both by military personnel and civilians alike.

Much deeper insights into the society can be inferred by studying housing, a topic which, however, is not devoid of problems. As a matter of fact, comprehensive overviews of these structures for Late Antiquity and the Early Islamic period are still missing. By contrast, a number of observations on Roman houses in Palmyra have already been put forward by Frézouls (1976b), Balty (1989, 407–12), Gawlikowski (1997a; 2007) and, more recently, Żuchowska (2011). A work aiming at exploring the *status quaestionis* of Late Antique and Early Islamic Palmyrene housing would inevitably encounter a number of hindrances, first and foremost, the uncertainty of their chronology and the limited data available from secondary literature. The evidence published so far represents only a small percentage of what has been brought to light. Excavations of private residential buildings started with the first archaeological investigations in Palmyra as early as the beginning of the 20th century. It should not be excluded that, in those occasions, post-Roman evidence were swept away to reach earlier levels. A large number of structures that can potentially be identified as houses stud the topographic plan produced recently by Schnädelbach (2010). Yet, most of these have never been studied. Despite of this, a thorough survey of the known remains through modern literature can still be useful to get an insight on the urban society living in Late Antique and Early Islamic Palmyra.

Housing: an overview of the evidence

The first building to have yielded traces of post-Roman houses is the Sanctuary of Baalshamīn, investigated by the archaeological team directed by Collart in the 1950s and 1960s. There, three large compounds (hereinafter Buildings A–C) encroached the northern courtyard (Grande Cour) of the sacred space (Collart and Vicari 1969, 83–8; Fig. 19). Two of them, Buildings A and C, which were located in the eastern and western porticoes, were dated by the excavators to the beginning of the 4th century on the basis

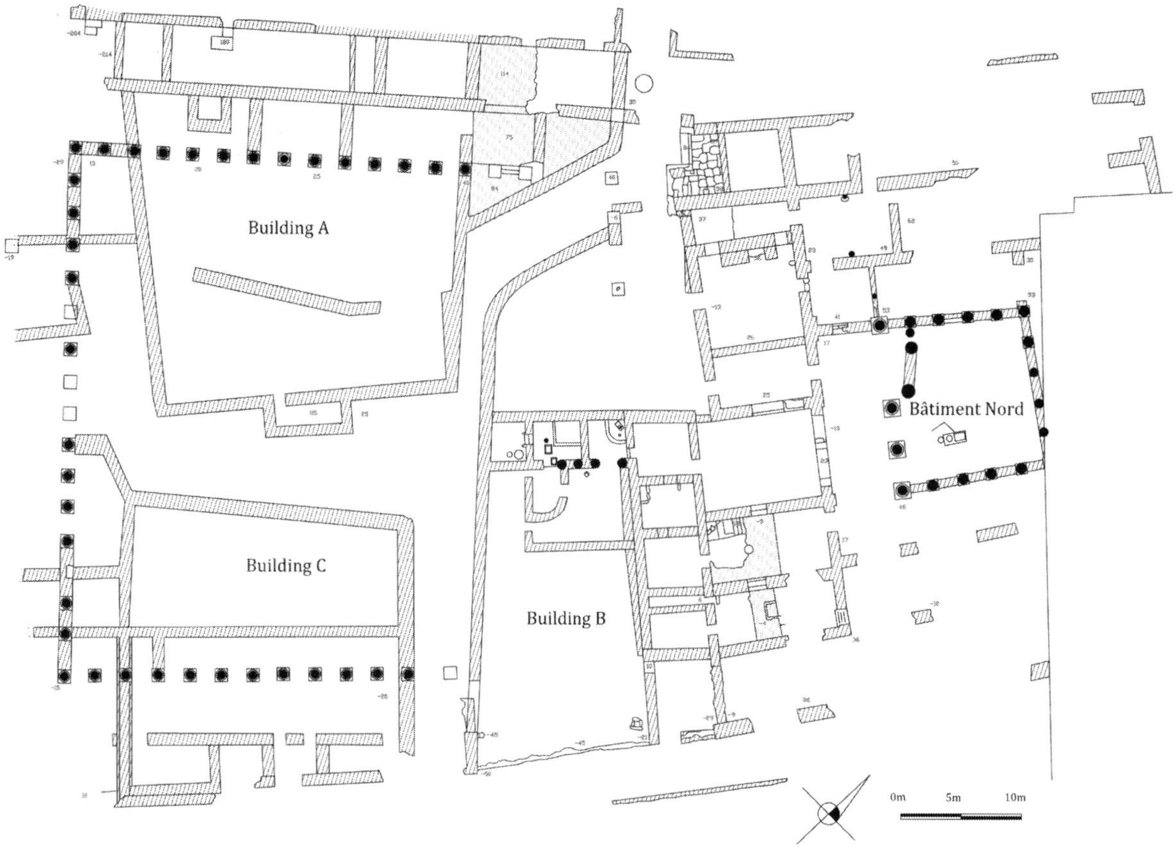

Figure 19. Grande Cour and Bâtiment Nord, Sanctuary of Baalshamīn (drawn by the author after plans at the Fonds d'Archives Paul Collart, Université de Lausanne).

of parallels with houses in the villages of northern Syria as well as a number of historically driven assumptions. Specifically, Collart believed that the occupation of the northern courtyard of the Sanctuary of Baalshamīn betrays the need of the population to find new residential areas where to live as a consequence of the shrinkage of the city after 273 (Collart and Vicari 1969, 94). The buildings are both characterised by open trapezoidal courtyards encroaching the Grande Cour and flanked by two or more rows of rooms. The court of Building A is said to have been turned into a meeting hall in the early 5th century.

Another house, Building B, also known as 'Quartier Arabe' in the final report of the excavations, occupies the northern portico of the Grande Cour (Fig. 20). Like the others, it consists of a large open courtyard. To the west of it was a row of rooms, communicating with the open courtyard via a 'vestibule'. The habitable surface of the building would have probably occupied also the rooms of the pre-existing Bâtiment Nord, located immediately to the south of the Hotel Zenobia. Building B was believed by Collart to have been built sometime between the 4th and the 6th century, to have been obliterated by an earthquake in the 10th century, and to have been restored in the 12th century. These conclusions, however, have never received general consensus by modern scholarship. A re-examination of the original documentation of the excavations has recently advanced the hypothesis that the building underwent destruction in the 6th century and was reconstructed in Umayyad time or slightly later. Numismatic evidence, pottery, and the epigraphic record seems to confirm this development. Although very little data remains to speculate on the chronology of Buildings A and C, it is plausible that these went through the same phases of constructions, destructions, and reconstructions (Intagliata 2017a).

Figure 20. Western wing of Building B (courtesy of Patrick Michel and Anne Bielman, Fonds d'Archives Paul Collart, Université de Lausanne) (cat. n. F/141).

A few years after the beginning of the excavations in the Sanctuary of Baalshamīn, the Syro-Polish team directed by Michałowski started the investigations ofthe Camp of Diocletian. The unearthing of the main road axis of the compound, the *Via Praetoria*, brought to light a number of structures interpreted as dwellings and productive areas that confirmed a widespread post-Roman occupation of the city (see Fig. 15). The plan of these structures remains not completely clear, as most of the buildings would have developed beyond the limits of the excavated area. The excavation of the stretch of the *Via Praetoria* from the Praetorian Gate to the *Groma* brought to light two walls built of *spolia* and narrowing considerably the width of the carriageway. Behind these walls, private residential buildings and productive areas were identified. To the northwest of the Praetorian Gate was a rectangular chamber 0.7m above the Roman level. It could be entered from the west and was paved with a flagging of reused building material. Several rectangular wells and two large jars set into the ground, one of which consisting of one jar inside the other forming a sort of 'thermos', have been uncovered in this sector. To the other side of the road was a 4m long room believed to be a kitchen because of the large amount of charcoal and pottery found, although the evidence described by the excavators do not exclude *a priori* a different function. Further to the west were other small chambers, five to the north and four to the south, the nature of which has never been clarified (Michałowski 1960a, 70–5).

The excavation of the area of the *Groma* yielded much more evidence, which can be briefly summarised as follow. To install new structures, the monument was subdivided into four separate rooms (each occupying one of its corners) by two narrow corridors crossing at right angle at its centre. The rooms are believed to belong to four different dwellings. One of them, located at the northern corner of the *Groma*, extended farther northeast, outside the limit imposed by the monument. The excavation of a chamber immediately to the north of the *Groma* unearthed a rectangular well delimited by four narrow blocks and flanked by a basin carved into a reused piece of architecture. Besides the presence of the basin, there is no other evidence mentioned in the report to support Michałowski's conclusion that this room was a worskshop. Caution must be exercised also on the presumed nature of another chamber, again a workshop according to Michałowski, situated against the east corner of the *Groma*. To the south corner of the monument is a small open court, inside of which was a rectangular room (Michałowski 1962, 54–77). To the west, the excavation of a chamber against the back wall of the southern portico of the *Via Praetoria* yielded a greenish glazed jug containing the 'Byzantine

Hoard'. This included the 27 gold coins and six pieces of jewellery, among which were two rings, two earrings, and one pendant in the shape of a cross (Michałowski 1962, 226–36; Skowronek in Krzyżanowska 2014, 60–4).

The stretch between the *Groma* and the *Forum* was also divided into three narrow corridors by two walls running east to west; the central one was left free for public circulation. To the north, between one of these two walls and the back wall of the northern portico of the street was a long courtyard (14.20 × 6.50m), which was interpreted as belonging to the house installed in the north corner of the *Groma*. To the south was a concentration of other rooms; one of them, at the very end of the southern portico of the *Via Praetoria*, had an unusual arrangement of four reused columns against the foundation wall of the Grande Porte. The columns could have supported arcades, possibly for a second storey (Michałowski 1963a, 41–60).

The chronological development of these buildings is difficult to follow. Originally, Michałowski put forward a broad 'Byzantine and Arab' chronology mostly because of the stratigraphic position of these structures and their building techniques. Later, Gawlikowski (1976b, 155; 1994, 136) proposed to date the structures to the Umayyad period, but did not exclude the possibility of their having been built during the Persian occupation of the region in the first quarter of the 7th century. He advanced the hypothesis that the structures were abandoned by the time of the destructions perpetrated by Marwān b. Muḥammad in 745. Later, 12th century constructions, which include the chamber with the two jars next to the *Porta Praetoria*, would have been installed on top of the Umayyad ones (Gawlikowski 1976b, 155). Recently, Genequand (2012, 49) has postulated the abandonment of the area to have a *terminus post quem* in the first half of the 9th century on the basis of the presence of polychrome glazed ceramic documented in the preliminary reports of the excavations (Michalowski 1960a, fig. 87; 1962, fig. 70).

The *Praetorium*, the base of the commander of the Camp of Diocletian, was uncovered in the mid-1970s (Fig. 18 – see also below, p. 78). The building represents a significant addition in the list of pieces of evidence on domestic architecture from Palmyra for being a clear case of encroachment in a pre-existing pagan sanctuary and a 'house of pretention'. Its first phase is believed to date back to the end of the 4th–beginning of the 5th century. It was installed in the largest free area of the Sanctuary of Allāth, between the temple and the northern wall of its *temenos*, making use of the eastern portico of the *Via Principalis* as its easternmost limit and annexing two rooms of the adjacent west barrack block. The core of the house, which had a second floor, is represented by a central L-shaped courtyard provided with a peristyle of six reused columns. The access to the building was through a wide entrance (1.61m), whose doorframe included a lintel featuring a cross in relief. A secondary entrance was located further south. The sector open to the guests, accessible from the southern porch of the courtyard, consisted of the small reception Room A3 (4.2 × 5.3m) separated from the narrow recess A4 (5.1 × 2.3m) by an arch that is not preserved. Room A2, located on the same side of the court, served as a dining area. To the east was a row of smaller chambers and a separate service quarter that consists of a kitchen (Room A14), a storeroom (Room A8), and a stable (Rooms A8–A9). The plan of the building is only apparently irregular and follows specific building criteria, first of all the use of a specific module (*quantitas*) that is the Persian-Babylonian foot.

After a disastrous earthquake the building was reconstructed. The renovation, or part of it, is dated by a coin that is probably an imitation of a *follis* minted at the time of Heraclius and Heraclius Constantine found in the partition wall closing the rear court of the structure. At that time, the second floor was abandoned and the inner arrangement of the building underwent significant transformations. These include the subdivisions of the courtyard into smaller units, the construction of a domed room blocking the secondary entrance, and the renovation of the main entrance. Further changes include the installation of *tanānīr* (sing. *tannūr*), pipes, and water basins, the reflooring of some rooms, and the blocking of passageways. Similar transformations occurred also later, before a further earthquake destroyed the house in the 11th century. Since then, the building remained abandoned until modern times, when two walls, probably garden fences, were constructed on top of its ruins (Kowalski 1994; 1995; 1999; for summary descriptions see, Sodini 1997, 486–7; Baldini Lippolis 2001, 245).

A number of walls with different orientations have been uncovered within the precinct of the Sanctuary of Nabū by the Syrian authorities (Fig. 21). Very little can be conjectured on these structures, as they have never been published in full and are documented in only one published plan (Bounni *et al.* 1992, pl. 8, fig. 12; Bounni 2004, 6). This shows a concentration of rooms to the north of the *temenos* area, between the *cella* and the row of shops opening onto the Great Colonnade. This might well have been a single habitation. Further rooms are visible to the south and east. The general layouts of these new constructions are difficult to pinpoint. The buildings are certainly post-Roman and belong to a phase when the sanctuary had already lost its original function. Wiegand *et al.* (1932, 108) had already reported the presence of late dwellings in the court of this sanctuary, without, however, providing any detailed description of the remains. Will (1966, 1414, n. 4) believed these houses to be contemporaneous with the structures unearthed by Michałowski in the Camp of Diocletian, while Gawlikowski (2009, 89) referred to them as built already in the 4th century. Among the lamps published in the final volume on the excavations of the sanctuary, six

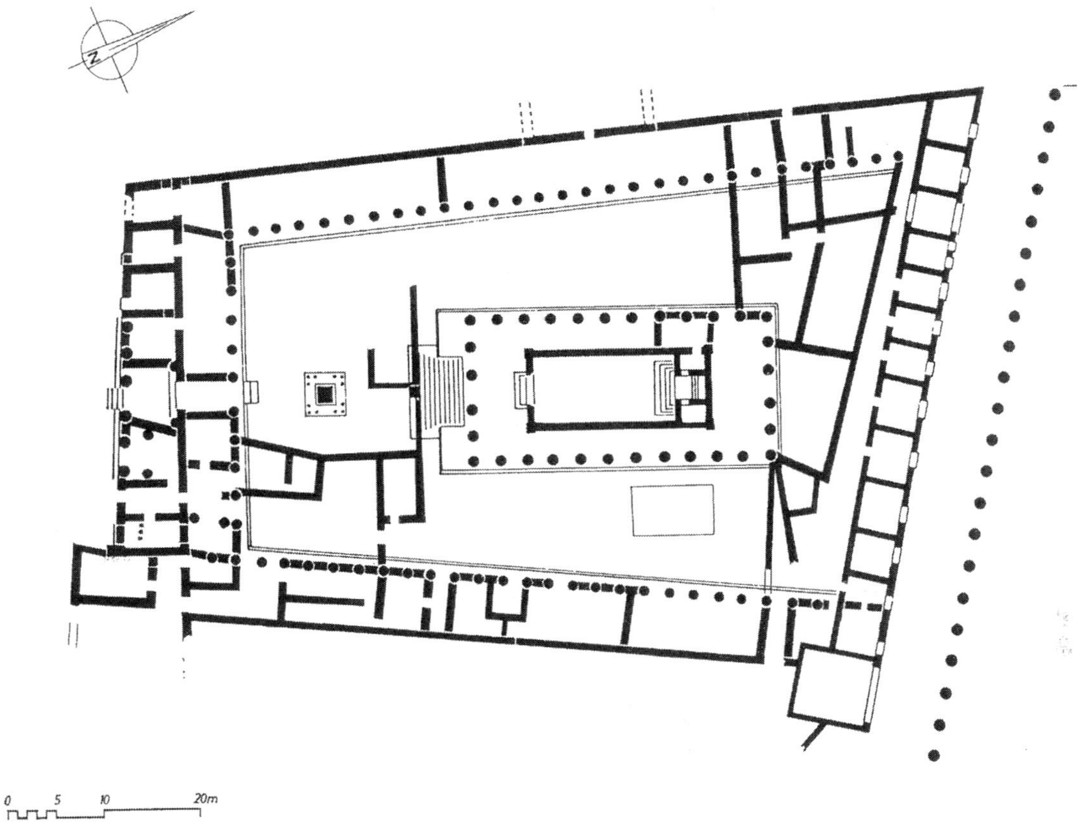

Figure 21. Sanctuary of Nabū, final stage of occupation (Bounni et al. *1992, pl. 22).*

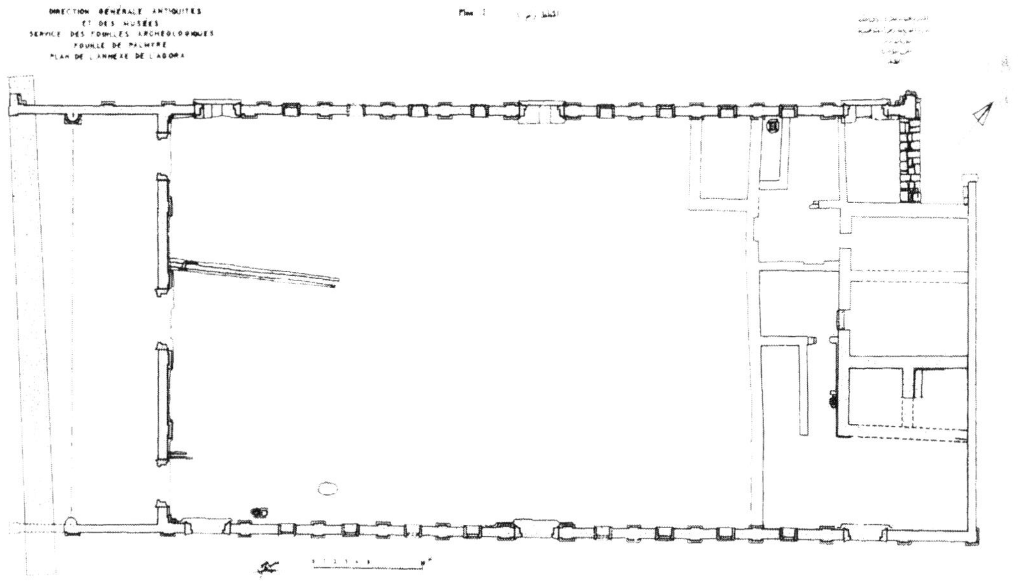

Figure 22. Annexe of the Agora *(Bounni and Saliby 1968, pl. 1).*

are generically dated to the 4th–5th centuries, thus proving a generic post-Roman chronology for the frequentation of the area. Five of them were found in the northeastern sector of the sanctuary, whilst the sixth in the area in front of the *propylaeum* (Bounni 2004, 103–5, ns 76–81). Later structures have also been identified in the area between the Sanctuary of Nabū and the Great Colonnade (see Fig. 13), but have not been published in full.

Residential units and possible workshops were also unearthed in the Annexe of the *Agora* (Fig. 22). Again, the structures are known only through a single plan drawn by Syrian authorities. This shows what appears to be a single building occupying the northeast quarter of the compound. A large, L-shaped courtyard was entered from the southeast and would have given access to a group of rectangular rooms of different size (Bounni and Saliby 1968, pl. i). The structure was originally dated to the Byzantine and Ayūbbid period. To Genequand (2008a, 4), however, no Ayūbbid material is visible in the two photographs of pottery published in the interim report, the latest dated artefact being a rounded lamp of the end of the 8th–first half of the 9th century. The scholar also questions Bounni and Saliby's conclusions on a two-phase occupation of these structures and advances the possibility that the buildings might have been in use without interruption from Late Antiquity into the Early Islamic period.

During the excavations of the Umayyad *Sūq* in 1977–1986, a complex of eight units was uncovered and interpreted as an Umayyad dwelling (al-As'ad and Stępniowski 1989, 209; fig. 1; Fig. 16). The largest room, very likely an open courtyard, was entered from the northwest and was provided with what appears in plan to be a rectangular well delimited by four narrow blocks. Further rooms develop around this court, but they open directly onto the carriageway of the Great Colonnade or to the east and not onto the court. Due to the inner layout of the building, and because of the lack of supportive evidence, the interpretation of this building as a house remains conjectural. Nothing excludes it to have had a different function, perhaps connected with the adjacent Umayyad *Sūq*.

The largest residential building uncovered in Palmyra that bears traces of post-Roman occupation, House F, was fully excavated by the Syro-Polish team in the mid-1980s (Fig. 23). The extensive residential compound occupies an entire block of the northwest quarter, stretching for a total

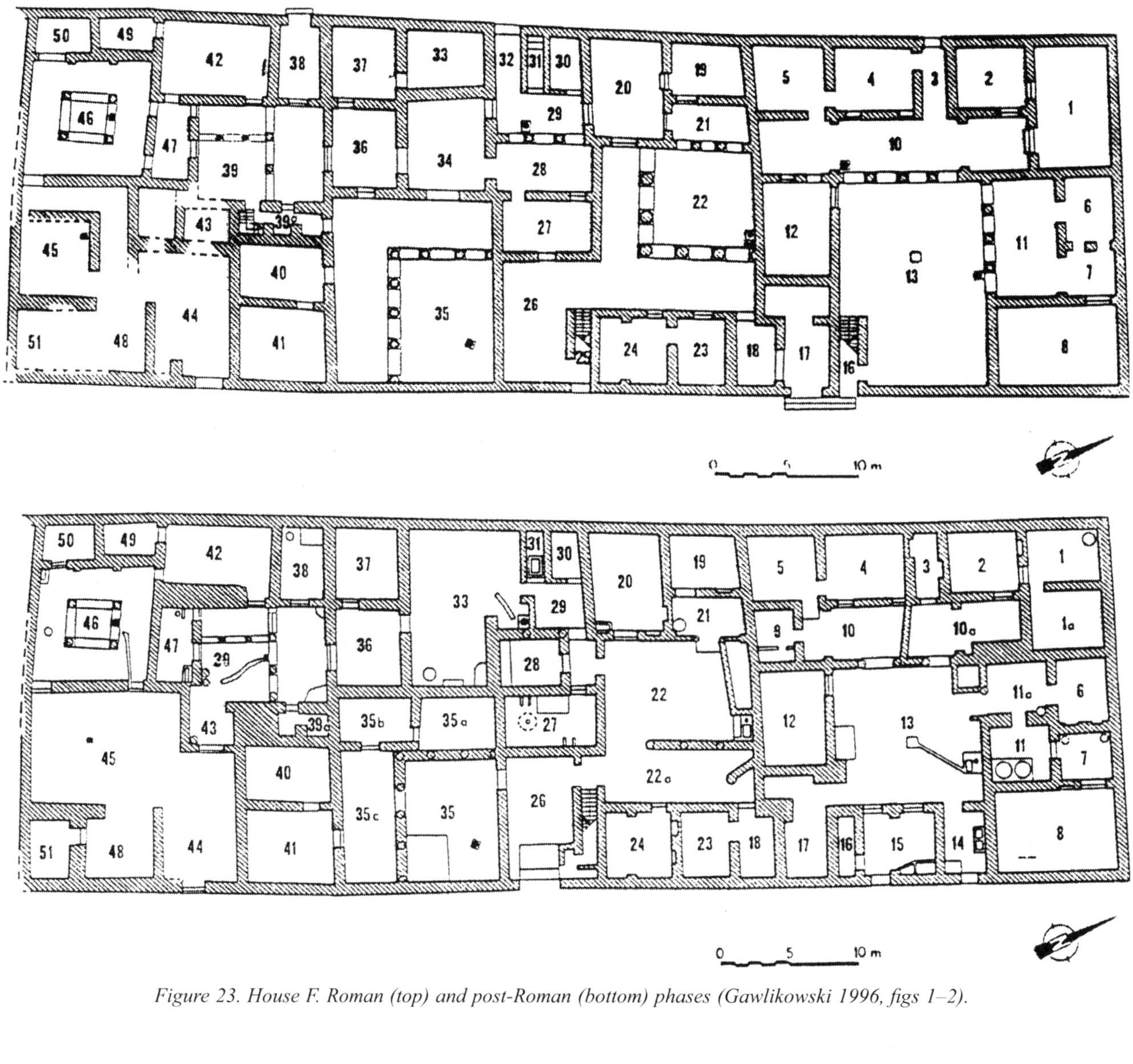

Figure 23. House F. Roman (top) and post-Roman (bottom) phases (Gawlikowski 1996, figs 1–2).

of more than 2000m^2. The building was constructed in the second half of the 2nd century; at that time, according to the excavators, the compound was a single residential unit owned by a rich member of the urban upper classes (Gawlikowski 1992a, 69; 1997a, 166). The house is believed not to have experience major alterations until the turn of the 7th century, when it was destroyed by an earthquake. Afterwards, it was transformed to accommodate more families. A detailed analysis of the numerous alterations that the building went through in the period under analysis would go beyond the scope of this short overview. Suffice it to say that phenomena such as the blocking up of *intercolumnia* of porticoes and doorways, and the subdivision of large rooms into smaller units became frequent and suggest a drastic change in the social status of the residents. Further, the house lost its original second floor. The building seems to have maintained the decorative apparatus of the 2nd century in its original position until the final abandonment of the block in the 9th century (Gawlikowski 1990a, 37–40; 1991a; 1991b; 1992a, 68–73; 1994, 133–41; 1996).

In the northern sector of the city, the excavation of the Suburban Market by the Syro-French archaeological team has yielded traces of residential activities (Fig. 25). The impressive compound (58 × 67m), the original phase of which dates back to the 2nd century, comprises at least 29 rooms developing around a large open central court. The building appears to have known a different function in Late Antiquity; the eastern wing was transformed into a cemetery, while the western one was used for residential and commercial purposes. At the time of maintenance interventions carried out on the nearby street, one of the east access to the building was enlarged (Delplace 2006–2007; 2013, 37–48).

The nearby southwest quarter was systematically explored only after 2007 by a Syro-Italian team. The excavations addressed a *domus*, the so-called 'Peristyle Building', the earliest phase of which dates back to the end of the 2nd–beginning of the 3rd century (Fig. 24). Both the plan of the building and the small finds, such as the numerous fragments of imported marbles and figurative stuccos, are informative

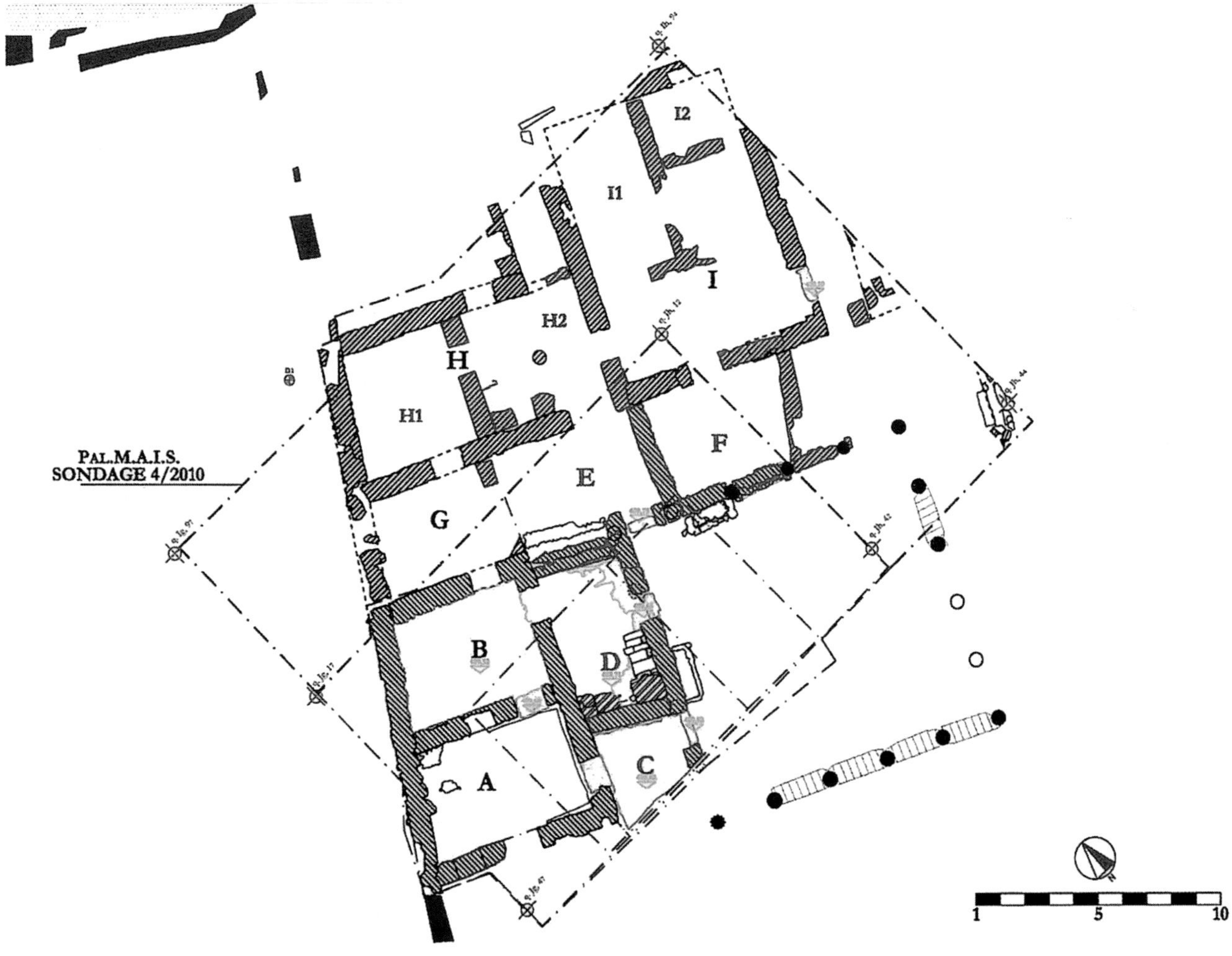

Figure 24. Peristyle Building (Grassi and al-As'ad 2013, 125, fig. 5).

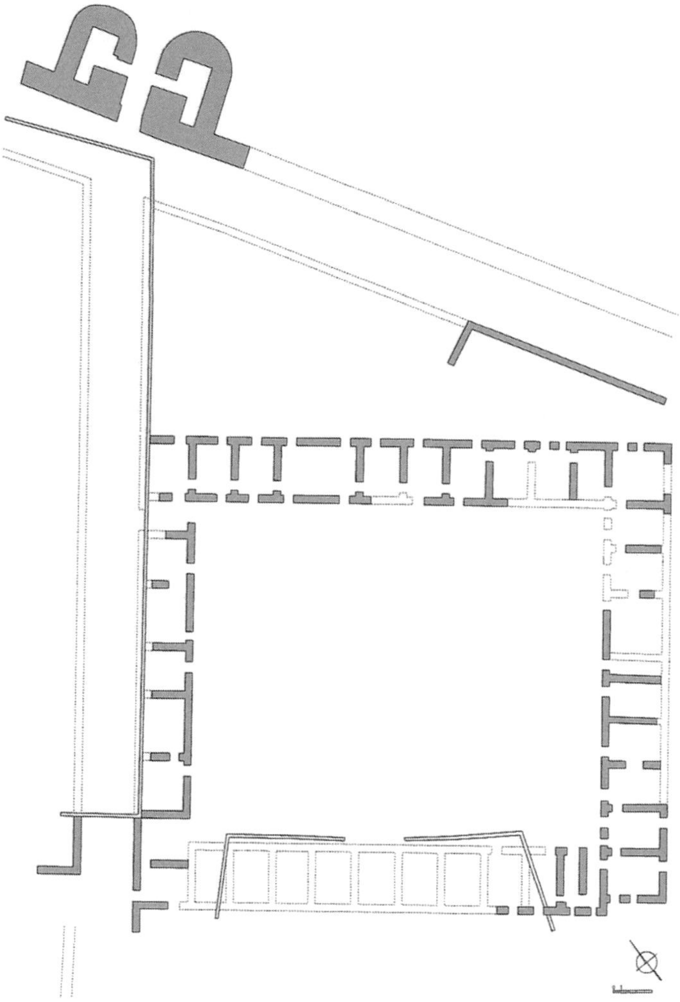

Figure 25. Suburban Market (Delplace 2013, 48, fig. 9).

on the wealth of the owner of the building in Roman times (Palmieri 2010; Nava 2015). The house underwent important spatial alterations up until the Early Islamic period. Because of the nature itself of the evidence, which most of the time consists of poor walls constructed with reused architecture, the exact dating of them is difficult to pinpoint. Four rooms (C–F) were installed in the northern and eastern porticoes of the open courtyard by using partition walls and blocking up *intercolumnia*. A staircase to the second storey was installed in Room D. The two largest excavated rooms of the compound, namely Room H and Room I, were divided into smaller units, respectively two and, possibly, four (Grassi 2009a; 2009b; 2010; 2011; 2012; Grassi and al-As ʿad 2013; Grassi *et al.* 2015, 1–7; 2012; Zenoni 2014).

Remarks on post-Roman Palmyrene housing

Setting of the buildings

Owing to the fact that private residential buildings did not develop on virgin soil and that pre-existing compounds were not completely removed to the foundations to be replaced by new structures, houses in Palmyra are characterised by a high degree of variability in terms of setting. For the sake of categorisation, it is possible to gather the evidence into two broad groups. Each of these present different solutions to the problem of the exploitation of the available space that are worthy of a brief discussion. The first group is represented by houses erected *ex novo* in disused public areas, such as civic or religious compounds and roads. Encroachment of private residential buildings into public space occurred at least as early as the end of the 4th–beginning of the 5th century as the evidence from the *Praetorium* suggests. The occupation of poor dwellings in the Camp of Diocletian proves the continuity of this practice well into the Early Islamic period. Buildings set into disused sanctuaries do not generally suffer from lack of space. The houses in the Sanctuary of Baalshamīn make free use of most of the available space of the Grande Cour. Their plans were allowed to develop almost freely, following construction patterns of their time. The *Praetorium* of the Camp of

Diocletian, a 'typical' peristyle house, and the confusing remains from the Sanctuary of Nabū offer further examples of this kind. Conversely, residential buildings installed into pre-existing roads have more spatial limitations. The houses in the *Via Praetoria* of the Camp of Diocletian develop only along the north and south sides of the road, leaving a narrow central lane free for public circulation. Similarly, the 'house' next to the Umayyad *Sūq*, in the westernmost section of the Great Colonnade, develops in the southern portico of the street but does not extend into its carriageway.

The second set of evidence consists of those dwellings that are simply the results of the renovation of pre-existing houses by means of a set of recurrent alterations such as the walling up of passageways, the blocking of *intercolumnia* of porticoes, the construction of partition walls, the raising up of floors, and the blocking of staircases. These phenomena, which are notably visible in the House F and in the Peristyle Building, offer important clues on the transformation of the social composition of the Palmyrene community, as we shall see. Yet, due to their ephemeral nature, they have proved to be extremely difficult to date. The majority of them have often been regarded as Early Islamic on the basis of their 'rustic' appearance. In fact, their appearance does not necessarily exclude *a priori* the possibility that they could occur earlier and then be maintained until the final abandonment of a building.

Building layouts

Variability clearly applies also to building layouts. In terms of plans, perhaps the most traditional compound remains the *Praetorium* of the Camp of Diocletian (Fig. 18). This, as seen, develops around a L-shaped peristyled courtyard; to reach the reception room, located in the southern wing, the visitors have to pass through the southern portico. The entrance to the courtyard was through a doorway on the east. Both the location of the entrance, which is not in axis with the centre of the courtyard, and the unusual shape of the courtyard might be intentional to promote privacy. The reason behind this arrangement is not dissimilar from the accesses '*en chicane*', or '*access en baïonette*', as they are known in modern literature, of Roman Palmyrene houses, which prevented people in the street from peeking into courtyards (Frézouls 1976b, 38; Balty 1989, 412; for Palmyra see Gabriel 1926, 85, fig. 3; fig. 5; pl. 15, Houses 38, 39 and 45; Frézouls 1976b, 37, fig. 3, Maison d'Achille; outside Palmyra see, for instance, Balty 1989, 412, Maison aux Consoles, Apamea; Goodchild 1960, Palace of the *Dux*, Apollonia). The main access of the *Praetorium*, however, was clearly conceived in order that only the southern area of the courtyard, where the reception hall of the house were located, would be visible from the street. The northern portico of the courtyard, which was deeper than the others and would have been provided the owner with 'a very comfortable place to spend time' (Kowalski 1994, 53) due to the daylight entering for most of the day from the south, seems to have been sheltered. The residents of the house would have been able to enjoy the amenity of their courtyard in this large recess away from prying eyes. Units of this kind are known also in the Roman period. A similar recess, not surprisingly orientated toward the south, can be found in the main courtyard of the 2nd century Maison d'Achilles, to the east of the Sanctuary of Bēl (Frézouls 1976b, 50).

All these features, that is to say the presence of a peristyled courtyard and large reception halls and the seeking for privacy, are all notable expression of the high social status of the owner. Despite the absence of strong evidence, the interpretation of the building as the *Praetorium* of the fortress is sound. The inclusion of this residence within the Camp of Diocletian, which was presumably still operational at that time, would be difficult to explain as an act of well-off civilians. *Praetoria* from other contemporary fortresses stand out for their opulence and, generally speaking, a standardised plan characterised by a central porticoed and an open courtyard surrounded by rooms of diverse function. Examples are scanty and include the buildings at *Iatrus* (Von Bülow 2007, 465, 467, figs 3, 4, citing Stanchev 1999), South Shield, and Vindolanda (Collins 2012, 91–3). If the late 4th–early 5th century chronology is regarded as valid, the location of the earlier, Tetrarchic *Praetorium* within the fortress remains, however, unknown.

The *Praetorium*, a rather modest official residential building, is certainly not typical of how Palmyrene houses in Late Antiquity and the Early Islamic period would have looked. Looking at the plans of the other Palmyrene houses, the first impression is that of a great simplicity and variability in layout, from fairly small dwellings to relatively large compounds of five or more units. A convergence in plan between post-Roman Palmyrene private residential buildings and their rural counterparts is often noticeable. Rural houses were usually characterised by a utilitarian architecture where space could be shared between humans and animals. The typical rural house in the Near East avoids 'gratuitous innovations, uses the simplest techniques to ensure a certain stability, and efficiently meets the most basic of family needs' (Petruccioli 2006, 68). It is, thus, not surprising that already in the 1960s Collart (1969, 84 citing Tchalenko 1953, 10–11, 12, n. 1) had stressed the striking resemblance between the Late Antique houses occupying the northern courtyard of the Sanctuary of Baalshamīn and the rural dwellings in northern Syria.

Private residential buildings could stand isolated, such as for example the houses in the northern courtyard of the Sanctuary of Baalshamīn (Fig. 19). More often, however, they are found clustered together in the same block and share the same courtyard. This pattern is exemplified by three apartments of four to five rooms in the northern section of the House F (Fig. 23, bottom). The dwellings, which are dated to the last stage of occupation of the building, could not be entered directly from the street. Rather, they were accessible from a shared courtyard (loc. 13) with a single entrance from the street. Medium-sized dwellings with four to five rooms of this kind are frequent in the Near East. At Pella in Jordan, for example, an entire quarter with mid-6th century houses was rearranged in the mid-7th century to accommodate smaller, two storey units entered through single accesses from shared courtyards (MacNicoll *et al.* 1982; Walmsley 1992; 2007b). Shared courtyards are common in the Umayyad Levant, as exemplified by the Umayyad House at Jerash, Building B, and the House in the Museum site in Amman Citadel (Gawlikowski 1986a; Bennett and Northedge 1977–1978, 175–7; Northedge 1992, 141–2, 151; Harding 1951).

A second pattern is evident from an analysis of the inner circulation of the southern part of the same building. In plan, it is possible to distinguish at least four clusters of twin-rooms (loc. 18 and 23; 19 and 21; 35a and 35b; 40 and 41) that could have been used as separate dwellings. The boundaries of the apartments are, however, not clear and a final publication of the remains from this block is essential to cast more light on the matter. Two twin-room dwellings of the same kind seem to be visible north to the shops 35–36 of the Umayyad *Sūq*, although nothing can exclude that they were part of a larger building. If proven right, the pattern of twin rooms would not be a prerogative of Palmyra. The Umayyad House at Jerash, for example, presents at least three sets of twin rooms, each opening toward the same courtyard. The front room could serve for daily activities, while the back room, with no windows, could be used for sleeping (Gawlikowski 1986a, 114). Less safe is the existence of one-room dwellings in Palmyra, which are frequent in the Near East (Richardson 2004, 59), but, admittedly, difficult to identify with a good degree of certainty.

The courtyard represents the most important spatial element in these buildings. These are normally simple open spaces with irregular shapes often imposed by pre-existing structures and were regarded as so essential that when the space allowed for a courtyard did not meet the expectations of the owners, walls were dismantled and rooms joined together (see, for instance, House F, loc. 33, 45. Gawlikowski 1994, 140; Fig. 23). They would have allowed for tasks such as animal stabling or limited productive activities, suggesting a low labour specialisation of the inhabitants. Like in modern urban centres, this space must also have had a social function, encouraging communal meetings between family members living in the same building.

Pre-existing courtyards were often rearranged into smaller rooms by subdivision (Petruccioli 2006, 84; 2007, 8–9). In this case, *intercolumnia* of porticoes were blocked and transversal partition walls constructed to transform the semi-open walking areas into close rooms. A minimal specialisation of the house is evident in the construction of shops within the courtyard, a trend that has already noted by Petruccioli (2006, 79; 2007, 6) for the Early Islamic period and labelled '*taberna* process'. In House F (Fig. 23), the addition of loc. 15 opened toward the street in courtyard 13 is illustrative of this transformation (Gawlikowski 1991a, 87–8). The vertical extension of the house through the addition of stairways into courtyards, Petruccioli's '*insula* process' (Petruccioli 2006, 80; 2007, 7), seems also to be attested. A staircase made of reused blocks was found in Room D of the Peristyle Building (Grassi and al-As'ad 2013, 119; Fig. 24), and against the northern wall of Room G in Building B in the Sanctuary of Baalshamīn (Intagliata 2017a; Fig. 19). The creation of a second storey to separate living quarters from stabling areas is often seen as one of the most characteristic aspects of the transformation of Roman into Medieval houses (Polci 2003, 106; e.g., House G, Pella, Walmsley 2007b, 520; House XVIII, Umm al-Jimāl, Brown 1998, 63). However, it must be stressed that earlier cases of this phenomenon are known (see e.g., the house at Ḥorvat Kanaf, about 5km to the northeast of the Sea of Galilee dated to the 5th–6th centures; Maoz 1993; Hirshfeld 1995, 27). Furthermore, it is noteworthy that the opposite seems to have happened in Palmyra. In the House F and in the *Praetorium* of the Camp of Diocletian staircases were apparently blocked in Umayyad times with the consequent loss of the second storey (Gawlikowski 1994, 136; Kowalski 1994, 58).

Houses as multi-functional units

Post-Roman houses are multi-functional compounds, capable, therefore, of hosting a wide range of activities. Particularly visible in the archaeological record remains the productive function, which is reflected by the presence of small-scale industrial installations, such as oil presses, storage facilities, and animal feeding equipment. In the original phase of the *Praetorium* (end of the 4th–beginning of the 5th century) the stables were clearly separated from the living quarters, suggesting attention to separating animals from their owners. Its reconstruction, following the disastrous earthquake of the late 6th–beginning of the 7th century, saw the fragmentation of the pre-existing space, the installation of storage facilities, and the raising up of new floors or removal of older ones to place water installations. The building became 'an ordinary family house, that needed more rooms as the family grew' (Kowalski 1994, 59), in which, however, activities of production and stockage became of primary importance. House F (Fig. 23) was probably destroyed by the same earthquake and underwent basically the same alterations: installations of productive facilities, such as oil presses, creation of stocking areas, and other minor additions (wells, *tanānīr*, cupboards hanging out from walls at different levels, and earthen/stone benches). Similar changes have been documented in the Peristyle Building in the southwest quarter (Fig. 24). Room B was paved with a red mortar floor. Rooms H and I, the largest compartments so far discovered, were subdivided in smaller units by means of partition walls. Houses in the *Via Praetoria* of the Camp of Diocletian shows similar features: jars installed immediately below walking levels, large mortars made with reused drums or capitals of columns, wells within the habitations, all lead to the conclusion that these small-scale changes were not exceptional occurrences in the city.

The post-Roman Palmyrene house as a 'barometer of social change'

A number of studies have recently been devoted to the social implications of the process of transformation of houses in Late Antiquity (Baldini Lippolis 2001; Bowes 2012, 19–33). The most common tendency nowadays is to see in the layout of private residential buildings the formal expression of a social class (Baldini Lippolis 2005, 12–22 – a 'barometer of social change': Bowes 2012, 16). Some doubts have recently been arisen, however, on their usefulness as mirror of the society due to the lacunose state of the majority of the archaeological evidence brought to light so far (Bowes 2012, 85; Grahame 2000, 2–3). Very few thoughts have been spared for the dwellings of more ordinary people (Hirschfeld 1995, 24; Ellis 2000, 73–113), as many of the studies conducted on the topic have been focused on the 'houses of pretension', which are rich urban *domus* belonging to members of the upper classes (Ellis 2000, 22–72). These seem to have experienced a surge in construction from the 4th century and continued to be built until the first half of the 6th century mostly in administrative centres (Bowes 2012, 87, 90). In contrast to Late Antiquity, very little has been written on housing of the Early Islamic period. The whole corpus of evidence, which has never been systematically surveyed, is scanty, consisting of very few case studies, some better studied than others. A convergence of the urban house plan with those located in rural settings has been noted, suggesting a ruralisation of the urban environment (Walmsley 2007a, 131–2). In line with these studies, it is worth investigating to what degree houses in Palmyra reflect the social composition of the community living in the city in the period under discussion, with particular focus on Late Antiquity, for which enough dated evidence is left to speculate.

Defining the social change: Roman versus Late Antique domestic architecture

The opulence reached by Roman dwellings in Palmyra would never be equated in later times. A good number of Roman aristocratic peristyle houses have been uncovered in the city, suggesting the existence of a rich aristocratic community living within the limits imposed by the inner city wall. The Maison d'Achille and the Maison de Cassiopée, to the east of the Sanctuary of Bēl stand out among the others for their monumentality (Frézouls 1976b, 36–45, 50). The former covers a total surface of more than 1600m^2 and is the most monumental private residential building unearthed in the city (Balty 1989, 410). Its 17 rooms develop inorganically around two porticoed courts, the biggest of them with a 3rd century mosaic featuring Achilles among the daughters of Lycomedes (Balty 1989, 409–10; Stern 1977, 5–26). Smaller *domus* (*c.* 500–1200m^2), also known as 'petite palais' (Balty 1989, 410), are attested in the northwest quarter. They share, on a minor scale, a certain degree of luxury. These are three houses out of 12 excavated by Gabriel at the beginning of the 20th century (Maisons n. 38, n. 39, and n. 45). The plans of the remaining nine residential buildings have not been published (Gabriel 1926, pl. 15; 85, fig. 3; 87, fig. 5; Balty 1989, 409). The house located to the southeast of the Theatre and the Peristyle Building in the southwest quarter can be also taken as examples of the same type (Frézouls 1976b, 45–9; Grassi and al-As'ad 2013).

The post-Roman houses diverge radically from their Roman counterparts. Private residential buildings had become all-encompassing units. Animals often shared the same roof with dwellers and productive installations were meant to answer the every-day basic needs of the micro-community living in each house. The subdivision of large *domus* into smaller units is informative of a dramatic social change. Reception halls, which would have been used prior to 273 for formal meetings between the house owners and their guests, now find no use and they begin to be partitioned into smaller rooms used for more practical needs. The subdivision of large units has been seen as the reflection of split inheritance; families are accommodated into small dwellings opening onto shared courtyards provided with single entrances, thus suggesting that they were related (Ellis 1988, 565–76; Gawlikowski 2007, 91). The installation of ovens, oil presses, and mangers is also informative of the less pretentious living conditions of the new owners. This phenomenon of social change has already been noted for Palmyra. Gawlikowski refers to it as the replacement of 'the landed aristocracy of the ancient city … [by] the middle-class of artisans and shopkeepers' (Gawlikowski 2009, 90; 1997c, 349).

Contextualising the evidence

Not only Roman houses in Palmyra differ considerably from the post-Roman ones, but also domestic architecture in Late Antique Palmyra does not easily match the pattern of transformation that affects élite housing in contemporary urban centres. This is characterised by a tendency toward architectural monumentalisation and display of wealth. Its better-known mark is the addition of new reception rooms, sometimes very large and often ending with one or more apses (Ellis 1988; 1991; 2000, 64). A tendency to build these rooms in the corner of the open courtyard of the house and immediately adjacent the street, in order both to facilitate the access of *clientes* in the private buildings and prevent them from reaching the more private sector of the building, has been noted (Özgenel 2007, 252–3; *contra* Bowes 2012, 44–5). The addition of these facilities would have changed the inner structure of buildings, so that in some cases the overall plan needed to be newly orientated. Construction of apsidal chambers goes hand in hand with an overall process of 'beautification' of the house, which include the addition of new elaborate mosaics and the extensive use of marble for decorating walls and floors.

A number of houses excavated in Antioch can be taken as representative of these transformations. Most of the research on domestic architecture in this site have interested structures located in the suburb of Daphne, where, according to written sources, the Imperial palace was located (Poccardi 1994, 997). Archaeological excavations of the first half of the 20th century were eager to retrieve the elaborate mosaics from these private buildings, showing little or no interest in the houses' inner layouts and the urban context in which they were set. As a consequence, the archaeological record now left of these buildings is particularly patchy. Late Antique mosaics have been retrieved from the Constantinian Villa (Levi 1947, 225–26; Stillwell 1961, 53; Barsanti 1994, 597–8), the House of the Bird-Rinceau (Levi 1947, 257–8, 366), the House of the Triumph of Dionysius (Levi 1947, 91–104, 278–9; Lassus 1984, 364), and the Yatqo Complex (Levi 1947, 279–83, 323; Lassus 1984, 362). The second phase (early 6th century) of the House of *Aiōn* saw the addition to the original 3rd century building of a corridor also paved with a mosaic floor. From the centre of the corridor, a large apse protruded to the northwest (Levi 1947, 355–6; Campbell 1988, 57–9). Conversely, in the House of the Mask some of the original mosaics were later (second half of the 4th century) covered by rich floors in painted stucco (Levi 1947 307–8).

At Apamea, Late Antique houses have survived in better conditions. Here, the aristocratic élite was often eager to express their social status through the construction of residential compounds embellished with the finest decorations. The Maison au Triclinos occupies an entire block of the city to the west of the Cathedral. The approximately 80 rooms of the complex are grouped around a large peristyled open court and two smaller courtyard. Some of the rooms stand out from the others for their rich mosaic floors and their walls covered in precious polychrome marble *crustae* (Balty 1969, 105–16; 2000, 178–80; Balty 1977, 70–4, 104–9, 114–17; 1997, 85–93). Less pretentious, but still remarkably impressive for their decorative richness and monumentality are the other peristyled houses excavated in the city, such as the Maison aux Consoles (Balty 1984, 19–38; 1997, 94–100), the Maisons aux Colonnes Trilobées (Raepsaet and Raepsaet-Charlier 1984, 181–201), the Maison aux Pilastres (Gisler and Huliwer 1984, 79–94), the Maison du Cerf (Donnay-Rocmans and Donnay 1984, 155–69), and the Maison des Chapiteaux à Consoles (Baratte 1984, 107–25). The material evidence collected during the excavation of these houses reflects the wealth and elevated social status of their owners. Expensive imported marbles are abundantly adopted for furniture, such as *sigma* tables, and floors and walls decoration. A tendency toward architectural experimentation can also be noticed. This is represented by the sporadic addition of unusual features such as tortile columns and large polylobate fountains. Polychrome or black and white mosaic floors showing either standard geometric decoration or more elaborate and less common iconography, are, again, ubiquitous.

Other urban sites have yielded less, but not least interesting evidence. The Promontory Palace at *Caesarea Maritima*, the earliest evidence of which goes back to the 1st century, originally developed around two large open courtyards. The plan would be eventually maintained throughout Late Antiquity with, however, some alterations, which include the addition of new mosaic floors (Lavan 1999, 155–8, esp. 157). The less pretentious House of Eusebius at Jerusalem is believed to have been constructed in the second half of the 5th century and includes more modest rooms with mosaicoed floors and walls (Avi Yonah 1976, 622–5; see in the same contribution the House of Anastasius). The main distinctive features of the so-called Trajan's Palace at *Bostra* (Buṣrā), believed to be a 5th–6th century building on top of a pre-existing Roman (2nd–3rd century) one, are its total surface (1850m^2) and the impressive Espace Triconque, a three-apsed reception room, to the south of the peristyled court. The latter remains a rare occurrence in Late Antique domestic architecture. These two features have recently brought to advance the hypothesis that this compound might have had a different function, perhaps secular or religious (Piraud-Fournet 2003, 1–40; 2007, 147–54, with further bibliography). Disruptive events, such as natural disasters, seem generally not to have affected the continuity in occupation of opulent houses in the Levant, as suggested by a building at *Sepphōris* located to the east of the Nile Festival Building. This was destroyed by an earthquake in the mid-4th century, but was soon rebuilt and its rooms paved with new mosaics (Netzer and Weiss 1995, 171).

The aristocratic houses of Roman time in Palmyra do not seem to have undergone these changes in Late Antiquity. People in the city do not show interest in a radical change of the plan of the buildings, which is something that one would expect if the members of the local élite were still living in their houses. No high-quality mosaics have been installed after 273, no reception halls enlarged, and no semi-circular apses added. The only 'house of pretention' in the city (the modest *Praetorium*) is that of a military officer. Like in the more monumental Espace Triconque in the Trajan's Palace at Buṣrā, the owner of the *Praetorium* could enter the reception room unseen through a lateral door from the outside. Nevertheless, the general disposition of the rooms of this building stands out for its extreme simplicity, small size and absence of an opulent decorative apparatus. The pattern of two rooms divided by an arch seems to recall more the local 'salles à alcôve' characteristic of private residential buildings of Ḥawrān (Villeneuve 1997, 269), than the opulent reception rooms of Apamea and Antioch. In addition, in stark contrast with what was noted in other cities where a significant surge in the construction of rich houses goes normally along with the maintenance of buildings of public utility (Bowes 2012, 71–6), at Palmyra the lack of aristocratic houses goes hand in hand with the absence of major public building activities.

All this seems to open the possibility of a drastic reduction in the number of members that had composed the Palmyrene local aristocracy in Roman time. The theory of a flight of aristocrats to the countryside can also be advanced, but remains difficult to support with the evidence so far brought to light in the surroundings of Palmyra. One of the main reason for this abrupt disappearance is likely connected to the disruptions that followed the events of 273, which must have caused substantial casualties among the Palmyrenes, some of whom were deported in Rome for the triumph of Aurelian in 274 (Hartmann 2016, 67). In any case, it would be dangerous to see in this transformation the complete end of the wealth of the Palmyrene community. Undoubtedly, a rich middle-class composed in all likelihood by merchants, shopkeepers, artisans, and soldiers must still have existed and might have formed the backbone of the new post-Roman Palmyrene élite. The study of houses, however, cannot be of any help to define in detail the social stratification of the Palmyrene community.

When did this social change start?

The crucial point of this discussion is to establish when this social change started. This is certainly not an easy task. In an attempt to explain the presence of rustic facilities in House F, Gawlikowski put forward the hypothesis that this process started in Late Antiquity, arguing that it might have been triggered by a natural disaster (Gawlikowski 1994, 136). More recently, he narrowed the chronology to the 6th–7th century (Gawlikowski 2009, 90; see also Gawlikowski 1997c, 349; 2007, 91). However, we should not exclude the possibility, which remains to be validated by future investigations, that a change in the social composition of the Palmyrene community happened much earlier.

Together with the absence of the process of 'beautification' of Late Antique aristocratic houses seen above, further archaeological evidence to support this theory comes from a rich Roman residence excavated by the Polish team immediately behind the Octostyle Portico in the northwest quarter. The building includes a large hall covered by a wide mosaic originally measuring over 9 × 5.50m in size (Gawlikowski 2004, 313). The mosaic, which features two central panels showing Bellerophon fighting the Chimera and a hunter shooting an arrow to a tiger, has been stylistically dated to the mid-3rd century. After 273, possibly as early as the beginning of the 4th century, the hall seems to have been transformed into a meeting place by a religious community devoted to the cult of the Anonymous God. To meet their needs, the newcomers modified the 3rd century mosaic floor with several poor quality additions, among them two black and white panels featuring two pairs of open bare hands, a symbol associated with the Anonymous God (Gawlikowski 2004, 318). The area was then renovated in the second half of the 4th century. In this phase, new rooms of domestic function were created by subdividing the space into smaller units through partition walls; *tanānīr* and wells were also installed. The new occupants found no use for the mosaic, which was covered with a more practical mortar floor (Żuchowska 2006, 445). This would suggest that the earlier aristocratic residents of the house moved away from their residence after 272–273 and point to a change of the social composition of the people who lived in this district as early as the 4th century.

Conclusions

In Palmyra, post-Roman domestic architecture seems to be in stark contrast not only with the monumentality of Roman houses, but also with the opulence of contemporary private residential buildings in other cities. This points towards a drastic shift in the composition of the Palmyrene society, which might have undergone a reduction in the number of the members of the local aristocratic élite. The starting date of this social change is difficult to pinpoint with the data available. We should not exclude, however, that this started as early as the 4th century. The evidence does not help clarify whether this event was sudden or gradual, but it might have been connected with the heavy casualties that occurred in 272–273. After this date, Palmyra was no more a wealthy caravan station as it used to be in Roman times, but had become a fortress city. The main priorities of its inhabitants changed abruptly. Their efforts were no more addressed to please the populations of the western empire with exotic and expensive products from faraway lands, but to meet the more practical needs of a garrison, as seen in the ensuing chapters. In this new scenario, then, Palmyra would have offered very few attractions to an aristocratic élite.

Chapter 4

Religious life and communities in Late Antique and Early Islamic Palmyra

Palmyra retained a prominent role as a religious centre after 273. Although the settlement did not reach the same status of cities of major Christian convergence such as al-Ruṣāfa, it certainly maintained an important role at a regional level. Palmyra is one of the earliest bishopric in central Syria and there is written evidence to suggest its involvement in the Christological debates of its time as early as the first half of the 4th century. At least eight churches were constructed in the city in Late Antiquity, one of which being one of the biggest building of its kind in Syria. Under the Umayyads, a mosque was built in the city centre, reflecting the advent of a sizable Muslim community. Christians and Muslims were not the only religious groups living in the city. Data from the epigraphic and archaeological records suggest the presence of Jews throughout Late Antiquity, and at least until the 13th century. A comprehensive reappraisal of the archaeological evidence and the written sources may help sketch a religious history of the city in Late Antiquity and the Early Islamic period.

Framing post-Roman Palmyra's religious history through written sources and epigraphic evidence

The epigraphic record suggests that pagan religious life continued seemingly without major interruption in the immediate aftermath of the Aurelianic disruptions. Two inscriptions from the Sanctuary of Bēl dated 272 and 273 mention a certain Septimius Ḥaddūdan as a symposiarch. The latest of them reports the direct support provided to the Roman troops besieging Palmyra by Septimius, 'who helped [the army of Au]relianus, the Caesar, [our lord]'; this action must certainly have helped Septimius Ḥaddūdan to assure a continuous and undisturbed involvement in the religious life of the city after the second Palmyrene revolt (*Inv.* 9, 40, n. 28; Gawlikowski 1973, 76–7; tr. Kowalski 1997, 41–2). Renovation works on pagan buildings are also known in the last quarter of the 3rd century. Two bilingual inscriptions, one of which dates back to 279–280, record the roofing of a Basilica of the god Arṣū, it being a section of the Great Colonnade dedicated to this local deity. This has often been taken as a proof that the Sanctuary of Arṣū, which was close to the *Agora* but outside the city wall, was still functioning at that time (al-Asʿad and Gawlikowski 1986–1987, 167–8, ns 7–8; on the chronology *contra IGLS* 17.1, 95–6, ns 80–1). The latest epigraphic evidence for pagan worship is provided by an altar dating back to 302 and dedicated by Avitus *optio princeps* to Zeus the Highest in the Sanctuary of Baalshamīn (*IGLS* 17.1, 163–4, n. 154).

Already at that time, Christianity was slowly begun its ascent. Sporadic mentions of Christian Palmyra in written sources appear as early as the first half of the 4th century. Caesar Baronius' *Martyrologium Romanum* recounts the martyrdom of Saints Libya, Eutropia, and Leonida in the city on the 15 July 303 (Baronius 1589, 264–5), but the reference to Palmyra is now believed to have been a typographical error of the writer (Lucchesi 1967, 1152–4). Marinus of Palmyra (Μαρῖνος Παλμύρων) is the first bishop of the city to be mentioned in the conciliar records as participant of the Council of Nicaea in 325 (Le Quien 1740, 2, 845; Devreesse 1945, 206; Fedalto 1988, 742; Turner (1899, 48) reports also the name Martinus; on the alleged connection with the Bānū Marīna, Shahīd 1984b, 345, n. 3).

The presence of a bishop from this city at such an early stage is informative of the role played by the settlement as a regional hub for Christianity at the time. As a matter of fact, the other two bishoprics known in the Palmyrene territory, *Euareia* (Ḥuwwārīn) and *Oresa/Oruba* (al-Ṭayyiba), were installed much later, respectively in the 5th and 6th centuries (Genequand 2012, 30). The process of Christianisation of the city is unclear, but it must have followed that of other territories in the desert fringe where, according to Sozomen, who wrote in the first half of the 5th century, the conversion of the local nomadic tribes 'appears to have been the result of their intercourse with the priests who dwelt among them, and with the monks who dwelt in the neighbouring deserts, and who were distinguished by their purity of life and by their miraculous gifts' (Soz., *EH*, 6.38; tr. Walford 1855, 310; Trimingham 1979, 86–100).

No written record survives to cast light on the religious life of the city in the second half of the 4th century, but the archaeological evidence points to major religious disruptions at that time. In the late 4th century, Palmyra was involved in the process of eradication of pagan worship, perhaps as a consequence of the edicts issued by Theodosius (Fowden 1978, 53; Chuvin 1990, 43–78; Trombley 1993, 1–97). On that occasion, the Sanctuary of Allāth underwent major disruptions. Its altar was cut horizontally to prevent further offering and the cult statue of Athena was deliberately mutilated. Its head was struck by numerous well-aimed blows to knock it off from the bust and disfigure its facial features (Gąssowska 1985, 115; see also, Sauer 2003, 49–52). The destruction of the essential elements of pagan worship was dated by Gąssowska mostly through numismatic evidence to the mid-380s. The scholar associated with the visit in 385–388 of Maternus Cynegius, who was *praefectus praetorio Orientis* and well-known physical executor of the anti-pagan measures undertaken by the emperor (Gąssowska 1985, 119). Yet, this hypothesis remains open to debate. In fact, the latest coin of the so-called 'Trésor du Temple d'Allat', a hoard found in the *cella*, within the debris of the latest destructive phase of the compound, has generically been dated to 383–395 (Krzyżanowska 2014, 55). Additional datable evidence on the end of pagan worship in Palmyra comes from the northwest quarter. The mid-3rd century mosaic in the Bellerophon Hall, had been later modified with low quality mosaic panels showing two bare open hands, a symbol commonly associated with the worship of this God. In the second half of the 4th century, however, the mosaic was covered by a mortar floor and the area acquired a more domestic nature (Gawlikowski 2004, 318; Żuchowska 2006, 445–8; see above, Chapter 3). No signs of destruction, however, have been recorded in this case.

The absence of evidence for pagan worship after the second half of the 4th century, associated with the predominantly Chistian nature of the Late Antique written sources, should not be considered as conclusive proofs of the abrupt end of paganism in Palmyra in this period. It cannot be ruled out *a priori* that the Palmyrene gods continued to be worshipped in this early phase. Looking at a much wider picture, it is clear that persistence of paganism remained particularly common in the Near East throughout Late Antiquity (Drijvers 1982, esp. 36; Trombley 1993; 1995). John of Ephesus (*EH*, 3.27), to cite an example, reports the eradication of the last sack of Paganism in Baʿalbak by the military officer Theophilus only in 597. Torturing and interrogating people accused of 'heathenish error', Theophilus was informed that 'numerous persons in every district and city in their land [practice Paganism], and in almost every town in the East, but especially at Antioch' (tr. Smith 1860, 210).

Unlike the 4th century, written sources on religious life in Palmyra in the 5th century are more abundant. In the account of the life of Alexander the Akoimetēs (*Alex. Akoim., 35*), the narrator recounts that the holy man, travelling with a group of followers through the Syrian steppe, was refused entry to the city because of the shortage of food. He refers to the Palmyrenes as 'Jews who call themselves Christians', the term 'Jews' probably intended as an insult rather than a reflection of the religious condition of the inhabitants (Gatier 1995, 454–5; see also Kaizer 2010, 119). Possibly in the same period (first half of the 5th century), bishop Cyriacus was in the city (Honigmann 1951, 146–7; Le Quien 1749, 2, 845). The man had been deposed in 403 by the Synod of the Oak for having supported the cause of John Chrysostom, the patriarch of Constantinople and was exiled in Palmyra in the same year (Pall., *Dial. John Chris.*, 20.35–8). The city very likely maintained its status of episcopal see throughout the 5th century, although only the name of bishop John is known. Theodorus, bishop of Damascus, signed for him the six canon of the Council of Chalcedon in 451 (Le Quien1740, 2, 845–846; *ACO 2.1.2.154;* 2.3.2.174).

The council of Chalcedon marked a significant shift in the fortunes of the Christological controversies of the 5th century. Besides issuing 27 disciplinary canons, it asserted the Orthodox Church doctrine postulating the existence of two natures in Christ against the heresy of Eutyches, who believed Christ to be a fusion of divine and human elements. In addition, it resulted in the deposing of the bishop of Alexandria, Dionysius, for his philo-Eutyches stance and appointing the pro-Chalcedonian Proterius. After the council, critics moved immediately against the newly formulated doctrine. The church that supported the teaching of Dioscurus in line with the orthodox position of Cyril of Alexandria was known with the name of Monophysite. Opposed to the Chalcedonians, the Monophysites believed in the presence of a single nature (φύσις) in Christ (Sellers 1953, 254–301). The Chalcedonian doctrine, however, was not challenged until the death of Marcian and the appointment of Leo to the throne in 457. In that year, Proterius was murdered, his body being burnt publicly in the hippodrome of Alexandria, and the patriarchal seat taken by the anti-Chalcedonian Timothy Aelurus (Sellers 1953, 274, n. 4). The death of Proterius was the subject of a letter signed by 12 bishops of the province *Phoenicia Libanensis*, among them John of Palmyra, and sent to emperor Leo. The bishops therein confirm their position rejecting the Chalcedon creed, but they distance themselves from the action of Timothy Aelurus in Egypt, who is described as an usurper and a tyrant (Le Quien 1740, 2, 845–6; *ACO* 2.5.46; Fedalto 1988, 742).

The Monophysite movement in the East strengthened in the second half of the 5th and the first decades of the 6th century thanks to an Imperial government that was mostly supportive of this heresy (Sellers 1953, 283). Illustrative of the stance of this is the issue of the *Henōtikon* by emperor Zeno (482) who attempted in vain to reconcile the two factions by re-aligning the Orthodox Church to the positions reached in the councils of Constantinople (381) and Ephesus (431) (Sellers 1953, 277). The efforts of Zeno and his successor Anastasius to appease the Monophysitic East were mostly motivated by practical considerations, first and foremost the strategic relative proximity of Syria to the Persian empire. Within this historical framework we should consider the construction of two remarkable pilgrimage sites by the Imperial authority, namely the *martyrion* of St Symeon the Stylite at Qalʿat Simʿān and Basilica A at al-Ruṣāfa, both roughly in the same time span, 470–490 (Bogisch 2005, 54, 62). Al-Ruṣāfa, situated *c.* 130km northeast of Palmyra, experienced an unprecedented building development during the 6th century with the growth of the cult of St Sergius, who was believed to have been martyred there under Diocletian. The shrine gradually became an important meeting place, especially for those nomadic communities living in the eastern borderlands among which the cult of St Sergius mainly spread. Palmyra must have certainly benefited economically from the mass of pilgrims visiting the shrine of St Sergius, perhaps acting as a road station for those travelling along the eastern frontier.

At the time of the exile of the Chalcedonian Elias from Jerusalem on 1 September 516 'the east was to all appearances Monophysite' (Frend 1972, 227). The position of the Imperial authority, however, changed abruptly under Justin I, who was determined to proclaim the definition of Chalcedon as the only faith of the empire. Justin's reaction against the Monophysite movement, which at that time saw in the patriarch of Antioch Severus one of its most fervent supporters, resulted in the deposition, exile, and murder of the majority of the Monophysite followers in a purge that lasted 2 years (518–519). The late Syriac sources Michael the Syrian (*Chr.* 9.13) and the author of the *Chronicle of Zuqnin* (3.19) report John (II) bishop of Palmyra's being exiled in 519 on that occasion, suggesting therefore the support of the Church of Palmyra for the Monophysite cause (Honigmann 1951 98, 147; Fedalto 1988, 742). A new persecution broke out in 521 and concluded with the end of Justin's reign (Frend 1972, 247).

In Justinianic time, the position of the Imperial authority did not change. After a first period of openness to the anti-Chalcedonian movement as a result of the influence of Theodora, wife of Justinian and adherent to Monophysitism, anti-heretic persecutions burst out again. In an Imperial edict issued on 6 August 536 Justinian banned Severus, Anthimus of Trebizond, and their supporters, and ordered all the copies of Severus' writing to be burnt (Frend 1972, 273). The list of the clergymen who approved this decision is known; the deacon and ξενοδόχος/*hospitalarius* of the Church of Palmyra (τῆς Παλμυρέων ἐκκλεσίας), Julian, was among them (Mansi 1762, 921; *ACO* 3.151). Overall, the first half of the 6th century represented a significant turning point for Palmyra. According to Malalas (*Chr.*, 17.2) and the later Theophanes (*Chr.*, 1.174), the emperor Justinian was responsible for restoring the churches in the city in 527–528. Indeed, the majority of the churches brought to light are now believed to have been constructed or refurbished at that time. The title ξενοδόχος/*hospitalarius* given to the deacon Julian of Palmyra hid the existence of charitable institutions in the city controlled by the Church. The Imperial renewed growing interest in the city, however, might not have been the only cause of the sudden increase in the number of ecclesiastical buildings. In other cities, their construction was often the result of the action of single or groups of well-off individuals aiming at manifesting their piety to an urban community that was thoroughly permeated with Christian values (Majcherek 2005, 146). However, no epigraphic material has so far been found in Palmyra that would allow us to link these individuals to particular acts of religious euergetism.

Compared to Justinianic times, the history of Christian Palmyra in the second half of the 6th century is rather obscure. In the *Notitia Antiochena* compiled by the patriarch Anastasius, the city is said to be under the jurisdiction of Damascus together with ten other urban centres; it occupies third place in the list after *Eliopolis* and *Abila*, and before *Laodikeia* (*sic*), suggesting its importance in the conciliar record (Honigmann 1925, 75; Vailhé 1907, 145). A further clue on the ecclesiastical position of Palmyra comes from a mid-6th-century Syriac codex belonging to the unidentified monastery of NṬP' DZGL said to be in the city's territory. The text is supposedly written 'in the days of the two holy and devout bishops Mār Jacob and Mār Theodore' (Wright 1872, 2.468–9, n. 585; Millar 2013, 23). These are known to have become bishops respectively of Edessa and *Bostra* (or 'the camp of the Saracens') (Millar 2013, 23) after the request of the prominent leader of the Jafnids al-Ḥārith b. Jabala to appoint two Monophysite monks to the bishopric seats. The two holy men are credited by other written sources with organising the Monophysite Church's hierarchy (Hoyland 2009, 130). Mār Jacob (Baradaeus) in particular is known to have been greatly devoted to this cause. John of Ephesus (*Jac. Bar.*, 693) claims that he ordained 100,000 clergymen and 26 bishops during his office, and it is after him that the Syrian Monophysites come to be called 'Jacobites' (Frend 1972, 287). Yet, no bishops have been appointed by the two for Palmyra at least until 566 (Millar 2013, 24). This would explain why, according to Millar (2013, 23), the Syriac passage does not refer to the bishop of Palmyra, as might be expected since the text was written in a monastery said to be near the city and possibly within its administrative jurisdiction, but to the itinerary bishops.

The fate of the religious community of Palmyra in the first decades of the 7th century is also uncertain. Nothing is known on the religious activities of the city under Persian rule at the beginning of the century, while little is left to speculate for the short time span comprised between the re-conquest of the East by Roman forces and the Islamic dominion. In 630, Heraclius held a council at *Hierapolis* to persuade a selected group of bishops to accept his Monothelite creed. One of the participants was Thomas, bishop of Palmyra (Mich. Syr., *Chr.*, 11.3; Fedalto 1988, 742). Plausibly while Thomas was still bishop, the body of St Anastasius was translated from Dastagerd in Persia to Jerusalem via Palmyra in 631 (*Anas. Per.*, 1.102–104; Millar 2008, 70–2; Kaizer 2010, 115–16). The relic of the saint carried by a pious monk is said to have performed a miracle in the city healing a blind man in seven days (*Anas. Per.*, 1.129–130).

The Islamic takeover of Palmyra in 634 did not result in any major break in the religious life of the city. According to al-Balādhurī (*Futūḥ*, 111–12), the inhabitants were granted the state of *dhimma*, which envisages a condition of subordination embodied in the payment of a poll tax, but also the freedom of person, legal status, property, and religion under an assurance of safety and security (Bosworth 1982, 41–5; Levy-Rubin 2011, 36). This seems to reflect a generalised trend in the newly conquered territories, where juridical Christian autonomy was overall respected and Christian Arab tribes retained their religious roots (Dick 1992, 90–1). As a matter of fact, although the Pact of ʿUmar banned formally the erection of new ecclesiastical buildings or the restoration of destroyed ones (Noth 1987, 291), church construction remained intensive at the time in the former Roman territory (Guidetti 2009, 3). No names of bishops are known for this period, but the city must have remained an important Christian hub. Michael the Syrian (*Chr.* 3.451, 453; Fedalto 1988, 742) reports the existence of two bishops at a later date, in early ʿAbbāsid time. These were Simeon, from the Convent of Mār Jacob of Cyrrhus, appointed by Cyriacus in 793, and John, of the Monastery of Mār Ḥanania, appointed by Dionysios (818). At the end of the 8th century, the poet Abū Nuwās (*Dīwān*, 1.250) on his way to Egypt from Baghdad still recorded the presence of churches in the city. A gap in written sources affects our knowledge on Muslim activities in the city. In *Bilād al-Shām* a substantial Christian community remained present throughout the Umayyad period (Humpreys 2010, 45–9). To cite some estimates, according to Ferré (1988), at the end of the 7th century Muslims in Syria did not exceed 200,000 people out of a population of 4 million. It is reasonable to believe that Muslims in Umayyad Palmyra were at first a minority and that conversion must have been slow, especially owing to the strong Christian traditions of the central Syrian region.

A number of religious communities coexisted throughout the century of Umayyad dominion in Palmyra, several archaeological items of evidence confirming this interaction. In the Suburban Market, the Syro-French team uncovered a large cemetery in the east portion of the building with around thirty burials dating back to no later than the 7th–8th centuries. The majority were orientated from east to west, following a Christian custom, but three had a north–south orientation suggesting, according to the excavators, that they might have been Muslims, or, at least, not Christian (Delplace 2006–2007, 107). The only presumed piece of evidence of intolerance against Christians in Palmyra found so far is reported in the *Praetorium* of the Camp of Diocletian. Here, roughly in the mid-7th century, the eastern entrance to the building was rebuilt and the lintel overhanging the passageway, which bore a carved Christian cross, was concealed (Kowalski 1994, 58; Gawlikowski 1977, 265 reports that the cross was chiselled away). The action has been tentatively connected to the order of the caliph ʿUthmān b. ʿAffān (r. 644–655) to remove crosses from walls of streets and significant urban buildings. Crosses were the target of Islamic antipathy mostly because, in being the universal sign of Christianity, they were consequently associated with the Byzantine empire (King 1985, 269; Griffith 1992, 126).

The lacunose state of written evidence cannot contribute more in tracing a religious history of post-Roman Palmyra. Unsurprisingly, what emerges from Late Antique written sources is predominantly a 'Christian history', as little is said on the existence of other religious communities. Even during the Islamic dominion, the Christian legacy of Palmyra remains very much alive through the pen of Muslim writers. Archaeological evidence, therefore, have to be considered as a necessary complement to written sources in order to trace a more exhaustive religious history of the city throughout Late Antiquity and the Early Islamic period.

The archaeological evidence

The Christian community

The Christian community and its places of worship; remarks on the location of churches

Churches constitute the majority of Late Antique buildings of public utility known at the site and hide the existence of a resourceful Christian community. Looking at a much broader context, the high presence of churches in Palmyra does not surprise. With the diffusion of Christianity, and especially form the second half of the 5th century, churches became the new urban landmark, constituting indispensable ornaments for cities, towns, and villages. In large metropoleis, the construction of a high number of churches is expected. At Rome, for example, 83 churches are known only in the 6th century (Guidobaldi 1994, 44). In eastern provincial cities, as well as in small towns and villages, churches are particularly numerous. Oft-quoted examples in modern literature include the villages of Umm al-Jimāl, where 15 churches have been identified (De Vries

1985, 251, 256), Rihāb, with ten churches (Piccirillo 1981, 54–60), and Khirbat al-Samrā', with eight (Humbert and Desreumaux 1990, 258–65). The construction of churches financed by members of urban communities became the new form of euergetism in Late Antiquity.

All the churches discovered so far at Palmyra are *intra muros*. Most of them are installed in earlier buildings that in some cases have had their plans considerably altered. Church I, for example, has an unusual plan that is dictated by its installation within a pre-existing 4th century civic building. The church installed in the Sanctuary of Bēl, and, if we want to accept Collart's conclusion, that in the Sanctuary of Baalshamīn, are the only that re-use earlier pagan buildings. The conversion of temples into churches is a practice that is attested across the empire and has traditionally been interpreted as the necessity to stress the triumph of Christianity over paganism (Deichmann 1939, 144). Yet, triumphalism might not have been the only reason (Jacobs 2013, 313). The process of conversion included first the deconsecration and purification of the place, a practice that is often difficult to discern in the archaeological record (Jacobs 2013, 287–9). Only then, the temple would have been restructured to serve as a church. Conversions were normally not invasive and often consisted only in the addition of an apse (Bayliss 2004, 33). The practice seems not to have been particularly widespread in the East (Deichmann 1939; Bayliss 2004, 36–8; Saradi 2006, 355–84; Jacobs 2013, 294–5). One of the earliest examples is represented by the conversion of the Temple of Zeus at Aizanoi, which was transformed into a church as early as *c.* 400 (Naumann 1979, 76–7; Rheidt 2003, 244). In some places, the process took longer than in others. At Athens, for examples, pagan temples were deconsecrated only at the end of the 5th century; the *Hepaisteion* and the *Erechtheion* were converted into churches in the late 6th–early 7th centuries (Saradi 2011, 273, with further bibliography). The installation of a church in the Sanctuary of Bēl might have been moved by a number of practical reasons. The sanctuary, with its majestic *c.* 200 × 200m *temenos* would certainly have been an impressing sight from any visitor approaching the monument from the Great Colonnade. Undoubtedly, the monumentality of the earlier compound would have provided a suggestive, no-cost setting to glorify Christianity to the detriment of the pagan past.

As for their location in the urban fabric, churches in Palmyra are situated along two main axes. Four of them open onto, or are located next to, the Great Colonnade. These include three small churches surveyed by Majcherek, the church in the Sanctuary of Bēl, and Church I in the northwest quarter. All are found next to public buildings or open spaces that would have encouraged communal meeting. The pattern of installing churches along wide colonnaded street is very diffused in the Late Antique Near East and beyond and found its origin as early as the 4th century. At Apamea the *Rotunda*, the *Atrium* Church, and the *Basilica* are all located along the *cardo* (Foss 1997, 211). Similarly, at Philippi, the mid-4th century Church of the Apostle Paul and the late 5th century Basilica A could be accessed by the main city's artery, the *Via Egnatia* (Brenk 2003, 9). In these and other sites, these streets would have provided the builders monumental backdrops for their churches, which would have thus enjoyed particular urban visibility (Jacobs 2014). The location along major thoroughfares would have been functional to provide easy access to the Christian community in case of public events such as religious processions or cities' fairs.

Three other churches, named by the excavators Churches II, III, and IV, open onto Church Street. This cluster of buildings has made scholars to believe on the existence of a veritable ecclesiastical quarter that emerged as early as the 5th century but developed fully only one century later (Gawlikowski 2001). The reasons behind the formation of this quarter in this specific area are obscure. It was certainly not moved by practical reasons. The 4–5m wide, narrow Church Street would have been difficult to access by the large mass of believers willing to participate to the liturgies officiated in these buildings. We can assume that one church had served as the cathedral and the others grouped around it in a later time.

Although little work has so far been conducted in the southern part of the city, it is safe to assume that the Christian community used to live there too. The excavation of the Peristyle Building in the southernmost section of the quarter has revealed that this sector of the city remained occupied until at least the 8th century (Grassi and al-As'ad 2013, with further bibliography). A cross was found carved on one of the columns of the porticoed open courtyard of the building (Fig. 44). So far, archaeological evidence would suggest that the focus of the Christian community was certainly to the north of the Great Colonnade, but it does not support conclusively an abandonment of the southern areas.

Churches in pre-existing pagan monuments

As already mentioned, two churches are believed to have been installed in pre-existing pagan sanctuaries in Palmyra, namely in the Temple of Bēl and in the Temple of Baalshamīn. The other major pagan sanctuaries *intra muro*, the Sanctuary of Allāth, in the Camp of Diocletian and the Sanctuary of Nabū in the city centre, do not seem to have undergone the same transformations. Little survives of the church installed in the Temple of Bēl (Amy *et al.* 1975, 157–60; Gawlikowski 1993, 153; 2001, 123; Westphalen 2009, 156–9; Jastrzębowska 2013). The inner arrangement of the church eludes us. It has often believed that the conversion of the pagan monument into a church resulted in the re-orientation of the axis of worship towards the east. This was achieved by adding a *baldacchino* to cover the altar on the east wall of the nave. A semi-circular groove ending in two squared cavities would be the only trace left of this installation (Fig. 26). At the centre of the *baldacchino* is the negative imprint of a cross. (Schlumberger 1935, 161; Lassus 1947, 246, 302; Leroy 1964, 82; 1965; Amy *et al.* 1975, 157–60; Westphalen 2009, 155–9). Yet, Jastrzębowska (2013) has recently confuted this well-rooted conclusion. The scholar believes that, although a *baldacchino* must have existed, this was not installed to protect the altar. The apse must have been situated in the southern *adyton* of the temple (Fig. 27), as indicated by four circular sockets about 0.12–0.13m in diameter marking the position of the altar screen and visible running east to west on the steps of the staircase leading to this room. A further element in support of this conclusion is the position of the mural paintings along the east and west walls, which are not found neither next to the northern *adyton* nor the *baldacchino*. The paintings feature standing hierarchical figures both isolated and in a group. The best preserved of these is on the west wall. It shows traces of two central figures, Mary on a throne and Christ. An angel stands immediately behind them (Fig. 28). Two more figures flank this central scene. Identification of these has often been attempted, yet, none of them with absolute certainty. Jastrzębowska (2013, 181) has recently interpreted the figure on the left as St Sergius paying homage to Christ.

The uninterrupted occupation of the Sanctuary of Bēl until the beginning of the last century represents a major obstacle to ascertaining the chronology of the church. The painting has stylistically been dated to the 6th century. An inscription dated to the 4th or 5th century within the *baldacchino* recites: '(Peace be with you), Holy Mother of God, full of Grace, made Lazaros, servant of God …' (*IGLS* 17.1, 55–6, n. 47; tr. rev. Kowalski 1997, 57). It may refer to the sole addition of the *baldacchino* or the erection of the church in its entirety (Westphalen 2009, 157). To the excavators, the church was erected in the 5th century and, thus, was already in function when the paintings were added (Amy *et al.* 1975, 159). Its activity ceased in 728–729, when an Arabic inscription was added on the east wall of the building (*Inv.* 9, 51, n. 39).

Our knowledge of the presumed church in the temple of the Sanctuary of Baalshamīn is even more blurred (Collart 1963, 154–8; Collart and Vicari 1969, 77–81; Fig. 29). Collart dated its construction back to the first half of the 5th century (Collart and Vicari 1969, 94). The building was re-orientated to the southeast following an axis of worship known from other churches in the city. A new entrance was cut into the west wall of the *cella*, and three small, not communicating rooms were installed in the former entrance, being a squared sanctuary, 3.9m large, and two lateral rooms, smaller than the sanctuary (3.5m). The two columns marking the entrance of the sanctuary would have supported a wide arch (not found) as several grooves on the columns would suggest. The entrance to the church would have been through a porch 4m deep (the *narthex*) erected with reused columns from the colonnades of the Grande Cour. The lateral porticoes of the pagan temple would have served as aisles, the former walls of the *cella*, which were not dismantled, as the limits of the *bema* of the new church. No new material was used to construct the church, which is entirely built with reused architecture.

Kowalski (1996) has questioned Collart's conclusions. On the basis of parallels from the villages of the Limestone Massif in northern Syria, he has suggested that the new building might have been hosted meeting halls for the élite strata of the population. Following Hanson (1978, 257), who argues that the transformation of pagan temples into churches is only safely attested after the mid-5th century, he rejects Collart's dating and proposes a 6th century chronology for the new building (Kowalski 1996, 221). The dating would be supported by the presence of a coin found on 12 October 1955 under the flagging of the *pronaos* in the temple. In Collart's notebook the coin is reported to be dated 582–602; in the final publication of the report it is said to be a pre–538 issue (Collart and Vicari 1969, 78, n. 1; Dunant 1975a, 110, n. 35; *Notebook* (*Excavation diary*), inv. n. 118). A criticism advanced against Collart's interpretation is that the alleged *bema* would have been completely isolated from the aisles, thus impeding the correct execution of any kind of liturgy (Kowalski 1996, 219).

Churches along the Great Colonnade

A second group of buildings includes four churches located along the Great Colonnade. Three of them have been identified in a field-survey by Majcherek and dated tentatively to the 6th century, but have never been excavated. They are characterised by apses orientated to the southeast and very limited sizes, suggesting perhaps their use as chapels rather than churches (Fig. 30). One is situated about 15m to the north of the Baths of Diocletian. In plan, it does not seem to open onto the Great Colonnade, but it is close enough to be included in this group. It is set at the junction of two roads on top of a pre-existing building. The church is mostly covered by a thick deposit of ash that has been interpreted by the surveyors as the result of the activities of the furnaces in the Baths of Diocletian. This conclusion, however, remains conjectural and needs to be verified through systematic excavation; if proven right it would open the possibility that the Baths of Diocletian were still operational when the church had already collapsed. The main outlines of the structure are visible on the ground. It has a width of 14m and a semi-circular apse of 5.5m in diameter. The length of the church could not be measured due to the poor preservation of the remains, but it is likely that it extends to the nearby side road leading to the Sanctuary of Baalshamīn. Neither aisles nor lateral rooms flanking the apse are visible (Majcherek 2005, 142).

The second unexcavated three-aisled church has been identified in the area next to the *Nymphaeum* near the

Tetrapylon (Section B of the Great Colonnade). It is a rectangular building (12 × 19m) with an apse semi-circular on the inside but polygonal on the outside. The church seems to have been built on top of an earlier building. Two bases of columns would mark the limit of the southern aisle (2.5–2.7m deep), but nothing would exclude them as being part of a later structure. The level of the floor of the church is considerably higher than that of the street onto which the building opens. Steps must have been compensated the difference in height (Majcherek 2005, 144).

Figure 26. Semi-circular groove marking the position of the baldaquin in the cella *of the Sanctuary of Bēl. (Pal.M.A.I.S. photo archive. Courtesy of the Pal.M.A.I.S. archaeological team, Università degli Studi di Milano).*

Figure 27. Southern adyton *of the Temple of Bēl (Pal.M.A.I.S. photo archive. Courtesy of the Pal.M.A.I.S. archaeological team, Università degli Studi di Milano).*

Figure 28. Painting on the eastern wall of the church, next to the southern adyton *(Jastrzębowska 2013, 190, fig. 7).*

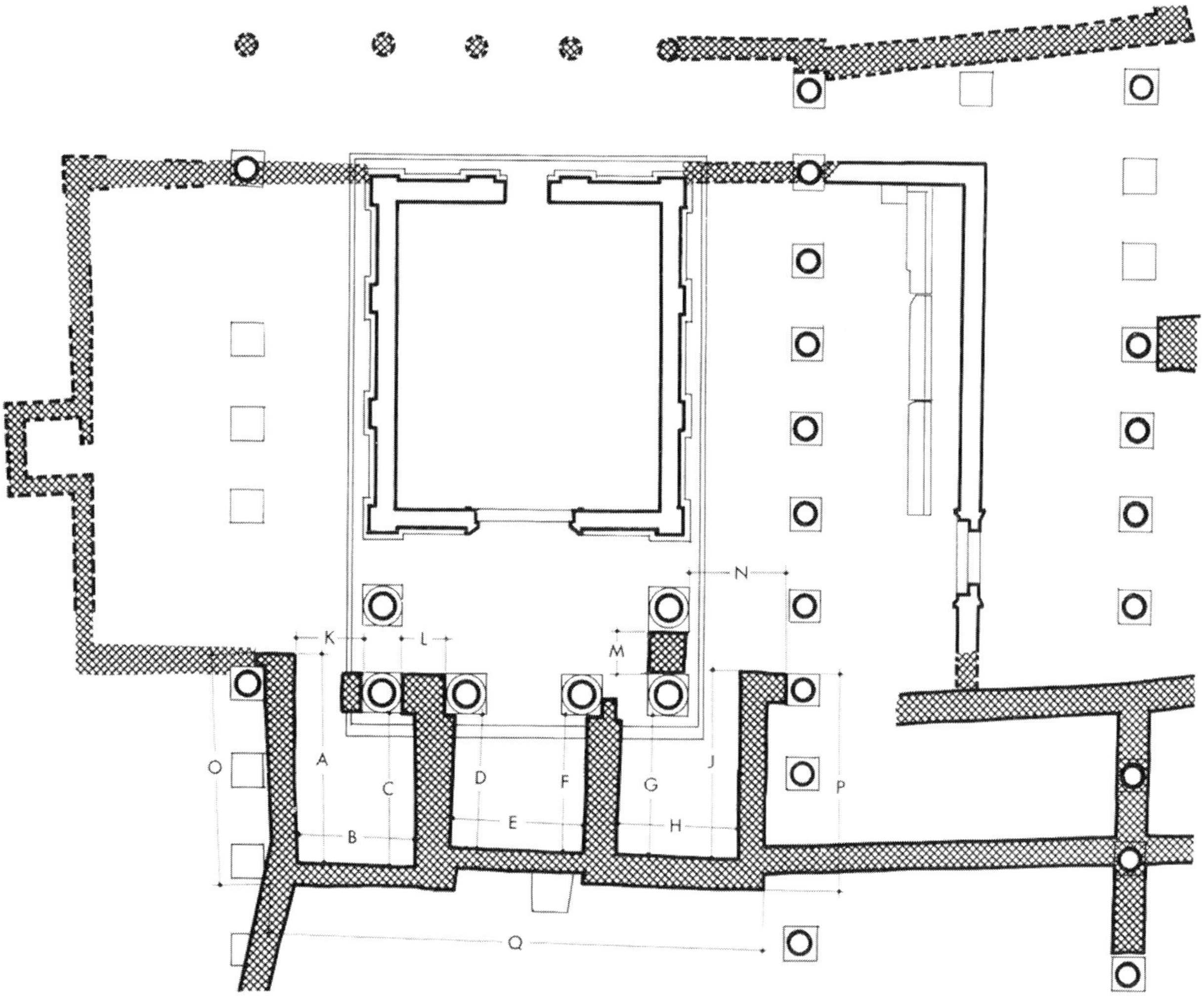

Figure 29. The presumed early 5th century church installed in the cella *of the Sanctuary of Baalshamīn (Collart and Vicari 1969, pl. 27).*

The third church is situated next to the Funerary Temple 173d, on the western wall of which it abuts and it is 21m in length. The church arrangement does not differ from that of the other two buildings described above. The stylobate of the building is still visible, together with the bases of two columns which define the limit of the north aisle. The outline of the apse, about 5.6m wide, was distinctly visible at the time of the survey. The blocking of the *intercolumnia* would suggest that the church underwent subsequent alterations (Majcherek 2005, 143).

The fourth church of this group, Church I has always been considered as part of an extended ecclesiastical quarter composed of three other churches (Church II–IV) and located in the northwest quarter (Gawlikowski 2001; Majcherek 2013, 252; Fig. 31). One of its main accesses, however, opened onto the Great Colonnade (Fig. 32). The building is installed on a pre-existing 2nd century rectangular civic basilica (21.57 × 12.77m) whose orientation follows that of the block (southwest–northeast). Its walls were in stone up to about 4m and in mudbrick in their upper part. The mudbrick section of the wall does not survive, while the stone wall section is preserved up to 3m. It is in a characteristic local variant of *opus emplectum*, which makes use of 1m-high courses of closely fitting narrow blocks alternated by narrower courses of bounders.

The civic building underwent substantial alteration in the 4th century, but only in the mid-6th century the apse was added, transforming the structure into a church. One of the main entrances to the new building was from the south, through a 1.75m wide doorway. A paved *atrium* with a portico composed of reused columns placed roughly 1m from the wall of the church would have embellished this side of the building. It was connected with the Great Colonnade to the south through a narrow paved passage, some 25m in length (Żuchowska 2006, 448–50). A second entrance was located on the northern side of the church; it opened onto a three-sided porticoed court, some 33 × 25m in size, accessible from a lateral street through a three-entranced gateway. A flight of three steps leading to a space some 5m wide would have preceded the access to the church.

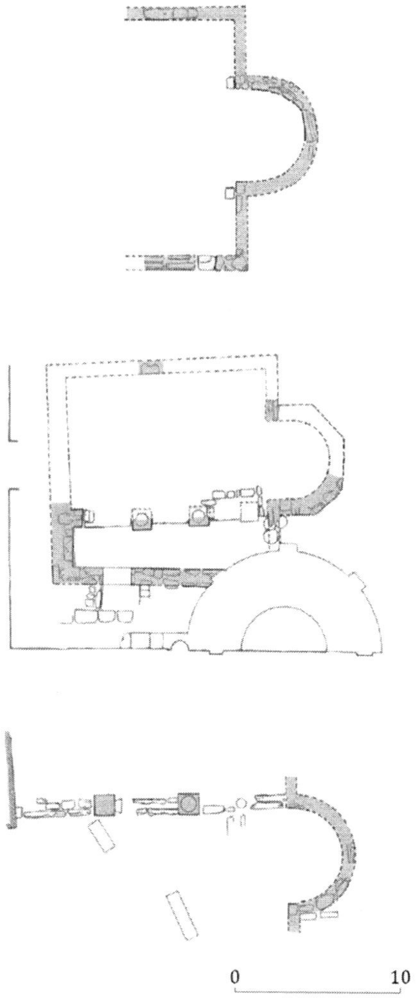

Figure 30. Churches along the Great Colonnade (Majcherek 2013, 26, fig. 3).

The court underwent confusing later phases, dated not later than the mid-6th century, which included the installation of a ceramic kiln and a stable. Finally, a third entrance to the church was located on the eastern side of the building.

The inner arrangement of the church consisted of a transverse hall with benches made of *spolia* plastered against the walls and the floor (Fig. 33). The apse was orientated to the southeast and is semi-circular on the inside but polygonal on the outside. It could be accessed through a 5.8m wide passage embellished with an arch that was supported by two piers with squared capitals. The original floor is missing where the wall of the *synthronon* would have been installed. The sanctuary extends into the hall through a *podium*, 0.45m high, accessible with a single step and provided with an altar screen. Two squared rooms flank the apse. They were neither accessible from the apse nor from the rectangular hall. Rather, the southern one was entered via a preceding room from the *atrium*, while the northern from the northern court. The building seems to have

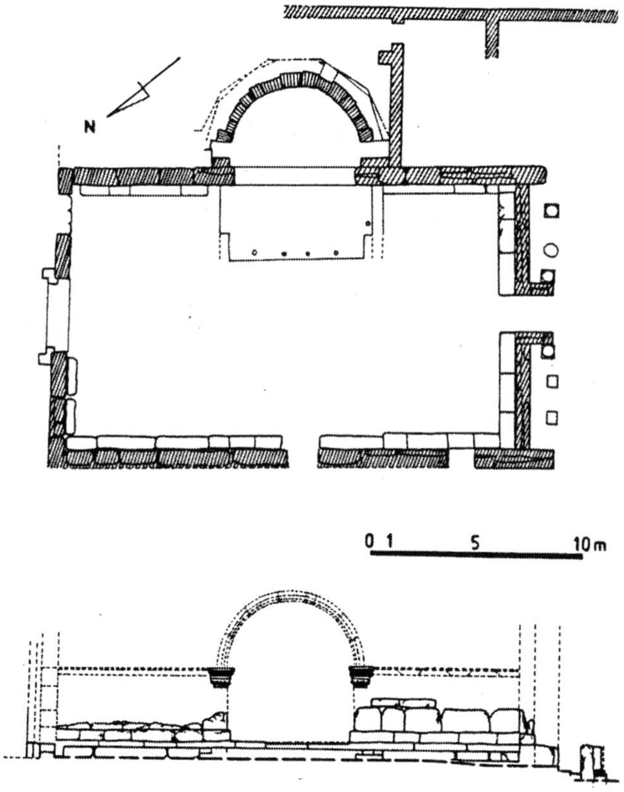

Figure 31. Church I (Gawlikowski 1990a, 41, fig. 2).

been abandoned in the 7th century. Its walls are believed to have collapsed two centuries later (Gawlikowski 1990a, 40–3; 1991a, 89–90; 1991b, 399–410; 1992a, 73–6; 1993, 155–6; 1994, 141–2; 1998, 209–10; 2001, 123–5; Duval 1992; Westphalen 2009, 160).

Churches opening onto Church Street

A cluster of three churches (Churches II–IV) has been exposed in the northwest quarter of the city. They all open onto the same lane, named appropriately 'Church Street' by the excavators. Church II is located about 75m to the northeast of Church I, two blocks to the east. It was installed on a pre-existing building whose original inner arrangement and function remain unknown. As a consequence, its plan is irregular; the aisles are not symmetrical and the east and west walls are not parallel. The building is orientated northwest–southeast, with the apse looking to the southeast. It had no access from the western side. It could be entered through three passageways cut into its northern wall and two doorways on its southern wall. In the preliminary report of the excavation, the construction of the church was believed to have occurred in the 8th century. This conclusion is based on the discovery of a coin found below a column reused as a step in front of the threshold of the southwest entrance (Gawlikowski 1998, 206; but this might simply be a later refurnishment, Genequand 2012, 27). A

Figure 32. Church I, entrance from the Great Colonnade (Sean Leatherbury/Manar al-Athar [available at <http://www.manar-al-athar.ox.ac.uk>]).

Figure 33. Church I, apse and interior (Sean Leatherbury/Manar al-Athar [available at <http://www.manar-al-athar.ox.ac.uk>]).

more recent statement by Gawlikowski (2001, 126, '*les églises II et III ont été intimement liées et sont selon toute apparence contemporaines*') might suggest, however, an earlier chronology. The abandonment of the church seems to have occurred in the course of the 8th–9th centuries.

The main building (23 × 17.3m, apse excluded) is divided into two aisles and a central nave by two rows of four reused columns that would have supported arches with archivolts situated about 5.1m above the floor level (Fig. 34). The columns have no bases and are set on top of flat slabs located about 0.6m below the floor. Two pairs of piers protruding from the east and west walls of the church at the end of each portico would have supported the last series of arcades. The floor of the nave is of plaster between the western wall and the first tier of the arcades, while, further east, it is paved with flagstones and reused architecture. The aisles are also similarly paved. A raised *podium* in flagstones extends into the nave from the apse. One of its paving slabs bears a Kufic inscription (a *basmala* in a poor state of preservation) dated to the first quarter of the 8th century, therefore providing a *terminus post quem* for the abandonment of the building. The presence of a groove in the *podium* suggests the existence of an altar screen 0.1m wide with a 1.55m wide open passage in the centre. A 6.3m wide arch resting on two piers marked the entrance to the apse. Its back wall would have been polygonal on the outside but semi-circular on the inside. It was abutted by a 0.5m *synthronon* in brick that largely survives. At the centre of the *synthronon*, three steps would have led to the bishop's throne (Gawlikowski 1997b, 196–7; 1998, 199–206; 2001, 126; Westphalen 2009, 160).

The main body of the church is associated with a number of annexed buildings that follow roughly a similar chronological development. It is abutted to the south by a 5 × 5m porticoed courtyard that pre-existed it. In its original stage, four 3.7m wide porticoes would have run around an open court. At a later time, the northern portico was included into the south wall of the church and almost all the *intercolumnia* of the other porticoes were walled up to create small rooms. A path of stone slabs running northwest–southeast was laid in the newly created open court. The occupation of the structure ended in the 8th or 9th centuries, when two lime kilns were installed (Gawlikowski 1997b, 194–6).

The ecclesiastical complex associated with Church II develops further east with a baptistery consisting of three intercommunicating rooms (Fig. 35). The compound is fairly extended, measuring 24m from east to west, that is more than the church itself, but only 9m from north to south. The first room is an open courtyard (9.4 × 7.8m) provided with a small peristyle of four columns. The room was entered from the church through two passageways, one opening onto the apse and the other onto the nave. South to the porticoed courtyard, another passageway would have given access to a 'waiting room' provided with benches on its north side and opening onto a court that possibly hosted a fountain. After crossing a second room, one could reach the core of the baptistery. This consists of three long and narrow rooms whose partition walls were dismantled at a later stage. They were each provided with a niche on the back wall. The central room features a floor paved with marble slabs and a stone vessel immediately next to the back wall. The southernmost room preserves a bowl set into a floor made of brick (Gawlikowski 1999, 195–6; 2001, 126).

The complex ends to the north with a wide-open area that served as a cemetery (described separately below, Gawlikowski 1999, 192–4). Six water tanks (each about 4 × 2m) were situated next to it. Their construction is believed to have been contemporaneous with the floors of Churches II and III. They fell into disuse at the same time as the two churches and were robbed of their stones in the 9th century or later (Gawlikowski 2000, 257).

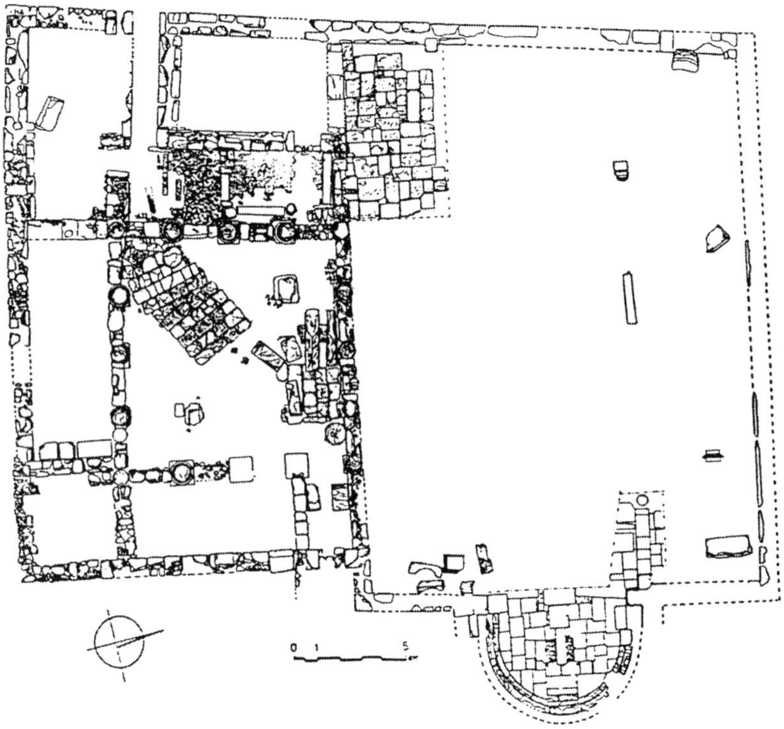

Figure 34. Church II and Courtyard G2 (Gawlikowski 1997b, 195, fig. 2).

Church III is situated in the same block of Church II, but 50m further to the north. It is orientated northwest–southeast with its apse looking to the southeast. Its west façade does not directly open onto the street, but is located 9m inside the block; access was, therefore, assured through an *atrium*. The building consists of a main body of about 21 × 23m (Fig. 36). It could be entered through three doorways on the western wall and two more passageways on each of the lateral walls. At a later stage, only one passage, the central one on the western side, was left open, while the others were blocked up. The main body was divided into two aisles and a central nave by four low, freestanding piers (each 0.75m thick and 1.1m long) on each side (Fig. 37). Two similar piers protrude at each end of the aisles from the east and west walls. The piers, now poorly preserved, would have supported a total of six arches with archivolts 6.4m wide.

The building is homogenously paved with a worn white plaster floor on a black ash bedding. This covers an earlier floor made with flagstones. At the centre of the nave lies a raised flagged walk orientated northwest–southeast. The apse is semi-circular and supported by radial buttresses on the outside (Fig. 38). It would have had a *synthronon*, of which only a few blocks of limestone remain in place. A monumental arch supported by lateral piers marked its access from the nave, while a low altar screen with a central *cancellum* isolated it. The sanctuary extended into the nave of the church with a raised *podium* paved with white plaster and provided with a portico with six small columns of black granite. Two lateral rooms would have flanked the apse. The northern one was entered from the north aisle through a passage 1.95m wide, flanked by two columns and two large basins. It was interpreted as the *martyrion* of the church and was also accessible from the apse through a narrow doorway. The south one was also accessible both from the northern aisle and the apse. At a later stage, its stone floor was removed and a well and water pipes were installed in it. According to the excavators, the church was constructed as early as the 5th century and was refurbished under Justinian. The final abandonment of the complex dates to the 9th century (Gawlikowski 2003, 284). This was preceded by a phase in which the area was used as a quarry for building material. Lime kilns were installed in the nave and two small rooms of unknown nature were constructed in the southeast and northwest corners of the church (Gawlikowski 2000, 250–5; 2001, 125–7; 2002, 258–63; 2003, 281–8; Westphalen 2009, 160–1).

Like Church II, the main body of Church III was associated with a number of dependencies. A rectangular 18m deep *atrium* provided with four porticoes and sunken in the centre would have ensured a monumental access to the church from the west (Fig. 39). The east and west porticoes of this structure were provided with eight columns with intercolumniation of 2.6m; the north and south porticoes were shorter and provided with only three columns with intercolumniation of over 4m. The western portico was 3.15m deep, without passages cut into its back wall. Both the south and north entrances to the *atrium* from the street were marked by arcades supported by piers. According to

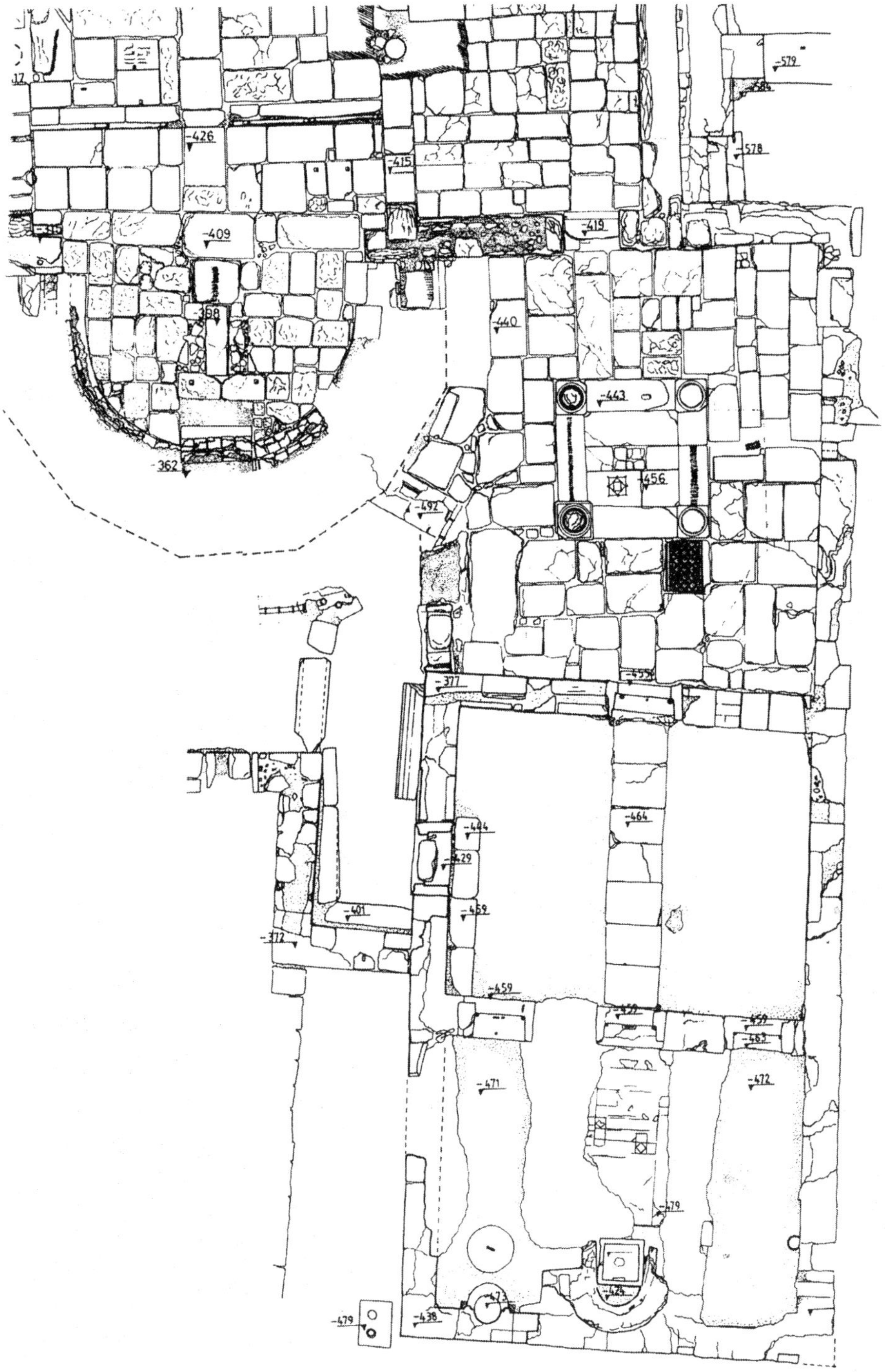

Figure 35. The baptistery of Church II (Gawlikowski 1999, 190, fig. 1).

the excavators, most of the *atrium* was constructed together with the church. At a later stage, the *intercolumnia* of the porticoes were walled up. A wall was also built between the two intermediate columns of the north and south porticoes, thus narrowing the street to its original width (4–5m) (Gawlikowski 2003, 285). A rectangular apsidal chapel (4.3 × 13.7m) opens onto the *atrium*. It shares part of its southern wall with the north wall of the church and ends with a semi-circular apse flattened on the outside and orientated to the southeast. Its entrance was from the west side and was marked by an arch. The history of the structure follows that of Church III. It was refurbished in the 6th century and remained in use until the early 9th century (perhaps as a mosque, Gawlikowski 2003, 287). Finally, to the north of

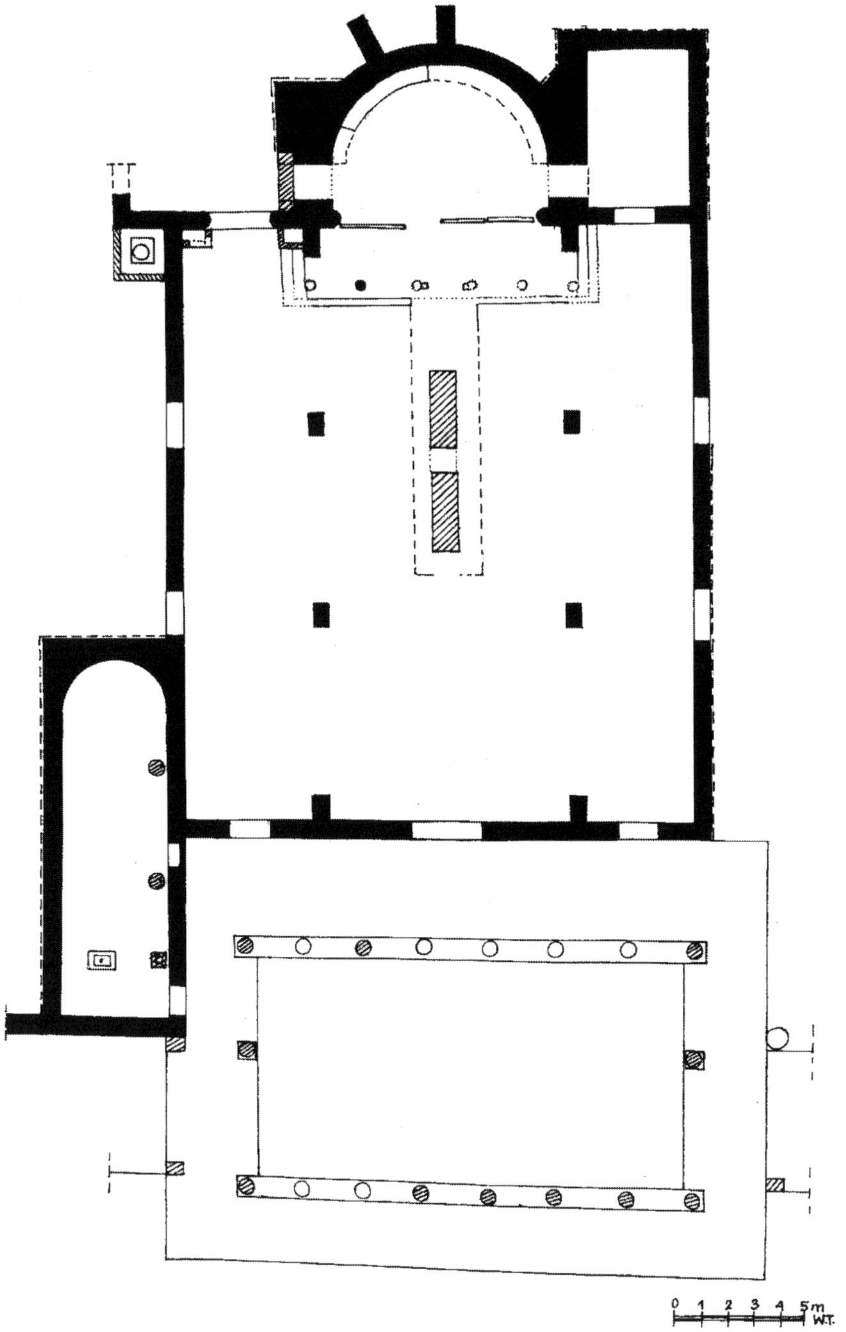

Figure 36. Church III (Gawlikowski 2003, 280, fig. 1).

the church was a compound that might have been used with residential purposes and served as an *episkopion*. Among the features of the compound, which still has to be fully investigated and published, are a peristyled courtyard and a large apsed hall accessible both from the courtyard and the *atrium* (Gawlikowski 2009; Majcherek 2013, 252).

Church IV, about 100m to the north of Church II, stands out for its monumentality (47.5 × 27.5m; Fig. 40). The building was first noticed by Gabriel and its plan published in 1926 (Gabriel 1926, pl. xvi). Wiegand surveyed it and published a second plan in 1932 (Wiegand 1932a, Taf. 18), and Lassus (1947, 168, 231) mentioned the building in its monumental work on the *Sanctuaries Chrétiens de Syrie*. Yet, the church would not be systematically excavated until 2007. The main building, situated on a pre-existing compound whose original arrangement is still unknown, is orientated northwest–southeast with the apse looking to the southeast. It is a single-apsed basilica with two aisles and a central nave divided by two rows of three monolithic columns every 8.5m (Figs 41 and 42). Two pairs of piers

Figure 37. Church III, interior (Sean Leatherbury/Manar al-Athar [available at <http://www.manar-al-athar.ox.ac.uk>]).

Figure 38. Church III, apse (Sean Leatherbury/Manar al-Athar [available at <http://www.manar-al-athar.ox.ac.uk>]).

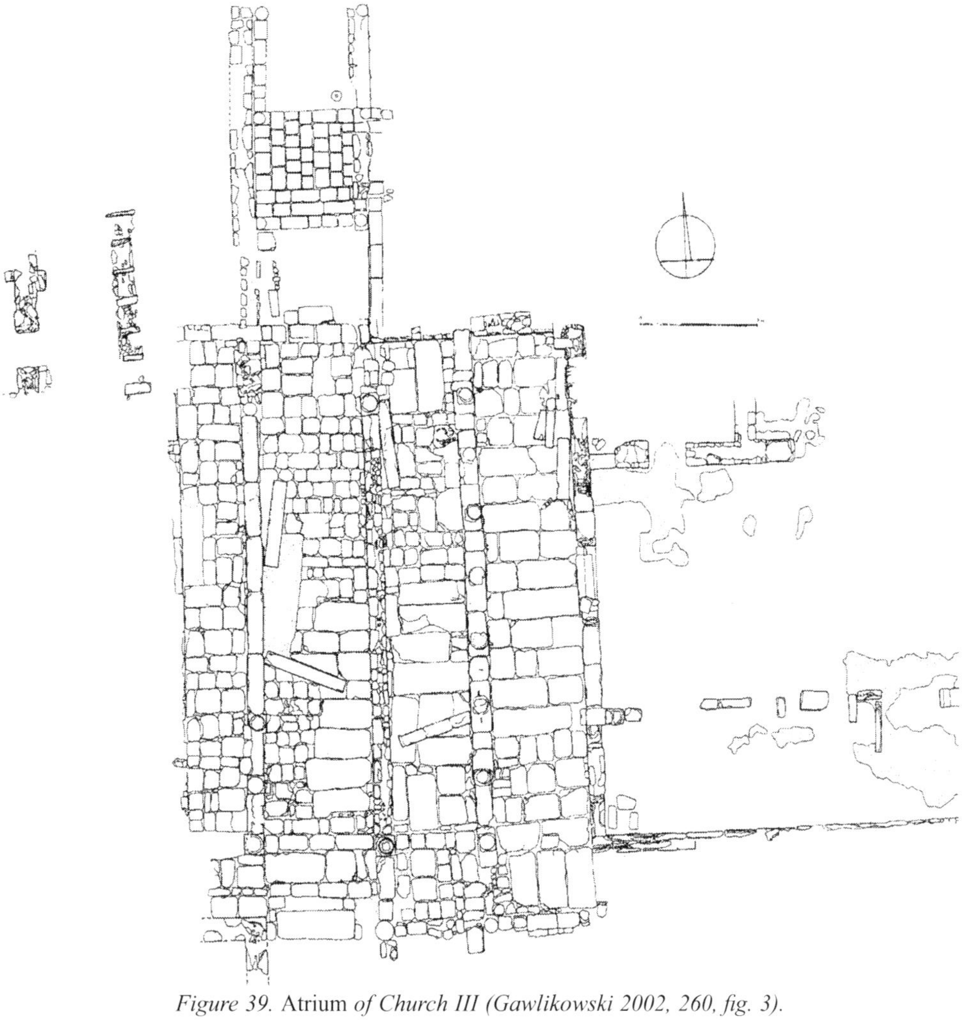

Figure 39. Atrium *of Church III (Gawlikowski 2002, 260, fig. 3).*

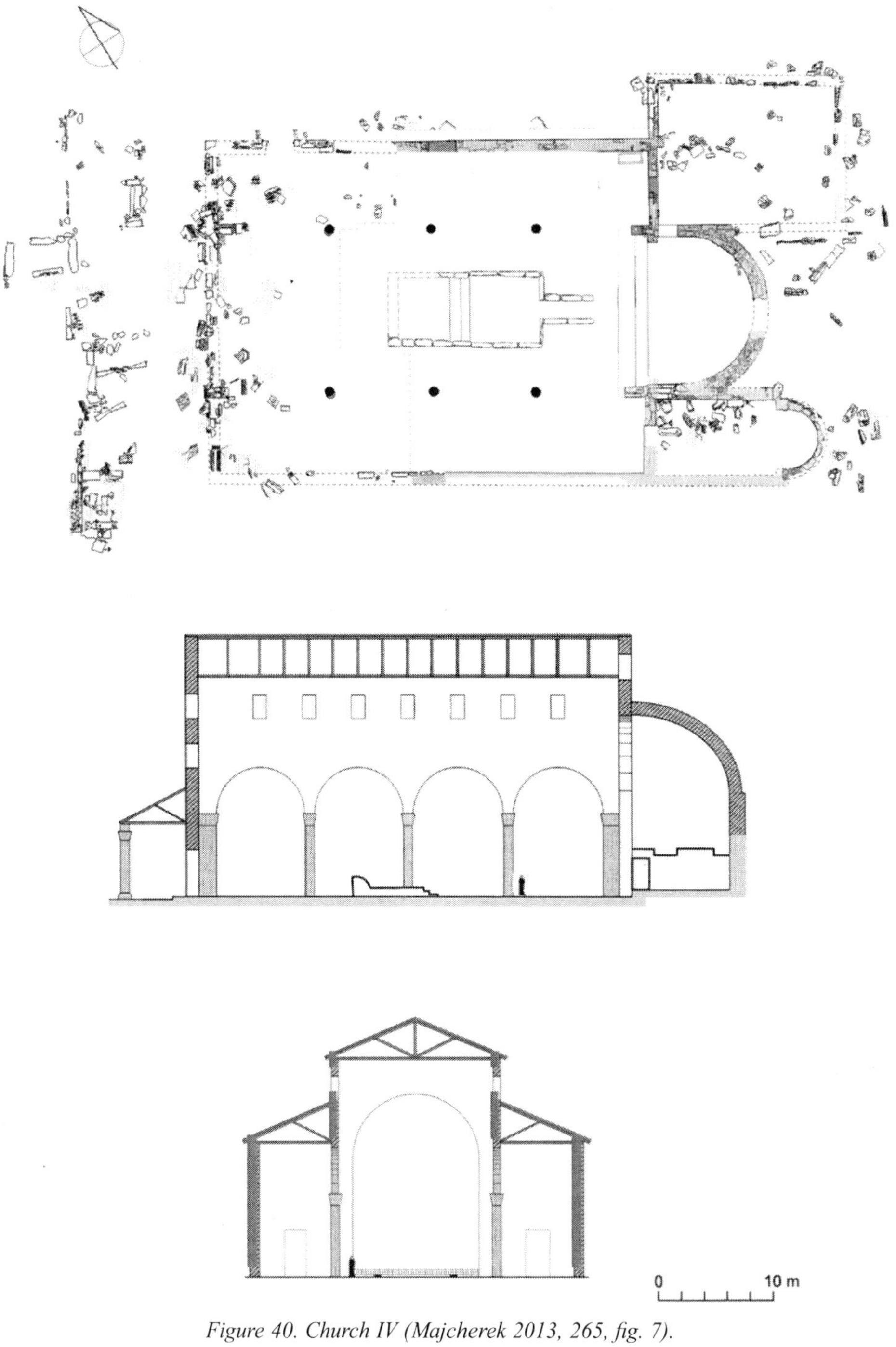

Figure 40. Church IV (Majcherek 2013, 265, fig. 7).

protrude at the end of each portico from the east and west walls of the building, providing supports for arcades. The church opened to the west through three passageways covered by a porch about 5.7m deep and with eight columns. The central entrance is wider (2.6m) than the lateral.

The apse is large (12.3m in width) and semi-circular on the inside but polygonal on the outside. It has a raised floor of flagstones, on which an altar screen would have stood, and is flanked by two rooms. These communicate both with the aisles and the apse. The southernmost room is rectangular, while the northern one culminates with a semi-circular apse. In this, a 5th–6th century reliquary was found, suggesting that the room functioned as a *martyrion*. The apse and the two joining rooms extend into a nearby street, thus blocking the traffic. A rectangular *bema* (*c.* 7.2m by 6.3m), now in a poor state of preservation, was located in the nave. Its western half, where the benches for the clergy were located, was raised and accessible through two steps.

Figure 41. Church IV from the west (Sean Leatherbury/Manar al-Athar [available at <http://www.manar-al-athar.ox.ac.uk>]).

Figure 42. Church IV from the east (Sean Leatherbury/Manar al-Athar [available at <http://www.manar-al-athar.ox.ac.uk>]).

The *bema* communicates with the *podium* with a narrow corridor. The roof of the church was tiled and situated 22–23 m from the ground. A tentative 6th century dating for the construction of the church has been proposed on the basis of written sources. In the Early Islamic period, the building was rearranged and occupied by new rooms, whose function is obscure. It has been suggested they might have served for residential or administrative purposes. The dating of the abandonment of the church has not been ascertained (Majcherek 2008; 2009; 2012; 2013, 253–6).

The Churches of Palmyra in their architectural context

It is possible to advance several preliminary hypotheses on the architectural context in which these buildings were conceived on the basis of the analysis of their plans and several architectural features. Such analysis has necessarily to exclude unexcavated churches, as well as those buildings whose plan is not clear or whose existence has been put in doubt. This would limit it to the four better-excavated churches in the northwest quarter (Churches I–IV), which are, however, poorly preserved owing to the characteristic building technique of the region, that is to say bricks on low stone walls (Butler 1929, 178–9).

Churches in Palmyra show a certain degree of homogeneity that generally fits into an architectural regional group (that of central Syria) characterised by remarkable influences from northern Syrian architecture (Butler 1929, 179; Krautheimer 1981, 147). The buildings in this group feature a standard three-aisled basilical plan divided by two rows of columns or piers and ending east with a semi-circular apse. This is often flanked by two lateral rooms (*pastophoria*) accessible from the aisles and sometimes from the apse itself (Lassus 1947, 54). A tendency has been noted (characteristic of northern Syrian churches) to mask the lateral rooms and the apse behind a flat back wall (Butler 1929, 187–9; Lassus 1947, 57). From the beginning of the 5th century onward, the lateral rooms show a neat specialisation of functions: one would have served as *diaconicon*, where objects for the liturgy would have been stored, the other as a *martyrion*, where the relics of martyrs would have been kept to be accessible to the believers (Lassus 1947, 162; Krautheimer 1981, 152; Beaudry 2005, 131). Not all the churches, however, followed this strict standardised model, and numerous variations divert from this pattern.

Church I in Palmyra consists of a central hall devoid of the typical tripartite division and an apse located on its eastern, longer wall. The unusual, transverse layout of the building is due to its installation in a pre-existing building, rather than the result of intentional planning (Gawlikowski 1990a, 43). As a matter of fact, transverse plans are not frequent in the East. They are sporadically attested in Ḥawrān, Commagene, Cappadocia and in the Wādī al-Naṭrūn (Fourdrin 1985, 319 ns 1–4). Yet, the most significant concentrations are to be found in Jabal al-Zāwiya (Apamene, Fourdrin 1985, 320–7) and further northeast, in the Ṭūr ʿAbdīn area (Bell 1982). In the former, nine churches out of ten (at al-Dānā, Btirsa, Shinsharaḥ, and al-Bāra) present a transverse plan; they are all provided with a projecting squared apse and no lateral rooms (Fourdrin 1985, 320–7). Phase I of the *Atrium* Church in Apamea provides a better parallel with Church I in Palmyra. The *Atrium* Church is believed to be dated to the first half of the 5th century on the basis of numismatic finds and the style of its decorative apparatus (Balty and Napoleone-Lemaire 1969, 9–22). As in Palmyra, the uncommon layout of the church is due to its installation in an earlier building (Fourdrin 1985, 327 n. 13). Churches in the Ṭūr ʿAbdīn area often present transversal halls and a tripartite eastern sanctuary. These include, among the others, the churches at Qarṭamin and Ṣalaḥ. The apse, however, in most cases protrudes from the back wall, which is rarely flat. By contrast, the apse and the two lateral rooms of Church I are masked by a flat back wall, recalling a disposition that, as already pointed out, is typical of northern Syrian ecclesiastical architecture. In contrast with Syrian architecture, the access to the two rooms was not via the main hall and, according to the excavators, neither from the apse (Gawlikowski 1990a, 42). Lateral rooms flanking the apse in Palmyra are only safely attested in Churches I, III, and IV (Gawlikowski 2003, 280, fig. 1; Majcherek 2008; 2009). The presence of a southern entrance monumentalised with a portico is also illustrative of conformity to a northern Syrian building tradition (Krautheimer 1981, 151). Occurrences of lateral porticoes are known, for example, in the churches of Burj Ḥaydar (mid-4th century – Tchalenko and Baccache 1979, pl. 18, fig. 36; Tchalenko 1990, 25–9), Dēḥes (mid-5th century – Tchalenko and Baccache 1979, pl. 201, fig. 337; Tchalenko 1990, 135–40), Ḥalabiyya (first half of the 6th century – Lauffray 1983, 95, 116, 118; 1991, 98, fig. 41), and al-Ruṣāfa (Basilica A, last quarter of the 5th century – Fowden 1999, 82; Basilica B, 518 – Kollwitz *et al.* 1958–1959, 24; Kollwitz 1959, 53–60; Donceel-Voûte 1988, 281–2).

The standardised tripartite single apsed basilical plan is exemplified in Church II. According to Westphalen, this building might have served as the cathedral of the city. His assumptions are based on the presence of a nearby cemetery and an annexed baptistery. This would give a special meaning to the building, it being the only structure of this type known in the city. The baptistery does not find precise parallels, but Gawlikowski (2001, citing Lassus 1947, 80; Epstein and Tzaferis 1991, 89–94; Khatchatrian 1962, n. 192) has traced good comparisons with the three-roomed baptisteries of Emmaus, Sussita-Hippos and Paros. The adjoining building to the north of the church might have served as the residence of the clergy (Lassus 1947, 233–4, 238). Similar but more monumental buildings are known, for example, from the Church of Saints Sergius and Bacchos at Umm al-Sarāb (dated to 489, Butler 1929, 47, ill. 45; King 1983, 124), the Church of Numerianus at Umm al-Jimāl (6th century, Butler 1929, 115–16), and the Cathedral at Ḥalabiyya (6th century, Lauffray 1991, 91–5).

Church III retains the same basilical plan, but instead of using columns to support the clerestory it makes use of piers, conveying the impression of a vast interior. This was an architectural program widely followed in Syria from the mid-5th century onward within a generalised process of architectural experimentation (Butler 1929, 70; Krautheimer 1981, 164; Grossmann 1973, 38 refers to it as the 'Weitarkandebasilica'). The most illustrative examples of this tendency in north Syria are in Qalb Lūza (dated to 480 – Butler 1929, 71–2; Tchalenko 1974; Tchalenko and Baccache 1979, pl. 260, fig. 423; Tchalenko 1990, 163–6), Barād (North Church, 561 – Butler 1929, 142, ill. 151), and al-Andarīn (Churches of Saints Michael and Gabriel, 5th century – Butler 1929, 81; 190, ill. 193; Church of the Holy Trinity, 5th century – Butler 1929, 80; 81, ill. 87; South Church – Butler 1929, 80; 209, ill. 209; Cathedral, about 560 – Butler 1929, 158–60; 159, ill. 170). Church III is flanked to the north by a chapel orientated to the east. The situation of this chapel is strongly reminiscent of that of three similar structures (so-called 'memorial chapels') in the Fountain Court Complex at Jerash (Crowfoot 1931, 10–11; pl. 1). Unlike Palmyra's Church III, however, these were accessible both from the *atria* and the churches.

Church IV is the largest church in the city as well as one of the largest churches in the whole of Syria. With its main body of 47.5 × 27.5m it falls into a peculiar group of buildings defined by Krautheimer (1981, 160) as 'cathedrals', and characterised by a tendency to monumentality. Similar buildings are attested in Qalb Lūza (main body: 16.56 × 30.91m), al-Andarīn (Cathedral: about 43 × 25m), al-Ruṣāfa (Basilica A: 54.4 × 28.6m – Ulbert 1986, 119; Basilica B: 48.5 × 25.7m – Fowden 1999, 87), Ruwayḥa (Church of Bizzos: 39.65 × 19.25m, mid-6th century – Tchalenko and Baccache 1979, pl. 289, fig. 472; Tchalenko 1990, 189–92), and Karratīn (Cathedral of St Stephen: about 60 × 26m – Butler 1929, 158). The homogeneity of this group has inclined scholars to believe in the existence of 'itinerant workshops' active in a 30–40 year span at the end of the 5th–beginning of the 6th century (Krautheimer 1981, 160).

A further feature that strongly links this building with a northern Syrian architectural tradition, and which requires separate discussion, is the occurrence of a *bema*. *Bemata* are stone or wooden platforms normally horseshoe-shaped and located in the nave of churches. They found their origin in 2nd and 3rd century synagogues and are widespread between the mid-4th and the first decades of the 7th century. Their function is still rather obscure, although it is now clear that they must have had a supporting role in the Syrian liturgy (Loosley 2012, 101). The majority of *bema* churches, 42 out of a total of 49 (excluding that of Palmyra) are to be found in the Limestone Massif in northern Syria. Most of them are in *Syria Prima* and *Syria Secunda* (Balty and Balty 2004). Only Basilica A at al-Ruṣāfa and the Citadel Basilica at Dibsī Faraj are in *Euphratensis*. The most recent work on *bema* churches by Loosley comes to the conclusion that these structures might have been associated with a school of design originating in Antioch (Loosley 2012, 39). The author also concludes that *bemata* are usually found in the oldest church of a settlement and that there is never more than one church with a *bema* in a settlement (Loosley 2012, 51–2). The *bema* in Church IV of Palmyra is remarkable in many ways (see Majcherek 2013, 255). The structure is not horseshoe shaped but rectangular and was entered via a sort of narrow corridor. One of the nearest parallel examples would be, among others, the rectangular *bema* in Fāfartīn (372), but its shape remains still far from that of Palmyra, since it has a semi-circular end (Tchalenko and Baccache 1979, pl. 43, figs 82–3; Tchalenko 1990, 41–5). A closer parallel is the *bema* in the Citadel Basilica at Dibsī Faraj (Harper 1975, 330, 331, fig. D). The reason for the deviation of the Palmyrene *bema* from the standard pattern is obscure. Looking at the distribution pattern, it is clear that the *bema* church in Palmyra is the southernmost instance known in Syria and the only example known so far in *Phoenicia Libanensis*. It is also one of the four occurrences, together with those at al-Ruṣāfa, Barād, and *Seleucia Pieria* (Çevlik), not in a provincial village but in a sizeable settlement, as well as one of the two instances known in episcopal sees (the other being al-Ruṣāfa). The *bema* church at Palmyra does not appear to be the oldest of the city, but it must certainly have been the most monumental.

Overall, the evidence from Palmyra points straight to an architectural tradition that is clearly regional and deeply influenced by northern Syrian building. Other features, however, are less common. Polygonal apses, for example, are scarcely attested in Syria. Occurrences in northern Syria include the apse of the Church of Saints Michael and Gabriel at al-Andarīn (Butler 1929, 81; 190, ill. 193). At Palmyra, polygonal apses are safely attested in Churches I, II, and in one of the three churches along the Great Colonnade (Gawlikowski 1992a, 72, fig. 3; 1999, 190, fig. 1; Majcherek 2005, 144). The most remarkable evidence of outside influence remains, though, the *atria* of Churches I and II. *Atria* are rarely attested in the region (Gawlikowski 2003, 285). Illustrative examples are to be found mostly in northern Syria: Khirbat Ḥass (Butler 1929, 37, ill. 36), Ruwayḥa (South Church, Tchalenko 1990, 185–8), Ḥalabiyya (Lauffray 1983, 51–6), and Apamea (*Atrium* Church – Balty and Napoleone-Lemaire 1969). Further south, they are attested at Jerash (*Propylaea* Church and the Fountain Church Complex – Crowfoot 1931, 6–16) and Pella (Civic Complex Church and East Church – MacNicoll *et al.* 1982, 103–110; 1992, 153).

A final note should be made on the decoration of these churches. It is noteworthy that their excavations do not seem to have brought to light any significant marble decoration comparable to churches in other major religious centres in Syria. This might partly be the result of the protracted occupation of these compounds. The state of preservation of Churches II and III is poor also because four lime kilns were set in these buildings at a later time. The choice of the place for the installation of these structures must not have been casual and might have been moved by the abundance of raw material available to be processed on the spot. The impressive Church IV has gone through a long process of refurbishment in the Early Islamic period that has considerably altered the inner arrangement of the building. The long occupation of this church must have affected the presence of this kind of evidence. This applies also for the church in the temple of the Sanctuary of Bēl. It is noteworthy, however, that unlike other major cities, such as Apamea or al-Ruṣāfa, which make use of new stones and marbles material cut *ad hoc*, in Palmyra all the building material was spoliated from earlier buildings (Gawlikowski 1993, 156). This is likely to be due to the financial limitations of the city. Palmyra was not a metropolitan see, a capital of a province, or a renowned pilgrimage centre, but it had become a more modest provincial city with, however, enough means to achieve important building projects.

To conclude, churches in Palmyra clearly adhere to an architectural form that appears to be strongly influenced by northern Syrian building traditions, although other less common features are also attested. There is very little variety in Palmyra either in plan or decoration. The centralised plan, known in other urban centres such as Apamea or Jerash is here missing. Decoration is mostly absent and far from the richness of the decorative pattern characteristic of some religious hubs in its vicinity, such as, for example, al-Ruṣāfa. Although this might have to do with the financial limitations of the city, it is also possible that it is the result of the long occupation that these buildings have experienced. The archaeological evidence brought to attention so far, however, confirms the ability of the city to cope with ambitious building projects, such as that of Church IV or the 24m long baptistery of Church II, its ability to attracting large-scale investment, and its overall considerable building vitality throughout Late Antiquity.

The Christian community: further evidence

Christian stone inscriptions, mostly funerary in nature, have been found in the cemetery next to the Archaeological Museum, the Great Colonnade, the Camp and the Baths of Diocletian, the Sanctuary of Bēl, and the Valley of the Tombs. Some bear biblical names, such as Jacob (*IGLS* 17.1, 378–9, n. 502), Symeones, Ioannes (*IGLS* 17.1, 146, n. 137; 346, n. 452; 376–7, n. 498; 377, n. 499), Sergios (*IGLS* 17.1, 146, n. 137), and Lazaros (*IGLS* 17.1, 55–6, n. 47), sometimes associated with engraved crosses (a practice which starts in Palmyra in dated inscriptions from the second half of the 5th century), acclamations to God (*IGLS* 17.1, 377–8, n. 500; 378–9, n. 502; 118, n. 106; 118, n. 107) and Christ (*IGLS* 17.1, 378, n. 501), and Christian formulaic sentences, such as 'Have courage, soul, no one is immortal' (Θάρσι, ψυχή, ὀδὶς ὀθάνvατος) attested twice (*IGLS* 17.1, 375–6, n. 496; 334–5, n. 435), or the more frequent '(Lord) give the rest to the soul of your servant' (ἀνόπαυσον τὴν ψυχὴν τοῦ δούλου σου) attested with variants five times (*IGLS* 17.1, 377–8, n. 500; 378, n. 501; 378–9, n. 502; 376–7, n. 498; 377, n. 499). Among them, is also the formula Εἷς θεός inscribed on one of the columns of Section C of the Great Colonnade, known mainly (but not solely) in the eastern Christian tradition (*IGLS* 17.1, 117, n. 105; Di Segni 1994, with further bibliography). Painted inscriptions on pottery bearing Christian names and symbols are also frequent. Personal names like Sergios (Dunant 1971, 124, n. 20; 125, ns 22–7), Ioannes (Dunant 1971, 124, ns 15–18), Symeones, appearing as a *diaconon* (Dunant 1971, 125, n. 28), George (Dunant 1971, 123, ns 8–11), Joseph (Dunant 1971, 126, n. 36), Elias (Dunant 1971, 124, n. 15), Abraham (Dunant 1971, 123, n. 8), Peter (Dunant 1971, 124, ns 19–20), Michael (Dunant 1971, 124, n. 19), and Daniel (Grassi *et al.* 2015, 32–3) are attested and, again, in some cases associated with Christian symbols, such as crosses or circles with eight spokes (Fig. 43).

As in other contemporary urban centres (King 1985; Jacobs 2013, 615–17), the engraving of crosses on walls, columns, and door lintels remained a widespread practice in Palmyra throughout Late Antiquity. A few examples suffice to illustrate that the tendency was common in the city and might have stemmed from the necessity of the Christian community to 'sanctify' or protect sensible places, such as pre-existing pagan sanctuaries, houses, and churches. We have already mentioned the barely visible cross engraved on one of the columns of the north portico of the courtyard in the Peristyle Building (see above, p. 50; Fig. 44). A lintel was erected on top of the entrance of the *Praetorium* of the Camp of Diocletian to bless the house and whoever was about to cross its threshold (Kowalski 1994, 58, pl. 19.2). Similarly, the right doorjamb of the entrance to a presumed *martyrion* from Church Street bears a simple cross (Fig. 45). A cross was also incised in one of the columns of the *narthex* marking the entrance of the presumed church in the *cella* of the Sanctuary of Baalshamīn (Collart 1963, 155; Collart and Vicari 1969, 78).

Small finds of Christian nature are rarely reported in secondary literature. The stamp for liturgical bread mentioned earlier in ch. 1 represents an interesting piece of evidence. The inscription on the artifact recites: '+ The blessing of the Lord upon us, amen' (+ ΕΥΛΟΓΙΑ Κ[ΥΡΙΟ]Υ ΕΦ ΗΜ[ΑC] ΑΜΗΝ) (Michałowski 1964a, 184, fig. 214; Galavaris 1970, 12). The location of this find is puzzling (in the Camp of Diocletian to the south of the main entrance of the *Forum*) and difficultly explicable. To this we should add the fragmentary golden pendant in the shape of a cross that was found in the late 7th century hoard in the same area, just some metres to the southeast of the *Groma*.

The Jewish community

The Jewish element is attested at Palmyra from Roman times (Hartmann 2001, 324–32, with further bibliography), and a number of pieces of evidence proves its presence in the city throughout Late Antiquity and the Early Islamic period. The excavation of a safely dated 4th century context in the Sanctuary of Allāth has yielded two complete, five nozzle rectangular lamps together with three other fragments. These were produced locally and bear identical decorations. Their upper sides feature a conch flanked by

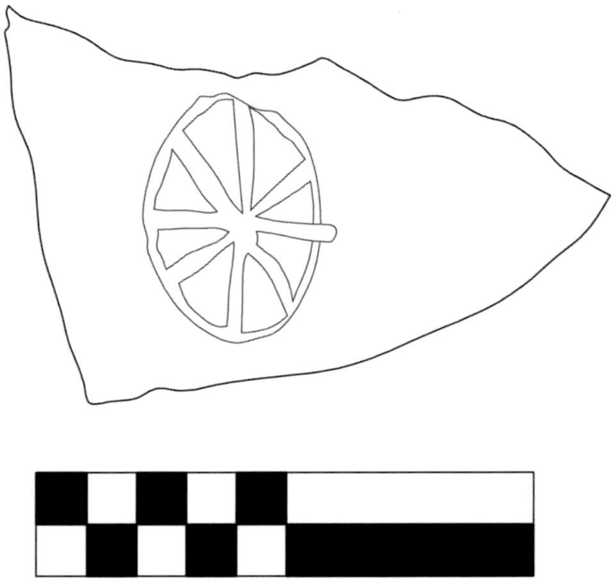

Figure 43. Eight-spoked wheel painted on a potsherd from the northern courtyard of the Sanctuary of Baalshamīn (redrawn by author after original sketch, Fonds d'Archives Paul Collart, Université de Lausanne).

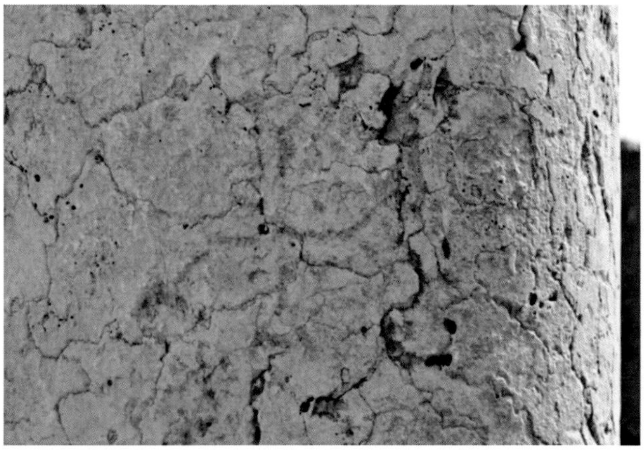

Figure 44. A barely visible cross with forked ends carved on one of the still standing columns of the Peristyle Building (Pal.M.A.I.S. photo archive. Courtesy of the Pal.M.A.I.S. archaeological team, Università degli Studi di Milano).

Figure 45. Right door jamb of the entrance to a presumed martyrion *from Church Street (Sean Leatherbury/Manar al-Athar [available at <http://www.manar-al-athar.ox.ac.uk>]).*

two seven-branched lampstands, *menorah* (Krogulska 1983; see also Daszkiewicz *et al.* 1995). The back is decorated with lines combined in various patterns (mostly herringbone). The five nozzles are black from use. The form is attested in Palmyra only once but the decoration finds no parallels (Krogulska 1983, 211; Amy and Seyrig 1936, 262, pl. l, 1).

Millar (2013, 100–1) has recently brought the attention to four Jewish inscriptions that are quotations from the Hebrew text of Deuteronomy 6–7 and 28: 'Hear of Israel, the Lord is our God, the Lord is one. And these words which I command you this day you shall write them on the doorposts and on your gates'. They were found, as prescribed by the *Shema*, on the lintel and doorjambs of a house in the northwest quarter. Their dating is uncertain, but it is safely included in our period of interest (*Ins. Jud. Or. 3*, Syr., 70–5, ns 44–7). A post-Roman Jewish inscription has also been found in the temple of the Sanctuary of Bēl, in the northern *adyton*. It recites: 'Ṣadiq, priest, son of Eleazar' and was probably engraved when the church had already been abandoned (pre-728/729) and before its conversion to a mosque in 1132–1133 (*Ins. Jud. Or.* 3, Syr., 75–6). The reason behind this inscription is obscure. Frey has advanced an association with the putative foundation of Palmyra by King Solomon and the desire of a priest to mark his passage in such a legendary site (*CIJ* 2, n. 824).

No synagogues have been safely identified in the city. Some scholars have regarded the doorway with the lintel bearing the Jewish inscriptions as the entrance for a building used as such (recently, Kaizer 2010, 117). Yet, there is no hard evidence to support this assumption (see *Ins. Jud. Or.* 3, Syr., 72–3). The plan of the ruins of the site by the Bureau Topographique des Troupes Françaises du Levant (1931) indicates a synagogue in the northwest quarter, in the spot where Church IV is situated (see Fig. 4). In the second half of the 12th century, Benjamin of Tudela (*It.*, 31) visited the city which at the time was 'surrounded by walls', very likely the *temenos* of the Sanctuary of Bēl. The writer reports that, 'in Tarmod there are about 2000 Jews. They are valiant in war and fight with the Christians and with the Arabs … Their head are R. Isaac Hajvani, R. Nathan, and R. Uziel' (tr. Adler 1907, 31). The Jews mentioned by the traveller might well have been the descendants of the Jewish community living in the city in Late Antique and Early Islamic times.

The Muslim community

Mosques: an overview of the evidence

Unlike churches, mosques have often failed to attract the interest of the archaeologist. As a result the information on these buildings is limited to very short and incidental references within wider scale work. Of the five buildings that have been interpreted as mosques in Palmyra, only one can be safely said to have covered such a role. This is the Congregational Mosque installed next to the Umayyad *Sūq* (Fig. 46). The building repurposed a pre-existing *caesareum* (Bounni 1971, 123; 1995, 17). For its construction, the back wall of the Roman building was re-orientated to the south to serve as a *qibla* wall, and a semi-circular *miḥrāb* 1.3m deep was installed in it. A second niche was found along the same wall, 2m further to the east, but it is not certain whether it was in use as a second *miḥrāb* or was simply a reused architectural element included into the wall. There is the possibility that a former mosque would have used the back wall of the Roman structure as the *qibla* wall and only later, when the Muslim community grew in size, was the decision taken to re-orientate the building and create a vaster place of worship. The inner arrangement of the building would feature a courtyard that re-uses the south row of columns of an earlier peristyle to mark the northern limit of the praying area. A rectangular room provided with a small *miḥrāb* was added to the south in a later time. The Umayyad chronology of the building is mostly given by its situation in the city and parallel examples with similar building in *Bilād al-Shām* (Genequand 2008a; 2009a; 2012, 52–7; 2013).

All the other attributions remain purely conjectural and, so far, are not supported by any firm evidence. Among

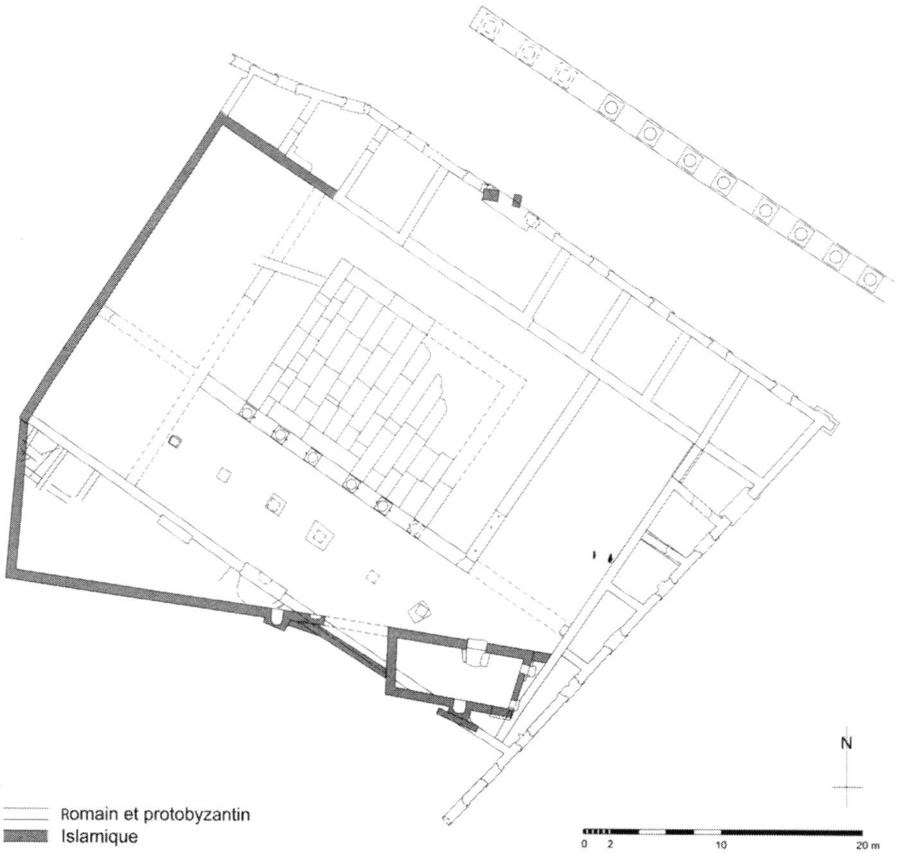

Figure 46. Congregational Mosque (Genequand 2013, 109, fig. 7).

these is shop n. 31 of the Umayyad *Sūq*, which has been interpreted as a small mosque because of the presence of a small quadrangular niche orientated to the southwest (al-As'ad and Stępniowski 1989, 208). The northwest chapel of Church III presents a distinctive arrangement of its south wall (two columns and a re-used altar set against it) that led the excavator to consider a possible re-use of the structure as a Muslim place of worship (Gawlikowski 2003, 287). Similarly, according to Gawlikowski (1995, 27), it is possible that the *Horreum* of the Camp of Diocletian was used as such. The building is divided into two areas by a row of pillars. The *qibla* wall is roughly orientated to the south but is devoid of any *miḥrāb*. These conclusions, however, have recently been contested (Genequand 2012, 49). Finally, a mosque was unearthed during the excavations of the easternmost section of the Great Colonnade by the Syrian authorities. It features a rectangular wall divided in two halves by a row of four columns of different sizes. The semi-circular *miḥrāb* of the building is orientated south and is fronted by an entrance (Saliby 1996, pl. 2; see Fig. 14).

Mosques: architectural considerations

Of the five aforementioned buildings, only the mosque next to the Umayyad *Sūq* can be safely regarded as a Muslim place of worship very likely dated to the Umayyad period. Genequand (2008a, 13–15; 2012, 63–6) has already clarified the architectural context in which the building was conceived. It is worth reconsidering his argumentations here. The mosque falls into a homogeneous group of buildings characterised by a standardisation of the length to width ratio which prevailed during the reign of Hishām b. 'Abd al-Malik – 724–743 (Walmsley and Damgaard 2005, 375). The group includes the mosques of Jerash (Walmsley 2003; Walmsley and Damgaard 2005; Walmsley 2007a, 84–6), Qaṣr al-Ḥayr al-Sharqī (Grabar *et al.* 1978, 46–51), al-Ruṣāfa (Sack 1996), and Amman, city centre (Northedge 1992, 63–9). These are characterised by modest size, between 1000m^2 and 5000m^2 (Walmsley and Damgaard 2005, 373), thus much smaller than other Muslim places of worship in major religious cities such as Damascus (15.75m^2), Harrān (some 10,000m^2), or Wāsiṭ (10.795m^2) (Northedge 1992, 68). Despite their lower ranking and limited financial resources, these centres were indeed of administrative significance; Jerash, for example, was the capital of a district of the *jund* al-Urdunn and also had a mint (Walmsley 2003, 111–12). To Walmsley and Damgaard, the prayer hall of the Jerash's mosque would have been large enough (38.9 × 13.8m = 536.83m^2) to host 450 worshippers, suggesting the presence of a sizable

Muslim population in a time when Muslim communities were in the minority (Walmsley and Damgaard 2005, 371).

The installation of congregational mosques next to strategic crossroads and near market places, as with Palmyra, is a frequent occurrence in antique urban centres. The congregational mosque at Jerash, for example, stands next to the south *Tetrakionion* square, at the intersection of the ancient Roman *cardo* and south *decumanus* (Walmsley and Damgaard 2005, 364). Shops have been found around the south *Tetrakionion* square and the western part of the south *decumanus* (Walmsley 2003, 112–13). Finally, the annexation of a smaller mosque next to the main building in medieval time and the likely abandonment of the former is also worthy of note. The same occurrence is attested at al-Ruṣāfa, where the original mosque was replaced by a smaller building in Ayyūbid times (Sack 1996, 33–7). In a different way, at Amman, the Umayyad Mosque was reduced in size in the late 9th–early 10th century resulting in the elimination of the third bay of the prayer hall (Northedge 1992, 66–8). To conclude, the archaeological record of Early Islamic places of worship at Palmyra is meagre, but nonetheless sufficient to confirm the presence of a sizeable Muslim community. In the Umayayd period, Palmyra retained a local importance and was at the centre of the Marwānids' urban development project. The abandonment of the original building and the construction of a smaller mosque can be connected to a process of gradual shrinkage of the population and an overall decline of the city in later times.

The Muslim community: further evidence

A part from mosques, there is little other published evidence to support the existence of a Muslim community at Palmyra. Epigraphic evidence is particularly meagre. The inscription found in the *cella* of the Sanctuary of Bēl and dated to AH 110 (728–729) is a prayer to God by ʿAbd al-Ṣamad b. ʿUbayd and Muḥammad b. Yazīd and dates the abandonment of the church to the first half of the 8th century (*Inv.* 9, 51, n. 39).

Burials

Archaeologically, besides the orientation and, perhaps, the grave goods, it is very difficult to distinguish among the burials of the religious communities living in Palmyra in Late Antiquity and the Early Islam. Generally speaking, burials in this period do not show any signs of the architectural monumentality that had characterised funerary structures in Roman times. Whether this was the result of the end of a gradual process or, rather, an abrupt change is difficult to establish due to the paucity of evidence and their chronology, which is normally from the 6th century onward. As discussed, beside one exception, graveyards and isolated burials are to be found within the city wall. Skeletons lie in an extended position in stone cists or, more frequently, in simple pits dug into the ground. Traces of wood have been found in several cases, suggesting the use of wooden coffins. No detailed descriptions of these cemeteries have ever been published and only mentions in interim reports are available in secondary literature.

The largest post-Roman graveyard (78 burials) is located outside the city wall, to the south of the modern Archaeological Museum (Fig. 47). Syrian authorities excavated it in the late 1960s. The published interim reports provide the reader with general descriptions of the burials and their grave goods. Most of the depositions (normally 2 × 0.6 × 0.5m in size) are in stone cists made with large, narrow blocks of limestone (sometimes reused) set vertically into the ground. The majority of the burials, which are all orientated east–west, have not yielded artefacts, while others present rich sets of grave goods consisting of bracelets and necklaces with coloured beads, bronze belt buckles, glass vessels, and pottery. The excavated area is believed to be only the southeast corner of a much extended quadrangular cemetery of 500m per side; modern private residential buildings covers the remaining section of the graveyard (al-Asʿad 1967; 1968; al-Asʿad and Ruprechtsberger 1987, 137–46). A wide 4th–7th century chronology for these burials has been put forward (al-Asʿad and Ruprechtsberger 1987, 137). According to the excavators, the presence of some artefacts, such as a glass vessel bearing an Arabic inscription ('*shukralla*'), suggest that the cemetery continued to be used

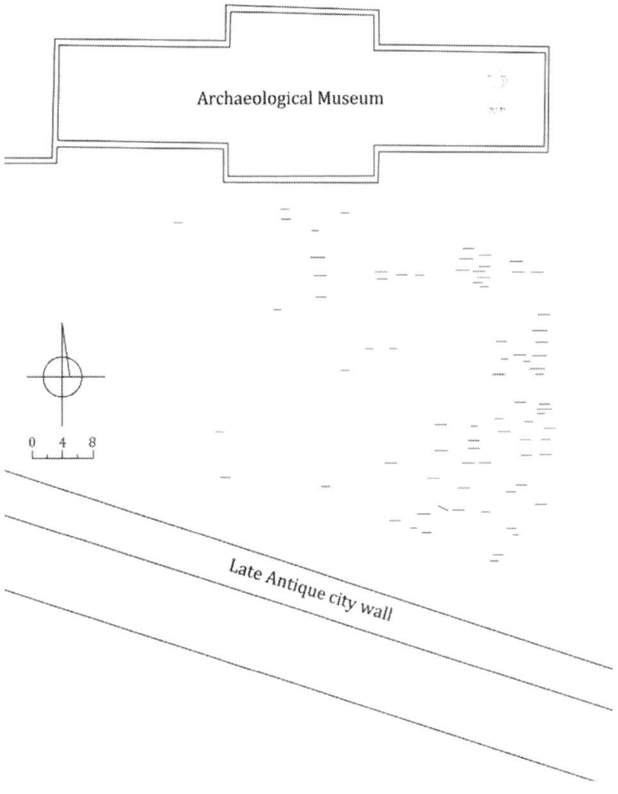

Figure 47. Byzantine Cemetery (redrawn after al-Asʿad 1968, pl. 1).

well into Umayyad times (al-Asʿad and Ruprechtsberger 1987, 137–8).

A graveyard set in the city centre has been brought to light by the Polish team between Churches II and III. The cemetery is 33m wide and divided in two halves by a wall running from east to west. The area was densely occupied before the 4th century, but it seems to have been an abandoned field by the time of the installation of the graveyard, which corresponds with the construction of Church II. As a matter of fact, burials were found set immediately on top of a 4th century fill. The access to the cemetery was through three doorways on the north wall of Church II. A total of seven burials orientated east to west has been exposed. Only two were found in stone cists covered with flat stones. The others were simple pit burials dug into the ground. With the exception of a young girl wearing copper earrings and a necklace of glass beads, no other grave goods have been found (Gawlikowski 1999, 192–4; 2000, 254–5). The paucity of artefacts is in stark contrast with the richness that had characterised Roman depositions. The position of the cemetery is understandable, given its proximity to the two churches, with which it is presumably contemporary, and the desire of the believers to be buried *ad sanctos*.

A further concentration of burials within the Late Antique city wall was uncovered in 2001 in the Suburban Market, next to the Dura Gate. In the 7th–8th centuries, the eastern section of the building was transformed into a cemetery, while the rest of the structure remained occupied by houses or shops. The cemetery included more than thirty burials orientated either north to south or east to west. According to the excavators, the different orientation would suggest that Christian and Muslim (or non-Christians) were here buried together. The burials often come in concentration of two or more depositions within a single room, whose entrance had been walled up. Bodies were sometimes deposited in wooden coffins, whose remains have been identified during the excavations. They were wrapped in clothes before being buried, some of which standing out for their rich material, such as silk and gold (Delplace 2006–2007, 106–7, 108; 2013, 40). The reason behind the position of this cemetery is puzzling. It might have to do with its general peripheral location and its vicinity to one of the main gates of the city.

Finally, isolated depositions within the urban limits are also attested. In the northwest corner of Church II a stone cist covered with flat stones has been uncovered containing two skeletons lying one upon the other. The skeletons were lying 'looking north, their feet towards the east' (Gawlikowski 1998, 203). The deposition occurred when the church was already abandoned and part of the floor had already been removed.

Conclusions

Very little is known of Palmyra's religious life in the 4th and 5th centuries. We are informed through written sources that the city remained an episcopal see and its bishops were involved in the Christological controversies of their time. Yet, written sources are not informative on the potential continuity of Paganism, nor on the presence of other religious community in the city, which have, however, left archaeological traces. In the 6th century, Palmyra saw a veritable surge in church building, possibly triggered by Imperial investment. Up to eight churches are believed to have been refurbished or constructed at this stage. One of these, Church IV, is indeed significant for its size alone, comparable with that of contemporary churches in other major Christian centres, such as Basilica B at al-Ruṣāfa (48.8 × 25.7m) and significantly vaster than other Syrian 'cathedrals' such as that of al-Andarīn (*c.* 43 × 25m) or, further north, Qalb Lūza (main body: 30.91 × 16.56m). The presence of a church of sizable proportion demonstrates the ability of the episcopal see to attract investment even for large building enterprises, and likewise confirms the overall building vitality of Palmyra in a period in which churches were the main public buildings to be constructed. The presence of a *bema* in the same church is an extraordinary occurrence in central Syria that may suggest the flourishing of a privileged dialogue in the region with one of the major centres of Christianity of the time, namely Antioch.

The archaeological evidence for places of worship in the Early Islamic period confirms the continuing local importance of the city after the Islamic takeover. The Congregational Mosque of Palmyra does not reflect only the religious necessity of an isolated Muslim community. Parallels with other buildings in *Bilād al-Shām* have shown that the erection of the building in Palmyra has to be interpreted as part of a large-scale process of urban development under the Marwānids. The importance of Palmyra at that time was possibly not administrative, as for other centres where congregational mosques are attested, but rather political. The city was in fact the centre of the Banū Kalb, the leading Arabic tribe renowned for its support of the Umayyad dynasty (Genequand 2008a, 14). The later construction of a more modest mosque to meet the need of a reduced population is consistent with the abandonment of the *intra muros* churches, suggesting a veritable decline of the city only after Umayyad times.

Chapter 5

The military

The military role of Palmyra increased considerably under the impulse of the Tetrarchic restrengthening of the frontier defensive system. This intervention prevented the complete abandonment of Palmyra and assured its survival up to the Islamic takeover. According to the *Notitia Dignitatum*, the city hosted the *Legio I Illyricorum* in the 4th century. Malalas and Procopius record that new troops were deployed in the city together with the *dux* of Emesa under the reign of Justinian. The importance of Late Antique Palmyra as a stronghold on the Persian frontier is often implicitly recognised by the majority of written sources. Nevralgic centre of the militarised city was the Camp of Diocletian, an imposing and architecturally pretentious fortress that was installed in the late 3rd–early 4th century in the western corner of the city. A detailed examination of its remains is key to the understanding of the historical development of the settlement in Late Antiquity.

The garrison at Palmyra

The military history of Palmyra in the 4th century is closely linked to that of the *Legio I Illyricorum*, a legion believed to be the result of the unification of the contingents from Pannonia left after the victory against Zenobia in 272 (Zos., *Hist. Nov.*, 1.52, 3; Ritterling 1925, 1406; Kowalski 1998, 189–94). It is still disputed when the installation of the legion took place. It has been suggested that the *I Illyricorum* was deployed in the city as early as the Aurelianic intervention in the city (Hartmann 2001, 409; Juchniewicz 2013, 194). Its main function would have been to prevent any further uprisings in the city after the second Palmyrene revolt. This conclusion is plausible, but remains to be proven. There is good chance that before, or during, the construction of the Camp of Diocletian, the legion was somehow involved in the military campaign in Egypt in 293–295 together with the *Legio XI Claudia*, *Legio VII Claudia*, *Legio IV Claudia*, and very likely *Legio I Italica*. After this campaign, either the legion was transferred in its entirety from Egypt to Palmyra or its detachment in Egypt met the rest of the unit that had already been moved to this city. There is also the possibility that the detachment joined the rest of the unit elsewhere and that only later was the *I Illyricorum* transferred entirely to the new destination (Lewin 2002, 92).

The earliest evidence of the existence of the legion is a late 3rd century funerary inscription from Aydın, ancient Tralles in southwest Anatolia, of a certain Aurelius Onesimus 'soldier of the *Legio I Illyricorum* and *tutor cessionarius*' (*ILS* 2.1038, n. 8875; Christol and Drew-Bear 2002, esp. 34–6). Presumably contemporary is the inscription of al-Azraq, in northern Jordan, which reports the construction of a *praetensio* by the soldiers of this and other legions that had taken part in the expedition to Egypt. The inscription presents a number of problems, not least the meaning of the word *praetensio*, which is still debated (Lewin 2002, 92 for extensive bibliography). Additionally, it does not specify whether the *Legio I Illyricorum* was working at the *praetensio* in its entirety or, as argued by Kowalski (1998, 190), was represented by a detachment.

The works for the construction of the Camp of Diocletian commenced during or after the event glorified in the inscription of al-Azraq. An inscription found on the lintel of the main entrance to the Temple of the Standards celebrates the construction of the '*castra*' by the *vir perfectissimus* and *praeses provinciae* Sossianus Hierocles on behalf of the two *Augusti* (Diocletian and Maximian) and the two *Caesars* (Constantius and Galerius). Since Sossianus Hierocles left his office in the province in 303, the inscription dates the construction of the fortress between 293 and 303 (*IGLS* 17.1, 132–1, n. 121; Dodgeon and Lieu 1991, 119; Kowalski 1997, 44–5; 1998, 191; Lewin 2002, 93 gives a narrower chronology). A striking similarity is noticeable between the inscription of Palmyra and the example discovered from the contemporary fort of Udhruḥ, base of the *Legio VI Ferrata*, 15km to the east of Petra (Kennedy and Falahat 2008, 159); in itself, this is a further proof of the existence of that centrally controlled 'grand scheme' of re-strengthening of the frontier reported by Malalas (*Chr.*, 12.40), 'on the frontiers, from Egypt as far as the borders of Persia, Diocletian built forts (*castra*) establishing in them frontier troops (*limitanei*); and choosing *duces*, he stationed one in each province within the ring of forts, with large numbers of men as a mobile reserve. And he set up inscriptions to the Augustus and the Caesar on the frontier of Arabia' (tr. Mann 1977, 14, n. 8; Kennedy and Falahat 2008, 166). Unlike the inscription from Udhruḥ, however, that of the Camp of Diocletian does not specify which legion the *castra* was meant to accommodate.

There is evidence for a military presence in Palmyra in the first quarter of the 4th century. The same Sossianus Hierocles mentioned in the foundation inscription of the *castra* is also reported to be responsible of the construction of the baths in the city centre (*IGLS* 17.1, 112–15, n. 100). The altar dedicated by Avitus *optio princeps* in 302 in the Sanctuary of Baalshamīn reveals that the religious compound was still functioning and proves the co-existence of civilians and soldiers in the settlement (*IGLS* 17.1, 163–164, n. 154). Besides Palmyra, two inscriptions dated to the first quarter of the 4th century report the presence of the soldiers from the *Legio I Illyricorum* in Egypt. One, on a bowl from Koptos, is a dedication to the *Tyche* by the inhabitants of Emesa in 316, 'for the safety of the detachments of the legions *III Gallica* and *I Illyricorum* which are under the command of Victorinus, *praepositus*' (*ILS* 2.1039, n. 8882; tr. Kowalski 1998, 192–3). The second is an inscription found in Aswān dated 26 May 321 and again dedicated to the *Tyche* for the safety of the same legions under the same *praepositus* (de Ricci 1903, 445, n. 67; for the chronology see Bagnall, Cameron *et al.* 1987, 177). The possibility that these detachments were already in Egypt as early as 300 should not be excluded. Brennan (1989, 200–1, esp. n. 14) associates the *Legio I Illyricorum* with the *miliarienses* mentioned in an inscription found at Elephantine.

The latest mention of the *Legio I Illyricorum* comes from the late 4th century *Notitia Dignitatum* (*Or.*, 32.30). This document represents the only piece of evidence that states specifically that this legion was garrisoned in Palmyra. Two more inscriptions from the city confirm a military presence throughout Late Antiquity. One was found on a block of imported tuff and refers presumably to building carried out under the *vir perfectissimus*, *dux Orientis*, Flavius Platanius Serenianus (*IGLS* 17.1, 297–298, n. 366). The inscription has been dated to 325 (Jones *et al.* 1971, 825 *contra* Seyrig 1950, 239; see below, p. 90). The text of the second, only recently published by Yon and tentatively dated to the 5th century, is rather fragmentary and difficult to interpret; it presumably mentions recruits (τίρωνας), soldiers (στ[ρατιώτας]) and officials ([ὀφφικι]αλίος) together with a *dux* and a governor (*IGLS* 17.1, 295, n. 359).

Written and epigraphic evidence suggests that Palmyra retained its role as a centre of recruitment for the army in the period under discussion (a practice that started well before the 270s, Edwell 2008, 50–62). The *Notitia Dignitatum* reports the presence of two troops of Palmyrene soldiers: the *Cuneus Equitum Secundorum Clibanariorum Palmyrenorum*, one of the *vexillationes comitatenses* (*Not. Dig., Or.*, 7.34), and the *Ala Octava Palmyrenorum*, an auxiliary unit stationed in the Thebaid (*Not. Dig., Or.*, 31.49). *Vexillationes comitatenses* enjoyed the legal privileges of the legions (Southern and Dixon 1996, 30–1). *Clibanarii* were heavily armoured shock cavalry equipped with a bow and lance (Bivar 1972). They had formed the backbone of Zenobia's army and were later included in the Roman army possibly as early as Aurelian's reign (Eadie 1967, 170–1; Elton 1996, 106). The presence of a troop of *clibanarii* from this city is confirmed by a funerary inscription in the Tombs of the Prophets at Jerusalem that mention an Anamos, 'κλιβανάρι(ο)ς [τρίτος?] Παλμύρας' (Clermont-Ganneau 1899, 364). It has roughly been dated by Clermont-Ganneau to the 4th or 5th century (Clermont-Ganneau 1899, 364–5). The *Ala Octava Palmyrenorum* might have been the result of the transformation of a former *Numerus Palmyrenorum* stationed in Coptos in 216 into a regular field unit (Rocco 2010, 145).

Written sources suggest the possibility of a reduction of the military presence in the 5th century. Malalas reports that Justinian 'ordered a *numerus* of soldiers to be stationed there with the *limitanei* (μετὰ τῶν λιμιτανέων), and also the *dux* of Emesa, to protect the Roman territories and Jerusalem' (Mal., *Chr.*, 17.2). The text is confusing, as it does not specify whether the troop of *limitanei* was there before the intervention of Justinian, or, less likely, was deployed together with the *numerus* of soldiers and the *dux* of Emesa. The term μετὰ can be translated either as 'with' or 'among' and modern literature has not yet, found a consensus (see for instance, Shahīd 1995, 172; *contra* Kowalski 1997, 51). In neither case is a *legio* mentioned. The installation of new troops in the city is echoed by Procopius (*Aed.*, 2.11.10–12), who appears less informed than Malalas, and later Theophanes (*Chr.*, 1.174, who follows Malalas). The action of deploying more troops can be seen as the attempt of the emperor to compensate for a reduction of the military strength of the city in a period of rising conflict between the Roman and Persian empires. This fits perfectly into a much broader trend that affected the majority of the forts along the eastern frontier as a consequence of the peaceful conditions in the 5th century. A gap of occupation and reduction in military presence is attested at the same time in numerous sites along the eastern frontier. The *vicus* at al-Lajjūn, for example, was mostly abandoned and the civilian settlement moved within the walls of the fort, whose military personnel must have been reduced (Crawford and Parker 2006). At the opposite end of the frontier, the *Legio IIII Parthica* at *Circesium* was moved elsewhere in the same period (*Not. Dig., Or.*, 35.24; Proc., *Bell.*, 2.5.1–4; Proc., *Aed.*, 2.6; Ulbert 1989, 293–5). The stretch of frontier from *Sura* (Sūriyya) to Palmyra does not seem to have experienced this gap due to the impulse given at the time by the shrine at al-Ruṣāfa; excavations at the fort of *Tetrapyrgium* have yielded ceramic material dated to the end of the 5th–beginning of the 6th century (Konrad 2001, 74–5). As already pointed out recently by Lewin (2011, 241), this, however, does not exclude the possibility that garrisons along this section were not kept under-strength. This generalised reduction of the Roman military presence saw the gradual emergence of the Arab allies as the main forces of policing of the eastern frontier (Lewin 2007).

Taking the text of Malalas literally, it seems that two forces, a group of *limitanei* and a *numerus* of soldiers, were quartered in the city in the first half of the 6th century. In addition, one of the two *duces* of *Phoenicia Libanensis* was residing there too – the other *dux* would have resided in Damascus (Greatrex 2007, 92). These two *duces* were at the time at the head of a large, regular field army. When Chosroes threatened the city of Antioch in 540, the *duces* of *Phoenicia Libanensis*, at that time Theocistus and Molatzes, are said to have converged on the city with a force of 6000 men (Proc., *Bell.*, 2.8.2; Liebeschuetz 1977, 497). Later, the same field army from *Phoenicia Libanensis*, this time under the command of the *duces* Rhecithancus and Theocistus, joined an expedition against Chosroe in Mesopotamia led by Belisarius (Proc., *Bell.*, 2.19, 33). The general's army also included a large force of Saracens led by Arethas (Proc., *Bell.*, 2.16.4). It is unclear where this regular field army was deployed, but it is reasonable to assume that at least part of this contingent would have been stationed together with one of the two *duces* at Palmyra. The settlement was certainly sufficiently defended and had the necessary facilities to accommodate a large army. Troops might have been quartered (presumably in part) in the Camp of Diocletian, which at the time underwent significant renovation: the inner arrangement of the *Horreum* was altered and the *Principia* was enlarged to accommodate more rooms.

It is not clear whether the two *duces* remained in charge after Justinian. In all likelihood this was probably not the case. In later times only one *dux* of *Phoenicia* is normally recorded by written sources (Goubert 1951, 95, 107, 277–9; Kowalski 1997, 52). Theophylactus Simocatta (*Hist.*, 2.3) mentions only Ilifred as *dux* of Emesa in 568. Not much later, in 570 an uprising around Edessa was led by the *dux* of *Phoenice* Germanus (Th. Sim., *Hist.*, 3.2.5). At that time considerable help in terms of military defence must have come from the nomadic element, the *foederati* Jafnids. These seem to have been active in the Palmyrene territory during the 6th and the beginning of the 7th century, but no strong evidence is left to support their effective military involvement in this area (Isaac 1990, 211). Similarly, there is no evidence to cast light on the fortunes of the garrison stationed in Palmyra in later times. It is reasonable to assume that the Roman forces abandoned the city as soon as Syria entered the Persian dominion. In the short time span comprised between the end of the Persian occupation and the Islamic takeover, either a small garrison of regular soldiers was quartered in the city or Palmyra was left to be defended by its inhabitants. On the strength of the city in the Early Islamic period there is little to conjecture, as written sources are silent in this regard.

The Camp of Diocletian

History of research

The Camp of Diocletian represents one of the most monumental post-Roman evidence of Palmyra. Its remains have often attracted the interest of travellers since the rediscovery of the city by Wood in the 18th century. Yet, scientific contribution on this monument would not appear until the first half of the 20th century. In 1931, Cantineau published a number of inscriptions from the fortress, including the foundation text of the *castra* by Sossianus Hierocles (*IGLS* 17.1, 132–3, n. 121). One year later, the compound was described in detail in the contribution based on three German surveys carried out in 1902, 1917, and 1928 by Wiegand and his team (Krencker 1932). At the time, the most impressive building visible on the ground was the Temple of the Standards.

In 1952, Starcky (1952, 18) lamented the lack of systematic excavations of the complex. These started under the direction of Michałowski only seven years later and lasted, not without interruptions, for about 30 years (1959–1987). Given the dimension of the concession (about 30,000m^2, Michałowski 1960a, 11), the excavation was not systematic but examined specific areas leaving a large plot of land unexposed. The works were carried out from east (*Porta Praetoria*) to west (*Principia*) and covered the total length of *Via Praetoria*, some sections of the *Via Principalis*, the *Principia*, the *Horreum*, several barrack blocks, and the Sanctuary of Allāth – including the later *Praetorium* installed within its *temenos*. Minor soundings were also carried out to cast light on the water supply system. The bulk of data of the Polish works are presented in a collection of eight monographs of the Research Centre for Mediterranean Archaeology in a preliminary fashion (Michałowski 1960a; 1962; 1963a; 1964a; 1966; Gawlikowski 1973; 1984; Sadurska 1977). Shorter interim reports have also been published in diverse journals, most of them being *Annales Archéologiques Arabes Syriennes* (Michałowski 1960b; 1960c; 1961–1962; 1963b; 1964b; 1967; 1969; 1971; Bernhard 1969; Sadurska 1972; 1973b; 1977; Daszewski 1972; Gawlikowski 1983c), *Études et Travaux* (Gawlikowski 1975b; 1976a; 1978; 1979a; 1979b; 1992b; Sadurska 1973a), and *Studia Palmyreńskie* (Gawlikowski 1969; 1985; Niepokólczycki 1969; Daszewski and Kołątaj 1970; Kołątaj 1975; Sadurska 1975; Krogulska 1985; Kowalski 1994), and in a number of conference proceedings (Gawlikowski 1976b; 1987a; 1987b). A few contributions by the members of the Polish team have been concerned to synthesise all these data. A praiseworthy attempt to provide a broad overview of the military presence in Late Antique Palmyra on the basis of written sources and archaeological evidence has been done by Barański (1994). Four years later, Kowalski (1998) published a summarising article on the Camp of Diocletian that also included valuable information on the excavations of several barrack blocks.

The results of the excavations of the Camp of Diocletian had the merit of having animated discussion on the military role of Palmyra after 273, its place in the framework of the defence of the eastern frontier, and its fate in post-Roman time. The 1960s were mostly dominated by scholarly debate on the nature of the remains that was stimulated by an article by Schlumberger (1962). The scholar believed that the Camp of Diocletian was in reality the residence of Zenobia and Odaenathos, a theory that would later be proven wrong in the course of the excavations. Schlumberger also believed that the term *castra* in the foundation inscription of the fortress does not refer to the military compound but to the city as a whole. Fellmann (1976) attempted to analyse the Camp of Diocletian in a much broader way, providing parallels to prove that the compound was indeed part of a well-established military architectural tradition and not an *unicum* in the empire. In the same contribution, Fellmann, supporting Schlumberger's discussion on the term *castra*, suggested that the area occupied by the military enclosure would have been too small to accommodate an entire legion and that at least part of the garrison must have been billeted within the civilian settlement. More recent publications by non-Polish scholars have often inclined toward Fellmann's broader approach to the study of the compound. These include the works by Kennedy and Riley (1990, 134–7), Gregory (1996, 189–95; 1997, E1.1–11), and Lenoir (2011, 74–80; 303).

Description of the remains

Setting of the compound

Due to the importance of the Camp of Diocletian for the period under analysis, it is useful to provide the reader with a summary account of its remains through an examination of secondary literature. The compound is installed on the eastern slope of a hill, on what had been in Roman times a suburban area at the edge of a necropolis (Fig. 48). It dominates Palmyra from higher ground and appears as an

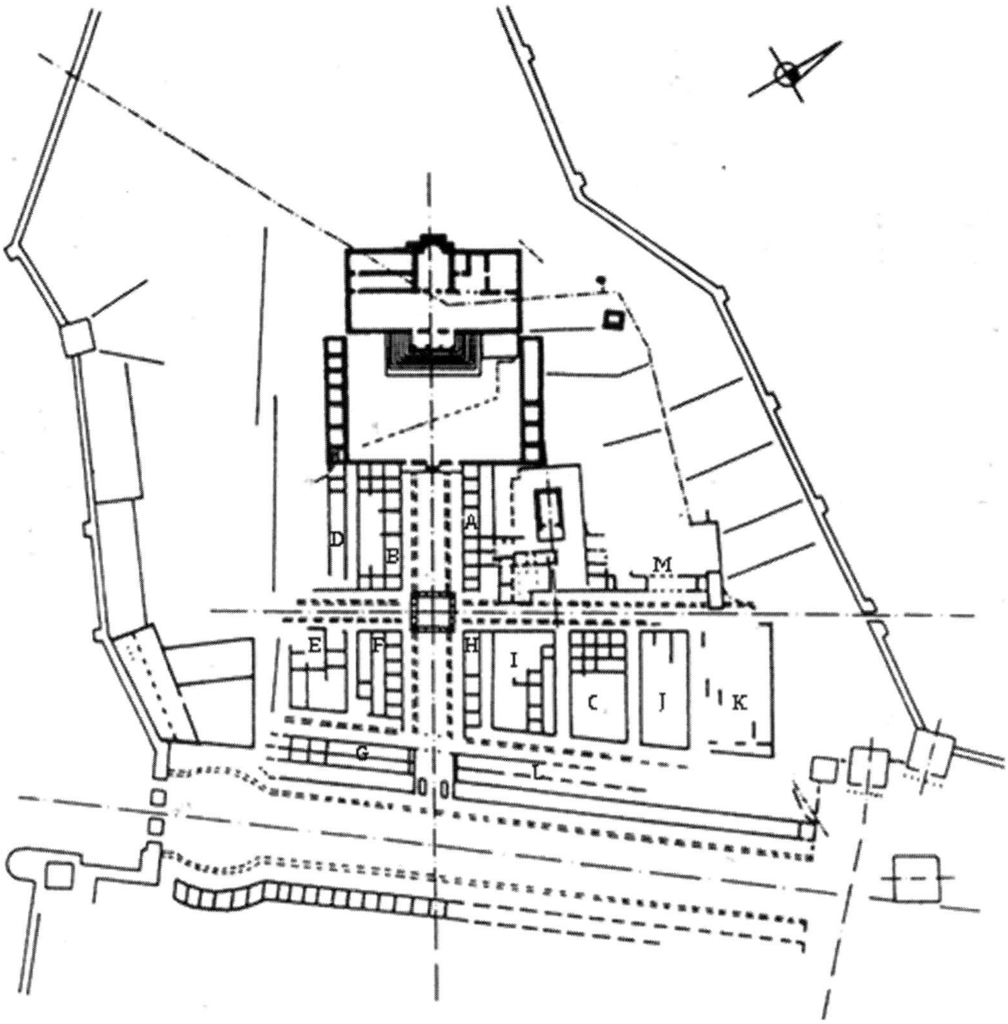

Figure 48. Camp of Diocletian. Letters indicate barrack blocks (Kowalski 1994, pl. 26).

appendix of Palmyra's urban circuit to the west. The area encircled by the wall is 6.4ha. Given the uneven terrain, however, not all this was built up and large plots of land to the north, east, and south were apparently left free of buildings. Nothing would exclude, however, that these areas were occupied by much less permanent structures, such as tents, which barely leave traces in the archaeological record.[1] The compound was constructed in an area occupied by earlier buildings. The *Via Praetoria* pre-existed the fortress (Michałowski 1962, 41–3; 1963a, 40). According to Filarska (1967, 108–9), the style of the capitals would suggest that the construction of the *Via Praetoria* took place as early as the 2nd century. The area later occupied by the *Forum* was formerly part of a 1st century artisan and residential quarter (Michałowski 1964a, 11–26; Krogulska 1985; 1997) and a 2nd–3rd century sanctuary dedicated to the Anonymous God (Gawlikowski 1973, 109). The desacralisation of public places for military purposes is not devoid of parallels in the empire: the installation of a fort in the Temple of Ammon at Luxor represents an example of this tendency taken to the extreme (Deckers 1973). Of the pre-existing buildings, thus, only the *Via Praetoria* and the Sanctuary of Allāth, as discussed below, seem to have been left in place.

The fortress remains isolated from the civilian settlement to the east through an arrangement of three rows of rooms parallel to the Transverse Colonnade. The rooms were constructed upon an earlier section of the city wall dismantled at the beginning of the 1st century (Gawlikowski 1975b, 378). They join the urban circuit to the south through a straight wall against which the *Horreum* abuts (Gawlikowski 1992b). Diverse interpretations have been put forward to explain this arrangement. Michałowski regarded the rooms as shops later filled in with debris to create a practical defensive system against attacks from the city (in Kowalski 1998, 195). Kowalski (1998, 205) considered as shops only the rooms opening onto the Transverse Colonnade; he interpreted the others as barrack blocks consisting of front and back rooms. Conversely, Lenoir (2011, 75) regarded the remains as three rows of shops, one of which has back-rooms. According to him, the shops were already abandoned by the time of the construction of the military complex. Yet, no safe theories can be put forward without the support of published archaeological data.

The limit of the Camp of Diocletian to the northwest (between the shops and the city wall) is marked by three funerary temples (86b [=D302], 86 [=D301], and 173c [=A201]). The space between the northernmost shop and the Funerary Temple 86 [=D301] was closed up with a partition wall pierced by an entrance, the so-called 'Water Gate' (Gawlikowski 1992b, 334). The whole arrangement had no defensive character but was presumably intended simply as a formal limit between the civilian settlement and the military compound. The situation of the Camp of Diocletian in the city recalls that at Dura Europos, where the fort is only partially isolated from the city by a wall of mud brick 1.65m thick (Lenoir 2011, 49). To the north, east, and south, the Camp of Diocletian is delimited by the urban circuit.

Reused architecture pillaged from nearby *hypogea* and other pre-existing buildings were used as building material for the construction of the Camp of Diocletian. A number of sculptural elements are firmly dated to only a couple of generations before the construction of the compound. This practice was regarded by Michałowski (1962, 15) as '*l'expression des sentiments du régime qui représentait le force de domination et la prépondérance sur la popolation*'. It is possible, however, that it might have primarily been guided by convenience. The use of *spolia* was not only permitted by law, but also recommended by the authors of military treatises (*C. Th.*, 15.1.36; *De re strategica,* 10.3; Pringle 1981, 133).

Gates

The main access to the Camp of Diocletian was via the Praetorian Gate (*Porta Praetoria*) which opens eastward (Fig. 49). The gate is installed immediately upon the earlier shops of the Transverse Colonnade and consists of a triple entrance divided by two rectangular pillars (Gawlikowski 1976a, 275). The southernmost lateral passage gave access to two small rooms to the south. The easternmost had a staircase, while the other has been interpreted as the room of the gatekeeper. Another room was accessible from the northern lateral passage (Michałowski 1960a, 21–2, 29). The Praetorian Gate gave access to a rectangular courtyard opening onto the *Via Praetoria* by means of two columns *in antis*. The façade of the gate is decorated with moulded door frames whose features had first inclined Michałowski (1960a, 76) to believe that it pre-existed the Camp of Diocletian. Yet, it is now generally agreed that the gate was constructed together with the fortress and adopted

Figure 49. Porta Praetoria *(Browning archive. Courtesy of the Palestine Exploration Fund) (cat. n. 67).*

extensively reused architecture in its construction (Kowalski 1998, 199). Michałowski recorded the presence of two small fragments of marble among the finds from one of the lateral rooms: a fragment of '*dallage en pierre noire aux tâches vertes*' (in all likelihood, *porfido verde antico*) and a laurel leaf in white marble, possibly from a mosaic. He believes that the fragments might have been part of the original decorative apparatus of the *Porta Praetoria* (Michałowski 1960a, 33, 36, fig. 34; Wielgosz 2013, 332, fig. 8).

Two other subsidiary entrances to the Camp of Diocletian are known. One is the *Porta Principalis Sinistra* of the fortress, located along the northern stretch of the urban circuit at the end of the *Via Principalis*. It has a single entrance and is flanked by two buttress towers. The one to the west is not bonded with the city wall and is, therefore, a later addition. The other access is between the Temple Tomb 86 and the northernmost shop along the western side of the Transverse Colonnade. It features a single entrance and has been named 'Water Gate', as several pipelines run through it and join the main water conduits running along the southern portico of the Great Colonnade. The remains of the gate include two reused jambs which share a foundation with a gutter carved in the middle (Gawlikowski 1992b, 334).

Street layout

The Camp of Diocletian develops in four irregular blocks formed by the intersection at right-angles of two colonnaded streets (Fig. 48). The *Via Praetoria* is the widest (11.6m; south portico 3.55m; north portico 3.6m) and runs for about 100m from east to west, connecting the Praetorian Gate with the *Principia* (Michałowski 1963a, pl. 1; Tabaczek 2001, 46–7). As already pointed out above, it is believed to have pre-existed the fortress. The *Via Principalis* (roughly 13m wide) stretches from the *Porta Principalis Sinistra* southward for about 150m and has only partially been uncovered on its northern stretch. According to the excavators, it was installed together with the fortress at the end of the 3rd–beginning of the 4th century. It divides the fortress into two irregular halves, the eastern one consisting mostly of barracks (Tabaczek 2001, 45, 47–8). Its construction resulted in the destruction of the eastern section of the *temenos* of the Sanctuary of Allāth (Gawlikowski 1977, 265).

The junction of the two streets is marked by a monumental *Groma* that was constructed as part of the Tetrarchic building project (Michałowski 1962,10–41; Fig. 50). The *Groma* is roughly a square (14.25 × 14.45m). It consists

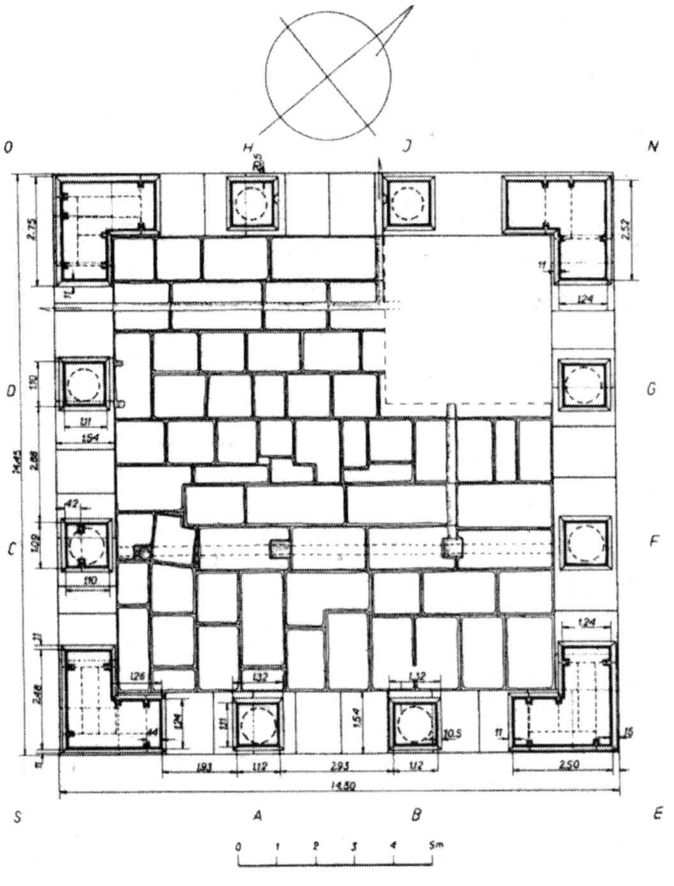

Figure 50. The Groma, *Camp of Diocletian (Michałowski 1962, 17, fig. 10).*

of four angular pillars and two interval columns along each side, all bearing Corinthian capitals. The decorative apparatus of the monument is particularly elaborate and consists of reused architecture. Among them an altar with an inscription dated 239–240 included in the foundations of the monument provides a convenient *terminus post quem* for the construction of the building (Michałowski 1962, 15).

The street arrangement is unusual as most of the time large forts develop around a T-shaped street layout terminating with a *Groma* that gives direct access to the *Principia*. The type is known by Lenoir as '*camps carrés avec principia centraux en face du croisement de deux vie*' (Lenoir 2011, 292). The problem of the street layout of the Camp of Diocletian was addressed by Fellmann, who found parallels in Britain (*castrum* of Portchester and *castellum* of Cardiff), Romania (*castellum* of Drobeta), and Egypt (Luxor). Among its examples Fellmann also mentions the Palace of Diocletian at Split, which he believes to have been influenced by contemporary military architecture (Fellmann 1976, 179–80; 1979). A closer parallel is represented by the Tetrarchic fort of Naj ʿ al-Ḥajar, in Egypt, whose street grid are almost an exact copy of that of the Camp of Diocletian. Its *Viae Praetoria* and *Principalis* are colonnaded and cross at a right-angle in a square marked by a *Groma*, while the *Principia* is at the very end of the *Via Praetoria* abutting the eastern wall of the fort (Wareth and Zignani 1992, 189, fig. 1; Mackensen 2009, 294, fig. 2). Other parallels can be found in the fort at ʿAyyāsh (Poidebard 1934, 85–7, 90, 149, pls 86–7; Gregory 1996, 151–2; 1997, D4.1; Lenoir 2011, 64–5) and the *castellum* of ʿAmsharaddī (Lander 1984, 145–6; Gregory 1996, 182–3; Lenoir 2011,70–1).

In the Camp of Diocletian, a third street runs along the row of shops, parallel to the Transverse Colonnade. It is 4.4m wide and has been dated to the 2nd century (Gawlikowski 1968, 296; Tabaczek 2001, 46). Besides, *viae vicinariae* no larger than 3m would have separated the barrack blocks, assuring circulation within the compound (Kowalski 1998, 199). When the fortress lost its military function, it was gradually transformed into a residential and productive complex. Houses and workshops, as seen in a previous chapter, occupied the whole length of the *Via Praetoria* from the Praetorian Gate to the Grande Porte.

Water installations

Water for the garrison could be obtained in a number of ways. A device for controlling the flow of water coming from the Western Aqueduct and channelled to the city (the so-called 'Water-House') was excavated to the north of the *Principia*, while a water reservoir was uncovered to the northwest corner of the *Forum*, partly on top of one of the steps of the monumental staircase leading to the Temple of the Standards (Barański 1997, 8). The installation of this reservoir, which is certainly later than the original phase of the Camp of Diocletian, is one of the arguments used by Kowalski (1998, 207) in support of the claim that 'the original design [of the fortress] was not prepared to meet the conditions of Palmyra', suggesting the lack of military experience in desert conditions of the *Legio I Illyricorum*. It is worth stressing, however, that it is likely for its acquaintance with desert conditions that the legion was chosen to join the military expedition to Egypt in 293–295.

The limits of the fortress also encompassed a spring located immediately beneath the 'Water-House', in the northwest sector. The spring is included within a squared stone structure (4 × 4 m). Its water spilled from a circular hole on the western wall of the room into a water reservoir 1.3m deep; from there, water could be drawn by using platforms installed on the northern and eastern sides of the room. Small finds inside the water reservoir would confirm the use of the spring until the Ayyūbid period (Barański 1997, 9).

A number of water lines are known to have been installed in the Camp of Diocletian. Barański has put forward a preliminary chronology of these conduits based on the typology of their pipes (Barański 1997, 8–15, pls 4–6). Three conduits (Barański's types A–C) run parallel with an east–west orientation immediately to the north of the spring. Conduit A consists of stone blocks with openings of 0.24m similar to those found along the Great Colonnade (Barański 1997, 8), while the other two are made of terracotta. Pipes D and E, made as well of terracotta, follow the same direction and pass over the western stylobate of the *Via Principalis*. A further concentration of pipes (Barański's types A, F–I, K) has been uncovered in the area of the Water Gate some of them (Barański's types A, G, and K) crossing it to join the main conduits along the southern portico of the great colonnade (Barański 1997, 10). Other water channels were found below the floor level of the *Principia* and across the *Forum* (Gawlikowski 1984, 15–16, 20; Daszewski and Kołątaj 1970, 74–7; Bernhard 1969, 71–5; Krogulska 1984, 78–81; Barański 1997, 8). According to Barański (1997, 11), post-Aurelianic conduits include those made with pipe types A, C, E, and H (late 3rd to mid-5th century or even later). Pipe type G is dated to the early 6th century and is possibly associated with the Justinianic intervention in the city (Barański 1997, 11–12). Pipe type F is much later in date, possibly ʿAbbāsid (Barański 1997, 12). Conduits made of pipe types A, G and F were connected to the Western Aqueduct.

Barracks

The four irregular quadrants formed by the intersection of the *Via Praetoria* and *Via Principalis* are mostly occupied by lodgings (Fig. 48). The inner arrangement of most of these structures remains unknown. Kowalski identifies 13 barrack blocks (A–M), two of them (G and L) abutting the row of shops along the Transverse Colonnade. With the exception of barrack block C, dated to the second half of the 4th century, no chronology for the other remains is given (Kowalski 1998, 205). Kowalski groups the barracks into different types on the basis of their dimensions and shapes:

1) a single row of rooms opens onto the *viae vicinariae* (barrack blocks H and D). Barrack block A is a variant. The single room would have served both as *papilio* and for storage;
2) two rows of rooms (barrack blocks G and L);
3) three rows of rooms (two rows of *papiliones* and a row of back-rooms; barrack blocks B, E, F, and J);
4) four rows of rooms (two rows of *papiliones* and two rows of back-rooms; barrack blocks I and C) (Kowalski 1998, 204–5).

A standard 5 × 4.8m room (24m^2) prevails. This figure is common in Tetrarchic forts. At al-Lajjūn, room sizes are generally between 16m^2 and 26m^2 (Groot *et al.* 2006, 184). At Palmyra, larger rooms are also attested in barrack blocks E, K, and M. Multi-roomed accommodation with up to four units serving as officers' suites have been also identified in barracks M (Kowalski 1998, 205). It should not be excluded that some of these rooms, especially those opening onto the streets, were in use as workshops, shops, or *tabernae*.

It is still open to debate whether the number of barracks (and, more generally speaking, the inhabitable surface within the fortress) would have been sufficient to provide accommodation for the whole unit or part of the garrison would have been billeted in town, as postulated by Fellmann (1976; *contra* Barański 1994, 13; Zanini 1995, 84, n. 35). Admittedly the latter explanation does not take into account two important points: 1) Late Antique legions were much smaller than earlier legions, 1000 against 6000 men (Southern and Dixon 1996, 31 with further bibliography; on the reduction of the area of forts in Late Antiquity see Kennedy and Riley 1990, 19); and 2) not all the garrison was necessarily accommodated in the fortress at the same time. A large number of soldiers might have been on duty somewhere else, either temporarily or permanently (Gregory 1995, 149; 1996, 434–46). Nonetheless, this does not help disentangle the issue. De Vries' reconstructed plan of the contemporary legionary fort of al-Lajjūn shows only in the eastern *praetentura* 16 half block with 16 rooms each, for a total of 128 rooms and more rooms are visible in the western half of the fort. The precise number of rooms in the Camp of Diocletian is difficult to estimate, but it is certainly lower than the figure from al-Lajjūn. It cannot be excluded that the undeveloped land surrounding the fortress might have been used to accommodate tents. For the time being, however, the possibility that part of the legion was billeted in town cannot be completely disproven with the archaeological data at our disposal.

The Horreum

The troops stationed in the Camp of Diocletian were strongly dependent on food supply from the countryside. The only published evidence that might be connected to the supply of foodstuff to the Camp of Diocletian is an *ostrakon* found by Wiegand and his team at the beginning of the 20th century. This bears an inscription referring to the quantity of a load of grain or similar foodstuff (Lehner 1932, 107, n. 1). Foodstuff was stored in a *horreum*, a warehouse, that lied in the southeast corner of the compound. The warehouse abuts the city walls to the south and the wall of the Transverse Colonnade to the east (Fig. 51). It was entered through one single opening pierced in the northern wall. Two other walls mark its northern and western limits. Their building technique is identical with that of the *Principia*, as well as the U-shaped towers and a number of repairs along the urban circuit. The rectangular hall occupies an area of more than 500m^2. It is divided in two aisles by a row of nine rectangular pillars orientated east–west that caused the building to be known as the 'Édifice à Piliers' in the first phases of the excavations. Both aisles were paved with flagging. In the northern one, six mills were installed; their existence is suggested by traces of wear on the floor, the remains of their supports, and their scattered fragments. In a later phase, after a partial destruction of the building, the number of mills was reduced to four; in the northern aisle additional pillars were installed flanking the original ones and set against the northern wall in order to reduce the span of the beams; a water basin was also installed in the southern aisle upon the flagging. Two Justinianic *folles* and two lamps associated with these levels would pinpoint the chronology of this phase to the second quarter of the 6th century. The Early Islamic period marked the end of the function of the building as a *horreum* and the beginning of a new phase represented by the partition of the two aisles into smaller units. A coin of Heraclius dated 639–640 found in one of these compartments would date this phase to post-634. Post-reform coins and pottery confirm the occupation of the building until its abandonment, which occurred in the 8th century. According to Gawlikowski, it is possible that the *Horreum* was at this time transformed into a mosque (Gawlikowski 1983b; 1986b; 1987a; 1992b; Kowalski 1998, 203–4, mostly based on Gawlikowski's 1986 preliminary report).

The peripheral position of the *Horreum* in the camp of Diocletian is not uncommon in Roman military architecture. The contemporary *horrea* of al-Lajjūn offers a good comparison. A striking parallel with the *Horreum* of Palmyra is offered by the fort of Krivina (*Iatrus*), base of the *Cuneus Equitum Scutariorum* (*Not. Dig., Or.*, 40.8), where the warehouse is located on the southern wall of the fort and is divided into two narrow rectangular aisles with a row of pillars (Von Bulow 2007; Rizos 2013, 662). The same inner arrangement is known at the later fort of Veliki Gradac (*Taliata*). In this case, however, the warehouse does not abut the wall of the fort, but is located just a couple of metres south of the eastern tower of the *Porta Praetoria* (Popović 1984, 275, fig. 5, in Dinchev 2007, 485).

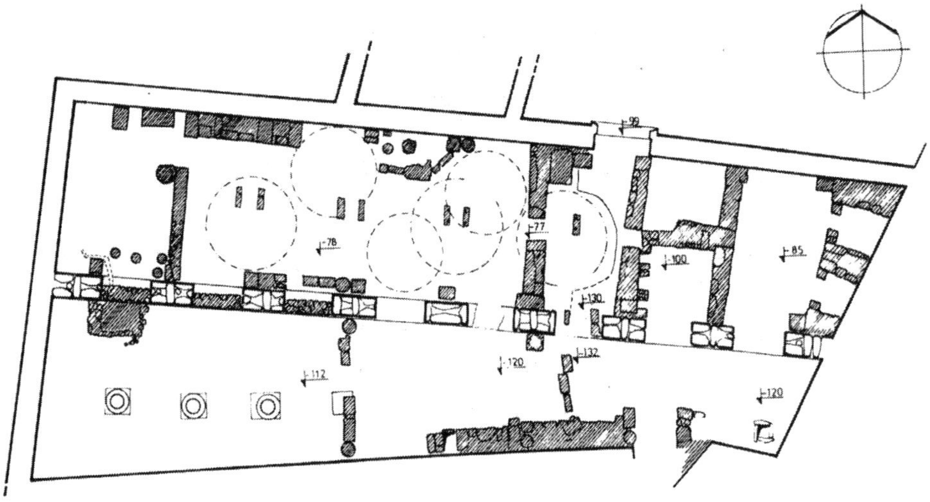

Figure 51. The Horreum *in its latest phase, Camp of Diocletian (Gawlikowski 1992b, 327, fig. 2).*

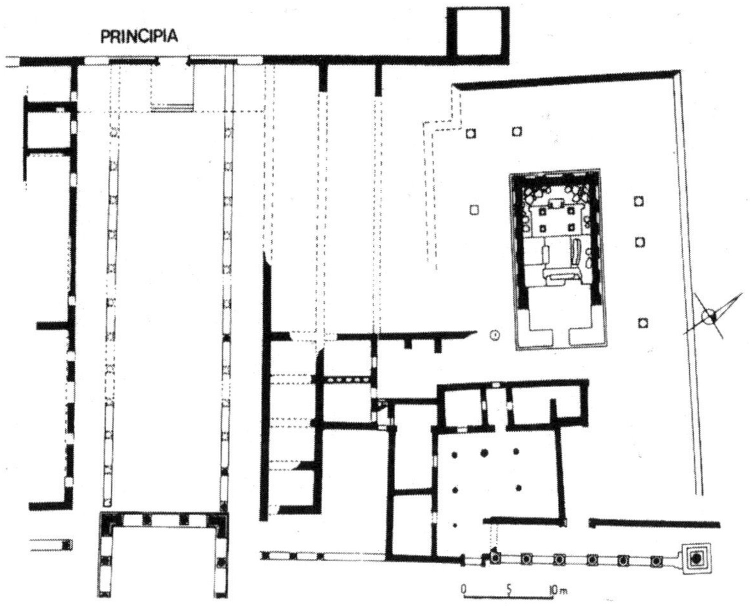

Figure 52. Sanctuary of Allāth, Late Antique phase, Camp of Diocletian (Kowalski 1994, pl. 27).

The Sanctuary of Allāth and the Praetorium

The Sanctuary of Allāth is situated in the northwestern quadrant of the Camp of Diocletian (Fig. 52). The original sanctuary consisted of a *temenos* and a chapel dating back to the 1st century BC. In the 1st and 2nd centuries the compound was monumentalised with four porticoes along the precinct walls, a *cella*, and a monumental entrance from the east. The temple underwent major alterations under Diocletian after a phase of destruction associated to the events of 273. The most important change at the time was the demolition of the eastern stretch of the *temenos* wall for the construction of the *Via Principalis* (Gawlikowski 1983a, 65). A new wall was built with an orientation 3° different from that of the former and six columns were set on top of a new stylobate. A honorific column dated epigraphically back to AD 64 was left in position untouched (Gawlikowski 1977, 257–8).

The decision to reconstruct the temple of Allāth after the destruction of 273 might have been motivated by the necessity for divine tutelage in unfamiliar surroundings (Stoll 2007, 466). The tendency of adopting local cults in new places of deployment is a frequent feature of Roman armies, which are prone to religious permeability (Stoll 2007, 452). The Arab deity Allāth is often represented in a warrior-like appearance also typical of Athena/Minerva (Teixidor 1979, 53–62; Starcky 1981, 565–8; Gawlikowski

1983a, 60; 1990, 2639–642; Kaizer 2002, 99–108; 2010, 121; emblematic of this practice is the inscription dedicated to *Helios Elagabalos* and Athena/Allāth from Cordoba, Milik 1967, 300–6). This straightforward transposition would make of Allāth more than a simple local cult by the soldiers, Minerva being included among the official gods worshipped in the army (but not included in official calendars such as the *feriale duranum*, Watson 1969, 131). A fitting parallel for the inclusion of the Sanctuary of Allāth within the limits of the newly established fortress is the temple of Azzanathkona at Dura Europos, constructed at the beginning of the 1st century. As for Palmyra, the construction of the *Principia* immediately to the south of this sanctuary did not mark the end of the religious activities of the building, which continued to be in use by both locals and soldiers until the destruction of the city in 256.

The Sanctuary of Allāth appears to have suffered pillage and destruction at the end of the 4th century. One of the main chronological indicator of this event is a coin of Aelia Flavia Flaccilla, first wife of Theodosius (376–386) found in the latest level of occupation of the temple in a gap between the floor slabs. Furthermore, a hoard of 45 Roman bronze coins was found in the northeast part of the *adyton*; with the exception of one mid-3rd century issue, all the others are dated to the 4th century, the latest being 383–392 (Krzyżanowska 1981; 2014, 52–5; Krogulska 2005, 123, n. 2). In addition a large quantity of 4th century lamp fragments, for a total of roughly 200 specimens, was found scattered all over the *cella* and associated with the same phase. It was also at that time that the cult statue of Athena was intentionally mutilated and disfigured. As already discussed above (see p. 47), the pillage of the sanctuary has been associated by the excavators with the coming to the city of Maternus Cynegius, *Praefectus Praetorio Orientis* in the mid-380s. The latter is well-known for having been a zealous physical executor of the anti-pagan measures undertaken by Theodosius I (Gąssowska 1982).

Changes occurred in the plan of the compound at the end of the 4th–beginning of the 5th century, when a private residential building was installed in the southeast corner of the sanctuary (Kowalski 1994; 1995; 1999). The structure consists of a central peristyled courtyard and two wings of rooms to the west and south. To the south it has direct access to a 4th century barrack block (see, Chapter 3). A fragment of the cult statue of Athena was found included in the western wall of one of its rooms in the western wing. The connection with a nearby barrack block and the presence of a peristyled courtyard has inclined Kowalski to regard the building as the *Praetorium*, the residence of the commander of the *Legio I Illyricorum* (Kowalski 1994, 52–3). The building appears to have been destroyed by an earthquake at the end of the 6th or beginning of the 7th century, refurbished twice (in the 7th–8th and in the 9th centuries), and abandoned after an earthquake that occurred in the 11th century.

The Principia

In a dominant position, at the western end of the *Via Praetoria*, were the fortress's headquarters (*Principia*). The *Principia* is a rectangular building measuring 75.9 × 62.5m and occupying a total area of 5190m² (Lenoir 2011, 77; Figs 53–4). It consists of three separate sections, namely an open court to the east (the so-called *Forum*), a cross-hall (the *Basilica*), and a row of rooms to the west, among them in central position is the *Aedes* or Temple of the Standards. The main access to the compound was through a monumental gate, the Grande Porte opening onto the *Via Praetoria* to the east and onto the *Forum* to the west (Michałowski 1963a, 21–43; Krogulska 1984, 86). From the *Via Praetoria*, a staircase with four steps would have led visitors to a wide platform presumably as wide as the street and 3.6m deep (Michałowski 1963a, 29–30; Lenoir 2011, 77, n. 43). The original building project of the staircase was changed in the course of its construction; a first was covered by a second, more monumental flight of steps (Krogulska 1984, 83–4, fig. 26). Recently, it has been suggested that the first phase of construction of the staircase, carried out by the soldiers of the *Legio I Illyricorum*, is dated before 293 (Jucniewicz 2013, 194). Although this theory remains plausible, there is no hard evidence in support of such chronology. The gate was provided with three entrances accessible from the platform, the central one being wider (2.6m) than the lateral (1.7m) and with two columns at the front. The façade looking east was richly adorned with moulded door frames and a triangular pediment on top of the central entrance.

The *Forum* is a large open courtyard (62.4 × 45.8m) at a level about 1.5m higher than the *Porta Praetoria* (Michałowski 1964a, 9). It was provided with two rows of seven rooms (probably *armamentaria*) along its south side; one, in the southeast corner, was a *latrina* (Michałowski 1964a, 9–52; Krogulska 1984). Further rooms would have been located along the north side. A 1m wide doorway between the *Basilica* and the southern wing of rooms of the court would have assured a subsidiary access to the *Forum*. The open court was originally planned to be porticoed on three sides (east, north, and south), but the plan was abandoned and the columns of the north and south sides were buried below the level of the court. Therefore, only the eastern side, the one onto which the Grande Porte opens, retained a portico. At the centre of the *Forum* would have stood a 3.1 × 3.95m platform which was raised 1.25m higher than the level of the court. On the western corner was a water reservoir added after the construction of the *Principia*; the structure was later covered by debris produced from the collapse of the eastern wall of the *Basilica* (Krogulska 1984, 78, 90). The western side of the *Forum* was dominated by a 3.9m high monumental staircase. It had 18 steps

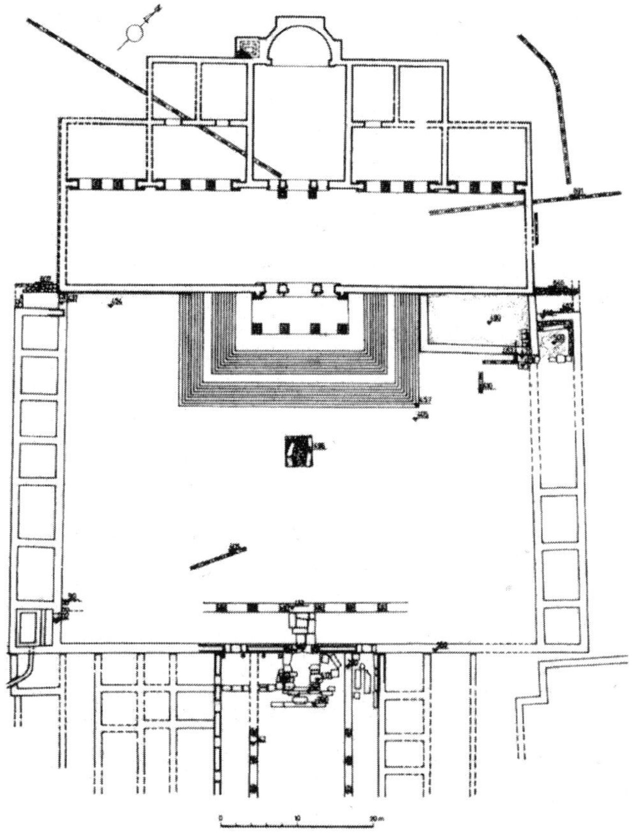

Figure 53. The Principia, *Camp of Diocletian (Gawlikowski 1984, annex VII).*

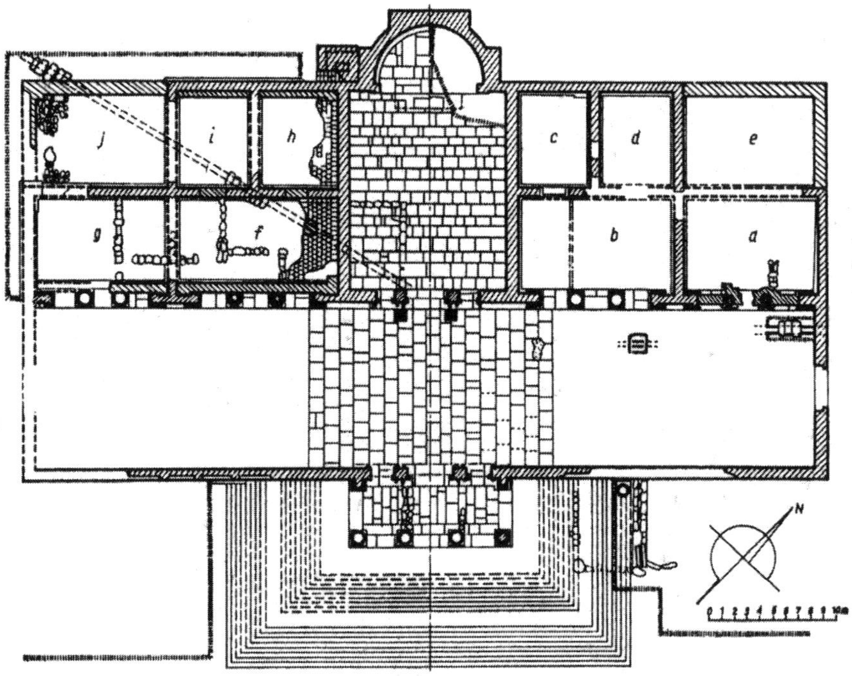

Figure 54. The eastern sector of the Principia *in its latest phase, Camp of Diocletian (Sadurska 1975, 117, fig. 3).*

separated by a 1m deep interval landing. The staircase would have terminated with a second landing 2.15m in depth; immediately on top of that would have stood a large paved platform (12.8 × 5.2m) with a four-columned portico (Gawlikowski 1984, 22–6).

A gate on top of this platform would have marked the entrance to the *Basilica*. This has three doorways, the central one larger and higher than the lateral ones (width 3.08m; height 6.5m against width 1.48m, 1.46m; height 2.95m). The decorative apparatus of this structure is particularly elaborate. The three entrances are surmounted by triangular pediments. Upon the pediments of the lateral doorways are two small niches. The architecture used for the erection of this structure was taken from at least four earlier buildings, possibly funerary temples, dated to the 2nd or beginning of the 3rd century (Gawlikowski 1984, 26–32).

The westernmost sector of the *Principia* consists of a rectangular cross-hall (*Basilica*) and, further west, two rows of rooms. It was installed upon an artificial mound about 4 m higher than the level of the *Forum* on the slope of the hill (Gawlikowski 1984, 34–9). The cross-hall is 60 × 11.9m and is paved with beaten earth with the exception of a raised flagging orientated east to west and connecting the entrance to the *Basilica* with that of the Temple of the Standards. This is accessible through a triple entrance. The central doorway was surmounted by a lintel that would have borne the foundation inscription of the *castra*. It was flanked by two pedestals that would have supported the statues of the emperors. The lateral entrances were surmounted by niches.

The Temple of the Standards (*Aedes*) is a rectangular hall in axis with the *Via Praetoria* and 11.9 × 14.5m in size (Fig. 55). It ended to the east with a semi-circular apse roofed by a semi-dome. The semi-circular area is raised from the rest of the structure to about 0.85m and

Figure 55. Temple of the Standards (Browning archive. Courtesy of the Palestine Exploration Fund) (cat. n. 69).

is accessed through a wide arch. The walls of the apse were embellished with three niches, each with triangular pediments. Flanking the *Aedes* to the south is a rectangular tower (2.6 × 3.2m; preserved height 10.3m), whose function is unknown. To the east and west of the Temple of the Standards are two rows of rooms which run parallel to the cross-hall. Excavations have revealed that they underwent two main phases of development. In the first, two symmetric rectangular units, interpreted as *scholae*, flanked the *Aedes*. They had the same size as the Temple of the Standards and were divided internally with a large room at the front and two smaller units at the back. The front room was entered through the cross-hall through two columns *in antis*. Two smaller symmetrical rooms stand further to the south and north. After a devastating fire the *Principia* were rearranged, but the function of the rooms was probably maintained. The whole compound was enlarged to the southwest and northeast and the inner arrangement of the rooms underwent important alteration (Gawlikowski 1984, 17–45). The chronology of this second phase has been pinpointed to the 6th century (Kowalski 1994, 201).

The *Principia* of the Camp of Diocletian has been the object of a number of wide-ranging studies aimed at a better understanding of its position in the framework of Roman military architecture (Fellmann 1958, 166; 1976, 180–9; Gawlikowski 1984, 62–69; Lenoir 2011, 340–1). Fellmann includes the building in a specific *forumtypus* (variant III) which developed in the 1st century and later became standardised and widely adopted. The type is characterised by an open court with flanking rooms, a cross-hall and one or two rows of rooms immediately behind it (Fellmann 1958, 166). Due to the widespread adoption of the type, parallels for the *Principia* of the Camp of Diocletian are numerous. One of the most fitting is offered by the earlier fort of *Lambaesis*, base of the *Legio III Augusta* (Gawlikowski 1984, 64–5). The north, east, and west sides of its open court (63.5 × 37.4m) are porticoed and are provided with a row of rooms each. The cross-hall was accessible through two staircases (not just one as in Palmyra) at the end of the east and west porticoes. It was divided into three aisles by two rows of columns. Through the cross-hall it was possible to access three rows of rooms along its south, east, and west sides. The room situated at the centre of the south side is the Temple of the Standards. As in Palmyra, the cross-hall and the group of rooms immediately behind it are on a higher level (about 3m) than the open court. The total surface covered by the *Principia* is impressive (9375m^2), making it one of the largest buildings of this kind in the empire (Lenoir 2011, 330–1).

Despite these similarities, however, the two *Principia* differ in a number of features. The compound of Palmyra does not stand at the centre of the Camp of Diocletian as in most forts and fortlets in Tripolitania and Numidia (Lenoir 2011, 343), but is off-centred. This position is rare but not unknown. Fellmann (1976, 180–3) cites parallels from Lympne in Britain, Luxor in Egypt, and *Iatrus* in *Moesia Secunda*. To these one could add the case of *Castellum Dimmidi* (Massʿad), Numidia (end of the 2nd century – Lenoir 2011, 223–7) and the aforementioned Najʿ al-Ḥajar in Egypt (Wareth and Zignani 1992). The forum of Palmyra is also flanked by *armamentaria* only on the north and south sides, making it more similar to the *principia* at the forts of *Gholaia* in Tripolitania or *Gemellae* in Numidia (Lenoir 2011, 152–60; 212–16). The three aisled cross-hall of the *Principia* of *Lambaesis* is an extraordinary occurrence not present in Palmyra. Further parallels from Dura Europos (Rostovtzeff 1934, pl. 3) and al-Lajjūn (Lain and Parker 2006) confirm Fellmann's conclusion that the standard plan of this *forumtypus* remained in widespread use until the 4th century. Yet, the Camp of Diocletian shows a clear tendency toward monumentality and decorative richness that is unparalleled in other military compounds and deserves further investigation.

The role of the Camp of Diocletian in the defensive system of the eastern frontier

The general layout of the Tetrarchic forts along the Syrian section of the eastern frontier, in which pragmatism in construction is predominant, has already been discussed in Chapter 1 (see above, pp. 8–9). The Camp of Diocletian stands significantly a part from these forts not only for its size (6.4ha, including undeveloped land) but generally for its ostentatious appearance. A deliberate tendency toward monumentality and decorative richness is expressed through its architecture. This is mostly true of the *Principia*, but it clearly applies to other features of the fortress. The *Porta Praetoria* presents a good example. Triple entrance gateways in themselves are extraordinary occurrences in the Near East. They are attested only in two other cities: *Amida* (Diyarbakır) and al-Ruṣāfa (Crow 2007, 446). The only known military installation with triple entrance gateways is the Tetrarchic fort of al-Lajjūn, modern Jordan, base of the *Legio IV Martia* (*Not. Dig., Or.*, 37.12). The fort had two triple entrance gateways, the *Porta Praetoria* and the *Porta Principalis Sinistra*. The other two gates (*Porta Principalis Dextra* and *Porta Decumana*) are provided with only a single portal. The *Porta Principalis Sinistra* (so-called 'North Gate') is the best preserved and would have been the most frequented entrance to the compound for 'the most official, commercial, and recreational traffic' coming from the cities of the agricultural plateau to the west of the fort (De Vries *et al.* 2006, 198). It is surely for this reason that this access was monumentalised with a triple access, to 'convey a message of military force and Imperial strength' (De Vries *et al.* 2006, 199). The monumentality of this gate would have been assured by two U-shaped towers flanking the entrance. Despite the Praetorian Gate of Palmyra lacking lateral projecting towers, it must have looked equally impressive. The priority of the architects was here given not to construct an unbreachable gate, but to impress whoever was about to pass through it. In stark contrast with the plain façade of the North Gate at al-Lajjūn, that of Palmyra is architecturally decorated and gives onto a rear squared courtyard which opens toward the *Via Praetoria* with two columns *in antis* (Gawlikowski 1976a, 276). This was certainly not meant to have any defensive purpose (vantage court) as the passage giving onto the *Via Praetoria* was open and not closed with a counter door. The porticoed street grid is a more frequent occurrence in near-eastern forts and, together with *gromae*, finds its origin in urban architecture (Fellmann 1976, 180; Bejor 1999). Al-Lajjūn represents again a good parallel with Palmyra. In this site an arched portico was uncovered in a stretch of the southern side of the *Via Praetoria*, but it is likely that a second portico also ran along the northern side (Parker 2006, 116–17).

The *Principia* represents the triumph of the architectural programme permeated by this tendency toward monumentality. To reach the focal point of the complex from the *Via Praetoria* (the Temple of the Standards) visitors had to cross two triple-accessed adorned gates which are nothing but theatrical façades around 1m thick (Grande Porte: 0.7m – Michalowski 1963a, 34; access to the cross-hall: 1.05m – Gawlikowski 1984, 24, fig. 3). They should also have been ready to climb two monumental staircases to reach a level around 4m higher than that of the *Porta Praetoria*. The cross-hall and the rows of rooms to the west are located on top of an artificial rectangular mound, *c.* 60 × 12m containing about 2000 cubic metres of rubble and soil (Gawlikowski 1984, 13) deliberately created to raise this part of the *Principia* from the rest of the fortress. This spectacular architectural solution has no parallel whatever in the Near East. A good (but earlier) comparison can only be found in northern Africa, the aforementioned *Principia* of the fort of *Lambaesis*.

The impressive architecture of the Camp of Diocletian is an element that has barely attracted the attention of scholars. Fellmann (1976, 186) believes that the monumental *Principia* would reflect the importance '*de l'armée romaine et de son influence decisive sur le gouvernement de l'empire à cette époque*'. Yet, he fails to explain why this large-scale monumentality occurs only in the Camp of Diocletian and nowhere else along the eastern frontier. Lenoir has recently stressed the uniqueness of the architectural apparatus of the *Principia* and suggested that the Camp of Diocletian might have served as the headquarters of the whole frontier defensive system. The same role, he says, had been fulfilled by the fort of Dura Europos along the Euphrates in the 3rd century (Lenoir 2010, 158). This, we believe, is a plausible theory which might also explain the necessity to deploy here one of the two legions of the province.

Yet, it is possible to push this conclusion further. The theatrical architecture of the Camp of Diocletian was clearly not conceived to please the soldiers already garrisoned in the fortress. Men of the *Legio IV Martia* were at ease even in the less impressive, but still monumental, fort of al-Lajjūn. It is thus legitimate to ask ourselves whether this architecture made to impress was instrumental in conveying a message of strength to the eyes of occasional visitors, such as chiefs of nomadic tribes willing to interact with the Roman military power and not well-acquainted with monumentally-scaled buildings.[2] Written sources inform us that the relations of Rome with local nomadic tribes were extremely volatile (Lewin 2007, 244–55). Changes of alliance were common and treaties were frequently broken (Isaac 1997, 447–51). It is possible that Palmyra served as one of the mediating points between the Romans and local *scenitae*, a role that, after all, it had already assumed before the Zenobian collapse and would be inherited in the 6th century by the pilgrimage centre of al-Ruṣāfa (Fowden 1999, 148–72, with further bibliography). Palmyra, which according to Procopius was 'well situated across the track of the hostile Saracens' would certainly have suited this role (Proc., *Aed.*, 2.11, 10–12; tr. Dewing 1961, 177). Admittedly, direct evidence to support interaction between Rome and the local nomadic element in Palmyra is almost absent. The only written evidence is very late but might be informative of earlier diplomatic relations. In 630, the body of St Anastasius was brought back to Jerusalem from Dastagerd via Palmyra (*Anas. Per.*, 1.102–4). The Dastagerd–Palmyra portage was led by a Saracen phylarch whose role was to protect the holy man and his precious luggage. Having reached Palmyra, the monk proceeded to *Arados* (Arwād) and then Tyre. The choice of Palmyra was presumably not casual and suggests the existence of a well-trodden track between the east and west in the 7th century.

Conclusions

The installation of the *Legio I Illyricorum* marked a shift in the main role of Palmyra, which was transformed from a caravan city to a military stronghold. This role was maintained throughout Late Antiquity, although written sources suggest that the general peaceful condition of the 5th century might have resulted in the reduction of the city's military strength. In the first half of the 6th century, the city served as the base for the backbone of the army under the control of one of the two *duces* of *Phoenicia*. Written sources have helped define the pivotal role of the city in the defence of the eastern frontier. The hypothesis that Palmyra in Late Antiquity 'sunk into … a trifling fortress', using Gibbon's words (Gibbon 1831, 117), stands on a very fragile ground. The Camp of Diocletian represents undoubtedly one of the most ambitious military project ever realised along the eastern frontier during the Tetrarchy. Although it was built mostly by adopting reused building material, the monumental pretentiousness of this compound is unrivalled in the panorama of Late Antique military architecture. A large, specialised workforce under the command of capable hands and extensive funding must have been required to clear the area from pre-existing monumental structures, lay new streets, create the artificial mound where the *Principia* would have stand, and move and reassemble reused architecture of heavy tonnage for the construction of new buildings. The completion of this impressive compound must have been perceived as an achievement at the time, rightly deserving to be celebrated in an inscription. The reasons behind the monumentality of the Camp of Diocletian has animated very little debate. It is possible, as suggested by Lenoir, that this reflects the role played by Palmyra as headquarters of the frontier defensive system. The architectural pretentiousness of the fortress might have been functional to impress occasional visitors willing to interact with the Roman authority. The fall of Palmyra in 272 must have shaken the fragile political balance of local nomadic societies. The construction of the Camp of Diocletian can, thus, be read as a conscious demonstration of power and an attempt to reassess the Roman authority in this area.

Notes

1 I am grateful to Eberhard Sauer for this suggestion.

2 I am grateful to Jim Crow for this suggestion.

Chapter 6

The city walls

The limits of the city in Late Antiquity and the Early Islamic period were imposed by the course of its circuit wall, known in modern literature with the name of 'Wall of Diocletian'. Nowadays this imposing fortification represents, together with the Camp of Diocletian, the most important physical legacy of the post-Roman city; since its dimensions mark considerably the topography of the ancient site, the ramparts have attracted the attentions of travellers and scholars alike since the late 17th century. The dating of this feature is still hotly debated. If it seems certain that the circuit wall remained in use throughout Late Antiquity, there are still doubts on the chronology of its construction and numerous renovations. The existence of the city wall is strictly linked with that of the city itself. The destructions of the city wall reported by written sources at the end of the Umayyad period, eventually coincided with the beginning of a decline of the city's fortune, which gradually shrank within the limits of the *temenos* of the Sanctuary of Bēl. A re-analysis of the written sources and the archaeological evidence may contribute to disentangle the issue on its chronology.

A still unresolved case: the chronology of the so-called 'Wall of Diocletian'

Seen from the air, the circuit wall of Palmyra has roughly the shape of half a circle with an appendix represented by a section surrounding the Camp of Diocletian. Von Gerkan (1935, 27) imaginatively describes it as having approximately the shape of the snout of a dolphin whose torso resembles the city itself. Its irregular course is the result of the necessity to avoid natural features as well as the choice of including within the urban perimeter specific buildings or sensible strategic areas. The wall was defended by two sets of projecting towers: buttress towers are normally bonded with the curtain wall, while U-shaped towers abut it and are consequently later in construction. Pre-existing structures (mostly tombs) are also integrated into the wall; there is little doubt that these were converted into defensive towers when the wall was constructed. Monumental gates and small posterns are located all along its circuit, providing easy access to the settlement from all sides.

Much has been written on the chronology of this defensive system based on the physical relations between the wall and the perimeter of the classical and Late Antique settlement, while only few contributions have advanced conclusions based on a systematic analysis of the building techniques. The first dating of the urban circuit was put forward by Wood (1753, 39), who believed the ramparts to be Justinianic in date. This conclusion would be taken as valid by Gabriel (1926, 74).

The first detailed analysis of the remains of the wall was undertaken by Fick (1932) in the early 20th century. On the basis of Fick's conclusion and a field survey, von Gerkan (1935) advanced the hypothesis that the wall was built hurriedly by Zenobia to stop the Aurelianic assault of 272. The theory of the Zenobian construction received general consensus among scholars until the mid-20th century; it was welcomed positively by Schlumberger (1935, 149–62), and later Starcky (1941, 24) and Seyrig (1950, 240–2). Seyrig went farther, hypothesising that the U-shaped towers were Justinianic additions to the ramparts. The association between the passage of Procopius and an inscription naming a Platanius Serenianus, *vir perfectissimus*, *dux Orientis* is the main evidence advanced in support of his conclusions.

By the beginning of the 1950s von Gerkan's hypothesis had already been widely accepted. In essence, however, was a new theory according to which the city wall would have been constructed as part of the Tetrarchic restorations of the city (Van Berchem 1954, 258, n. 1; Duval 1946, 55, n. 2; Starcky 1949, 43, n. 3). This conclusion was drawn by van Berchem in 1954; the arguments of this scholar in support of this dating mostly arose from an analysis of written sources:

> *la ville fut mise à sac, et l'arrêt complet de la civilisation palmyrénienne, observable dans les nécropoles, prouve que la population fut, sinon totalement éliminée, du moins réduite à ses éléments les plus misérables. L'érection du rempart a, de toute évidence, suivi la catastrophe*'. (Van Berchem 1954, 259)

According to van Berchem, the Zenobian city was much extended and limited by another wall whose remains are still visible to the south of the Wādī al-Qubūr. His theory became widely popular and within a decade it was generally accepted by the scientific community.

This prevailing model, however, has recently been questioned on the basis of the examination of the building techniques. Zanini (1995) believes that the city wall was the result of at least three building interventions. A first wall would have been constructed by Zenobia and later destroyed by Aurelian. At a later stage, the Camp of Diocletian was fortified. Yet, the city remained without ramparts until the reign of Justinian. The emperor would rebuild the wall and add U-shaped towers. Recently, Juchniewicz (2013) has argued that the pre-existing city wall was built under Aurelian by the *Legio I Illyricorum* to prevent the pillaging of the city, and that, on the basis of a study of the building techniques, the chronology of the U-shaped towers is Tetrarchic and not Justinianic (see also Intagliata 2017b). The debate on Palmyra's inner wall, thus, remains open. A number of observations can still be put forward on the basis of the latest studies and a fresh re-examination of the written sources and the archaeological evidence.

Written sources

The contribution that the analysis of written sources has had in the hotly debated chronology of the ramparts has been remarkable, but has dimmed the importance of a thorough examination of the archaeological remains. As a matter of fact, archaeological excavations along the urban circuit has seldom been conducted and scientific studies on the evidence still in place, for example mortar, are non-existent. The study of Palmyra's urban circuit must start from a careful and critical re-examination of the information contained in written sources as it is evident, and must be stressed at this early stage, that the descriptions of the walls given by ancient authors are often misleading, contradictory, and fail to provide any clue at all to their chronology.

Historia Augusta, Vita Aureliani (2.26, 4) describes the Palmyra's fortifications in a letter supposedly written by Aurelian to Mucapor. In it, the emperor tries to justify the long time spent in the siege of the settlement:

> 'It cannot be told what a store of arrows is here, what great preparations for war, what a store of spears and of stones; there is no section of the wall that is not held by two or three engines of war, and their machines can even hurl fire'. (tr. Dodgeon and Lieu 1991, 96)

Shorter and less detailed is a passage by Zosimus (*Hist. Nov.*, 1.54), in which it is simply reported how, 'the people of Palmyra jeered that it [the city] could not be taken' (tr. Buchanam and Davis 1967, 32–3). Leaving aside the problem of the reliability of these texts (Hartmann 2001, 379–82), it is evident that the passages do not state either that the wall was constructed by Zenobia or that the wall stormed by the Aurelianic troops was actually the inner urban circuit.

Yet, should we decide to consider these two conclusions as valid, we would still face a number of issues. Specifically, it would remain puzzling how a 2.50m thick wall provided with 2.50m projecting buttress towers would have been considered sufficient to stop an assault by a Roman army and allies allegedly led by the emperor himself. As a matter of fact, Palmyra's buttress towers would have hardly been able to accommodate any pieces of artillery. In the latter half of the 4th century, Vegetius (*Epit.*, 4.29) reports the existence of two types of torsion siege engines used in defending city walls, namely the *ballista*, a bolt-firing, two-arm catapult, and the onager, a one-arm, stone-throwing engine, often known as *tormentum muralium* (Marsden 1969, 197; 1971, 245, n. 1). Ammianus (*Res Gest.,* 24.4, 1–7) describes their use in his account of Julian's campaign in the Near East and later Procopius (*Bell.*, 5.21, 14–19) reports their being used by Belisarius in Rome against the Goths' attack of 537. Both were large pieces of artillery of heavy calibre and particularly difficult to move, Ammianus (*Res Gest.*, 19.7, 6–7) informatively uses the words *ars difficillima* referring to the task of moving four *onagri* during the siege of *Amida* in 359 (Marsden 1971, 264). Furthermore, they would have required a large, specialised crew (Marsden 1969, 191–198). At least eight men were necessary to work an onager, while a crew of expert *ballistarii* might have been more numerous.Vegetius (*Epit.*, 2.25) reports that, in the *antiqua legio*, eleven men were needed to arm a *carrioballista* (ballista mounted on a wagon or with four wheels) and aim it. We are also informed that the recoils of machine of such size could inflict serious damage to the towers in which they were installed (Amm. Marc., *Res Gest.*, 23.4, 5). The space of about 5m^2 provided by the towers in Palmyra would certainly not have been sufficient to set up these heavy engines and give their crew enough room to move. One should also add to the count the presence of archers on the towers, whose mobility would have been necessary to provide enfilading fire at targets at closer range than that of heavy artillery (Marsden 1969, 117).

Written sources inform that the ramparts of Palmyra remained in use throughout the 4th and 5th century. In the *Life of Alexander the Akoimētes*, it is recounted that the inhabitants of Palmyra 'closed the gates of the city' at the approach of the holy man and his group (*Alex. Akoim.*, 35). According to Procopius (*Aed.*, 2.11, 10–12), the city was strengthened 'with defences which defy description' under Justinian. As already seen, this much discussed passage has been taken by Starcky and others as proof of a renovation of the city wall by the emperor, and in particular the addition of U-shaped towers. In his work, Procopius, however, does not specify the exact nature of these defences as he does, for instance, in describing the re-fortification of the city of *Dara* (Croke and Crow 1983, 151; Whitby 1986, 752–3). Both the use of a formulaic sentence, extremely common in his accounts (Roques 2011, 112, n. 46; 205, n. 151; Gregory 1995, 18–19), and the conciseness of the passage cast doubt on the reliability of this author, who probably never visited Palmyra (Zanini 1995, 54). Indeed, it has already been noted on numerous occasions that Procopius' panegyric work should be treated with reservation (see, for instance, Barnea 1960; Croke and Crow 1983). Specifically, it has been stressed that the author tends to attribute works that had been carried out by Anastasius and Justin I to Justinian (Croke and Crow 1983, 146; see, for instance, al-Ruṣāfa, Karnapp 1976, 51–3, and *Dara et al.* 1983; *contra* Whitby 1986, 771–2).

It is notable that Malalas (*Chr.*, 17.2) further mentions the Justinianic renovation to the city. The writer, who seems to be better informed than Procopius, recounts how:

> the emperor appointed an Armenian named Patrikios as *comes Orientis* in Antioch. He gave him a large sum of money with instructions to go and reconstruct the city in *Phoenice* on the *limes*, known as Palmyra, and its churches and public baths. He ordered a *numerus* of soldiers to be stationed there with the *limitanei*, and also the *dux* of Emesa, to protect the Roman territories and Jerusalem. (tr. Jeffrey *et al.* 1986, 245)

Interestingly, in Malalas (and later Theophanes) the strengthening of the ramparts of the city is not mentioned at all. This is certainly not to be interpreted as a careless omission of the author. Malalas takes generally great care in recounting restorations of city walls. In reporting the reconstruction of *Silvan/Martyropolis* (Mayyāfāriqīn) a few lines later he specifies, for example, that the emperor 'constructed its walls and colonnades for they had fallen into ruin in the course of time, and transferred an eastern *numerus* there' (Mal., *Chr.*, 18.5, tr. Jeffrey *et al.* 1986, 246–7). In this case, both the texts of Malalas and Procopius agree on a Justinianic restoration of the ramparts (Gregory 1996, 69). Therefore, it seems unreasonable to conclude that Malalas would have omitted reporting the restoration of the city walls in Palmyra, especially if they would have 'defied description' as Procopius claims.

As far as later written sources are concerned, Palmyra's city wall is frequently mentioned in the accounts of the conquest of the city by Khālid b. al-Walīd in 634. Undoubtedly, most of these sources are written much later than the events narrated and several of them certainly contain fictional information. Even so, the large amount of sources that refer to Palmyra's ramparts leaves us in little doubt that Palmyra's city wall was still standing in the Early Islamic period. During the Islamic takeover, Palmyrene fortification (or the action of the inhabitants to fortify themselves) is mentioned in al-Ṭabarī (*Tā'rīkh,* 4.2109), al-Balādhurī (*Futūḥ,* 111–12), al-Ya'qūbī (*Tā'rīkh*, 2.134), Yāqūt (*Mu'jam*, 1.832), al-Wāqidī (*al-Maghāzī*, 1.44), and Ibn A'tham al-Kūfī (*Kitāb*, 1.140–2). The accounts of al-Ṭabarī, al-Balādhurī, and al-Ya'qūbī are devoid of substantial detail. Yāqūt reports the frustration of the general for not being able to penetrate Palmyra's defences. In the account of the conquest of the city by al-Wāqidī, the author reports a speech allegedly given by the governor of the city to the inhabitants. The man is confident that the besiegers will never be able to take the city as '[the] fortification is impregnable; there is no way through it for anyone'. Ibn A'tham al-Kūfī too reports the frustration of the general at the impossibility of penetrating the city's fortifications: 'when the next day came, he [Khālid b. al-Walīd] rode out leading some of his companions, and moved around the city [trying to find a weak point], but Khālid could not find any strategem against them owing to the strength of the walls …'. It seems likely, then, that the city was at the time still sufficiently fortified to resist to the Islamic threat.

The city wall reported by Arabic sources has to be identified with the Late Antique urban circuit that surrounded the latest phase of development of the settlement before its 10th century reduction. Later repairs are notable along the whole course of the circuit wall and, although not exactly datable, they suggest the necessity of maintaining functional the ramparts over a long time. Not surprisingly, Palmyra's ramparts represented to Khālid b. al-Walīd a major obstacle to subjugating the city. Relying on al-Balādhurī's and al-Ṭabarī's claims, his army must have been very small, counting about 500–800 men (al-Balādhurī, *Futūḥ*, 110; al-Ṭabarī, *Tā'rīkh*, 4.2108–2110, referenced in Donner 1981, 126, 314 n. 185; other sources mentioned by Donner provide greater numbers).

The Late Antique ramparts of the city were still standing in 744, when al-Walīd b. Yazīd was advised to flee to Palmyra because the city was well-fortified (al-Ṭabarī, *Tā'rīkh*, 9.1796; Ibn 'Asākir, *Tā'rīkh*, 63.337–8). Finally, the ramparts are said to have been destroyed at the end of the Umayyad dynasty after Palmyra had revolted against Marwān b. Muḥammad (Yāqūt, *Mu'jam*, 1.829; al-Ṭabarī, *Tā'rīkh*, 9.1895–6; al-Hamadānī, *al-Iklīl*, 124; Ibn al-Faqīh, *Mukhtaṣar*, 110; Ibn al-Shiḥna, *al-Durr al-Muntakhab*, 275–6). All sources reporting the episode recount that the demolition uncovered the tomb of a woman richly adorned with a large number of robes and jewellery. Among her tresses was a sheet of gold (or copper) bearing the inscription, 'In the name of Allāh, I am Tadmur b. Ḥassān. Allāh may humiliate whoever enters in my house' (the text of the alleged inscription varies; this is from Ibn al-Faqīh, *Mukhtaṣar*, 110). It was the profanation of this tomb that, according to written sources, caused Marwān b. Muḥammad to be killed by 'Abd Allāh b. 'Ali and 'Āmir b. Ismā'yl al-Ḥārithi al-Musālī (al-Hamadānī, *al-Iklīl,* 124; Ibn al-Faqīh, *Mukhtaṣar*, 110; Yāqūt, *Mu'jam*, 1.829).

Relying on most of the Arabic writers, the destruction of Palmyra's wall must have been substantial. Al-Hamadāni (*al-Iklīl*, 124) reports that the discovery of the tomb of Tadmur b. Ḥassān was made after the city wall had been destroyed and 'at the base of the wall'. The same is reported by the other sources with very little variation (Ibn al-Faqīh, *Mukhtaṣar*, 110; Yāqūt, *Muʿjam*, 1.829; Ibn al-Shiḥna, *al-Durr al-Muntakhab*, 275–6). The inclusion of pre-existing tombs into the city wall is particularly common and, thus, does not surprise (Bounni 1970–1971). Yet, archaeological evidence brought to light so far does not seem to confirm this version of events. The city wall is in general still clearly visible along its entire course, suggesting that the narration of the episode has perhaps been exaggerated. As a matter of fact, some years later, the city could resist the attack of Bassām b. Ibrāhīm, who was sent by ʿAbd Allāh b. ʿAlī to capture Abū Muḥammad al-Sufyānī. Again in that occasion, the walls are said to have been damaged (Genequand 2012, 46 with further references).

Description of the remains

Due to the doubtful reliability of written sources, the systematic examination of the urban circuit cannot ignore a close examination of its remains. Particularly useful for this task are the results of the surveys carried out by an Italian team from Sapienza, Università di Roma at the end of the 1980s. The surveys were conducted within the framework of a wider project founded by Centro Nazionale delle Ricerche that aimed at a thorough photographic documentation of Byzantine structures in the Levant. The team was directed by Fernanda de' Maffei, Professor of Byzantine Art at La Sapienza from 1973 to 1990, and included Italo Furlan, Antonio Iacobini, Andrea Paribeni, and Enrico Zanini (Zanini 1995, 80, n. 6). Investigations in Palmyra focussed principally on the city wall in 1987 and 1990 and produced an impressive amount of photographic material. These were later integrated into the Centro di Documentazione di Storia dell'Arte Bizantina, an archive initiated in 1996 thanks to the efforts of Mara Bonfioli and now under the care of Alessandra Guiglia and Antonio Iacobini (Iacobini 2012; Paribeni 2012; Zanini 2012). The accurate geo-location of these photographs with the help of the topographic work of Schnädelbach (2010) allows a detailed reconstruction of the course of the wall for *c.* 3.2km. The remains photographed in these surveys can be grouped in three sections. The northern one runs from the Sanctuary of Bēl to the Camp of Diocletian. The western section surrounds this fortress and stretches further to the west to protect the peak of the hill. The southern section runs parallel to the Wādī al-Qubūr, which provides an additional natural defence for the settlement.

The northern section

The northern section, between towers [A308] and [A201], is about 1.5km in length (Fig. 56). Its remains are certainly the most visible of the whole urban circuit. It underwent considerable restorations from the 1980s until recently; as a consequence, the legibility of its structure has partly been obscured (see e.g., [A212] in Juchniewicz *et al.* 2010, fig. 24). In the photographs taken by Crouch (1975a, 27, fig. 18.a) at the beginning of the 1970s, it appears still partly covered in debris. Yet, already by the time of de' Maffei's visit, about 20 years later, its entire course was clearly visible. Overall, the curtain wall survives in good condition with the exception of the sector between tower [A301] and

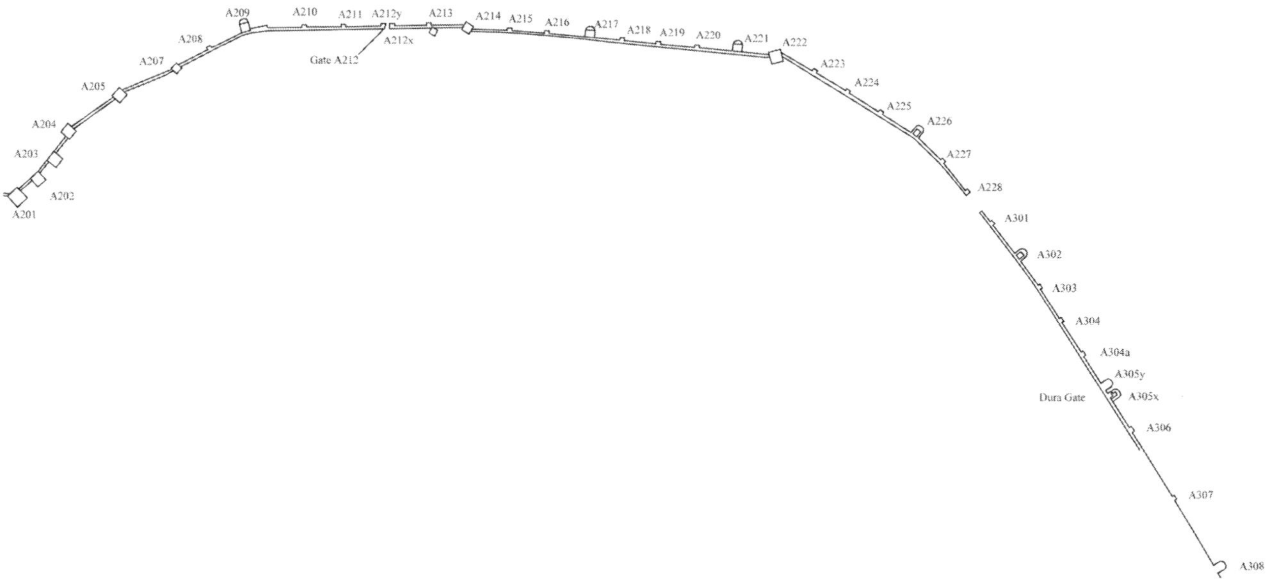

Figure 56. Northern section of the city wall, location of towers and gates (redrawn after Schnädelbach 2010).

[A228], which was destroyed for the construction of the main road leading to the site. The course of the wall located in the oasis is obliterated by a modern pathway leading to private orchards and gardens that was laid on top of it in modern days. The section includes 22 buttress towers, eight U-shaped towers, and at least 11 pre-existing structures incorporated in the curtain wall. Ten of these structures are tower tombs, while one remains unidentified. Two gates with U-shaped and buttress flanking towers, provided the main access to the settlement; two additional openings, later walled up and devoid of any defensive structures, are located next to towers (between [A222] and [A221], and between [A207] and [A205]).

Buttress towers are normally bonded with the curtain wall and do not survive for more than four courses. Two exceptions are the towers flanking the opening [A212], which clearly abut the curtain wall and, therefore, are later than it. U-shaped towers seem to be better preserved; they have been the object of extensive restoration works throughout the last three decades. They project for 10–11m and are normally 8–9m in width. Their ground floor is provided with an inner chamber that was brick vaulted and accessible via an opening located either in their east or west sides; therefore, the ground chamber could not be accessed directly from the city. A second floor was reachable by an inner staircase that in most cases remains well-preserved. Three narrow, splayed windows on the north, west, and east sides of each tower would have provided light for the ground chamber. Unlike buttress towers, which are normally located at intervals of 30m, the location of U-shaped towers is less regular. Normally, there are three buttress towers at interval between U-shaped towers (*c.* 120m), but this is not always the case.

Beside buttress and U-shaped towers, pre-existing buildings were incorporated in the structure of the ramparts. Most of these are located in the westernmost stretch of this section of the wall, the one nearest to the Camp of Diocletian, and consist of monumental tombs. The absence of other defensive structures in this section of the wall would suggest that these buildings were converted to function as defensive towers. With the exception of tower [A201], whose structure is still to some extent fairly legible, normally tombs do not survive for more than four courses. Two of them have recently been excavated by the Syrian authorities (al-As'ad 2013, 17–18). Tower [A222] has recently been interpreted as the *castellum aquae* of the northern aqueduct conveying water to the city from Biyār al-'Amī (Juchniewicz *et al.* 2010, 56; Juchniewicz and Żuchowska 2012, 68; see above, Chapter 1).

The western section

The western section of the city wall encompasses the Camp of Diocletian and runs from tower [A201] to tower [A101] for 0.75km (Fig. 57). It sits on the steep eastern slope of a hill. As for the northern section of the ramparts, the wall is about 2.5m thick on average. It would have included a total of 12 buttress towers, one postern, and four pre-existing structures, of which two are monumental tombs and the others remain unidentified. The curtain wall and the towers have never been the object of systematic restoration nor excavation. All the structures photographed appear to be in poor state of preservation but one ([A104]). A piercing between towers [A112] and [A111] provides an opening for a modern pathway leading to the *Principia* of the Camp of Diocletian.

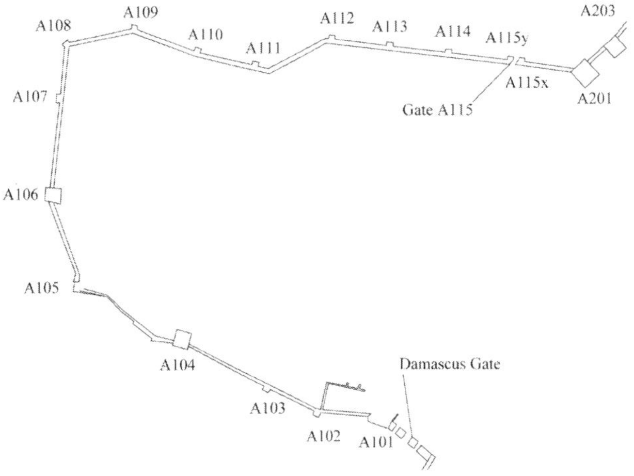

Figure 57. Western section of the city wall, location of towers and gates (redrawn after Schnädelbach 2010).

Buttress towers have standard shape and size and do not differ considerably from those located along the northern section of the ramparts. They project about 2.5m and are normally 4m in width. All but one are bonded with the curtain wall. The towers along the slope generally survive in fairly good condition up to six courses, while the outlines of those on top of the hill are barely visible on the ground. U-shaped towers are not present in this section of the wall possibly because of the steepness of the slope and because this area's not requiring any additional defence. The only access to the Camp of Diocletian through this section of the wall is represented by a simple opening, [A115], about 4m in width and flanked by two buttress towers. The importance of this postern to the understanding of the relative chronology of this section of the city wall is discussed below.

The southern section

The southern section of the city wall visible in the archival material runs parallel to the Wādī al-Qubūr for 0.85km, from the Damascus Gate to tower [A416] (Fig. 58). It has been the object of very little excavation or restoration and a great part of it is still covered by collapsed architecture and soil. This makes the analysis of its building techniques particularly challenging. The section visible in the photographs available includes 11 buttress towers, five U-shaped towers and three

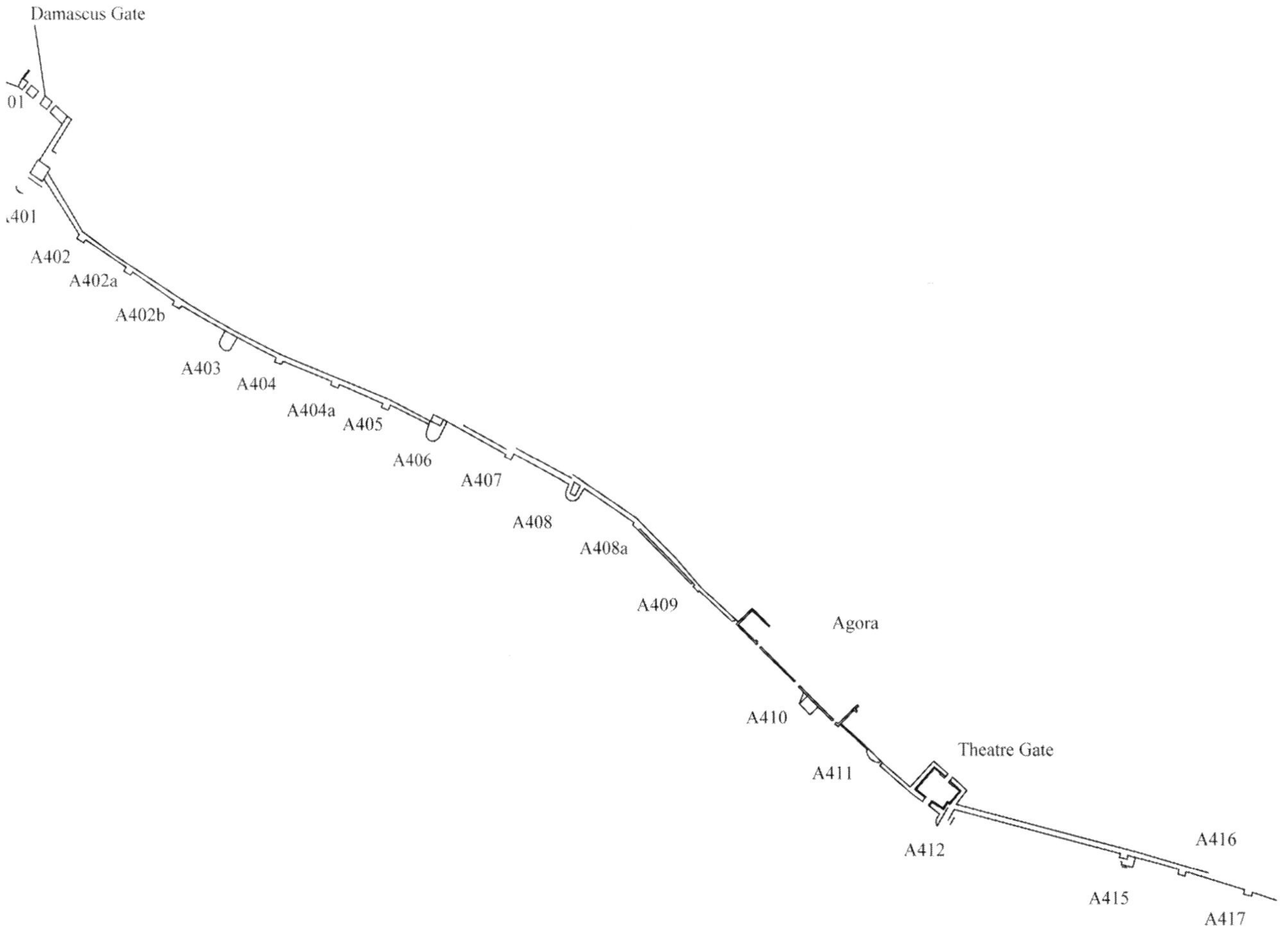

Figure 58. Southern section of the city wall, location of towers and gates (redrawn after Schnädelbach 2010).

pre-existing structures. Two monumental gates provide access to the city from the south, namely the Damascus Gate and the Theatre Gate, which is still partly standing.

The general state of preservation of the buttress towers is poor. Most of them are still covered in debris and only their rectangular outlines are recognisable on the ground. Only one, [A410], abutting the south wall of the *Agora*, survives up to six courses. On top of one of them, [A402a], is a pathway leading from Wādī al-Qubūr to the site. Despite their meagre preservation, there is little doubt that most of these towers are bonded with the curtain wall and are, therefore, contemporary with it. With the exception of the tower [A410], all of them appear to have an average width of 4.5m and project about 2.5m from the curtain wall. Like most of the towers in the northern and western sections, they are normally found every 30m, although in some cases the distance can be greater.

U-shaped towers are equally badly preserved or not entirely visible. With the exception of [A408], which is 12 courses high, they generally survive for no more than two or three courses. Tower [A408] is provided by a rectangular ground chamber that, unlike other similar towers of the northern section, has no access from the outside. It was entered through a stone staircase from the first floor of the tower. The towers are situated at irregular intervals of one to three buttress towers. Pre-existing structures include an imposing tower tomb in tower [A401], an unidentified structure integrated in tower [A406], and, as said above, the southern wall of the *Agora* and its Annexe.

Access to the settlements from the south was assured by two gates that stand out for their exceptional plan compared to other entrances to the city. This is probably not a coincidence since it was through these two gates that visitors from Damascus would have entered the city. The Damascus Gate, of which very little is visible on the ground, was a triple-entranced gate. It is certain that the gate was flanked to the east by the U-shaped tower [A401], but it is unknown whether another tower would have stood to the west of it. By contrast, the Theatre Gate is much better preserved. Its plan is more complex than the gates seen so far. It consists of a single entrance that opens into a rectangular vantage court and a second gate which makes use of a pre-existing honorary arch later strengthened for defensive purpose. The gate was originally flanked by two U-shaped towers, of which only that to the east is visible on the ground. The curtain wall has been very little excavated and is barely visible on the ground; it generally stands for no more than two courses. Yet, in a number of places, the wall survives at greater height, allowing speculation about the building technique in use. As for the rest of the ramparts, it has an average thickness of 2.5m.

An excavation was conducted in 1963–1964 along this section of the urban circuit. This resulted in the uncovering of towers [A417], [A418], and the stretch of curtain wall in between. The wall is reported to be cut at its mid-point by a postern that is about 1m wide (Bounni and Saliby 1965, 136, pl. 3). [A417] is a buttress tower bonded with the wall whose measurements on the Syrian plan (projection 2.5m; width 11m) do not match with those reported more recently by Schnädelbach (projection *c.* 2.5m; width 4.5m).

Building techniques

BT1–4

The photographs preserved at the Centro di Documentazione di Storia dell'Arte Bizantina prove to be enough detail to advance a number of preliminary observations, to be validated by autoptic analyses, on the building techniques in use for the construction of the ramparts. It is possible to identify at least four distinct building techniques (henceforth BT1–4), whose pattern is recurrent and easily distinguishable. Three of them (BT1, BT3, and BT4) have already been identified in a previous study by Zanini (1995, 68–70). An attentive scrutiny of their location allows to shed more light on their relative chronology and advance conclusions on the dating of the urban circuit.

The first building technique (BT1) is characterised by two faces of narrow blocks of greyish limestone laid normally in stretcher bond wihout mortar in the junctions (Fig. 59). The core of the wall is filled with small stones 0.1m to 0.2m in size mortared together. It is notable that the coursing is regular, although the height of each course varies. The wall constructed with this technique was certainly not built in a haste. The blocks have been carefully laid; joints are normally centred on the block in the course below. The result is a structure which from the outside resembles a rough pseudo-isodomic wall. At least from the photographs it seems that no reused material was employed for this building technique. BT1 is adopted extensively in the curtain wall and buttress towers throughout the whole course of the city wall. Exceptions are the stretch surrounding the Camp of Diocletian and the U-shaped towers in BT4. The wall constructed with this building technique survives up to two or three courses. An inscription from the re-used tomb [A207] provides a *terminus post quem* of 212 for walls of BT1 construction (*Inv.* 4, 2, n. 3). As already pointed out by Zanini (1995, 65), this characteristic form of *opus emplectum* is local and seems to have been in use in monumental civic buildings and, mostly, tombs.

Walls in BT2 masonry consist of narrow blocks of whitish limestone set typically in stretcher bond without mortar in the junctions and arranged in regular courses. The core of the wall is composed of small stones mortared together. From an examination of the photographic material available, it seems that no reused building material was employed for this building technique. BT2 masonry is visible immediately on top of courses in BT1 in the northern and southern sectors of the city wall (Fig. 59). By contrast, it seems not to have been in use in the curtain wall encompassing the Camp of Diocletian. The superimposition of the two building techniques is particularly notable in the northern section of the city wall (Figs 59, 65). This building tradition is technically associated with BT1 in its use of narrow blocks and a rubble core, but adopts a different limestone building material. The technical similarity between the two makes wonder whether these were built at the same time; interpreting this superimposition as an intentional choice to please the eye should be avoided, because in several places the coursing is irregular. It is possible that the builders simply decided to construct the wall using limestone from different quarries because of the lack of available building material.

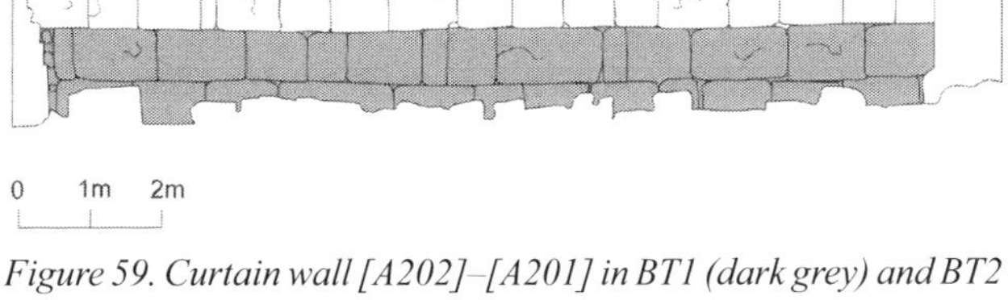

Figure 59. Curtain wall [A202]–[A201] in BT1 (dark grey) and BT2 (white) (drawn from cat. n. 870805a, Centro di Documentazione di Storia dell'Arte Bizantina, Sapienza Università di Roma).

Figure 60. Curtain wall [A201]–[A115x] in BT3 (cat. n. 901009a, Centro di Documentazione di Storia dell'Arte Bizantina, Sapienza Università di Roma).

Figure 61. Northern section, tower [A209] in BT4 (cat. n. 871219a, Centro di Documentazione di Storia dell'Arte Bizantina, Sapienza Università di Roma).

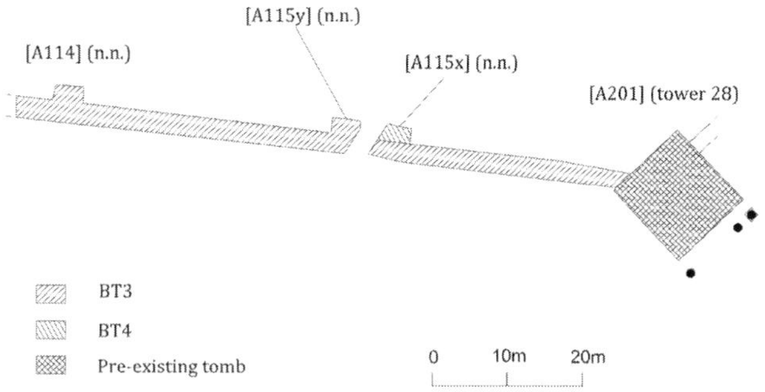

Figure 62. Northern access to the Camp of Diocletian (redrawn after Schnädelbach 2010).

The third building technique (BT3) adopted for the construction of the city wall makes use of small blocks of reddish limestone placed generally in stretcher bond without mortar in the junctions. The two faces of the wall are consolidated by a core of mortared small stones. The regularity of the coursing is broken by the inclusion of blocks of larger size, probably reused, whose edges are carefully cut to be integrated into the structure of the wall. The laying of the blocks is particularly accurate and must have required time and a specialised workforce. This building technique is adopted solely for the curtain walls and buttress towers surrounding the Camp of Diocletian. The only exception is constituted by the buttress tower [A115x] flanking the northern entrance to the fortress. which is built in BT4 and abuts the curtain wall.

The wall built in BT3 is not contemporary with the construction of the Camp of Diocletian (Figs 62–3). The northern gate of the fortress, [A115], is pierced through the curtain wall and is clearly later than it. The opening is in line with the *Via Principalis*. It is reasonable to assume that the postern was constructed to provide access to the *Via Principalis* and that the two features are contemporary. A Tetrarchic chronology for this opening is corroborated by an analysis of the building technique adopted for the buttress tower [A115x] to the east of the opening. The tower was added to the original ramparts to flank and protect the opening with which is contemporary. Its building technique is the same as that used for the U-shaped towers (BT4) and found parallels in Tetrarchic buildings from the Camp of Diocletian, as discussed below. This implies that BT3 is earlier than the Diocletianic restorations, but no exact dating of the ramparts can be postulated without a proper excavation of the remains.

The fourth building technique is the most diagnostic. Walls in BT4 are characterised by two faces made of courses of closely-fitting narrow blocks of whitish limestone laid with a header and stretcher technique and a core of mortared rubble (Figs 61, 64, 66). Blocks set at right-angles are normally located every 1–3 stretched blocks. This expedient was adopted to consolidate the structure and make the wall more resistant. Every three or four courses a single course of narrow, rectangular blocks is included, thus breaking the monotony of the structure of the wall. One of the main characteristics of this technique is that it makes abundant (if not solely) use of reused building material. As a consequence, it often happens that the coursing is not regular or the height of the courses varies. Two expedients are frequently adopted to compensate for this: 1. the edges of reused blocks are cut in order to be included more easily in the structure of the wall (as seen in BT3); 2. smaller blocks are added to create 'secondary' small courses and, thus, regularise the structure of the wall. BT4 is adopted for the U-shaped tower, tower [A115x] and the strengthening and extension to the south of the Theatre Gate. The same technique was in use for repairing several stretches of the curtain wall (in [A302]–[A301], [A228]–[A227], [A227]–[A226], and [A225]–[A224]). In the stretch comprised between towers [A408a] and [A409], in the southern section, a second wall was constructed with this technique against the pre-existing curtain.

Juchniewicz (2013, 196) has already pointed out briefly that this particular building technique finds two important parallels in Palmyra. The first comes from the warehouse of the Camp of Diocletian, whose west and north walls are built with this technique. In the *Principia* of the same fortress, the similarity is even more striking. Here courses of narrow blocks with the technique seen in the warehouse alternate courses of narrower rectangular blocks. The two expedients to compensate for the irregularity of the coursing are adopted extensively in the back wall of the building (see, for instance, Kolątaj 1975, fig. 5; Fig. 64). The original phase of the *Horreum* was found to be contemporary with the construction of the fortress. The dating of the *Principia* is proven both by archaeological evidence and, as seen above, an inscription on the lintel of the Temple of the Standards dating back to 293–303. A Tetrarchic dating for this building technique is also supported by other elements. Tower

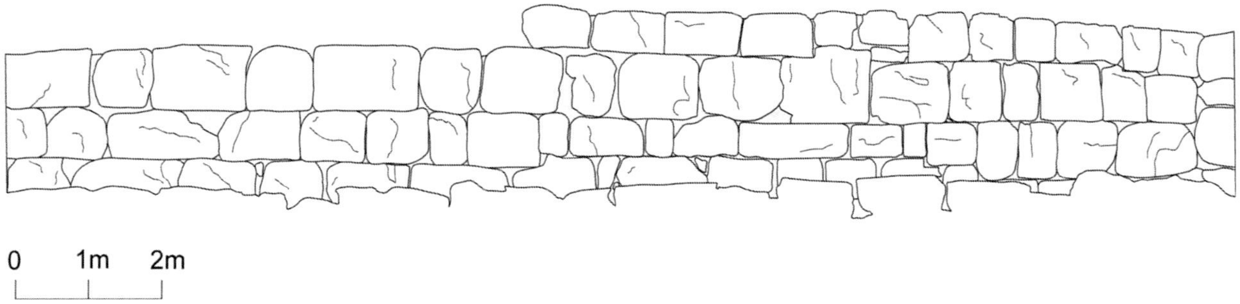

Figure 63. Curtain wall [A201]–[A115x] in BT3 (drawn from cat. n. 901008a, 901009a, Centro di Documentazione di Storia dell'Arte Bizantina, Sapienza Università di Roma).

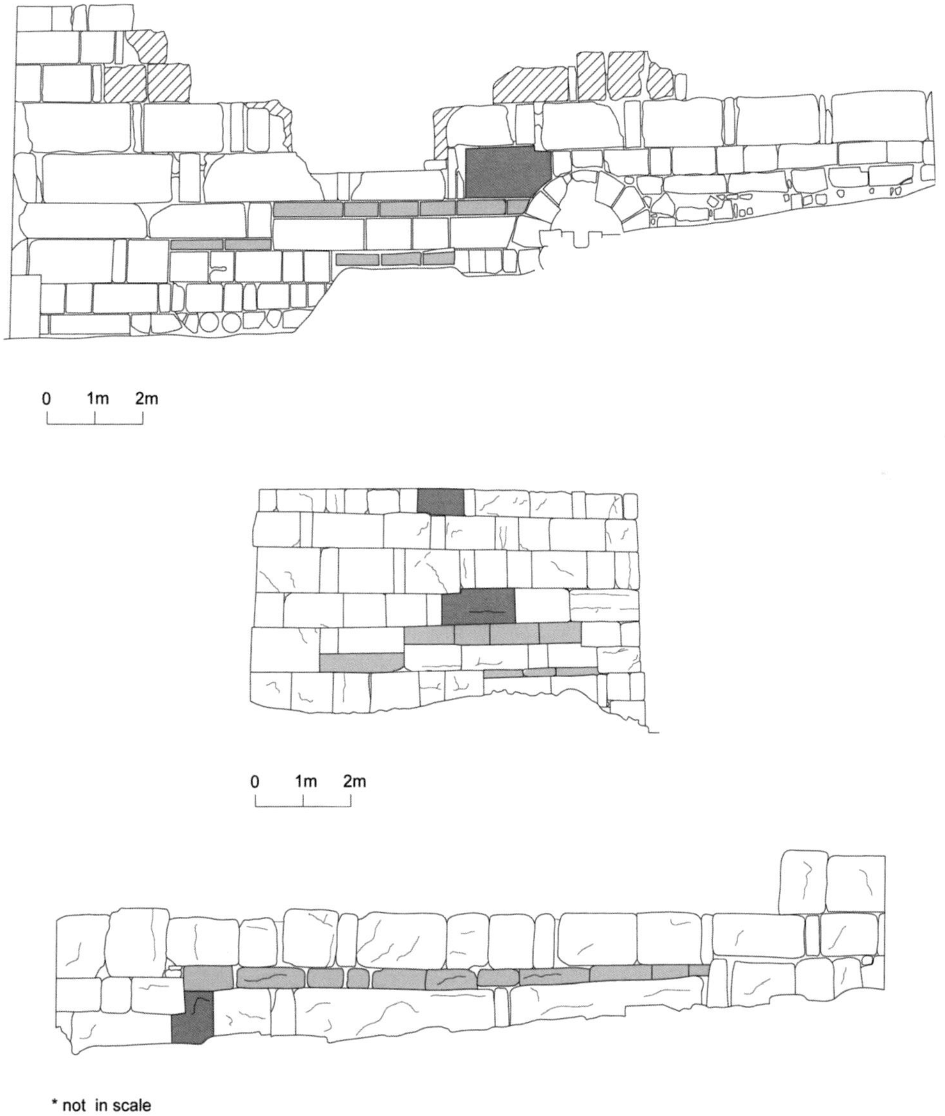

Figure 64. Comparisons between structures in BT4. Blocks coloured in red and light blue indicate the two expedients used to regularise coursing. Top: back wall of the Principia *of the Camp of Diocletian (redrawn from Kołątaj 1975, fig. 5); centre: south wall of the Theatre Gate (drawn from cat. n. 871013a, Centro di Documentazione di Storia dell'Arte Bizantina, Sapienza Università di Roma); bottom: repairs in curtain wall [A225]–[A224] (drawn from cat. n. 900505a, Centro di Documentazione di Storia dell'Arte Bizantina, Sapienza Università di Roma).*

[A115x], which was added to the original curtain to protect the new postern [A115] contemporary with the construction of the *Via Principalis*, is built in BT4 masonry (Figs 62, 67). It is also noteworthy that the last phase of construction of the Theatre Gate, whose plan is strikingly similar to that of other gates to be found in Tetrarchic forts, as seen below, is also in BT4 (Figs 69–71). There is, we believe, substantial proof that the 'Justinianic' U-shaped towers and the repairs of the city wall with BT4 are, in reality, contemporary with construction technique visible in the Camp of Diocletian, dated through archaeological and epigraphic evidence to the end of the 3rd–beginning of the 4th century.

Later repairs

Finally, a number of later repairs that adopt extensively reused building material are visible along the whole course of the ramparts. These are not homogeneous and do not occur in a fashion which enables recognition of any regular building pattern. No chronology for them can be put forward without autoptic analysis and targeted excavations. Perhaps the most curious of these is visible in the wall stretching between towers [A406] and [A407], in the southern section of the city wall. Here, at least two rows of reused drums of columns were placed horizontally above the original curtain wall (Fig. 72). A similar case of reuse is visible in wall b27 of the northern courtyard of the Sanctuary of Baalshamīn and in the Congregational Mosque, where the drums are, however, set vertically into the ground (Intagliata 2017a, 189; Genequand 2008a, 12, fig. 10). It goes without saying that these parallels are not sufficient to pinpoint an Umayyad dating for this restoration, which, however, remains tempting, especially considering the historical development of the city. Yet, repairs like these suggest that the city wall underwent maintainance intervention over a long time span.

Figure 65. Northern section, curtain wall in BT1 and BT2 [A208]–[A201] (cat. n. 900333d bis, Centro di Documentazione di Storia dell'Arte Bizantina, Sapienza Università di Roma).

Palmyra's city wall and Late Antique military architecture

The city wall of Palmyra is not isolated in the context of Late Antique military architecture and parallels can easily be drawn with cities and fortresses all over the empire. However, it should be stressed that a comparative analysis of towers and gates might be useful to reach a better understanding of the architectural background in which the wall was constructed, but does not help pinpoint any exact dating. Buttress and U-shaped towers are particularly common structures in the Roman world and they are attested over a long time span. The same, perhaps with the exception

Figure 66. Southern section, tower [A408] in BT4 (cat. n. 871328a, Centro di Documentazione di Storia dell'Arte Bizantina, Sapienza Università di Roma).

Figure 67. Western section, gate [A115] (cat. n. 870804a, Centro di Documentazione di Storia dell'Arte Bizantina, Sapienza Università di Roma).

Figure 68. Northern section, curtain wall in BT1 and BT2 [A205]–[A204] (cat. n. 870809a, Centro di Documentazione di Storia dell'Arte Bizantina, Sapienza Università di Roma).

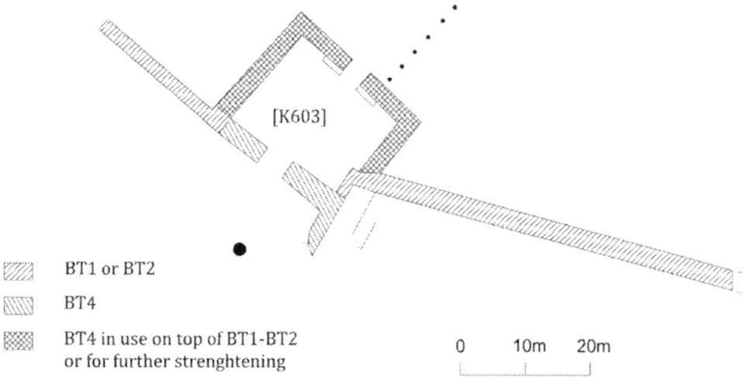

Figure 69. Theatre Gate (redrawn after Schnädelbach 2010).

Figure 70. Southern section, Theatre Gate, arch (cat. n. 871015a, Centro di Documentazione di Storia dell'Arte Bizantina, Sapienza Università di Roma).

of the Theatre Gate, applies for the openings along the circuit wall.

Buttress towers

As discussed above, buttress towers are normally associated with the earliest phase of construction of the city wall (BT1–3 masonry; see e.g., Fig. 61). They project normally for 2m to 2.7m and are found at intervals of about 30–35m. A number of them would be later incorporated into U-shaped towers. The lowest part of these structures, the only section still preserved, lacks of any inner chamber. The poor state of preservation of these towers does not allow to determine with certainty whether or not they were provided with a room on the ground floor accessible from the wall-walk. Yet, their modest size (*c.* 5m^2) would have hardly been enough for such purpose.

Buttress towers such as those at Palmyra occur frequently in Greek and Roman military architecture. They are known since the Hellenistic period and Roman engineers started adopting them only from the end of the reign of Gallienus (Todd 1983, 61–5; Lewin 1991, 15). At Jerash, the curtain wall of which has been dated by Seigne to the beginning of the 4th century (Seigne 1992, 341), Fisher (1938, 12) documents more than 101 towers of this type. They are reported to be 6m square and situated at regular intervals of 17–22m. Similarly, the city wall of Dibsī Faraj presents solid buttress towers occurring every 30m. Compared to those at Palmyra, they are slightly bigger, projecting from the ramparts by about 3–4m. They have been dated by Harper to Tetrarchic times on the basis of the parallel from Palmyra (Harper 1975, 326). The walls of *Zenobia* (Ḥalabiyya) might have included similar towers in their eastern section (Lauffray 1983, 127). In smaller forts, buttress towers sometimes occur as interval structures between corner towers. Examples include *Kastron Mefaa*, dated to the second half of the 3rd or beginning of the 4th century (Bujard 1995), *Aditha* (Lenoir 2011, 117), and Khirbat al-Zona (both undated) (Parker 1986, 45–6). Exception made for those at *Kastron Mefaa* (Umm al-Raṣāṣ), which are smaller, all the other towers project from the wall by about 2m. The use of buttress towers normally solid in their lower part is a widespread building tradition easily

Figure 71. Southern section, Theatre Gate, east side (cat. n. 871002a, Centro di Documentazione di Storia dell'Arte Bizantina, Sapienza Università di Roma).

Figure 72. Southern section, curtain wall [A406]–[A407] (cat. n. 901216d, Centro di Documentazione di Storia dell'Arte Bizantina, Sapienza Università di Roma).

found also in the western empire: examples include those of the city of Barcelona, Lugo, Astorge, Saragossa, and León (Todd 1983, 61). The most emblematic case is certainly that of the Aurelianic wall of Rome; this features 381 squared towers with a solid lower part and a chamber at the top, 7 × 7.6m in size and projecting from the rampart by 3.35m (Todd 1983, 61). Whether this circuit was inspired by Late Antique eastern tradition or earlier examples from southern Italy, for example *Paestum,* is uncertain.

The pattern of close-set buttress towers projecting outward is a building tradition commonly found in 3rd–4th century civilian settlements and military installations all over the empire. Juchniewicz's conclusion on an Aurelianic construction of these towers and the associated curtain wall has, however, to be revised (see, for instance, al-Ruṣāfa; Gregory 1995, 178). It has already been pointed out that the construction of the ramparts with buttress towers is the result of at least three distinct and well-recognisable building interventions (BT1–3), and not just one. Furthermore, Tetrarchic restorations (BT4) on the supposed Aurelianic city wall are clearly visible in several stretches of the curtain wall immediately above courses in BT1 and BT2, suggesting that the original city wall suffered considerable destruction at a certain time. These destructions are difficult to explain historically with a *terminus post quem* of 273 and a *terminus ante quem* of *c.* 300 (or even earlier). It would be much more reasonable to believe that these occurred during the Aurelianic events of 273 and that repair was undertaken about 20–30 years later under the tetrarchs. A refortification of a much reduced sector of the Roman city in the third quarter of the 3rd century remains, thus, a reasonable hypothesis. Yet, that this occurred hastily is implausible given the data provide by the archaeological record.

U-shaped towers

U-shaped towers in Palmyra have standard sizes; they project from the curtain wall by about 11m and have a width of about 9–10m (Figs. 61, 66). They preserve a rectangular room on the ground floor of *c.* 4–5m × 6–7m accessible from the outside through a single narrow passageway, the doorframe of which was often being reused, or through an inner staircase from the first floor. The front (most exposed) wall is normally thicker than the sides. The presence of entrances toward the outside is puzzling, and could be explained by the decision to avoid piercing the pre-existing city wall. Such an operation not only would have undermined the stability of the wall itself, but it would have required much more effort than constructing the entrances anew. In case of attack, the defenders would simply have needed to block up the entrances, a practice that is visible in most of these structures (Zanini 1995, 68). The upper storeys were likely to have been accessible from the wall-walk. Several towers have been partly preserved to a level where three vertical openings are visible (Fick 1932, 39, figs 37–9). Their internal splayed shape, which would have allowed more light to enter, would suggest a use as small windows for ventilation and light (Gregory 1995, 153; Lauffray 1983, 97).

Towers of this type are normally found from the end of the 3rd century onwards and are characteristic of Late Antique fortifications. Most of them are used throughout Late Antiquity and later adopted, with substantial alterations, in the Early Islamic period (Lander 1984, 181; Genequand 2006a). Yet, in the Levant, U-shaped towers seem to have been diffused especially in Tetrarchic times. A good example is the fort of al-Lajjūn in Jordan, the circuit of which includes four fan-shaped corner towers and 20 U-shaped towers projecting about 10m from the curtain wall. Unlike Palmyra, their ground-floor inner chamber was accessible through a doorway from inside the fort, while the second floor could be accessed by a staircase outside the tower, against the curtain wall (De Vries *et al.* 2006). Identical structures are visible in the Tetrarchic fort of Udhruḥ, about 15km to the east of Petra, Jordan (Kennedy and Falahat 2008). Examples of U-shaped interval towers in Syria include Khān al-Manqūra (Kennedy and Riley 1990, 181–3), and the earliest phase of the fort at al-Bakhrā', also dated to the Tetrarchic period (Genequand 2012, 73–9). In the Mesopotamian frontier, it is worth mentioning the city of *Singara* (Shinjār), whose ramparts have been tentatively dated to a pre-363 period and include 21 U-shaped towers (Oates 1968, 99–106). Other Tetrarchic examples are known outside our area of analysis and include in Egypt the forts at Luxor (al-Saghir *et al.* 1986, pl. 14), Qaṣr Qārūn (Lander 1984, 190), and Naj' al-Ḥajar (Mackensen 2009). The urban circuit of Babylon in Old Cairo, which also include similar structures, has never been object of systematic study (De Vries *et al.* 2006, 210 citing Butler 1902, 240). The bulk of the evidence for U-shaped towers comes, however, from lower *Moesia*, where Lander was able to identify nine examples, all falling within a 100km radius; further north, the only example attested in *Noricum* is in Zwentendorf (Lander 1984, 218).

What makes the remodelling of the city wall of Palmyra different from the case studies mentioned above is that U-shaped towers do not replace all the pre-existing buttress towers, but are alternated with them. This seems to have been a widespread pattern in later times and at a small number of sites in the Levant. In northern Mesopotamia, *Amida*, the construction of which commenced before 337, presents buttress towers every 50m and measuring 1.50 × 1.20m alternated with U-shaped towers (Gabriel 1940, 99; Crow 2007, 435). The same pattern is visible at *Resaina/Theodosiopolis* (Rā's al-A'yn) (Gregory 1997, 89–91), the ramparts of which have tentatively been dated to the 4th century on the basis of comparanda (Gregory 1996, 93). Much later, the hotly debated early 6th century ramparts of the city of *Dara*, in today's Mardin Province, Turkey, show the same pattern of large U-shaped towers that project from the curtain wall by about 10m, intervalled normally by two buttress towers (Crow 1981; Croke and Crow 1983; *contra* de' Maffei 1985, 115, 140–4; Whitby 1986). The same arrangement is visible at *Constantina/Tella* (Viranşehir) (Crow 2007, 444). Finally, two more examples are worthy of note: al-Ruṣāfa and Mayyāfāriqīn. At these sites buttress towers are alternated with bigger towers of different shapes and sizes. The early 6th century wall urban circuits of al-Ruṣāfa include buttress towers that are known to have been solid up to the first floor, where they were provided by a 9m² room, and bigger triangular, U-shaped, circular, and rectangular towers (Karnapp 1976, 19; Hof 2009, 820). At Mayyāfāriqīn, which according to Procopius was strengthened by Justinian, only two small squared towers are known between towers C (polygonal in shape) and D1 (U-shaped) (Gabriel 1940, 213–17). Gabriel suggests that towers of this shape would have existed in other sections of the curtain, but they would later have been demolished (Gabriel 1940, 215).

A further note should be made on the chronology of Justinianic urban circuits. It has been noted not without reason by Crow that fortifications in Syria which are firmly believed to be Justinianic, namely Qinnasrīn and Ḥalabiyya (Feissel 2000, 98), have very little to share with this pattern, and thus with Palmyra (Crow 2007, 444; Lauffray 1983, on Ḥalabiyya; Fourdrin 1994, on Qinnasrīn). Both these sites present rectangular projecting towers, access to which was provided by a staircase included in the ramparts. Towers of the same kind, and almost the same size, have been found at Dibsī Faraj and dated through comparison and building techniques to Justinianic times (Harper 1975, 326). If in Palmyra the pre-existing buttress towers are integrated into U-shaped structures, at Dibsī Faraj the squared towers had been razed to the ground to leave space for the Justinianic ramparts. A rapid glimpse at several parallel examples suggests, thus, that a Tetrarchic date for the U-shaped towers of Palmyra would perfectly fit into the general architectural military tradition of the time. In addition to this, it is legitimate to question whether the addition of these structures and the decision to keep the pre-existing buttress towers in Palmyra might have been the first stage of creating an architectural formula which would be repeated from Mesopotamia and Syria through the following two centuries.

Gates

A number of gates would have provided access to the city. One of the most imposing was certainly the Damascus Gate, which was provided with a triple entrance and pre-existed the curtain wall. As already discussed above (see p. 81), triple gates are particularly rare in Late Antiquity. For visitors willing to access the Camp of Diocletian, the Damascus Gate would have been only the starting point of a monumental route that, passing through the Transverse Colonnade, the *Porta Praetoria*, and the *Via Praetoria*, would have culminated with the *Aedes* in the *Principia*. For travellers directed to, or stopping by Palmyra, it would have served as a magnificent entrance into the city. Other accesses along the curtain wall are simple openings pierced into the curtain wall, sometimes flanked by buttress towers that are rarely later converted into U-shaped towers.

The Theatre Gate, is, however, more peculiar. To the north, it makes use of a pre-existing triple arch dated to 171–236 (Filarska 1967, 157). This would have given onto a colonnaded street [K600] leading toward the Theatre. The arch was later reinforced on its northern side and its lateral passage closed and embellished with two niches. To the south of this structure was a vantage court which included a pre-existing structure to the southeast. The wall in BT4 that closes this court to the south is pierced by a single passageway embellished by a doorframe. In Schnädelbach's plan a U-shaped tower abuts this structure to the east (Schnädelbach 2010, 53), and is mirrored by a similar structure to the west of the entrance (now not visible anymore on the ground). The asymmetry of these two U-shaped towers and the reuse of a honorary arch have been regarded by Crouch as diagnostic features of the gate, which is said to be comparable with the Justinianic West Gate at Leptis Magna (Crouch 1975a, 23). There are, however, substantial differences between the two. At Leptis Magna the vantage court is just a simple corridor. More important, the use of this gate (with a vantage court and two openings) associated with U-shaped towers is known from much earlier and better fitting Tetrarchic examples. These are limited to the large settlements and forts already discussed above and include, to cite some, *Singara* and *Amida* in Mesopotamia, Luxor and very likely Qaṣr Qārūn in Egypt, *Abrittus, Iatrus,* and *Dinogetia* in lower *Moesia*. A Tetrarchic dating of this gate based on typological comparison would perfectly bear examination of its building techniques. BT4 masonry, characteristic of a Diocletianic building intervention, as discussed above, is used in the strengthening of the arch, in the top-most courses of the vantage court and in its south wall. It therefore seems likely that the gate experienced at least two important construction phases: in the first, a pre-existing arch was included in the ramparts; only later was the vantage court created by adding the southern wall, strengthening the arch and building the two U-shaped towers.

Several remarks on the so-called 'wavy wall'

Final observations must be made on the remains of a wall visible outside Palmyra's ramparts to the north of the Camp of Diocletian and within the city's perimeter in the northwest quarter. The feature, known as 'wavy wall' for its irregular course, is built on top of pre-existing structures and is said by various scholars to have been constructed after the destruction of the main ramparts of the city at the end of the Umayyad period (Gabriel 1926, 77–8; von Gerkan 1935, 29–30; Crouch 1975a, 11). There is little evidence to support this conclusion that, thus, remains open to discussion (recently Genequand 2012, 50–1). A survey of the Polish archaelogical team in the northwest quarter resulted in identifying an open air channel running alongside the inner face of this wall and beginning from the Camp of Diocletian. The channel is said to have been connected to the Western Aqueduct and to be visible running to the north of the modern Hotel Zenobia (Gawlikowski 1998, 210–11).

Conclusions

Palmyra's urban circuit had been one of the main reasons behind the survival of the settlement throughout the conflicting Late Antiquity and Early Islamic period. The chronology of this feature is still hotly debated. If information provided by ancient written sources remain unreliable, a scrutiny of the archaeological remains allows for more solid conclusions on its chronology. On the basis of the analysis of archival photographs of the urban circuit, it seems reasonable to conclude that the first phase of the wall, with buttress towers, was constructed in different phases somewhen in the 3rd century and not under Diocletian. The construction of the wall does not seem to have occurred hastily. It is possible to note a certain attention in levelling its courses and laying carefully its blocks. At a later time, the wall was restored and strenghtened with the addition of imposing U-shaped towers. A close examination of the building tecnique adopted for these structures has validated a Diocletianic chronology. The Justinianic reconstruction of the city wall reported by Procopius (but not by Malalas or Theophanes), does not seem to have left visible traces on the ground. As far as the later history of the city is concerned, there is little archaeological material left to speculate. Although later repairs along the whole course of the ramparts would reflect the necessity to maintain the city wall functional over a long time, it is very difficult to pinpoint exact dates. Numerous written sources report that Palmyra remained an important fortified place and refuge until the mid-8th century, when the city wall was said to be demolished by Marwān b. Muḥammad. The destructions reported by written sources are, however, not visible on the ground and might perhaps have been exaggerated.

Chapter 7

Palmyra after Zenobia: a history

This chapter presents a brief account of the history of Palmyra throughout Late Antiquity and the Early Islamic period by collating the evidence analysed so far in a more diachronic, rather than thematic, fashion. The chapter will deliberately omit the events before 272–273, on which there is already a vast literature, and will focus on the period following the second Palmyrene revolt. What particularly emerges from the following patchy historical account is its non linearity. The historical narrative of the city after the 3rd century is best described as a succession of cycles of decline and renewal, in which the military, on the one hand, and the advent of Christianity, on the other, played a crucial part. Constant adaptability to changed wider political, cultural, and administrative circumstances is perhaps the common thread that better define the development of Palmyra 'after Zenobia' and assured its survival throughout the period under discussion.

Prologue: the destructions of 273

According to two written sources, namely Zosimus (*Hist. Nov.*, 1.61–2) and the author of the *Vita Aureliani* (31.5–9), the fall of Zenobia and the second Palmyrene revolt (272–273) had dramatic repercussions on the city itself. Zosimus reports a letter, presumably not genuine (Will 1966, 1409), written by the emperor to a fictional character, Cerronius Bassus (Paschoud 1996, 156). Therein, Aurelian accounts the sack of the 'temple of the Sun', in all likelihood the Sanctuary of Bēl, and the massacre of the inhabitants of Palmyra by a *Legio III*. Conversely, the author of the *Vita Aureliani* reports the bloodless conquest of the city, but states that Palmyra was razed to the ground. Scholars have frequently been inclined to minimise the claims of alleged devastation reported by these sources. Will (1966, 1413–14) argued that the hypothesis of total destruction of the city is not consistent with the archaeological evidence. The scholar noted that the most important buildings of the settlement do not present any sign of destruction associated with this event. A quarter of a century later, Kowalski (1997, 44) would echo Will's conclusion but noted traces of destruction datable to the third quarter of the 3rd century in a number of buildings. He argued that the event did not mark the end of the city and that continuity is attested in the epigraphic record. Since Kowalski's work, new items of evidence associated with Aurelian's military intervention have accumulated; it is worth considering them here.

After the events of 273, monumental building stopped abruptly. Structures in the process of being constructed, such as the Theatre or the Great Colonnade remained largely incomplete (Barański 1994, 9; Żuchowska 2000, 191, 192, fig. 7). Columns ready to be brought to the city are still visible lying horizontally in the quarries to the north and northwest of Palmyra, suggesting their sudden abandonment (al-As'ad and Schmidt-Colinet 1992, 141–2). The city shrank to almost half its original size. The Hellenistic Quarter south of Wādī al-Qubūr was abandoned, albeit presumably not completely at first. Gradually, Palmyrene art and culture came to a halt (Hartmann 2016, 65–7).

There is evidence of destructions in the archaeological record demonstrating that the city was affected by a disruptive event in this period. A *caravanserai* brought to light in Hellenistic quarter shows traces of destruction dated to the end of the 3rd century that might be associated to the Aurelianic event (Schmidt-Colinet *et al.* 2013, 303). Evidence found within the perimeter of the inner city wall supports this bleak picture. As already noted by Kowalski, levels of destruction dated to the early 270s have been found in the Sanctuary of Allāth (Gawlikowski 1983a, 61), in the *Agora* (Seyrig 1940, 242), and possibly in the Theatre (Will 1966, 1413–14; *contra* Kowalski 1997, 44). In the northwest quarter, not far from the Bellerophon Hall, a wooden box opened '... as if emptied by a robber ...' was found containing several gold fragments, a stylus, a bronze seal ring, and four coins minted under Gallienus (260–268) (Gawlikowski 2004, 323). Further south, a thick level of charcoal was uncovered in the Great Colonnade (Section C) and, again, associated to this event (Żuchowska 2000, 187).

Repairs of buildings are attested in the epigraphic record in the late 3rd–early 4th century and may be connected with the same episode. Two of them are bilingual and recount the renovation of the 'great basilica' of Arṣū by several members of the tribe of Maththabōlioi in 279–280. The inscriptions probably refer to a section of the Great Colonnade dedicated to the god, whose temple stood close to the *Agora* but outside the inner city wall (*IGLS* 17.1, 95–6, n. 80–1). A third inscription, dated 328, reports restoration works to the octostyle portico by Flavius Diogenes. The structure is reported to have been 'ruined for a long time' before repairs were carried out (*IGLS* 17.1, 114–115, n. 101). This renovation follows a phase of substantial destruction dated to the second half of the 3rd century (Żuchowska 2006, 445). Overall, the archaeological record seems to prove that Palmyra experienced some disruptions in the late 3rd century that may be connected with the repression of the second revolt by Aurelian's troops in 273. That said, however, even with new archaeological evidence, a total destruction of the city seems unlikely. The alleged claims of the *Historia Augusta, Vita Aureliani*, according to whom the city was completely razed to the ground should, therefore, be received with careful reservation.

The immediate aftermath

Broad consequences of the fall of Palmyra in the East

The fall of Palmyra was not an event of purely local significance, but had broader implications that considerably altered the economic and political stability of the Levant. One of the most visible consequences was the end of the long range caravan trade (Young 2001, 182–4). The last inscription mentioning caravan activities is dated to the 260s; it was dedicated by the council and people of Palmyra to a certain Septimius Worōd for having secured the safe return of a number of caravans at his own expenses (*IGLS* 17.1, 81–4, n. 67). After this, we hear no more of caravans in the epigraphic record. Restorations of a row of shops in the Basilica of Arṣū is believed to be proof that Palmyra was still regarded as a source of potentially lucrative investment (al-As'ad and Gawlikowski 1986–1987, 167–8). Eventually, the treaty signed by Diocletian in 297 with the Persians, which established Nisibis as the sole trade point between the two empires, would put an end to any hope the city might have had of reviving its commercial prosperity (Frézouls 1980, 383; Gawlikowski 1983a, 68). As a consequence of this agreement, the caravan trade moved northwards and the central Syrian caravan routes were abandoned (Sartre and Sartre-Fauriat 2008, 93).

A second consequence was political. The fall of Palmyra had caused considerable unrest among Arab tribal communities. Palmyra had served the Romans as a stabilising force among local nomadic societies and this event must have significantly affected their fragile political balance. General unrest is reflected by the almost sudden cessation of Aramaic at Palmyra and former Nabatean territory, and the decrease of Safaitic and Thamudic graffiti (Graf 1989, 158–9). Any attempt to cast light on the diplomatic implications of this episode is, however, confronted at the outset by the lack of substantial evidence and the chronology of the written sources, which is mostly Early Islamic and, therefore, written at a much later date than the events recounted. However, these sources are particularly rich in detail of the political development of the time and provide valuable insights not available elsewhere (Bowersock 1983, 132–3; Hartmann 2001, 332–51). The sources mention the involvement in the Palmyrene affairs of a powerful confederation of tribes known under the name of Tanūkh. These were originally settled in northwest Arabia and only later moved to al-Ḥīra and the middle Euphrates. During Zenobia's reign, the confederation was led by Jadhīma, 'king of the Tanūkh', as described in an inscription from Umm al-Jimāl (*PAES*, 37–40, n. 41). Relations between this confederation and the Palmyrenes must have been frequent. In a Manichaean manuscript in the Chester Betty Library in Dublin dated around 272, the 'Queen of Thamor' (Zenobia), is said to have supported the installation of a Manichaean community at Abidar, in the territory controlled by Amarō, i.e. the nephew and successor of Jadhīma, 'Amr b. 'Adī, first Naṣrid ruler (Tardieu 1992, 17). Later sources suggest, however, that the two communities were not on friendly terms. The lengthy account of the fall of Zenobia by al-Ṭabarī (*Tā'rīkh*, 1.757–61) is particularly informative on this. The writer recounts the murder of the husband of Zenobia (al-Zabbā' in Arabic literature) by Jadhīma, who would in turn be killed by Zenobia herself. 'Amrū b. 'Adī took revenge of his uncle and marched against Zenobia, who killed herself during the ensuing turmoil.

It is noteworthy that the *Historia Augusta, Vita Aureliani* (28.2) reports the existence of a contingent of Saracens who allied with Aurelian and contributed to the attack to Palmyra. It would not be surprising if, among these Saracens, were also members of the Tanūkh tribe (Bowersock 1983, 134–7). A later alliance with the Tanūkh would easily be explicable as the Roman attempted to fill the military vacuum left by the annihilation of the military power of Palmyra. Al-Mas'ūdi recounts that 'Amrū b. 'Adī was made king by the Romans (al-Mas'ūdī, *Murūj*, 3.274–5); his successor, Imrū' al-Qays, was buried not far from the fort of Namāra, near Roman territory in 328, suggesting that the two powers were on friendly terms at the time (Shahīd 1984a, 31–54, with further bibliography). Despite the Tanūkhid military support, however, the political situation of *Syria Phoenice* in the last quarter of the 3rd century must have remained profoundly unstable, given that it prompted Diocletianic, as we shall see, to intervene in the Near East.

Continuity after the Aurelianic disruptions

The events of 272–273 brought about the end of Palmyrene commercial prosperity, but they did not mark the complete abandonment of the city nor a total end of the everyday activities of its inhabitants. The city retained its juridical status; numerous Diocletianic milestones found on the road Homs–Palmyra, refer to the city as a *colonia* (see above, p. 21). In the Sanctuary of Bēl, a bilingual inscription dated March 273 reports that Septimius Ḥaddūdan, a local 'illustrious senator', presided at the symposium of Bēl as a symposiarch and 'helped [the army of Au]relianus, the Caesar, [our lord] ...' (tr. Kowalski 1997, 41; Gawlikowski 1973, 78). Septimius Ḥaddūdan had been recorded with the same title in another inscription dated March 272, i.e. before the second Palmyrene revolt (Gawlikowski 1973, 76; Kowalski 1997, 41). The inscriptions suggest that members of the élite who distinguished themselves as allies of the emperor during the Palmyrene revolts maintained their status and position in the civic administration that was, therefore, still functioning. A bilingual inscription dated to 274 or 279 engraved in the doorway of the tomb of Malkū, in the southwest necropolis, refers to the cession of five *loculi* of the *hypogeum* from a woman and his family, a practice that had been common in Roman times (Gawlikowski 1970, 211; Ingholt 1935, 106–8; Kowalski 1997, 43). The aforementioned roofing of the 'basilica' of the temple of Arṣū by several members of the tribe of the Maththabōlioi in 279–280 suggests that buildings were being restored and that the tribal system remained at the base of the Palmyrene community (see above, p. 98).

The 4th century

The first half of the 4th century

The survival of Palmyra after the turbulent events of 273 owes very little to private investment. The aristocratic élite was in all likelihood considerably reduced in Late Antiquity, as proven by the absence of aristocratic residences. The reasons for the survival of the city must be sought in the involvement of the Imperial authority, which under Diocletian was busy strengthening the defences of the eastern frontier. The increased Roman military presence along the Syrian frontier has been differently explained by modern literature (Lewin 2007, 243–4). Some scholars believe that it had to do with the growing threat of the Saracens, whose movements on the fringe of the empire had greatly affected the security of this border area (Parker 2006; Gichon 2002 on *Limes Palaestinae*). Others have argued that the activities of the local nomadic element must have been limited to minor acts of banditry and that the presence of the army can be better explained by the necessity of patrolling the roads and, more broadly, economic security (Isaac 1997, 459; Kennedy, D. L. 1992; Young 2001, 130–3). Lewin (2007, 244) reached a mediation between these two positions, stressing the multiple functions of the Late Roman army in the East, able not only to protect the local economy but also, 'to cope with banditism, to settle conflicts between pastoralists and sedentarists [and] as a defensive system aiming to intercept potential attacks by the Saracen tribes'. The nomadic threat is certainly not to be underestimated. Between the late 3rd and the end of the 4th century, the Tanūkhids remained allies of Rome (Shahīd 1984b, 465–521). Their support, however, seems not to have been enough as the constant Saracen threat prompted Diocletian to intervene personally in the Near East with a targeted military campaign as early as May/June of 290. On that occasion, the emperor also established an arms factory at Damascus (*Pan. Lat.*, 3.11, 5, 4–5; 7.1; Dodgeon and Lieu 1991, 107).

In a later stage, Diocletian was responsible for substantial building programs aimed to strengthen the defences along the border. These also concerned Palmyra. At this time, building intervention in the settlement included the construction of the Camp of Diocletian and the Baths of Diocletian by the *vir perfectissimus* and *praes provinciae* Sossianus Hierocles in 293–303. It has been argued that the building program also included the city wall, which was repaired and strengthened with imposing U-shaped towers (see Chapter 6). A garrison, the *Legio I Illyricorum*, was quartered in the city, presumably on this occasion or even earlier. The Camp of Diocletian might have hosted only part of the legion and, in all likelihood, was also intended to be a conscious demonstration of power in a land that had formerly been characterised by exteme conflict. The presence of the army must have drastically affected the everyday life of Palmyra's inhabitants to an extent that is barely discernible from the evidence at our disposal. Military personnel are attested in the city, suggesting the expected high degree of interaction between civilians and the army. The official Avitus dedicated an altar to Zeus in 302 in the Sanctuary of Baalshamīn, which, at the time, must still have been functional (*IGLS* 17.1, 163–4, n. 154). Another inscription found in the depôt of the Museum of Palmyra in 1950 by Seyrig mentions a certain '... *Flavius Platanius Severianus*, *vir perfectissimus*, *dux Orientis* ...' (Seyrig 1950, 239; *IGLS* 17.1, 297–8, n. 366). Seyrig's dating to the Justinianic period was revised a few decades later to 325 (Jones *et al.* 1971, 825). The title *vir perfectissimus* indicates that the dignitary belonged to the *ordo equestris*; *dux Orientis* that he commanded the units on the eastern border (Jones *et al.* 1971, 825–6) A Serenianus mentioned by Ammianus Marcellinus (*Res Gest.*, 26.5, 3; 10, 2) as the *dux Orientis* of *Phoenice*, was probably the same person (Kowalski, 1997, 46; Jones *et al.* 1971, 825). A further official inscription written in Latin from the Sanctuary of Allāth reports the construction of an unidentified building

([- - -]S/[- - -] ANUS/[- - -] constituit) (*IGLS* 17.1, 147, n. 139).

Life in the civilian settlement continued, albeit much reduced from that of Roman times. The renovation of the Octostyle Portico in block E by the λογιστής (lat. *curator*) Flavius Diogenes dated 328 would suggest not only that restoration in the city continued, but also that the settlement still preserved a functional *curia* that appointed dignitaries within the rank of the civic administration (*IGLS* 17.1, 114–15, n. 101). The renovation has been associated with the resurfacing of the section of the Great Colonnade in front of the Octostyle Portico (Żuchowska 2006, 448). Restoration works were carried out at the end of the 3rd and beginning of the 4th century after widespread destruction between this structure and the site of Church I. These included the enlargement of Bellerophon Hall, the installation of a new mosaic floor, and the overall rearrangement of the area (Żuchowska 2006, 445). Other early 4th century traces of occupation are meagre and come mostly from the same quarter. The Eastern Building appears to have been constructed in the 2nd century, abandoned in the late 3rd–early 4th century, to be reoccupied in the 4th century. It was later covered by the structures of Church II and its annexed baptistery. In its 4th century phase, the area had already lost its monumental appearance. One of its rooms, G.3.10, was rearranged to include two pottery kilns, whose rectangular floors have been found 1.5m below the 6th century church and associated with diagnostic ceramic material (Gawlikowski 1998, 205; 2000, 255–6).

Christianity is attested in written sources from the first half of the 4th century. Bishop Marinus was listed as a participant of the Council of Nicaea in 325 (Le Quien 1749, 2, 845; Devreesse 1945, 206; Turner 1899, 48; Fedalto 1988, 742). Yet, no archaeological evidence has so far been uncovered which would suggest the presence of churches or other religious buildings associated with them in the city before the 5th century. Although the city life was concentrated within the perimeter of the newly restored city wall, two inscriptions suggest that the surroundings of the city would also have been frequented to a certain extent. One in the southwest necropolis (Hypogée de Dionysos [=R254]), whose content has never been published, was reported by Ingholt to be dated to 22 April 312 (Ingholt 1932, 16–17). The other mentions the opening of the gate in the same tomb on 20 September 333 (Ingholt 1932, 17 = *IGLS* 17.1, 394, n. 527).

The second half of the 4th century

There is very little evidence to cast light on the history of the city in the second half of the 4th century. The only occurrences of Palmyra in written sources are in the *Notitia Dignitatum* and the *Tabula Peutingeriana*. Although it is generally agreed that the former reflects the military situation after Jovian's treaty with the Persians in 363, it is possible that several troops recorded in this document might have been stationed in the *Pars Orientalis* before this date (Dodgeon and Lieu 1991, 340). This could be the case of the *Legio I Illyricorum*, as already argued, whose prefect seems to have been stationed in Palmyra under the command of the *vir spectabilis dux Phoenici* (*Not. Dig., Or.*, 32.30). The document also reports the existence of a *Cuneus Equitum Secundorum Clibanariorum Palmirenorum* under the *vir illustrious magister militum per Orientem* (*Not. Dig., Or.*, 7.34) and an *Ala VIII Equitum Palmyrenorum* under the *dux Thebaidis* (*Not. Dig., Or.*, 31.49). In the *Tabula Peutingeriana*, Palmyra is depicted as a double-towered city, suggesting its logistic importance in the *cursus publicus*. The city is reported to be 19 *milia* from the station of *Harae* (Arāk), on the way to Sūriyya (*Sura*), and 32 *milia* from *Heliarama* (Qaṣr al-Ḥayr al-Gharbī), on the way to Damascus (*Tab. Peut.*, seg. 10–11). It was also connected to *Centum Putea*, which is a road station on the way to Apamea.

Archaeological evidence for this period comes mainly from the northwest quarter. At that time, the mosaic of the Bellerophon Hall in block E was covered with a floor of dark grey mortar. A room lying north of this area was provided with two *tanānīr* and a lavatory, while between the later Church I and the Bellerophon Hall a long, narrow room paved with a floor of dark grey mortar was installed (Żuchowska 2006, 447). The archaeological record from the Sanctuary of Allāth is particularly rich and has suggested that the destruction of its temple must have occurred in the mid-380s. The event has been associated with the visit to the city of Maternus Cynegius, *praefectus praetorius Orientis*, and has been regarded as the result of the anti-pagan measures taken by Theodosius I (Gąssowska 1988). This was followed in the late 4th–early 5th century by the installation of a private residential building, which has been identified as the *Praetorium* of the Camp of Diocletian (Kowalski 1994). That said, it should not be excluded that paganism remained a practice in Palmyra. So far, all would suggest that, although life continued in Palmyra without major interruption, the vitality of its community must already have been greatly reduced from the first half of the century.

The 5th century

The 'dark age'

The 5th century is regarded as a period of general peace in Syria (Greatrex and Lieu 2002, 31–61). Relations between the Roman and Persian empires flourished so that Arcadius (395–498) appointed the Persian king Yazdegerd I as formal guardian of the safety of his son and future emperor Theodosius II in 408 (Greatrex and Lieu 2002, 32–3). Priscus (fr. 19, Suda A 3803) reports that in the mid-5th century the newly elected *magister militum per orientem* Ardaburius

> 'since ... received this office in time of peace, ... turned to self-indulgence and effeminate leisure. He amused himself with mimes and conjurors and stage spectacles and, spending his days in such shameful pursuits, he took no thought at all for things that would bring him glory'. (tr. Greatrex and Lieu 2002, 46)

At that time the Tanūkh's power, still allied of Rome, was declining. In the 5th century, the role of providing security along the fringe of the desert was mostly in the hands of the nomadic Salīḥids. These seem not have encountered major difficulties in pursuing the task. Written sources mention only sporadic raids carried out by the Saracens allied with Persians. Jerome (*Ep.* 126) reports a Saracen raid in Egypt, Palestine, *Phoenicia*, and Syria in 411 without providing information on its origin (Greatrex and Lieu 2002, 35). Other sporadic attacks are reported by Priscus (fr. 10.9–15) in 447/448 – followed by negotiations in 452 (fr. 26) and by Evagrius (*HE*, 3.2 [100.6–9]) and Isaac of Antioch (*Hom.*, 11.32–47) in about 474 (Greatrex and Lieu 2002, 35, 35–47). Major conflicts between Rome and Persia in 421–422 and 440 occurred only further north, involving mainly the cities of northern Mesopotamia. This relative period of peace is generally associated with a time of economic growth in the Levant. Lands in marginal areas began to be agriculturally exploited to meet the needs of a rising population (Ward-Perkins 2001, 320–7). New networks of villages emerged on the fringe of the Negev desert in Palestine and on the Syrian Limestone Massif (Decker 2009, 174–203).

If it is true that across the Roman East for the 5th century urban and rural settlements 'peace meant prosperity' (Sarris 2011, 126), this cannot be said for military installations along the eastern frontier. In some stretches of the eastern frontier, forts, as discussed above (see p. 9), may have experienced an overall reduction of their strength, generally followed by a proportional reduction in the civilian settlements associated with them. As a matter of fact, one of the key elements in the choice of a fort's location was the availability of specific goods (mostly foodstuff, clothes, arms, and building material). Some were produced by the soldiers themselves, such as timber or bricks, while others needed to be purchased from natives, thus stimulating the local market (Whittaker 1994, 101; for the impact of the army on the cities along the eastern frontier see, Janniard 2006, esp. 135–43). *Canabae* and *vici*, i.e. civilian settlements associated with military installations, were, then, an indispensable support for the life of the garrison providing soldiers also with leisure activities in bathhouses, bars, and brothels (Macmullen 1963, 92; Hanel 2007). With the reduction of the army and the consequent halt in military demands, the local market collapsed and civilian settlements associated with fortresses underwent a period of stagnation.

This phenomenon appears to be clearly visible in Palmyra. The reduction of the city's garrison corresponded to an overall period of decline in the city's fortune reflected both in written sources and archaeological evidence. The often quoted text by Procopius (*Aed.*, 2.11.10–12) mentioning restorations undertaken by Justinian because the city 'had come to be almost completely deserted' is the only passage that directly claims that Palmyra had suffered a decline in urban life. Malalas (*Chr.*, 17.2) and later Theophanes (*Chr.*, 1.174) would be more succinct in describing this episode, but they both give a clue on this using the verb ανανέωση, meaning 'to restore'. Other sources provide further evidence. The author of the life of Alexander the Akoimētes recounts how the holy man and his group of brethren were prevented from entering the city by its inhabitants because of the paucity of food: 'the citizens, having seen from a distance a mass of brethren (and thus being Jews who call themselves Christians) approaching them, closed the gates of the city saying to each other, "Who is capable of feeding all these; if they only entered our city we would all starve"' (*Alex. Akoim.*, 35; tr. Kowalski 1997, 48; on the reliability of this source see Fowden 1999, 74, esp. n. 76). In 403, Palladius (*Dial. John Chris.*, 20.35–8) reports that Cyriacus was exiled to Palmyra for his stance against orthodoxy. Finally, we are informed that in the mid-5th century Theodorus, bishop of Damascus, signed on behalf of John of Palmyra the sixth canon of the council of Chalcedon in 451 (Le Quien 1740, 2, 845–6; *ACO* 2.1.2.154; 2.3.2.174) as well as a letter concerning the matter of the death of Proterius in 457 (Le Quien 1740, 2, 845–6; *ACO* 2.5.46; Fedalto 1988, 742). That the bishop could not move from Palmyra on either of these occasions may be seen as further proof of the troubling period the city was undergoing. Several of these texts, such as that in the life of Alexander the Akoimētes, report episodes which admittedly make us question the reliability of their authors. Nonetheless, it is noteworthy that all of them seem to agree in depicting a city which was certainly not at its peak of prosperity.

Archaeological evidence is, so far, consistent with that of written sources and supports this picture. Only two buildings of a certain significance are believed to have been constructed sometime in the 5th century, that is to say Church III and the church in the Sanctuary of Bēl. Yet, Church III was abandoned in the same century and later renovated in the 6th, while very little evidence can be firmly associated to the first stage of the church in the Sanctuary of Bēl. Other buildings show signs of disruption and abandonment in the century under discussion or even earlier. The fill of the Eastern Building (see above, p. 100) has yielded material consistently dated to the late 3rd–early 4th century. No continuous occupation into the 5th century has been recorded. Church II would be erected in the 6th century immediately on top of this fill. Between Churches II and III lies an almost empty area. The excavation of its fill has yielded potsherds dated no later than the early 4th century. At the time of the construction of Church II, this area was converted into a graveyard. The Bellerophon Hall and its neighboring structures show important traces of occupation in phases IV (second half of the 4th century) and VI (6th century) but reduced and confused activities in the phase in between. These are limited to the laying of a new floor in parts of loc. A13–A14 and A22, and a wall that cuts the floor of loc. A15. Continuity is, however, recorded in House F. According to the excavators, the house survived in its original 2nd century stage until the 6th century, when major changes occurred after an earthquake. A full investigation of the water line running along the Great Colonnade, which was connected to the most important city's water supply system in Late Antiquity (the Western Aqueduct) would possibly provide more evidence to add to this list. Either if the stone conduit is believed to be later replaced by a Justinianic pipeline because broken or silted up (Barański 1997, 11) or if it is considered the Justinianic replacement of an earlier, mid-4th century pipeline (Juchniewicz and Żuchowska 2012, 67), there remains an obscure phase of disruption in between that points to the 5th century. There seems to exist, therefore, a strong link between the military presence and the prosperity of the civilian settlement (Lewin 2011, 262). This becomes clearer if one examines the evidence of the 6th century. The installation of the *dux* of Emesa in the city and a *numerus* of soldiers coincides with the beginning of a period of building which has no precedent in the history of Late Antique Palmyra.

Further 5th century evidence

There is no other safely dated evidence to cast light on 5th century Palmyra apart from the epigraphic record. This remains meagre, consisting of just four funerary inscriptions bearing exact dates (*IGLS* 17.1, 374–6, n. 494–7), and other inscriptions of various nature generically dated to the same century (*IGLS* 17.1, 119, n. 112; 167, n. 158; 295, n. 359; 377–9, n. 500–2). These are all in Greek. One of them deserves special attention. It is dated to 20 February 469 and refers to the death of a certain Maranios, son of Maneos (*IGLS* 17.1, 375–6, n. 496). Maranios' father bears the title ἔκδικος. This was normally a title conferred by the *praefectus praetorio* to assume the responsibilities of the *curator civitatis* (Kowalski 1997, 50) and suggests the existence of a functional civic administration. Another inscription reports the burial of a certain Odaenathos, a name which hides strong links with the city's Roman past, on 30 June 442 (*IGLS* 17.1, 374, n. 494; *Inv.* 9, 130, n. 213; Kowalski 1997, 49; Avram 2001–2003, 246). Some features, for example the material of the supports (marble), suggest that at least three other inscriptions were more official; yet, all of them are too fragmentary to put forward any conclusions on their nature (*IGLS* 17.1, 119, n. 112; 167, n. 158; 295, n. 359).

The 6th and the first three decades of the 7th century

The first half of the 6th century

The events of the 6th century threatened the security along the border that was achieved in the previous century. Hostilities broke out when the Persian ruler Kavādh, who had regained power in 498–499, was refused financial support by Anastasius (r. 491–518) (Greatrex and Lieu 2002, 62). Although the Persian army was mostly mobilised in Mesopotamia during the resulting conflict, Naṣrid raids under the guidance of al-Mundhir were carried out further south as soon as Anastasius took the throne and were later intensified (Greatrex and Lieu 2002, 51, 71–86). Byzantium reacted by securing an alliance with the fervent Monophysite dynasty of the Jafnids. These officially replaced the Salīḥids as *foederati* of Byzantium in 529, when their ruler, al-Ḥārith b. Jabala (529–569), was made supreme φύλαρχος upon a confederation of allied tribes (Proc., *Bell.*, 1.17.46–8. Greatrex and Lieu 2002, 88). The new alliance contributed to the successful challenge to Naṣrids' supremacy in the territory by defeating al-Mundhir and his army in 554 near Qinnasrīn (Mich. Syr. *Chr.*, 9.33; Greatrex and Lieu 2002, 129–30).

Jafnid activities are known in the Palmyrene region in the mid-6th century. Jafnid rulers are known from inscriptions from Qaṣr al-Ḥayr al-Gharbī, al-Ḍumayr, and al-Ruṣāfa (Genequand 2006b, 77–8). We are informed by Procopius (*De Bel.*, 2.1, 6) of disputes which arose between the two tribal powers over control of grazing areas said to stretch south of Palmyra: '... This country which at that time was claimed by both tribes of Saracens is called *Strata*, and extends to the south of the city of Palmyra .... Now Arethas maintained that the place belonged to the Romans, proving his assertion by the name which has long been applied to it by all (for *Strata* signifies 'a paved road' in the Latin tongue), and he also adduced the testimonies of men of the oldest times. Alamoundaros, however, was by no means inclined to quarrel concerning the name, but he claimed that tribute had been given him from of old for the pasturage there by the owners of the flocks.' (tr. Dewing 1914, 261–3; see also, Bauzou 1993, 32). The toponym *Strata* refers to the region crossed by the 'route des khāns' stretching from Palmyra to Damascus. The episode, which occurred before the outbreak of the war between Rome and Persia in 540, has led scholars to suppose that regular patrolling units had already been withdrawn from this area and that this borderland was left to be defended by the Roman allies (Liebeschuetz 1977, 489; Fowden 1999, 66–7. Lewin 2011, 245). Still, it is important to note that archaeological evidence from the northern stretch of the eastern frontier, would suggest that the *castra* along this line of defense, such as *Tetrapyrgium* and *Cholle* (al-Khulla), remained occupied until the final withdrawal of the Romans from the area (Konrad 2001).

As far as Palmyra itself is concerned, Procopius (*Aed.*, 2.11, 10–12) informs us that Justinian restored the city with 'defences which defy description' and supplied it with 'abundant water' (tr. Dewing 1961, 177; see also, Proc., *Aed.*, 2.4, 1). Malalas (*Chr.* 17.2) recounts that the emperor gave a large sum of money to the new *comes orientis* Patrikios, to reconstruct Palmyra's churches and public baths. He also reports that Justinian ordered a *numerus* of soldiers to be quartered in Palmyra together with the *limitanei* and the *dux* of Emesa 'to protect the Roman territories and Jerusalem' (tr. Jeffreys *et al.* 1986, 245). Theophanes (*Chr.*, 1.174) would follow Malalas in accounting the restoration of Justinian on behalf of Patricius the Armenian in AM 6020 (527–528). The presence of one of the two *duces* in Palmyra suggests that the garrison in Palmyra must have been substantial. The military presence in the 6th century is relatively well-attested in the archaeological record of the Camp of Diocletian. After a devastating fire, the *Principia* were enlarged to the southwest and northeast, and the inner arrangement of the compound underwent important alterations in Justinianic times. At the same time, the *Horreum* was refurbished. The number of mills was reduced from six to four, additional pillars were installed flanking the original ones to strengthen the building and a water basin was placed in the southern aisle.

Imperial euergetism and military presence helped revive the fortune of the civilian settlement. Archaeological evidence, sometimes uncertainly dated, supports the meagre epigraphic record at our disposal (*IGLS* 17.1, 376–7, n. 498; 377, n. 499; 379–80, n. 503) to draw a clearer picture of Palmyra in this century. The process of Christianisation represents the most vivid example of this urban revitalisation. Some of the churches in the northwest quarter are believed to have been constructed in the 6th century, while Church III, was refurbished at the same time. Three smaller churches or chapels along the Great Colonnade have tentatively been dated to the same period. Similarly, paintings were added in the church installed in the Sanctuary of Bēl. The area between the Octostyle Portico and Church I underwent important alterations associated with the transformation of the quarter into an ecclesiastical complex. A narrow *atrium* was built to the south of Church I; the south wall of the octostyle portico along the Great Colonnade was monumentalised with reused framing elements; the floor of the whole area was levelled (żuchowska 2006, 448–50). Other facilities associated with these buildings were constructed in the area. Six large water tanks were discovered between Church II and III (Room G.3.3) and are believed to have been in use to supply water to these two buildings. They apparently fell into disuse when the churches were abandoned in the 9th century or later. Ecclesiastical sources attest the presence of charitable institutions in the city mentioning the existence of Julianus, ξενοδόχος/*hospitalarius* of the 'Church of Palmyra' (Mansi 1762, 921; *ACO 3.151*).

The second half of the 6th and the early 7th century

The conflict between Byzantium and Persia and their Saracen allies remained a constant feature throughout the second half of the 6th century. Al-Mundhir b. al-Ḥārith (568–581) took control of the Jafnid confederation after al-Ḥārith b. Jabala's death. The alliance with the tribal chief proved to be indispensable to Rome's meeting the Naṣrids' threat; a withdrawal of al-Mundhir's forces in 572–575 greatly weakened the Roman defences along the eastern frontier. The conflict continued intermittently under Tiberius (574–582) and Maurice (582–602), reaching a stop only after a treaty signed in 591 that lasted about ten years (Greatrex and Lieu 2002, 174). This protracted period of conflictuality must have had negative repercussions on the Palmyrene borderland and justifies the strengthening of the monastery in Jabal al-Bil ʿās in 574–575 (Mouterde 1942–1943, 84). Nonetheless, it is not clear if these conflicts affected Palmyra itself. The biased dating of the archaeological evidence and the paucity of written sources are certainly not helpful in outlining a history of the city in this period.

The continuity in occupation of major buildings (especially churches and their nearby dependencies), suggests that, despite the major military tensions along the frontier, the Palmyrene community continued its life as usual. Doubtless, the settlement remained a renowned religious centre, as it appears in third place in the list of the *Notitia Antiochena* after *Elioupolis* and *Abila*, and before *Laodikeia* (Honigmann 1925, 75; Vailhé 1907, 145). The Jafnid presence in the Palmyrene area remains attested. A Syriac codex said to belong to a monastery near Palmyra (TWDMR), very likely in the far north of *Phoenicia Libanensis*, mentions King Abokarib (MLK' 'BWKRYB), the brother of al-Ḥārith b. Jabala (Wright 1872, 2. 468, n. 585; Millar 2013, 24–5). At the end of the 6th or the beginning of the following century, an earthquake wrought considerable damage to the city. Levels of destruction have been recorded in the Camp of Diocletian (*Praetorium*, Kowalski 1994, 57), and in the city centre (House F, Gawlikowski 1992a, 74; western stretch of the Great Colonnade, al-As ʿad and Stępniowski 1989, 206; Church I, Gawlikowski 1992, 74; Sanctuary of Baalshamīn, Intagliata 2017a).

The first three decades of the 7th century prior to the Islamic takeover saw the Persians gradually taking control of most of the Levant. The Sasanian occupation of Syria (613–628) and the subsequent Byzantine control of the region until the Islamic conquest have left no evidence in Palmyra (Gawlikowski 2009, 89). The presence of the Jafnid element seems to be confirmed by two Arabic sources, Ḥamza al-Hiṣfahānī (*Tāʾrīkh*, 121) and Abū al-Fidāʾ (*Taqwīm al-Buldān*, 128–30), who both report that al-Ayham b. Jabala b. al-Ḥārith ruled over the city in the early 7th century. Shahīd (1995, 651) believes that the name of this individual must be read as Jabala b. al-Ayham, whom Ḥamza al-Hiṣfahānī reported to have ruled for about 27 years from 609. Yet, neither the accuracy of this interpretation nor the reliability of these admittedly late sources can be proven with the evidence at our disposal.

The city remained Monophysite in this period as proven by the account of Michael the Syrian, according to whom, at the Council of Hierapolis (630) Heraclius attempted to persuade a group of Monophysite bishops, among them Thomas of Palmyra, to accept his new Monothelite's creed (Mich. Syr., *Chr.*, 9.3; Fedalto 1988, 742). Between spring 630 and 2 November 631, the body of St Anastasius was translated from Dastagerd in Persia to Jerusalem via Palmyra by a monk. A φύλαρχος accompanied him in the stretch from Persia to Palmyra (*Anas. Per.*, 1.102–4). Having reached the settlement, the relic is said to have performed a miracle healing a blind young man in seven days (*Anas. Per.*, 1.129–30). This is the last event reported by written sources before the capitulation of Palmyra in the hands of Khālid b. al-Walīd a few years later.

Early Islamic Palmyra

The Islamic takeover

The invasion of Syria by the Islamic force was initiated by the first caliph Abū Bakr, presumably as early as 633. Most of the sources agree that the caliph dispatched four armies under the commanders ʿAmr b. al-ʿĀṣ, Yazīd b. Abī Sufyān, Shuraḥbīl b. Ḥasana, and Abū ʿUbayda b. al-Jarrāh. ʿAmr b. al-ʿĀṣ marched to Palestine and, later, Egypt, while the others and their armies to modern-day Syria and Jordan. The Syrian force was later joined by another general, Khālid b. al-Walīd, who entered the region in 634 from Iraq (Donner 1981, 111–27). Written sources seem to disagree on the route taken by the general. The crucial point of the debate is whether Khālid b. al-Walīd's route was via Dūmat al-Jandal, today in northwest Saudi Arabia, or Palmyra. Supporting evidence exists for both these itineraries and a conclusive position cannot be taken solely on the basis of the texts available (Donner 1981, 121, 124).

The account of the conquest of Palmyra is abundantly recorded in written sources and represents an important literary topos in the narration of the *futūḥ* (Ibn ʿAsākir, *Tāʾrīkh*, 2.80; al-Balādhurī, *Futūḥ*, 111–12; Ibn al-Faqīh, *Mukhtaṣar*, 125; Ibn Aʿtham al-Kūfī, *Kitāb*, 1.140–142; al-Ṭabarī, *Tāʾrīkh*, 4.2109; al-ʿUṣfurī, *Tāʾrīkh*, 1.124; al-Wāqidī, *al-Maghāzī*, 1.44; al-Yaʿqūbī, *Tāʾrīkh*, 2.134; Yāqūt, *Muʿjam*, 1.832. A further source is the poem by al-Qaʿqāʿ b. ʿAmr reported in Ibn ʿAsākir, *Tāʾrīkh*, 2.132). Of these sources, the passage in Ibn al-Faqīh's *Mukhtaṣar* is the vaguest, as it provides the reader only with a short list of cities said to have been subjugated by the general, including al-Muḍayyaḥ, Ḥuṣayd, Bishr, Qurāqir, Suwā, Arāk, and Palmyra. Al-Ṭabarī, al-Yaʿqūbī, Yāqūt, al-Wāqidī, and Ibn Aʿtham al-Kūfī report that the city was well fortified at the time of the conquest. Yāqūt in particular describes the frustration of the general at his inability to storm the city wall. All of the sources agree that the settlement is conquered by treaty (*ṣulḥan*) and not by force (*ʿanwatan*) by the Muslim army. The reason for this, according to at least Yāqūt and al-Wāqidī, is the impregnability of the ramparts. Al-Balādhūrī provides more detail on the *ṣulḥan*, recounting that the general 'wrote them (the Palmyrenes) a statement guaranteeing their safety on condition that they be considered *dhimma* people, that they entertain Moslems and that they submit to them' (tr. Hitti 1966, 171).

The details of the process of the conquest are omitted by all authors but two, namely Ibn Aʿtham al-Kūfī and al-Wāqidī, who disagree in describing the episode. Ibn Aʿtham al-Kūfī's *Kitāb al-Futūḥ* contains the longest account of the event and the only detailed narration of a fight between the Muslim force and the inhabitants of Palmyra. In the passage, special attention is paid to stress the aggression of the Romans (*rūm*), who 'attacked Khālid b. al-Walīd like fierce lions'. This is probably a rhetorical expedient to allude to the extraordinary fighting qualities of the conquerors, who eventually defeated the Palmyrenes. Five people are said to have lost their life during the battle. These are four Muslim brothers from the Banū Sadūs: Saʿīd, Qays, al-Ḥajjāj, Sāʾib b. al-Ḥārith, and ʿAbd Allāh b. ʿAbd Shams, brother of Jarīr b. ʿAbd Allāh al-Bajilīʾ. An allusion to a fight between the two parties is also found in a poem on the day of the conquest of Damascus supposedly written by al-Qaʿqāʿ b. ʿAmr and reported by Ibn ʿAsākir (*Tāʾrīkh*, 2.132). The text reports the slaughtering of the Romans in Damascus and Palmyra, but it is problematic, as already stressed by Donner, since al-Qaʿqāʿ is a member of the Banū Tamīm, who is believed to have left Syria before the conquest (Donner 1981, 317–18, n. 225).

The narration of the conquest of the city by al-Wāqidī reports the putative speech of the governor of Palmyra, al-KarKar, given to its inhabitants; these are invited to open the gates and surrender to Khālid's army. Unlike Ibn Aʿtham al-Kūfī, in al-Wāqidī's account no fight is involved. Again the passage is not devoid of elements that aim to stress the integrity and probity of the conquerors; these are in stark contrast with the behaviour of the Palmyrenes, who are depicted as selfish double-crossers. The governor is reported to have said:

> '... our people speak about their righteousness, their justice, their good reputation and that they do not seek corruption. Our fortification is impregnable; there is no way through it for anyone. However, we are afraid about our palm trees

and crops [outside the city]. It will not be harmful to us if we make a peace treaty with those people. Then, if our people achieve a victory, we can break this peace treaty; if [victory is] with the Arabs, we are safe with respect to them'.

The people of Palmyra then agreed to open the gate to the general and pay a tribute in gold and silver (al-Wāqidī, *al-Maghāzī*, 1.44).

Accounts of the capitulation of Palmyra were written solely from the point of view of the conquerors. As with all narrations that fall within the historiographical theme of the *futūḥ*, the main reasons for their writing transcend their importance as historical sources. The texts aim at justifying the rule of the Muslims over the non-Muslims, providing private individuals and families with an account of glorious deeds of ancestors which could be used to legitimize their high social or political status, and exhorting engagement in the *jihād* (Donner 1998, 177–9). At least two points from these texts are worthy of notice in the light of archaeological evidence. The first is the frequent allusion to the impenetrability of the city wall, (see pp. 85–6). The second is the reference to the *ṣulḥan* that Khālid b. al-Walīd is said to have stipulated with the inhabitants of Palmyra. The *ṣulḥ-ʿanwa* theme is common in Early Islamic narratives, since it was regarded as a critical factor in determining the tax status of a land (Donner 1998, 171). As far as our case study is concerned, the presence of this term suggests that the conquest of the city was a mere handover agreed by both parties. The archaeological record would so far support the hypothesis of a smooth transition of powers, as opposed to the disrupting conquest by Aurelian about three centuries earlier. Traces of destruction associated with this event have never been individuated and evidence suggests that the inhabitants of the settlement were not affected by major changes in their everyday lives, at least not in the short term.

The Islamic control (634–750)

After the Islamic conquest, the city was included in the *jund* of Homs (al-Muqaddasī, *Aḥsan*, 159). Throughout the century that follows, written sources refer to the city as under the control of the powerful Banū Kalb, a Yemenite tribe from northwest Arabia attested in the Palmyrene since the 6th century (associations of Palmyra with Banū Kalb can be found in Agapius, *Kitāb*, 515; Ibn ʿAsākir, *Tāʾrīkh*, 17.326; 63.337; al-Iṣfahānī, *al-Aghānī*, 17.112; 20.120; al-Ṭabarī, *Tāʾrīkh*, 9.1796, 1893). The first move of ʿUmar b. al-Khaṭṭāb as a caliph after the death of Abū Bakr in August 634 was to dismiss Khālid b. al-Walīd from the supreme command of the Muslim forces. This title was conferred on Abū ʿUbayda who, however, kept Khālid in charge of the cavalry. The *Chronicle of 1234* reports that after the fall of Damascus, dated by Sayf and his sources to 635, an army led by Khālid b. al-Walīd set out from this city to Jordan, al-Balqāʾ, and the Ḥawrān. The army wanted to loot these territories, but Abū ʿUbayda opted to make the people tributaries instead (*Chron. 1234,* 248–249). The army is said to have later passed via Baʿalbak and Palmyra to reach Homs, which was conquered by treaty after a siege. The order of Abū ʿUbayda must have been almost contemporaneous with Yazīd b. Abī Sufyān in guarding Damascus with a garrison. According to al-Ṭabarī (*Tāʾrīkh*, 4.2154–5) and, later, Ibn ʿAsākir (*Tāʾrīkh*, 2.132), Yazīd on his own initiative sent a detachment to Palmyra under the command of Dḥya b. Khalīfa al-Kalbī. The inhabitants of the city are said to have made peace agreements with them.

Not much later, during the struggles between Muʿāwiya and ʿAlī (the great *fitna*, 656–61), Palmyra appears as a place of confrontation between the two aspirant caliphs in al-Ṭabarī (*Tāʾrīkh*, 6.3447), and later in Ibn al-Athīr (*al-Kāmil*, 3.317). Al-Ḍaḥḥāk b. Qays was dispatched by Muʿāwiya, who ordered him to 'traverse the region below Wāqiṣa and attack every Bedouin whom he came upon who recognised the authority of ʿAlī' (tr. Hawting 1996, 201). Al-Ḍaḥḥāk is said to have led and army of 3000 men and have passed by al-Thaʿlabiyya to reach al-Quṭquṭāna (between Mecca and al-Kūfa). There he attacked a certain ʿAmr b. ʿUmays b. Masʿūd, who was making a pilgrimage with his family and a group of horsemen of ʿAlī. As a retaliation, ʿAlī sent Ḥujr b. ʿAdī al-Kindī against him together with an army of 4000 men. The two met at Palmyra; after a fight and some losses, al-Ḍaḥḥāk fled with his men at night.

The city would not appear again in written sources until the civil war between ʿAbd al-Malik b. Marwān and ʿAbd Allāh b. al-Zubayr. Ibn ʿAsākir (*Tāʾrīkh*, 55.261) reports that Banū Umayya was at the time under the protection of the people of Palmyra and how ʿUbayd Allāh b. Ziyād was able to persuade al-Ḍaḥḥāk b. Qays, who was on ʿAbd Allāh b. al-Zubayr's' side, to leave Damascus and take control of the city. Abū Mikhnaf, quoted by al-Ṭabarī (*Tāʾrīkh,* 7.482), recounts that the Umayyads had been driven out of Mecca, Medina, and the Ḥijāz by ʿAbd Allāh b. al-Zubayr and had found refuge at Palmyra. There Marwān was persuaded by ʿUbayd Allāh b. Ziyād to secure an oath of allegiance from the people of the city and those of the Banū Umayya who were still supporting him and to fight against the usurper. The caliph met al-Ḍaḥḥāk b. Qays at Marj Rāhiṭ, near Damascus, in 684, defeated, and killed him and most of his men. The passage in al-Ṭabarī represents the most circumstantial narration of the event. Much later, Ibn al-Athīr (*al-Kāmil*, 4.125) would take as accurate Abū Mikhnaf's narration and succinctly report the same episode. Abū Mikhnaf's account alone regards Palmyra as the refuge of Banū Umayya and the place where ʿUbayd Allāh b. Ziyād met Marwān. All the other sources recounting the episode inform us that the event took place in Damascus (Wellhausen 1963, 113–200, esp. 177). There is no evidence to support the accuracy of Abū Mikhnaf's account that, if proven to be reliable, would suggest that the city had at the time enough political authority and military strength to reverse a situation that even the caliph believed to be desperate.

After Marj Rāhiṭ, the Qays, who during the battle had suffered considerable losses, were seeking revenge against the Yemenites who had supported ʿAbd al-Malik, and especially against the Kalbites led by Ḥumayd b. Ḥurayth b. Baḥdal, the leader of Yazid's *shurṭa* (Crone 1980, 94). Actively involved in the fights against the Banū Kalb were mainly the Banū ʿĀmir, guided by Zufar b. al-Ḥārith al-Kilābī, who established himself in Qarqisīyā after the battle, and the Banū Sulaym, whose leader was ʿUmayr b. Ḥubāb. The latter had at first been on ʿAbd al-Malik's side but after Marj Rāhiṭ defected and joined Zufar b. al-Ḥārith (Wellhausen 1963, 201–2). The intertribal conflict that followed would remain a constant element in the Early Islamic period. As far as the history of Palmyra is concerned, however, it is worth looking at its early stage of development. The feud arose when Zufar b. al-Ḥārith attacked a settlement at al-Muṣayyakh, killing 20 Kalbites. As a retaliation, the Kalbites massacred several members of the Banū Numayr (one of the branches of the Qays in Syria), who were living with them in Palmyra. Al-Iṣfahānī recounts this event. In book 17 (112–13), the writer claims that Ḥumayd b. Ḥurayth b. Baḥdal went to Palmyra with the Kalbites, broke an existing treaty between the two tribes, and massacred Banū Numayr. In another place, the episode is recounted differently and in more detail. Ḥumayd b. Ḥurayth b. Baḥdal is said to have gone to Palmyra and to have imprisoned the people of the Banū Numayr. He left them in the custody of a Kalbite, a certain Maṭar b. ʿAwṣ, who is described as an extensive murderer. In a moment of anger, Ḥumayd commanded Maṭar to kill the prisoners. He realised only one hour later the potential consequence of his order and immediately sent a knight to Palmyra to prevent the slaughter. By the time he reached the city, however, Maṭar had already executed 60 men (al-Iṣfahānī, *al-Aghānī*, 20.120–121).

Although the two versions of the episode contain several discrepancies, they seem to agree on at least two points: 1. the Banū Kalb was living in the city with other tribal groups (which seems to be plausible; even Banū ʿĀmir seems to have been living in Palmyra among people of the Banū Kalb, al-Ṭabarī, *Tāʾrīkh*, 9.1796; Ibn ʿAsākir, *Tāʾrīkh*, 63.337); 2. the late 7th century saw the rising of inter-tribal tensions which affected the settlement itself. The latter point seems to be generally confirmed by archaeological evidence. Three published hoards of coins from Palmyra have chronological *termini post quem* that are interesting for the purpose of this discussion. One of them, found in the Camp of Diocletian, includes fragments of jewellery as well as 27 gold coins minted between the reign of Phocas and the mid-7th century; the latest issue is a *solidus* dated to the 8th indiction of the reign of Constants II (649–650) (Michałowski 1962, 63; Skowronek in Krzyżanowska 2014, 60–6). The others were found in the northwest quarter and consist respectively of about 750 and 18 silver Sasanian *dirhams*. They were collected during the Persian occupation of Syria and closed before the monetary reform of ʿAbd al-Malik (Gawlikowski 2002, 266–9; 2005, 463; 2009, 91; 2014, 71–120). These hoards cannot with certainty be associated specifically with the event recounted by al-Iṣfahānī. Yet, their burial might reflect the situation of tension that the city was undergoing in the last quarter of the 7th century.

Palmyra, however, remained somehow prosperous throughout the period of Umayyad dominion. A *sūq* was installed in the westernmost stretch of the Great Colonnade and a mosque was built nearby. Evidence of continuity of occupation has been found in all the residential buildings of the city and in pre-existing abandoned areas. Similarly, the Camp of Diocletian shows important traces of occupation in this period. This growth is not surprising, especially considering the direct political link between the Kalbites and the Umayyad family (Genequand 2012, 67). Also, it seems to be paralleled in other contemporary cities (both major urban realities, e.g., Jerusalem, al-Ruṣāfa, and secondary centres e.g., Jerash or Pella).

Palmyra is further mentioned during the conflict between al-Walīd b. Yazīd (743–744) and the usurper Yazīd b. al-Walīd, who eventually managed to obtain the caliphate. Most of the Kalbites seem to have supported the former, although some of its members joined the opposition together with the Qays. Almost all the sources recounting the events of the third *fitna* report that during Yazīd's uprising, al-Walīd was suggested to refuge in Palmyra, which was well-fortified (Ibn ʿAsākir, *Tāʾrīkh*, 63.337, 338, 345; al-Ṭabarī, *Tāʾrīkh*, 9.1796; al-ʿUṣfurī, *Tāʾrīkh*, 2.548). Yet, al-Walīd refused, according to al-Ṭabarī and Ibn ʿAsākir, because Banū ʿĀmir, who had rebelled against him, lived in the city (al-Ṭabarī, *Tāʾrīkh*, 9.1796). He then chose to flee to al-Bakhrāʾ where he met his death by the men of Yazīd. Apparently, the Kalbites who were with al-Walīd at al-Bakhrāʾ deserted because they did not want to fight against members of their own tribe. The only account that disagrees with these passages is that of Agapius (*Kitāb*, 511–12). The author recounts that al-Walīd was killed at Palmyra.

The reign of Yazīd b. al-Walīd was one of short duration. After 6 months the caliphate was taken over by his brother, Ibrāhīm b. al-Walīd (744). Ibrāhīm was supported by Sulaymān b. Hishām, general and son of ʿAbd al-Malik who fought the Byzantines in northern Mesopotamia, and, *inter alia*, the Kalbites of Palmyra. Opposition to Ibrāhīm came from the governor of Mesopotamia, Marwān b. Muḥammad b. Marwān, who inclined to support the candidacy to the caliphate of one of al-Walīd b. Yazīd's two sons. When Sulaymān b. Hishām executed them in Damascus, Marwān decided to march on the city, where he was given the oath of allegiance by its inhabitants and was raised to the caliphate. Agapius (*Kitāb,* 514–15) reports that by that time, Ibrāhīm b. al-Walīd and Sulaymān b. Hishām had already fled to Palmyra in refuge. In the city, they found the support of the Kalbites. From there, they would later go back to Damascus, to swear their allegiance to Marwān and end the opposition (al-Ṭabarī, *Tā'rīkh,* 9.1892; Ibn ʿAsākir, *Tā'rīkh,* 15.83; Agapius, *Kitāb,* 515).

After these events, a two-year rebellion led by Thābit b. Nuʿaym, the *wāli* of Palestine, broke out in 745. The new uprising forced Marwān to march to Syria and subdue the cities that had rebelled against him. He started from Homs. The Kalbites of Palmyra made clear their political stance against the current caliph, who was dependant on the Qays' support, by sending a contingent of 1000 cavalrymen to protect the city. The troop is said to have entered Homs 'on the night of the ʿId al-Fiṭr in 127' (6 July 745) and been under the command of Dhuʾāla b. al-Aṣbagh b. Dhuʾāla al-Kalbī. With him were three of his sons, Ḥamza, Dhuʾāla, and Furāfiṣa along with Muʿāwiya al-Saksakī, ʿIṣma b. al-Muqshaʿirr, Hishām b. Maṣād, and Ṭufayl b. Ḥāritha (al-Ṭabarī, *Tā'rīkh,* 9.1892–1893). Eventually, Homs surrendered to Marwān after a siege. Sources disagree on the fate of Dhuʾāla and the other Kalbites after this event. According to Ibn ʿAsakir, Dhuʾāla was killed and crucified in front of the gate of the city (Ibn ʿAsākir, *Tā'rīkh,* 17.326; see also Ibn Ḥabīb, *Muḥabbar,* 484; Crone 1980, 156). Yet, al-Ṭabarī (*Tā'rīkh,* 9.1895–6) recounts that Dhuʾāla and at least one of his sons, Ḥamza, were still alive after the capitulation of Palmyra shortly after. Having relieved Damascus and Tiberias and defeated Thābit b. Nuʿaym in Palestine, Marwān moved then to Palmyra.

The conquest of the dissident city is reported in detail by al-Ṭabarī (*Tā'rīkh,* 9.1895–6) and very synthetically by Ibn ʿAsākir (*Tā'rīkh,* 19.80) in discussing the life of Zumayl b. Suwayd al-Kalbī. Marwān first camped with his troops at Qasṭal, not far from Homs and later marched on Palmyra. Before moving from Qasṭal, however, the caliph made sure he had enough fodder and water for the march, because he had been informed that Kalbites had spoiled all the wells in the area. The capitulation of Palmyra was secured by treaty through the intercession of al-Abrash b. al-Walīd. Some of the Kalbites did not accept the treaty and fled to the desert: among them were ʿIṣma b. al-Muqshaʿirr, Ṭufayl b. Ḥāritha, who had both participated in the action at Homs, and Muʿāwiya b. Abī Sufyān b. Yazīd b. Muʿāwiya, the son in law of al-Abrash. By contrast, Yāqūt (*Muʿjam,* 1.829) reports that the city was taken by force and its population massacred. Archaeological evidence on the destruction associated with this event, as well as the alleged demolition of the city wall ordered by the caliph immediately afterwards, remains, however, absent. The destruction perpetrated by Marwān had been substantial in Syria (Ibn ʿAsākir, *Tā'rīkh,* 11.145), but they did not altogether prevent further rebellions from breaking out. In the year following the capitulation of Palmyra, Sulaymān b. Hishām claimed the caliphate for himself. He managed to take Qinnaṣrīn supported by the people of al-Ruṣāfa. Nonetheless, he was eventually defeated by Marwān and fled to Persia via Homs and Palmyra (Agapius, *Kitāb,* 517–18; Ibn ʿAsākir, *Tā'rīkh,* 22.395; Theoph., *Chr.,* 1.422). The events that followed brought about the collapse of the Umayyad dynasty, which ended with the death of Marwān in early August 750.

Epilogue: Palmyra after the fall of the Umayyad dynasty

The end of the Umayyad dynasty coincides with a reversal in the fortune of the city. Explanation for this has to be sought, we believe, primarily in the consequent collapse of the Kalbites' power associated with the Umayyads, who were slaughtered in the aftermath of the ʿAbbāsid accession to the caliphate. Despite the 740s tensions with Marwān, the Banū Kalb remained loyal to the Umayyad dynasty. At the end of July 750, a pro-Umayyad rebellion broke out against the ʿAbbāsids which involved also the Kalbites from Palmyra. Leading the uprising were Abū al-Ward al-Kilābī and Abū Muḥammad al-Sufyānī. The rebels, however, were defeated in the Qinnasrīn region by ʿAbd Allāh b. ʿAlī in late July 751. Abū al-Ward al-Kilābī was killed along with 500 of his followers, while Abū Muḥammad al-Sufyānī was able to flee with his men and the Kalbites to Palmyra. There, he resisted the attack of Bassām b. Ibrāhīm, who was sent by ʿAbd Allāh b. ʿAlī to take the city, and later fled to the desert (Cobb 2001, 46–8). The transfer of the capital from Damascus to Baghdad and the consequent move of the interest of the caliphate from Syria to Iraq might count as other reasons behind the city's collapse (Grimme 1886, 20).

Very little evidence survives to cast light on the post-Umayyad period of the city. The last bishop known from Palmyra, John (III) from the monastery of Mār Ḥanania, is said by Michael the Syrian (*Chr.,* 3.453) to have been consecrated in 818. The city centre seems to have been deserted already by the mid-9th century, although minor activities are attested in some places, such as the Camp of Diocletian. By the end of the 10th century the settlement might already have shrunk into the Sanctuary of Bēl (Gawlikowski 2009, 91). A number of inscriptions dating to 1132–1133 indicate the transformation of this compound into a fortress (*Inv.* 9, 54–5, n. 54; Huart 1929, 237–44; Sauvaget 1931, 143–8) and the conversion of the temple into a mosque (*Inv.* 9, 55–6, n. 55). The fortress on top of Qalʿat b. Mʿān, overlooking the city from the north was possibly constructed in the 13th century and experienced important structural addition, including a new gate, up until the occupation of the site by Fakhr al-Dīn in the 16th–17th centuries (Bylinski 1994; 1999). On medieval Palmyra, Ṣafī al-Dīn (*Marāṣid*, 1.200) writes, 'at present, its people live in its fortress, which has a stone wall. Its gate has two stone door panels. It also has granaries that remain to the present. They have a river that irrigates their palm trees and gardens' (similarly, see Ibn al-Shiḥna, *al-Durr al-Muntakhab*, 275–6). Al-Dimashqī (*Kitāb*, 39) gives a generic description of a mosque, which is probably not the one installed in the temple of Bēl, since it is reported to have a square plan. The settlement would survive in that condition for about nine centuries until the early 1930s, when French authorities would transfer its inhabitants to a newly erected town next to the abandoned ruins.

Chapter 8

Conclusions: Palmyra in perspective

Despite showing continuity with the earlier urban tradition, Late Antique cities in the East differ from their Roman counterparts for being 'small, fortified, Christian, and Imperial' (Zanini 2003, 214). In the Early Islamic period, pre-existing cities saw the addition of two important components in the urban fabric, namely the mosque and the *sūq*, and witnessed the continuity of the process the street grid's disintegration. How these changes affected Palmyra has already been discussed at length in the preceding chapters. The following wider, but necessarily brief and incomplete, overview of a selection of cities in Syria, which show continuity of occupation throughout Late Antiquity and the Early Islamic period, may help set our case study in a broader context.

Late Antiquity

A number of cities are recognised in written sources as renowned administrative and religious centres in Late Antique Syria. Two of these were of considerable size and held prominent statuses. Apamea extended for some 255ha. The walled city of Antioch, one of the largest cities in the Mediterranean, was double this size (Mango 2011, 96, fig. 3; 97, tab. 1; Foss 1992, 192). In both cities, the street pattern of earlier periods was well maintained. At Antioch, a new floor of basalt blocks was laid in the main colonnaded street and newly constructed porticoes were embellished with floors in *opus sectile* after the earthquakes of 526 and 528 and the capture of the city by the Persians in 540 (Lassus 1972, 148–51). Similarly, Apamea's Roman urban axis, a long colonnaded *decumanus* stretching in a north–south direction for about 2km, underwent major reconstructions to exhalt its *decor* throughout Late Antiquity. In 459, it was embellished with a *c.* 100m long mosaic and painted walls (Duliére 1974; Reekmans 1969). Much later, after a devastating earthquake, important renovations were carried out under Justinian, including the laying of new paving in part of the road, the covering of the mosaic floors with marble, the installation of a new drainage system and the construction of a *Tetrastylon* (Balty 1981, 46–84; Foss 1997, 207–8).

Among recreational buildings, baths seem to have left the most visible traces in the archaeological record. So far, in Antioch, seven bathing facilities, opulently adorned, have been discovered both inside and outside the city wall; yet, more are known through written sources. Although, for some of them, the chronology remains disputed, the majority seem to have survived, sometimes with major alterations, throughout Late Antiquity (Saliou 2014). Evidence from Apamea confirms the importance attributed to the practice of bathing by its urban community throughout the period under discussion. The 1200m^2 excavation of the bath complex in the northeast quarter would suggest that the compound was built in the 2nd century but remained in use throughout Late Antiquity with, however, a considerable reduction of its bathing area (Paridaens and Vannesse 2014, with further bibliography).

One would expect both Apamea and Antioch to be characterised by a high degree of social dynamism. In the archaeological record, however, evidence for the existence of an urban élite prevails. In Apamea, the process of beautification of existing large houses, such as the Maison au Triclinos, the Maison aux Consoles, the Maisons aux Colonnes Trilobées, the Maison aux Pilastres, the Maison du Cerf, and the Maison des Chapiteaux à Consoles, is very much in evidence. This included the addition of apsidal chambers, monochrome and polychrome mosaics, and the adoption of extensive marble decoration. In Antioch, evidence for houses of pretention is mostly associated with the presence of rich mosaics and painted stucco decorations in the Constantinian Villa, the House of the Bird-Rinceau, the House of the Triumph of Dionysius, the Yatqo Complex, the House of *Aiōn*, and the House of the Mask. The remains suggest the existence of an urban élite eager to express its status and flaunt its wealth through the construction of opulent private residential buildings (see above, p. 33).

Although maintaining the urban tradition remains the norm in both cities in Late Antiquity, new buildings started making their appearance. At Antioch, the earliest stronghold of Christianity in Syria, Imperial patronage seems to have been a key agent for urban development and church-building was often chosen as a means of manifesting the emperors' Christian piety. The list of churches and monasteries in the city and its vicinity is long (Downey 1961, 656–9). A number of churches are reported by written sources to be of Imperial foundation. Construction of the Μεγάλη Ἐκκλησία begun by Constantine in 327 and concluded around 341, when the building was dedicated. It had a roof gilded on the outside (thence also the name *Dominicum Aureum*) and was richly decorated (Downey 1961, 342–9); according to Kleinbauer (1973, 114), this became the prototype of aisled tetraconch churches in Syria and northern Mesopotamia. In the 6th century, Justinian and his wife Theodora were said to be responsible for the construction of the Theotokos Church, the Church of Saints Cosmas and Damian and the Church of the Archangel Michael (Downey 1961, 525–6). Archaeology at Apamea, which is more abundant, offers a glimpse of the elaborateness and monumentality that characterised churches in major cities. The Cathedral, built in the early years of the reign of Justinian by Bishop Thomas along the *decumanus* and about 500m from the *cardo*, had a domed tetraconch plan; it was entered via a monumental staircase and a porticoed courtyard embellished with a fountain and floor mosaics in its roofed areas (Balty 1981, 105–19, with further bibliography). Similar opulence would have characterised the *Rotunda*, which opened directly onto the *decumanus* (Balty 1981, 146–8; Foss 1997, 211).

The 'average' *poleis* in Syria could certainly not compete in grandeur and splendour with major cities like Antioch and Apamea. Yet, their development reflects urban processes already noted for larger 'mega-cities'. Their size varied: the walled area of late antique Qinnasrīn (*Chalcis*), to cite one, was some 80ha, while that of *Zenobia* (Ḥalabiyya) did not exceed 10ha (Mango 2011, 96, fig. 3; 97, tab. 1). A number of these *poleis* retained exceptional religious, administrative, or military statuses that triggered their urban development. From a mere fort along the eastern *limes*, base of the *Equites Promoti Indigenae* (*Not. Dig. Or.* 33.27), and alleged place of martyrdom of St Sergius (Georg. Cypr., *Descr. Orb. Rom.*, 882–3), al-Ruṣāfa was dramatically transformed in the 5th and 6th centuries to host the relics of the saint. Qinnasrīn, which has only recently been subjected to systematic excavations (Rousset 2012), retained such an exquisite military character in Byzantine times that modern secondary literature has made the city the centre of a presumed 'inner' defensive system, the controversial 'Limes de *Chalcis*' (Mouterde and Poidebard 1945).

The plan of these cities developed mostly within the physical limits provided by their circuit walls. Like Antioch and Apamea, existing cities maintained relatively intact their Roman urbanistic legacy. At *Bostra*, the major thoroughfares were largely respected, despite some minor invasion onto the roofed porticoes (e.g., the Nouveau Prétoire; Blanc *et al.* 2007, 21), and a major *Tetrapylon* was built in the 4th century at the crossroads between the main east–west axis and a north–south colonnaded street (Dentzer *et al.* 2007, 265–6, with extended bibliography). Similarly, new cities maintained the urbanistic aesthetic of earlier times. At al-Ruṣāfa, porticoed streets were laid along the urban circuit, while the interior of the city consisted of a fairly regular pattern of major roads, in places animated by monumental arches (Westphalen 2006). At Ḥalabiyya, which according to Procopius (*Aed.*, 2.8, 8) was greatly restored by Justinian, the two main colonnaded streets still crossed at right angles in a square marked by a *Tetrapylon* (Lauffray 1991, 35–42; Zanini 2003, 204; recently Blétry 2010, 253, fig. 3).

Bathing facilities remained common occurrences in medium-sized cities. The array of public buildings uncovered at Ḥalabiyya includes a bath complex and a gym, both of Justinianic foundation. The former is situated in the northeast quadrant of the settlement immediately next to the east wall of the ramparts and it was richly decorated. It consisted of a large rectangular *frigidarium* accessible from a narrow corridor (the *apodyterium*) to the west. It was connected to the south with a series of rooms with semi-circular ends, which would have served as *tepidarium* and *caldarium*. The baths were connected to the north with the gym, which consisted of a large open courtyard surrounded by rooms on its east, west, and north sides (Lauffray 1991, 113–29). *Bostra* was home to two major bath complexes: the Therme du Sud and the Therme du Centre, both richly adorned and occupying extensive surface areas (the first, 8000m^2; the second, 7000m^2). At its peak of development, the Therme du Centre counted some 34 rooms, including a large gym and a vast *latrina* whose capacity exceeded 100 seats (Broise and Fournet 2007; Fournet 2007, 243–4, with further bibliography).

Very little has been documented on private residential buildings. Data is lacking for Dibsī Faraj, where a number of houses were uncovered, but not fully published. One of them, a 'rich house', using Harper's words, was provided with an attached bath; it was constructed in the early 4th century and abandoned only some years later, when the new church was built in the southwest corner of the Citadel (Harper 1975, 325). Lauffray's work at Ḥalabiyya identified 11 houses scattered *intra muros*. One of them, the so-called 'Maison de l'Ours' or 'Maison du Lion' is characterised by a large porticoed court surrounded by lateral rooms. Also noteworthy is a complex of habitations located to the north of the unexcavated *Forum*. Although the inner arrangement is difficult to determine, it is still possible to follow the development of at least four residences consisting of no more than seven communicating units each (Lauffray 1991, 135–41). At *Bostra*, the pretentiousness of the 5th–6th century Trajan's Palace with is eclectic 'espace triconque', its unusual size, and its rich decorative apparatus must certainly have represented an exception in the panorama of the city's private residential buildings (Piraud-Fournet 2003, 1–40; 2007, 147–54).

As in Antioch and Apamea, churches remain an ubiquitous presence in smaller urban centres. At *Bostra*, three churches have so far been excavated. Two of them, the so-called Cathédrale de l'Est and the Church of Saints Sergius, Leontius, and Bacchus had monumental centralised plans, while the other, the church to the northeast of the South Bath, is a mono-apsidal basilica. Vast spaces and the use of rich decorative apparatus are characteristics found, to various degrees, in all three of these compounds (Blan *et al.* 2007, 137–46; Farioli Campanati 2007, 155–60; Farioli Campanati and Masturzo 2007, 217, with extensive bibliography). Ḥalabiyya counted at least two. One, interpreted as the cathedral and built under Anastasius, consisted of an imposing *atrium*, a *narthex* and a main building of 38.5 × 21.5m (Lauffray 1991, 49–95). The second church (so-called Église Ouest) was much smaller (19.5 × *c.* 31m); despite being not as richly adorned architecturally as the latter, its three-aisled, mono-apsidal main body was accessible through an open court and a *narthex*, and was provided with a small dependent baptistery flanking the apse (Lauffray 1991, 97–111). Dibsī Faraj's Citadel Basilica, had an exceptional main body of 41.5 × 29.5m and was richly adorned with mosaic floors bearing animal and stylised floral motifs. The second church of the city (so-called *Martyrion* Basilica), was relatively less impressive. Measuring 51 × 23.75m, this narrow basilica included a rich array of mosaic floors mostly adorned with geometric decorations (Harper 1975, 330–4). Of the four churches known at al-Ruṣāfa, Basilica A (54.4 × 28.6m) is one of the biggest early Christian churches in the whole of Syria (Ulbert 1986; for more recent discussion and bibliography see, Fowden 1999, 80–7). The church, located in the southeastern section of the city, would have included a richly adorned *martyrion*, a large porticoed courtyard, and a cross-in-square baptistery. The pretentiousness of the compound and the attention granted to large open areas functional for receiving large masses of pilgrims are justified by the role of the church, to which the remains of the saints were translated to rest in the early 6th century.

The case study of Androna (al-Andarīn) warns us against adopting arbitrarily the modern label of 'city' for Late Antique settlements. The site is located on the western fringe of the central Syrian steppe, between the Orontes and the Euphrates. It is reported to have been a *mansio* between Palmyra and *Chalcis* by the Antonine Itinerary and a κώμη, a village, in a 6th century floor mosaic inscription (Mouterde and Poidebard 1945, 60–3; Salame-Sarkis 1989, 322–5). Although it never received the status of *polis*, it was characterised by exceptional size (about 160 ha) and extraordinary urban features. It has an orthogonal plan delimited by two circuit walls – an inner and an outer one. At the centre of the settlement stands a *kastron*, a fort built by a certain Thomas in 558–559. The compound covers an impressive area of about 6000m^2; it has a square plan with four polygonal projecting corner towers and two interval rectangular towers on its north and east sides. Two entrances were located on the south and west sides and were flanked by rectangular towers. Double-storey living and working rooms were placed against the four walls. At the centre of the open court delimited by these rooms stands one of the dozen churches known in the settlement. It is a richly adorned, triple-aisled mono-apsidal basilica with two rows of arcades supported by limestone capitals (see Strube 2003; 2008; Mango 2011, with further bibliography).

Opposite the *kastron* to the west is the Byzantine Bath erected in 558–559 by the same Thomas responsible for the construction of the military compound. The building consists of an entrance court, a *frigidarium* with two rectangular pools, a *tepidarium*, and a *caldarium* with six semi-circular and rectangular pools. The decorative apparatus of the complex included imported marble, mostly from the Sea of Marmara, of which some 500kg have so far been recovered, wall paintings, and glass wall mosaics (Mango 2002; 2003; 2008; 2011). Private residential buildings excavated in the city show a certain degree of luxury and include large reception halls and rich mosaic floors (Strube 2003, 89–93; 2008, 59). The expansion of the settlement in the 5th and especially the 6th century resulted in a major exploitation of the fertile surroundings which is reflected in the increase of field irrigation (especially *qanawāt* and reservoirs: Mango 2008, 75–9; 2011, 103–22). The demands of the military markets might have been the first cause for the prosperity of this rural settlement. Surplus produced by the village could have been used to supply nearby military centres such as Chalcis (Mango 2011, 116).

Early Islamic period

The fate of existing cities in the Early Islamic period is mixed (see the summary in Walmsley 2007a, 76–90). By the second half of the 6th century, the urban *status quo* created during the peaceful conditions of the previous century underwent drastic changes in the two major centres of Antioch and Apamea. Both had already experienced major disruptions as a consequence of earthquakes and were severely affected by Persian raids. Antioch underwent major destructions during the Persian attack of 540; the city was restored by Justinian but capitulated again under the Persians in 610 and was conquered in 638 by Muslim forces. In this new political scenario, Antioch became a frontier city of renowned importance, hosting a permanent garrison. Despite its significance, the history of the city under the Umayyads remains obscure (see, in particular, Kennedy 1992). Albeit little, there is structural evidence to suggest a dramatic change in the quality of urban life and a reduction in urban activity. Buildings of rather modest quality (private residential structures, shops, and productive areas) invade the main streets and former public buildings such as the Hippodrome and the city's baths (Foss 1997, 194, with further bibliography). Written sources recount that Apamea was spared from the destructions of Chosroes. Yet, the city was deprived of much of its movable wealth. Apamea is reported to have been eventually destroyed by Adarman, general of Chosroes, in 573, conquered in 611 by the Persians, and, some 25 years later, overcome by the Muslims (Foss 1997, 206). The archaeological record suggests continuity of life and typical post-Classical urban transformations. Industrial installations, small shops, and private residential buildings started invading open monumental spaces, such as the *Agora* and the *decumanus*, where blocking walls were installed in its porticoes. Other public buildings went out of use. The *Nymphaeum* was covered in debris and later occupied by a burial, while the *Latrina* was abandoned after the 7th century. The opulent houses of the Late Antique aristocracy were subdivided into smaller units, perhaps to accommodate new families, and productive and storage facilities of rural character were installed (Foss 1997, 209–10, with further bibliography). At the dawn of the Islamic era, both Antioch and Apamea were not deserted, but lost their privileged status to the advantage of Qinnasrīn and Homs, which became the capitals of two *ajnād* (Walmsley 2007a, 74).

Other cities underwent major reconstructions. Al-Ruṣāfa was greatly refurbished after Hishām b. ʿAbd al-Malik took the caliphate in 724. A transept-type mosque, 56 × 40m in size, was constructed occupying part of the courtyard of Basilica A, therefore linking the new Muslim place of worship to the existing Christian sacred topography. The building makes extensive use of *spolia* from the ruined Basilica A, which had experienced destructions by an earthquake not long after its construction. Material from the same building was also reused for the construction of a nearby *sūq*, likely contemporary with the mosque, in the western courtyard of Basilica A (Sack 1996; Ulbert 1986; 1992). The construction of a *sūq* under Hishām b. ʿAbd al-Malik is not a prerogative of al-Ruṣāfa and is proof of a programmatic urban building revival in the region. Outside the urban circuit, Hishām b. ʿAbd al-Malik was responsible for the construction of a residence, which recent geophysical surveys have proved to extend for about 3km^2 (Sack and Becker 1999; Gussone and Müller-Wiener 2012, with further bibliography).

There is a significant gap in the data, which is difficult to overcome in order to understand the development of medium-sized cities in Early Islamic times. At Dibsī Faraj, the Early Islamic phase is much present, but not published in full. A large L-shaped building was constructed in the Citadel, making use of material dilapidated from earlier structures. This is partly installed in the pre-existing Citadel Basilica, whose nave and aisles served as an open courtyard (Harper 1975, 333). In addition, the baths underwent important changes in their nature; their extent is difficult to appreciate in Harper's report. Reflooring and opening of new doorways are documented, however (Harper 1975, 330). Similarly, the case study of *Bostra* discussed briefly above, does not seem to have left much trace of its Umayyad past. Despite the visible remains of the Mosque of ʿUmar being certainly later in date (12th–13th century), two inscriptions dated to the first half of the 8th century suggest building activities in the period under discussion (Korn 2007, 284). Other secondary centres show evident traces of continuity in occupation, which is sometimes represented by monumental construction (Walmsley 2007a, 83–4). The Umayyad Mosque at Jerash is one example of this. Built in stone and some 40 × 45m in size, it was located next to the ancient *Tetrakionion* of the city. Close to the new mosque, a number of shops were constructed, extending into the *Tetrakionion* Square (Walmsley 2003; Walmsley 2007a, 84–6; Walmsley and Damgaard 2005). A second example of a building project that went far beyond the small-scale private building activities of Early Islamic cities is to be found at Baysān, ancient *Scythopolis*, where a new marketplace comprising 20 lined shops preceded by a portico was built at the time of Hishām b. ʿAbd al-Malik (Tsafrir and Foerster 1997, 138–40).

Conclusions – Palmyra in perspective

Palmyra survived the events of 273 and grew to host a sizable urban community. It qualifies as a *polis* by written sources and developed to become one of the earliest bishoprics in the region, having in the 6th century at least eight churches. The city developed within its ramparts, making use of its pre-existing Roman street pattern. The Great Colonnade, the main Roman thoroughfare, was maintained and kept in use. Little is left for conjecture on the single bath complex known at the site, the Baths of Diocletian. The tendency toward opulence expressed in this compound, with the extensive adoption of reused marble material and the monumental access, recalls, albeit on a more modest scale, contemporary and later examples in the region.

Palmyra's exquisite military character, however, makes this city stand out from the others. Here, the military sphere merged physically with the civilian one. An imposing and architecturally elaborate fortress was constructed within the boundaries of the ancient city and to the detriment of pre-existing religious buildings, occupying an extensive part of the civilian settlement. Unlike al-Andarīn, where the *intra muros kastron* was built by civil initiative, and al-Ruṣāfa, which was transformed from a military fortress into a pilgrimage centre, in Palmyra the military became the main agent for urban development and trigged Imperial investments. The *praeses provinciae* was responsible for the construction of both the fortress and the baths in the city centre under Diocletian.

The relationship between the military and the civilian spheres was particularly strong and somehow symbiotic. The relative period of stability caused by the peaceful condition of the 5th century in Syria resulted in the shrinkage of the garrison of the city and an obscure phase for the civilian settlement. Yet, when necessity moved the Imperial authority to re-establish a regular garrison in Palmyra, the settlement revived. The city's historical development seems to reflect, then, the growing preponderance of the military component in Late Antique cities. The urban community, of which, admittedly, still very little is known, had to adapt to changed political and economic circumstances. The flux of wealth that had been channelled into the city through long distance trade in Roman times stopped abruptly in the late 3rd century. Associated with this event is the end of the construction and embellishment of rich private residential buildings. This reflects an important change in the social stratification of the city and the drastic reduction of the existing Palmyrene urban aristocracy. Not surprisingly, the only 'house of pretension' with a peristyled courtyard built anew in Late Antiquity in the city is that of a military officer. The army became the new engine of economic growth. The garrison in the city, which, in the 4th century, consisted of a legion and, in the first half of the 6th century, of part of the backbone of the regular Byzantine army in the province, might have found in the city the main source for supplies and recreational activities.

The alleged bloodless conquest of the city in 634 by the Muslim forces did not mark a drastic shift in the city's fortunes. The circuit wall seems to have been left intact and no major levels of destruction are known from the city centre. Palmyra maintained its fame as a fortress throughout Umayyad times, as written sources report it to have been used as a safe place by several political refugees. Yet, the collapse of the Roman eastern frontier meant that a garrison had no more reason to exist. The new political scenario and the consequent re-establishment of East-West trade routes must have had largely positive repercussions for Palmyra's economy. A solid class of merchants must have played a significant part in its economic life. At the time, the importance of Palmyra was also political, as the city was the base of the Banū Kalb, who supported the caliphate in Damascus. Throughout the Umayyad caliphate, the city experienced a process of rebuilding that saw the construction of a mosque in the city centre and a *sūq*. The existence of the mosque-*sūq* pair is not surprising and finds parallels in numerous other contemporary settlements. Inter-tribal conflicts exacerbated by political tensions might have occurred in Palmyra in the late 7th century, written sources and the burial of a number of hoards confirming their occurrence. Yet, this did not prevent altogether the city's survival. Eventually, the rise to power of the ʿAbbāsid dynasty marked the end of the political support received by Palmyra from the central power. As a consequence of Kalbite uprisings, the city was besieged; its walls are said by written sources to have been destroyed, although this event does not seem to be confirmed by the archaeological record. Evidence of continuity does exist after the mid-8th century: Christianity remained alive and a number of buildings were renovated in the city centre. However, the built up area gradually shrank and its inhabitants eventually moved into the better protected *temenos* of the Sanctuary of Bēl. Besides the characteristic military and political role that Palmyra assumed throughout Late Antiquity and the Early Islamic period, it seems, therefore, that the settlement behaved not dissimilarly from other contemporary medium-sized cites, demonstrating permeability in the face of the generalised changes that occurred as a result of profound transformation in the administrative, religious, and cultural structure of the Levant.

Bibliography

Abbreviations of written sources and epigraphic *corpora*

Abū al-Fidā', *Taqwīm al-Buldān* = Abū al-Fidā, *Taqwīm al-Buldān*, ed. H. O. Fleischer, 1831. Leipzig: F. Chr. W. Vogel.

Abū Nuwās, *Dīwān* = Abū Nuwās, *Dīwān Abū Nuwās*, ed. E. Wagner, 2001–2006. Beirut–Berlin: Das Arabische Buch.

ACO = *Acta Conciliorum Oecumenicorum*. 1914–1940. Strasbourg: de Gruyter.

Agapius, *Kitāb* = Agapius, *Kitāb al-'Unwān*, ed. and tr. (French) A. A. Vasiliev, 1912, *Patrologia Orientalis* 8 (2.2), 399–547.

AE = *L'Année épigraphique*. 1889–. Paris: Leroux, Presses Universitaires de France.

Alex. Akoim. = 'Life of Alexander the Akoimetes', ed. and tr. (French) E. de Stoop, 1909. *Patrologia Orientalis* 6, 641–705.

Amm. Marc., Res Gest. = *Ammianus Marcellinus, Res Gestae*, ed. and tr. J. C. Rolfe, 1935–1940. London-Cambridge, MA: Heinemann, Harvard University Press.

Anas. Per. = Flusin, B. 1992. *Saint Anastase le Perse et l'Histoire de la Palestine au début du VIIe siècle*. Paris: Editions du Centre National de la Recherche Scientifique.

Ibn 'Asākir, *Tā'rīkh* = Ibn 'Asākir, *Tā'rīkh Madīnat Dimashq*, ed. 'U. G. al-'Amrawī, 1995–2000. Beirut: Dār al-Fikr.

Ibn A'tham al-Kūfī, *Kitāb* = Ibn A'tham al-Kūfī, *Kitāb al-Futūḥ*, ed. M. 'A. Khān and 'A. W. Bukhārī, 1968–1975. Hyderabad: Osmania Oriental Publications Bureau.

Ibn al-Athīr, *al-Kāmil* = Ibn al-Athīr, *al-Kāmil fī al-Tā'rīkh*, ed. C.J. Tornberg, 1866–1871. Leiden: Brill.

al-Balādhurī, *Futūḥ* = *al-Balādhurī*, *Futūḥ al-Buldān*, ed. M. J. de Goeje, 1866. Leiden: Brill. Tr. P. K. Hitti, 1916. New York: Longmans Green.

Benj. Tud., *It.* = Benjamin of Tudela, *Itinerary*, ed. and tr. M. N. Adler, 1907. London: H. Frowde.

C. Th. = *Codex Theodosianus*. Ed. R. Mommsenn, 1962 (3rd ed.). Berlin: Weidmann.

Chr. Zuq. = *Chronicle of Zuqnin*, ed. J.-B. Chabot, 1933. Tr. R. Hespel, 1989. Paris: Peeters.

Chron. 1234 = *Chronicon ad annum Christi 1234 pertinens*, ed. J.-B. Chabot, 1916–1920. Paris: Ex Typographeo Reipublicae.

CIJ = J. B. Frey 1936–1952. *Corpus Inscriptionum Judaicarum*. Rome: Pontificio Istituto di Archeologia Cristiana.

CIL = *Corpus Inscriptionum Latinarum*. 1852–. Berlin,

CIS = *Corpus Inscriptionum Semiticarum*. 1881–1962. Paris.

De Re Strategica = *De Re Strategica*. Ed. and tr. G. T. Dennis, 1985. Washington: Dumbarton Oaks, Research Library and Collection.

al-Dimashqī, *Kitāb* = al-Dimashqī, *Kitāb Nukhbat al-Dahr fī 'ajā'ib al-Barrwa-al-Baḥr*. Ed. M. A. F. Mehren, 1923. Leipzig: Harrassowitz.

Evagr. *HE.* = Evagrius, *Historia Ecclesiastica*, ed. J. Bidez and L. Parmentier, 1898. London: Methuen. Tr. M. Whitby, 2000. Liverpool: Liverpool University Press.

Ibn al-Faqīh, *Mukhtaṣar* = Ibn al-Faqīh, *Mukhtaṣar Kitāb al-Buldān*, ed. M. J. Goeje, 1885. Leiden: Brill.

Georg. Cyp., *Desc. Orb. Rom.* = George of Cyprus, *Descriptio Orbis Romani*, ed. and tr. E. Honigmann, 1939. Bruxelles: Institute de Philologie et d'Histoire Orientales et Slaves.

Ibn Ḥabīb, *Muḥabbar* = Ibn Ḥabīb, Muḥammad, *Kitāb al-Muḥabbar*, ed. I. Lichtenstädter, 1942. Hyderabad: Dā'irat al-Ma'ārif.

al-Hamadānī, *al-Iklīl* = al-Hamadānī, *al-Iklīl al-Juz' al-Thāmin*, ed. N. A. Faris, 1940. Princeton, NJ: Princeton University Press.

Ḥamza al-Iṣfahānī, *Tā'rīkh* = Ḥamza al-Iṣfahānī, *Tā'rīkh Sinī Mulūk al-Arḍ wa'l-Anbiya'*, ed. and tr. J. M. E. Gottwald, 1844–1848. Leipzig, St Petersburg: Leopoldum Voss.

Hier., *Synec.* = Hierocles, *Synecdemos*, ed. and tr. E. Honigmann, 1939. Bruxelles: Institute de Philologie et d'Histoire Orientales et Slaves.

HA Aurelianus. = *Historia Augusta Vita Aureliani*, ed. and tr. F. Paschoud, 1996. Paris: Les Belles Lettres.

IGLS 5 = L. Jalabert, R. Mouterde, with C. Mondésert 1959. *Inscriptions Grecques et Latines de la Syrie. Emésène*. Paris: P. Geuthner.

IGLS 17.1 = J.-B. Yon 2012. *Inscriptions Grecques et Latines de la Syrie. Palmyre*. Beirut: Presses de l'IFPO.

ILS = H. Dessau (ed.) 1892–1916. *Inscriptiones Latinae Selectae. Berlin*: Weidmann.

Ins. Jud. Or.3 = D. Noy and H. Bloedhorn 2004. *Inscriptiones Judaicae Orientis III; Syria and Cyprus*. Tübingen: Mohr Siebeck.

Inv. = *Inventaire des inscriptions de Palmyre* (1–9 by J. Cantineau; 10 by J. Starcky; 11 by J. Teixidor; 12 by A. Bounni and J. Teixidor). 1930–1975. Beirut–Damascus.

Isaac, *Hom.* = Isaac of Antioch, *Homelies*, ed. and tr. G. Bickell, 1873. Giessen: W. *Keller.*

al-Iṣfahānī, *al-Aghānī* = al-Iṣfahānī, *Kitāb al-Aghānī*, ed. N. al-Hūrīnī, 1867–1869. Cairo: Būlāq.

Jer. *Ep.* = Jerome, *Epistulae*, ed. I. Hilbert, 1996. Vienna: Vienna Academy of Science.

John Eph., *EH* = John of Ephesus, *Ecclesiastical History*, ed. W. Cureton,1853. Oxford: Oxford University Press. Tr. P.R. Smith, 1860. Oxford: Oxford University Press.

John Eph., *Jac. Bar.* = John of Ephesus, *Life of Jacobus Baradaeus*, ed. E. W. Brooks, 1924. *Patrologia Orientalis* 18. Paris: Firmin-Didot.

Josh. Styl., *Chr.* = Joshua the Stylite, *Chronicle*, ed. and tr. W. Wright, 1882. Cambridge: Cambridge University Press. Tr. F. R. Trombley and J. W. Watt, 2011. Liverpool: Liverpool University Press.

Mal., *Chr.* = John Malalas, *Chronographia*, ed. H. Thurn, 2000. Berlin: de Gruyter. Tr. E. Jeffreys, M. Jeffreys and R. Scott, 1986. Melbourne: Australian Association for Byzantine Studies.

al-Masʿūdī, *Murūj* = al-Masʿūdī, *Murūj al-Dhahab wa Maʿādin al-Jawhar*, ed. and tr. (French) C. B. de Meynard and P. de Courteille, 1861–1877. Paris: L'Imprimerie Impériale.

Mich. Syr., *Chr.* = Michael the Syrian, *Chronicle*, ed. and tr. (French) J.-B. Chabot, 1899–1910. Paris: Ernest Leroux.

al-Muqaddasī, *Aḥsan* = al-Muqaddasī, *Aḥsan al-taqāsīm fī maʿrifat al-aqālīm*, ed. M. J. de Goeje, 1906. Leiden: Brill.

Not. Dig. = *Notitia Dignitatum*, ed. O. Seeck, 1876. Berlin: Weidmann.

PAES = E. Littmann (ed.) 1914. *Publications of the Princeton University Archaeological Expeditions to Syria, div. 4 'Semitic inscription', sect. A*. Leiden: Brill.

Pall., *Dial. John Chris.* = Palladius, *Dialogue on the life of John Chrysostom*, ed. and tr. A.-M. Malingrey and P. Leclercq, 1988. Paris: Editions du Cerf.

Pan. Lat. = *Panegyrici Latini*, ed. R. B. Mynors, 1964. Oxford: Clarendon Press.

Priscus = Priscus of Panium, in R. C. Blockley 1981–1983. *The Fragmentary Classicising Historians of the Later Roman Empire*. Liverpool: F. Cairns II, 222–376. More recent ed. by P. Carolla 2008. Berlin, New York: Walter de Gruyter.

Proc., *Aed.* = Procopius, *De Aedificiis*, ed. and tr. H.B. Dewing, 1961. London-New York: William. More recent edition by D. Roques 2011. Alessandria: Edizioni dell'Orso.

Proc., *Bell.* = Procopius, *De Bellis*, ed. J. Haury, 1963–1964. Leipzig: In aedibus B. G. Teubneri.

Ṣafī al-Dīn, *Marāṣid* = Ṣafī al-Dīn, *Marāṣid al-Iṭṭilāʿ ʿalā Āsmāʾ al-Amkina wa-al-Biqāʿ*, ed. T. G. J. Juynboll, 1852–1864. Leiden: Brill.

Soz., *EH* = Sozomen, *Ecclesiastical History*, ed. J. Bidez, 1983. Paris: Éditions du cerf. Tr. E. Walford. London: Henry G. Bohn.

Steph. Byz., *Ethnika* = Stephanus of Byzantium, *Ethnika*, vol. 4 (Π-Y), ed. and tr. (German) M. Billerbeck and A. Neumann-Hartmann, 2016. Berlin: de Gruyter.

Ibn al-Shiḥna, *al-Durr al-Muntakhab* = Ibn al-Shiḥna, *al-Durr al-Muntakhab fī tāʾrīkh mamlakat Ḥalab*, ed. J. E. Sarkis, 1909. Beirut: Imprimerie Catholique.

al-Ṭabarī, *Tāʾrīkh* = al-Ṭabarī, *Tāʾrīkh al-Rusul wa-al-Mulūk*, ed. M. J. de Goeje *et al.*, 1879–1901. Leiden: Brill. Tr. VV. AA., 1989–2007. Albany: SUNY Press.

Tab. Peut. = *Tabula Peutingeriana*, ed. E. Weber, 1967. Graz: Akademische Druck- und Verlagsanstalt.

Theop., *Chr.* = Theophanes, *Chronographia*, ed. C. de Boor, 1884. Leipzig: B. G. Teubnneri.

Th. Sim., *Hist.* = Theophylact Simoncatta, *Historiae*, ed. M. Whitby and M. Whitby, 1986. Oxford: Oxford University Press.

al- ʿUṣfurī, *Tāʾrīkh* = al- ʿUṣfurī, *Tāʾrīkh*, ed. A. D. al- ʿUmarī, 1967. Najaf: Maṭbaʿat al-Ādāb.

al-Wāqidī, *al-Maghāzī* = al-Wāqidī, *Kitāb al-Maghāzī*, ed. W. Nassau Lees, 1854. Calcutta: F. Carbery, Bengal Military Orphan Press.

al-Yaʿqūbī, *Tāʾrīkh* = al-Yaʿqūbī, *Tāʾrīkh al-Yaʿqūbī*, ed. 1960: Beirut: Dār Ṣādr, Dār Bayrūt.

Yāqūt, *Muʿjam* = Yāqūt, *Kitāb Muʿjam al-Buldān*, ed. F. Wüstenfeld, 1866–1873. Leipzig: F. A. Brokhaus. Tr. G. Le Strange, 1890. London: Alexander P. Watt.

Veg., *Epit.* = Vegetius, *Epitoma Rei Militaris*, ed. and tr. M. D. Reeve, 2004. Oxford: Clarendon Press.

Zos., *Hist. Nov.* = Zosimus, *Historia Nova*, ed. and tr. F. Paschoud, 2000. Paris: Les Belles Lettres. Alternative tr. J. J. Buchanan, H. T. Davis, 1967. S. Antonio: Trinity University Press.

Secondary literature

al-Asʿad, K. 1967. 'Ḥawl al-maqbara al-bīzanṭya fī ḥadiqat Mat-ḥaf Tadmur'. *Annales Archéologiques Arabes Syriennes* 17, 55–60.

al-Asʿad, K. 1968. 'Mudhakira ḥawl al-maqbara al-bīzanṭya al-Muktashfa fī ḥadiqat Mat-ḥaf Tadmur 1967–1968'. *Annales Archéologiques Arabes Syriennes* 18, 129–132.

al-Asʿad, K. and Gawlikowski, M., 1986–1987. 'New honorific inscriptions in the Great Colonnade of Palmyra'. *Annales Archéologiques Arabes Syriennes* 36–37, 164–171.

al-Asʿad, K. and Ruprechtsberger, E. M. 1987. 'Palmyra in spätantiker, oströmischer (byzantinischer) und frühislamischer Zeit'. In E. M. Ruprechtsberger (ed.). *Palmyra, Geschichte, Kunst und Kultur der syrischen Oasenstadt. Einführende Beiträge und Katalog zur Ausstellung*. Linz: Gutenberg, 137–148.

al-Asʿad, K. and Schmidt-Colinet, A. 1992. 'Joint archaeological mission at Palmyre in 1991–1992'. *Chronique Archéologique en Syrie: publication spéciale consacrée aux rapports annuels de l'archéologie en Syrie* 1, 140–142.

al-Asʿad, K. and Stępniowski, F. M. 1989. 'The Umayyad Suq in Palmyra'. *Damaszener Mitteilungen* 4, 205–223.

Alchermes, J. 1994. 'Spolia in Roman cities of the late empire: legislative rationales and architectural reuse'. *Dumbarton Oaks Papers* 48, 167–178.

al-Asʿad, W. 2013. 'Some tombs recently excavated in Palmyra'. *Studia Palmireńskie* 12, 15–24.

Amy, R. and Seyrig, H. 1936. 'Recherches dans la nécropole de Palmyre'. *Syria* 17, 229–266.

Amy, R., Seyrig, H. and Will, E. 1975. *Le temple de Bel à Palmyre*. Paris: P. Geuthner.

Avi Yonah, M. 1976. *Encyclopedia of Archaeological Explorations in the Holy Land. II*. Jerusalem: Israel Exploration Society and Massada Press.

Avram, A. 2001–2003. 'Inscription funéraire Byzantine de Palmyre'. *Studii Clasice* 37–39, 245–249.

Bagnall, R. S., Cameron, A., Schwartz, S. R. and Worp, K. A. 1987. *Consuls of the Later Roman Empire*. Atlanta, GA: Scholars Press.

Baldini Lippolis, I. 2001. *Ladomus tardoantica. Forme e rappresentazioni dello spazio domestico nel città del Mediterraneo*. Imola: Bologna University Press.

Baldini Lippolis, I. 2005. *L'architettura residenziale nelle città tardo antiche*. Rome: Carocci.

Baldini Lippolis, I. 2007. 'Private space in Late Antique cities: laws and building procedures'. In L. Lavan, L. Özgenel and A. Sarantis (eds). *Housing in Late Antiquity: from palaces to shops*. Leiden: Brill, 197–237.

Balty, J. 1977. *Mosaïques antiques de Syrie*. Bruxelles: Centre belge de recherches archéologiques à Apamée de Syrie.

Balty, J. 1984. 'La maison aux consoles'. In J. Balty (ed.). *Apamée de Syrie: bilan des recherches archéologiques, 1973–1979: aspects de l'architecture domestique d'Apamée: actes du colloque tenu à Bruxelles les 29, 30 et 31 Mai 1980*. Bruxelles-Paris: Centre belge de recherches archéologiques à Apamée de Syrie, 19–40.

Balty, J. and Balty, J.-C. 1977. 'Apamée de Syrie, archéologie et histoire. 1. Des origines à la Tétrarchie'. In H. Temporini (ed.). *Aufstieg und Niedergang der Römischen Welt* II.8. Berlin: de Gruyter, 103–134.

Balty, J. and Balty, J.-C. 2004. 'Nouveaux exemples de bêma Syrien'. In J. M. Blázques Martínez and A. Gonzáles (eds). *Sacralidad y arqueología. Homenaje al Prof. Thilo Ulbert al cumplir 65 años*. Murcia: Universidad de Murcia, 447–457.

Balty, J.-C. 1969. 'L'édifice dit "au triclinos"'. In J. Balty (ed.). *Apamée de Syrie; bilan des recherches archéologiques 1965–1968. Actes du colloque tenu à Bruxelles les 29 et 30 avril 1969*. Bruxelles: Centre belge de recherches archéologiques à Apamée de Syrie, 105–116.

Balty, J.-C. 1981. *Guide d'Apamée*. Bruxelles: Centre Belge de Recherches Archéologiques à Apamée de Syrie.

Balty, J.-C. 1989. 'La maison urbaine en Syrie'. In J.-M. Dentzer and W. Orthmann (eds). *Archéologie et histoire de la Syrie II. La Syrie de l'époque achéménide à l'avènement de l'Islam*. Saarbrüken: Saarbrüken Drukerei und Verlag, 407–422.

Balty, J.-C. and Napoleone-Lemaire, J. 1969. *L'église à atrium de la grande colonnade*. Bruxelles: Centre Belge de Recherces Archeologiques à Apamée.

Barański, M. 1994. 'The Roman army in Palmyra: a case of adaptation of a pre-existing city'. In E. Dąbrowa (ed.). *The Roman and Byzantine Army in the East: proceedings of a colloquium held at the Jagiellonian University, Kraków in September 1992*. Krakow: Uniwersytet Jagiellonski, Instytut Historii, 9–17.

Barański, M. 1995. 'The Great Colonnade of Palmyra reconsidered'. *ARAM* 7, 37–42

Barański, M. 1997. 'The Western aqueduct in Palmyra'. *Studia Palmireńskie* 10, 7–17.

Baratte, F. 1984. 'La maison des chapiteaux á consoles'. In J. Balty (ed.). *Apamée de Syrie. Bilan des recherches archéologiques 1973–1979. Aspects de l'architecture domestique d'Apamée. Actes du colloque tenu á Bruxelles les 29, 30 et 31 Mai 1980*. Bruxelles: Centre Belge de Recherches Archéologiques á Apamée de Syrie, 107–125.

Baronius, C., 1589. *Martyrologium Romanum, ad nouam kalendarii rationem, et ecclesiasticae historiae ueritatem restitutum. Gregorii XIII pont. max. iussum editum. Secundaeditio*. Antwerp: Ex officina Christophori Plantini.

Barnea, I. 1960. 'Contributions to Dobrudja history under Anastasius I'. *Dacia* 4, 363–374.

Barsanti, C. 1994. 'I mosaici di Antiochia: riflessioni sulla documentazione archeologica superstite'. *Proceedings of the Associazione Italiana per lo studio e la conservazione del mosaico* I, 318–323.

Bauzou, T. 1993. 'Epigraphie et toponymie: le cas de la palmyrène du sud-ouest'. *Syria* 70, 27–50.

Bauzou, T. 2000. 'La "Strata Diocletiana"'. In L. Nordiguian and J.-F. Salles (ed.). *Aux origins de l'archéologie aérienne. A. Poidebard (1878–1955)*. Beyrut: PUSJ, 79–91.

Bayliss, R. A. 2004. *Provincial Cilicia and the Archaeology of Temple Conversion*. British Archaeological Report S1281. Oxford: Archaeopress.

Beaudry, N. 2005. 'Formes architecturales et géographie historique: l'église de Bassit et le corpus nord-Syrien'. In J.-P. Sodini, F. Baratte, V. Déroche, C. Jolivet-Lévy and B. Pitarakis (eds). *Travaux et Mémoires 15. Mélanges Jean-Pierre Sodini*. Paris: Association des amis du centre d'histoire et civilisation de Byzance, 119–136.

Bejor, G. 1999. *Vie colonnate. Paesaggi urbani del mondo antico*. Rome: G. Bretschneider.

Bell, G. L. 1982. *The Churches and Monasteries of the Ṭur 'Abdin*. London: Pindar Press.

Ben Abed-Ben Khader, A. 1999. *Karthago, Carthage. Les mosaiques du parc archéologique des thermes d'Antonin*. Tunis: Institut National d'Archéologie et d'Art.

Benbabaali, D. 2005. 'La gestion de l'eau dans l'oasis de Palmyre, Syrie'. *Villes et Territoires du Moyen-Orient* 1 [available at <http://www.ifporient.org/node/418>; accessed, 19/12/2016].

Bennett, C. M. and Northedge, A. 1977–1978. 'Excavations at the citadel, Amman, 1976'. *Annual of the Department of Antiquities of Jordan* 22, 172–179.

Bernhard, M.-L. 1969. 'Fouilles Polonnaises à Palmyre 1967'. *Annales Archéologiques Arabes Syriennes* 19, 71–75.

Bessard, F. 2013. 'The urban economy in southern inland greater Syria from the seventh century to the end of the Umayyads'. In L. Lavan (ed.). *Local Economies? Production and Exchange of Inland Regions in Late Antiquity*. Leiden: Brill, 377–421.

Bivar, A. D. H. 1972. 'Cavalry equipment and tactics on the Euphrates frontier'. *Dumbarton Oaks Papers* 26, 271–291.

Blanc, P.-M., Dentzer, J.-M. and Sodini, J.-P. 2007. 'La grande église à plan centré (ou "cathédrale de l'Est")'. In J. Dentzer-Feydy, M. Vallerin, T. Fournet, R. Mukdad and A. Mukdad (eds). *Bosra. Aux portes de l'Arabie*. Beyruth: Presses de l'IFPO, 137–146.

Blanc, P.-M., Fournet, T., Dentzer-Feydy, J. and Vallerin, M. 2007. 'Le "nouveau prétoire"'. In J. Dentzer-Feydy, M. Vallerin, T. Fournet, R. Mukdad and A. Mukdad (eds). *Bosra. Aux portes de l'Arabie*. Beirut: Presses de l'IFPO, 213–214.

Blétry, S. (with Duval, H., Prost, E., Provost, S., Riba, B., Serdon, V., Shouwhan, Y. and Veyrac, A.) 2010. 'Trois années de recherches á Zénobia-Halabiyé (Syrie), ville forteresse proto-byzantine sur le limes oriental'. *Semitica et Classica* 3, 249–264.

Bogisch, M. 2005. 'Qalat Seman and Resafa/Sergiupolis: two early Byzantine pilgrimage centers'. In I. Volt and J. Päll (eds). *Byzantino-Nordica 2004: Papers presented at the international symposium of Byzantine studies held on 7–11 May 2004 in Tartu, Estonia*. Tartu: Tartu University Press, 52–72.

Bosworth, C. E. 1982. 'The concept of *dhimma* in early Islam'. In B. Braudeand and B. Lewis (eds). *Christians and Jews in the Ottoman Empire, Vol. 1. The Central Lands*. New York: Holmes & Meier, 37–54.

Bounni, A. 1967. 'En mission à Palmyre: Bilan de dix années de fouilles'. *Archéologia* 16 (May–June), 40–49.

Bounni, A. 1970–1971. 'Antiquités Palmyréniennes dans un texte Arabe du Moyen Âge'. *Mélanges de l'Université Saint-Joseph* 46, 331–339.

Bounni, A. 1971. 'Un noveau panorama de Palmyre'. *Annales Archéologiques Arabes Syriennes* 21, 117–128.

Bounni, A. 1990. 'Le sanctuaire de Nabū à Palmyre'. In F. Zayadine (ed.). *Petra and the Caravan Cities: proceedings of the symposium organised at Petra in September 1985 by the Department of Antiquities of Jordan and the Iconographic Lexicon of Classical Mythology (LIMC) with the financial support of UNESCO*. Amman: Department of Antiquities, 157–169.

Bounni, A., 1995. 'Vierzig Jahre syrische Ausgrabungen in Palmyra'. In A. Schmidt-Colinet (ed.). *Palmyra. Kulturbegegnung im Grezbereich*. Mainz: P. von Zabern, 12–20.

Bounni, A. 2004. *Le sanctuaire de Nabu. Texte*. Beirut: Institut d'Archéologie du Proche-Orient.

Bounni, A. and al-As'ad, K. 1982. *Palmyre: histoire, monuments et musée*. Damascus: Dar al-Fikr.

Bounni, A. and Saliby, N. 1965. 'Six nouveaux emplacements fouilles à Palmyre (1963–1964)'. *Annales Archéologiques Arabes Syriennes* 15, 121–38.

Bounni, A. and Saliby, N. 1968. 'Fouilles de l'annexe de l'agora à Palmyre. Rapport préliminaire'. *Annales Archéologiques Arabes Syriennes* 18, 93–102.

Bounni, A., Seigne, J. and Saliby, N. 1992. *Le sanctuaire de Nabū à Palmyre. Planches*. Paris: P. Geuthner.

Bowersock, G. W. 1983. *Roman Arabia*. Cambridge, MA: Harvard University Press.

Bowes, K. D. 2012. *Houses and Society in the Later Roman Empire*. London: Bristol Classical Press.

Brandes, W. 1989. *Die Städte Kleinasiens im 7. und 8. Jahrhundert*. Amsterdam: J. C. Gieben.

Brenk, B. 1987. '*Spolia* from Constantine to Charlemagne: aesthetics versus ideology'. *Dumbarton Oaks Papers* 41, 103–109.

Brenk, B. H. 2003. *Die Christianisierung der Spätrömischen Welt. Stadt, Land, Haus, Kirche und Kloster in frühchristlicher Zeit*. Wiesbaden: Reichert.

Brennan, P. 1989. 'Diocletian and Elephantine: a closer look at Pococke's puzzle (IGRR 1.1291 = SB 5.8393)'. *Zeitschrift für Papyrologie und Epigraphik* 76, 193–205.

Broise, H. and Fournet, T. 2007. 'Les thermes du Sud'. In J. Dentzer-Feydy, M. Vallerin, T. Fournet, R. Mukdad and A. Mukdad (eds). *Bosra. Aux portes de l'Arabie*. Beyruth: Presses de l'IFPO, 219–224.

Brown, R. M. 1998. 'A large residence (house XVIII)'. In B. de Vries (ed.). *Umm el-Jimal: a frontier town and its landscape in northern Jordan, vol. 1 fieldwork 1972–1981*. Portsmouth, RI: Journal of Roman Archaeology Supplemetary Series 26, 195–204.

Bujard, J. 1995. 'La fortification de Kastron Mayfaa/Umm ar-Rasas'. *Studies in the History and Archaeology of Jordan* 5, 241–249.

Bulliet, R. W. 1975. *The Camel and the Wheel*. Cambridge, MA: Harvard University Press.

Butler, A. J. 1902. *The Arab Conquest of Egypt and the Last Thirty Years of the Roman Dominion*. Oxford: Clarendon Press.

Butler, H. C. 1929. *Early Churches in Syria. Fourth to seventh Century*. Princeton, NJ: Department of Art and Archaeology of Princeton University.

Byliński, J. 1994. 'Survey of the Arab castle in Palmyra 1993'. *Polish Archaeology in the Mediterranean* 5, 144–155.

Byliński, J. 1995. 'A IIIrd century open-court building in Palmyra excavation report'. *Damaszener Mitteilungen* 8, 213–246.

Byliński, J. 1999. 'Qal'at Shirkuh at Palmyra: a medieval fortress reinterpreted'. *Bulletin d'Études Orientales* 51, 151–208.

Cameron, A. 1985. *Procopius and the sixth century*. Berkeley, Los Angeles, CA: University of California Press.

Cameron, A. 1993. *The Mediterranean world in Late Antiquity AD 395–600*. London: Routledge.

Cameron, A. 2003. 'Ideologies and agendas in Late Antique studies'. In L. Lavan and W. Bowden (eds). *Theories and Practice in Late Antique Archaeology*. Leiden: Brill, 3–21.

Cameron, A. 2011. *The Last Pagans of Rome*. Oxford: Oxford University Press.

Campbell, S. D. 1988. *The Mosaics of Antioch*. Toronto: Pontifical Institute of Mediaeval Studies.

Cantineau, J. 1934. *Le dialecte arabe de Palmyre*. Beirut: Institut Français de Damas.

Cantino Wataghin, G. 1999. 'The ideology of urban burials'. In G. P. Brogiolo and B. Ward-Perkins (eds). *The Idea and the Ideal of the Town between Late Antiquity and the Early Middle Ages*. Leiden: Brill, 147–180.

Carle, G., 1923, 'De l'alimentation en eau de Palmyre dans les temps actuels et anciens'. *Geographie* 40, 153–160.

Cerutti, A. 2014. 'Preliminary data for the Brittle Ware from the new excavations in the south-west quarter of Palmyra (Syria)'. In N. Poulou-Papadimitriou, E. Nodarou and V. Kilikoglou (eds). *LRCW 4: Late Roman coarse wares, cooking wares and amphorae in the Mediterranean. Archaeology and archaeometry. The Mediterranean: a market without frontiers*. British Archaeological Report S2616. Oxford: Archaeopress, 643–648.

Chabot, J.-B. 1907–1933. *Documenta ad Origines Monophysitarum Illustrandas*. Paris: Ex Typographeo Reipublicae.

Christol, M. and Drew-Bear, T. 2002. 'Le tutor cessionarius des Tralles'. *Tyche* 17, 31–38.

Chuvin, P. 1990. *Chronique des Derniers Païens. La Disparition du Paganisme dans l'Empire Romain, du Règne de Consantin à celui de Justinien*. Paris: Les Belles Lettres/Fayard.

Claude, D. 1969. *Die byzantinische Stadt im 6. Jahrhundert*. Munich: C. H. Beck.

Clermont-Ganneau, S. C. 1899. *Archaeological Researches in Palestine During the Years 1873–1874. With Numerous Illustrations from Drawings made on the Spot by A. Lecomte du Noüy*, vol. I. London: Palestine Exploration Fund.

Clermont-Ganneau, S. C. 1900. *Recueil d'Archéologie Orientale*, vol. III. Paris: Ernest Leroux.

Coates-Stephens, R. 2003. 'Attitudes to *spolia* in some Late Antique text'. In L. Lavan and W. Bowden (eds). *Theory and Practice in Late Antique Archaeology*. Leiden-Boston: Brill, 341–357.

Cobb, P. M. 2001. *White Banners. Contention in 'Abbāsid Syria, 750–880*. Albany, NY: State University of New York Press.

Collart, P.1963. 'Réutilisation chrétienne d'un grand sanctuaire de Palmyre'. *Atti della Pontificia Accademia Romana di Archeologia. Rendiconti* 35, 147–159.

Collart, P. and Vicari, J. 1969. *Le Sanctuaire de Baalshamin à Palmyre: Topographie et architecture*. Rome: Institut Suisse de Rome.

Collins, R. 2012. *Hadrian's Wall and the End of Empire: the Roman frontier in the 4th and 5th centuries*. New York: Routledge.

Combe, É., Sauvaget, J. and Wiet, G. 1931. *Répertoire chronologique d'épigraphie arabe*, vol. I. Cairo: Institut Français d'Archéologie Orientale.

Crawford, P. and Parker, S. T. 2006. 'The east *vicus* building (Area P)'. In S. T. Parker (ed.). *The Roman Frontier in Central Jordan. Final Report on the Limes Arabicus Project, 1980–1989*. Harvard, MA: Harvard University Press, 247–258.

Crouch, D. P. 1975a. 'The ramparts of Palmyra'. *Studia Palmireńskie* 6–7, 6–44.

Crouch, D. P. 1975b. 'The water system of Palmyra'. *Studia Palmireńskie* 6–7, 151–186.

Croke, B. and Crow, J. 1983. 'Procopius and Dara'. *Journal of Roman Studies* 73, 143–159.

Crone, P. 1980. *Slaves on Horses: the evolution of the Islamic polity*. Cambridge: Cambridge University Press.

Crow, J. 1981. 'Dara, a late Roman fortress in Mesopotamia'. *Yayla* 4, 12–20.

Crow., J. 2007. 'Amida and Tropaeum Traiani: a comparison of Late Antique fortress cities on the lower Danube and Mesopotamia'. In A. G. Poulter (ed.). *The Transition to Late Antiquity: on the Danube and beyond*. Oxford-New York: Oxford University Press, 435–458.

Crowfoot, J. W. 1931. *Churches at Jerash. A Preliminary Report of the Joint Yale-British School Expeditions to Jerash, 1928–1930*. London: British School of Archaeology in Jerusalem.

Dagron, G. 1977. 'Le christianisme dans la ville Byzantin'. *Dumbarton Oaks Papers* 51, 1–25.

Daszewski, W. A. 1972. 'Les fouilles Polonaises à Palmyre en 1968–1969'. *Annales Archéologiques Arabes Syriennes* 22, 129–150.

Daszewski, W. A. and Kołątaj, W. 1970. 'Wstępny raport z wykopalisk Polskiej Misji Archeologicznej w Palmyrze w 1968 r'. *Studia Palmireńskie* 4, 69–77.

Daszkiewicz, M., Krogulska, M. and Raabe, J. 1995. 'Technology and typology of common-ware pottery from Palmyra'. In H. Meyza (ed.). *Hellenistic and Roman Pottery in the Eastern Mediterranean – Advances in Scientific Studies*. Warsaw: Polish Centre of Mediterranean Archaeology, Warsaw University, 41–59.

De Ricci, S. 1903. 'Bulletin épigraphique de l'Egypte Romaine. Inscriptions Grecques (1896–1902)'. *Archiv für Papyrusforschung* 2, 427–452.

De' Maffei, F. 1985. 'Le fortificazioni sul limes orientale ai tempi di Giustiniano'. *Corso di Cultura sull'Arte Ravennate e Bizantina: seminario internazionale di studi* 32, 109–150.

De' Maffei, F. 1990. 'Zenobia e Annoukas: fortificazioni di Giustinano sul medio Eufrate. Fasi degli interventi e data'. In F. de' Maffei, C. Barsanti and A. Guiglia (eds). *Milion. Studi e ricerche d'arte Bizantina. Costantinopoli e l'arte delle province orientali*. Rome: Edizioni Rari Nantes, 135–177.

Debaine, F. and Jaubert, R. 2006. 'La degradation de la steppe: hypotheses et evolution du couvert vegetal'. In R. Jaubert and B. Geyer (eds). *Les marges arides du croissant fertile. Peuplement, exploitation et contrôle des resources en Syrie du Nord*. Lyon: Maison de l'Orient Méditerranéen, 149–165.

Decker, M. 2009. *Tilling the Hateful Earth. Agricultural Production and Trade in the Late Antique East*. Oxford, New York: Oxford University Press.

Deckers, J. G. 1973. 'Die Wandmalerei des tetrarchischen Lagerheiligtums im Ammon-Tempel von Luxor'. *Römische Quartalschrift für Christliche Altertumskunde und für Kirchengeschichte* 68, 1–34.

Deichmann, F. W. 1939. 'Frühchristliche Kirchen in antiken Heiligtümern'. *Jahrbuch des Deutschen Archäologishen Instituts* 54, 105–136.

Deichmann, F. W. 1976. 'Il materiale di spoglio nell'architettura tardo antica'. *Corso di Cultura sull'Arte Ravennate e Bizantina: seminario internazionale di studi* 23, 131–146.

Delplace, C. 2006–2007. 'La fouille du marché suburbain de Palmyre (2001–2005)'. *Annales Archéologiques Arabes Syriennes* 49–50, 91–111.

Delplace, C. 2013. 'Les recherches de la mission archéologique Française à Palmyre'. *Studia Palmireńskie* 12, 37–48.

Dentzer, J.-M. 2000. 'Le développement urbain en Syrie á l'époque Hellénistique et Romaine: modèles "occidentaux et orientaux"'. *Bulletin d'Études Orientale* 52, 159–163.

Dentzer, J.-M., Dentzer-Feydy, J. and Vallerin, M. 2007. 'Le tétrapyle et la place ronde'. In J. Dentzer-Feydy, M. Vallerin, T. Fournet, R. Mukdad and A. Mukdad (eds). *Bosra. Aux portes de l'Arabie*. Beyrut: Presses de l'IFPO, 265–266.

Devreesse, R. 1945. *Le patriarcat d'Antioche; Depuis la paix de l'Eglise jusqu' à la conquête Arabe*. Paris: J. Gabalda et Cie.

De Vries, B. 1985. 'Urbanization in the basalt region of north Jordan in Late Antiquity: the case of Umm el-Jimal'. *Studies in the History and Archaeology of Jordan* 2, 249–256.

DeVries, B., Godwin V. and Lain, A. 2006. 'The fortifications of el-Lejjun'. In S. T. Parker (ed.). *The Roman Frontier in Central Jordan. Final report on the Limes Arabicus Project, 1980–1989*. Harvard: Harvard University Press, 187–211.

Di Segni, L. 1994. 'Εἷς θεός in Palestinian inscriptions'. *Scripta Classica Israelica* 13, 94–115.

Dick, I. 1992. 'Retombées de la conquête Arabe sur la chrétienté de Syrie'. In P. Canivet and J.-P. Rey-Coquais (eds). *La Syrie de Byzance à l'Islam. VIIe–VIIIe siècles: actes du colloque international Lyon-Maison de l'Orient méditerranéen, Paris-Institut du monde arabe, 11–15 Septembre 1990*. Damascus: Institut Français de Damas, 89–95.

Dinchev, V. 2007. 'The fortresses of Thrace and Dacia'. In A. Poulter (ed.). *The Transition to Late Antiquity in the Danube and Beyond*. Oxford: Oxford University Press, 479–546.

Dodge, H. 1988. 'Palmyra and the Roman marble trade: evidence from the baths of Diocletian'. *Levant* 20, 215–230.

Dodgeon, M. H. and Lieu, S. N. C. 1991. *The Roman Eastern Frontier and the Persian Wars, AD 226–363. A Documentary History*. London, New York: Routledge.

Donceel-Voûte, P. 1988. *Les pavements des églises byzantines de Syrie et du Liban: décor, archéologie et liturgie*. Louvaine-la-Neuve: Départment d'Archéologie et d'Histoire de l'Art, College Erasme.

Donnay-Rocmans, C. and Donnay, G. 1984. 'La Maison du Cerf'. In J. Balty (ed.). *Apamée de Syrie. Bilan des recherches archéologiques 1973–1979. Aspects de l'architecture domestique d'Apamée. Actes du colloque tenu á Bruxelles les 29, 30 et 31 Mai 1980*. Bruxelles: Centre Belge de Recherches Archéologiques á Apamée de Syrie, 155–169.

Donner, F. M. 1981. *The Early Islamic Conquest*. Princeton, NJ: Princeton University Press.

Donner, F. M. 1998. *Narratives of Islamic Origins. The Beginnings of Islamic Historical Writing*. Princeton, NJ: Darwin Press.

Downey, G. 1961. *A History of Antioch in Syria, from Seleucus to the Arab Conquest*. Princeton, NJ: Princeton University Press.

Drijvers, H. 1982. 'The persistence of pagan cults and practices in Christian Syria'. In N. G. Garsoïan, T. F. Mathews and R. W. Thomson (eds). *East of Byzantium: Syria and Armenia in the formative period.* Washington: Dumbarton Oaks, Center for Byzantine Studies, Trustees for Harvard University, 35–43.

Dulière, C. 1974. *Mosaïques des portiques de la Grande Colonnade: Section VII, 16–17*. Brussels: Centre belge de recherches archéologiques à Apamée de Syrie.

Dunant, C. 1971. *Le sanctuaire de Baalshamin à Palmyre, III. Les inscriptions*. Rome: Institut Suisse de Rome.

Dunant, C. 1975a. 'Les monnaies'. In C. Dunant and R. Fellmann. *Le sanctuaire de Baalshamin à Palmyre, VI. Kleinfunde/Objets divers*. Rome: Institut Suisse de Rome, 103–110.

Dunant, C. 1975b. 'Les inscriptions sur céramique'. In C. Dunant and R. Fellmann 1975. *Le sanctuaire de Baalshamin à Palmyre, VI. Kleinfunde/Objets divers*. Rome: Institut Suisse de Rome, 119–128.

Dussaud, R. 1930. 'L'aménagement des ruines de Palmyre'. *Syria* 11, 203–205.

Dussaud, R. 1931. 'Le déblaiment du temple de Bêl à Palmyre'. *Syria* 12, 191–192.

Duval, P.-M. 1946. *Cherchel et Tipasa: recherches sur deux villes fortes de l'Afrique romaine*. Paris: P. Geuthner.

Duval, N. 1992. 'Une église nouvelle attribuée au début du IVe siècle à Palmyre (Syrie)'. *Bulletin Monumental* 150, 413–415.

Eadie, J. W. 1967. 'The development of Roman mailed cavalry'. *Journal of Roman Studies* 57, 161–173.

Edwell, P. M. 2008. *Between Rome and Persia; the Middle Euphrates, Mesopotamia and Palmyra under Roman Control*. London, New York: Routledge.

Ellis, S. P. 1985. 'The palace of the Dux at Apollonia and related houses'. In G. Barker, J. I. Joyd and J. Reynolds (eds). *Cyrenaica in Antiquity*. Oxford: British Archaeological Reports, 15–25.

Ellis, S. P. 1988. 'The end of the Roman house'. *American Journal of Archaeology* 92, 565–576.

Ellis, S. P. 2000. *Roman Housing*. London: Duckworth.

Elsner, J. 2000. 'From the culture of *spolia* to the cult of relics: the arch of Constantine and the genesis of Late Antique forms'. *Papers of the British School at Rome* 68, 149–184.

Elton, H. 1996. *Warfare in Roman Europe, AD 350–425*. Oxford: Clarendon Press.

Epstein, C. and Tzaferis, V. 1991. 'The baptistery ad Sussita-Hippos'. *Atiqot* 20, 89–94.

Farioli Campanati, R. 2007. 'L'église des Saints Serge, Bacchus et Léonce et le palais "episcopal" Saint-Serge'. In J. Dentzer-Feydy, M. Vallerin, T. Fournet, R. Mukdad and A. Mukdad (eds). *Bosra. Aux portes de l'Arabie*. Beyruth: Presses de l'IFPO, 155–160.

Farioli Campanati, R. and Masturzo, N. 2007. 'L'église des thermes du Sud'. In J. Dentzer-Feydy, M. Vallerin, T. Fournet, R. Mukdad and A. Mukdad (eds). *Bosra. Aux portes de l'Arabie*. Beyruth: Presses de l'IFPO, 217.

Fedalto, G., 1988. *Hierarchia ecclesiastica orientalis, vol. II. Patriarchatus Alexandrinus, Antiochenus, Hierosolymitanus*. Padova: Edizioni Messaggero.

Feissel, D. 2000. 'Les édifices de Justinien au témoignage de Procope et de l'épigraphie'. *Antiquité Tardive* 8, 81–104.

Fellmann, R. 1958. *Die Principia des Legionsslagers Vindonissa und das Zentralgebäude der römischen Lager und Kastelle*. Brugg: Vindonissa Museum.

Fellmann, R. 1976. 'Le "camp de Dioclétien" à Palmyre et l'architecture militaire du Bas-empire'. In P. Ducrey, C. Bérard, C. Dunant and F. Paschoud (eds). *Mélanges d'histoire ancienne et d'archéologie offerts à Paul Collart*. Lausanne: Bibliothèque Historique Vaudoise, 173–191.

Fellmann, R. 1979. 'Der Diokletianspalast von Split im Rahmen der spätrömischen Militärarchitektur'. *Antike Welt* 10, 47–55.

Fellmann, R. 1987. 'Der Palast der Königin Zenobia'. In E. M. Ruprechtsberger (ed.). *Palmyra, Geschichte, Kunst und Kultur der syrischen Oasenstadt; Einführende Beiträge und Katalog zur Ausstellung*. Linz: Verlagsanstalt Gutenberg, 131–136.

Ferré, A. 1988. 'Chrétiens de Syrie et de Mésopotamie aux deux premiers siècles de l'Islam'. *Islamochristiana* 14, 71–106.

Fick, A. 1932. 'Zur Stadtmauer'. In T. Wiegand (ed.). *Palmyra: Ergebnisse der Expeditionen von 1902 und 1917*. Berlin: Im Verlag Heinrich Keller, 37–40.

Filarska, B. 1967. *Études sur le décor architectural à Palmyre* (=*Studia Palmireńskie* 2). Warsaw: Warsaw University Press.

Fisher, C. S. 1938. 'Description of the site'. In C. H. Kraeling (ed.). *Gerasa, City of the Decapolis. An Account Embodying the Record of a Joint Excavation Conducted by Yale University and the British School of Archaeology in Jerusalem (1928–1930) and Yale University and the American Schools of Oriental Research (1930–1931, 1933–1934)*. New Haven, CO: American Schools of Oriental Research, 11–25.

Foss, C. 1997. 'Syria in transition, A.D. 550–750. An archaeological approach'. *Dumbarton Oaks Papers* 51, 189–269.

Fourdrin, J.-P. 1985. 'Les églises à nef transversale d'Apamène et du Tur 'Abdin'. *Syria* 62, 319–335.

Fourdrin, J.-P. 1994. 'Une porte urbaine construite *à* Chalcis de Syrie *par* Isidore de Milet le Jeune (550–551) (with an epigraphic appendix by D. Feissel)'. *Travaux et Mémoires du Centre de Recherche d'Histoire et Civilisation Byzantines* 12, 299–307.

Fournet, T. 2007, 'Les thermes du Centre ("Khân ed-Dibs")'. In J. Dentzer-Feydy, M. Vallerin, T. Fournet, R. Mukdad and A. Mukdad (eds). *Bosra. Aux portes de l'Arabie*. Beyruth: Presses de l'IFPO, 243–254.

Fournet, T. 2009a. 'Les bains de Zénobie à Palmyre. Rapport préliminaire – août 2009' [available at <http://balneorient.hypotheses.org/604>, accessed 18/05/2014].

Fournet, T. 2009b. 'Résumé de T. Fournet' [available at <http://balneorient.hypotheses.org/1124>, accessed 18/05/2014].

Fowden, E. K. 2004. 'Christian monasteries and Umayyad residences in Late Antique Syria'. In G. Fowden and E. K. Fowden (eds). *Studies on Hellenism, Christianity and the Umayyads*. Athens: de Boccard, 175–192.

Fowden, G. 1978. 'Bishop and temples in the eastern Roman Empire AD 320–435'. *Journal of Theological Studies* 29, 53–78.

Fowden, G. 1999. *The Barbarian Plain. Saint Sergius between Rome and Iran*. Berkeley, CA: University of California Press.

Frend, W. H. C. 1972. *Therise of the Monophysite Movement. Chapters in the History of the Church in the Fifth and Sixth Centuries*. Cambridge: Cambridge University Press.

Frézouls, E. 1976a, 'Questions d'urbanisme palmyrénien'. In E. Frezouls (ed.). *Palmyre. Bilan et perspectives. Colloque de Strasbourg, 18–20 Octobre 1973, à la mémoire de Daniel Schlumberger et de Henri Seyrig*. Strasbourg: AECR, 191–207.

Frézouls, E. 1976b. 'À propos de l'architecture domestique à *Palmyre'*. *Ktema* 1, 29–52.

Frézouls, E. 1980. 'Les fonctions du Moyen-Euphrate à l'époque Romaine'. In J. Margueron (ed.). *Le Moyen Euphrate: zone de contacts et d'échanges: actes du colloque de Strasbourg, 10–12 Mars 1977*. Leiden: Brill, 355–386.

Gabriel, A. 1926. 'Recherches archéologiques à Palmyre'. *Syria* 7, 72–92.

Gabriel, A. 1927. 'Kasr el-Heir'. *Syria* 8, 302–329.

Gabriel, A. 1940. *Voyages archéologiques dans la Turquie orientale*. Paris: de Boccard.

Galavaris, G. 1970. *Bread and the Liturgy: the symbolism of early Christian and Byzantine bread stamps*. Madison WI: University of Wisconsin Press.

Gąssowska, B. 1982. 'Maternus Cynegius, Praefectus Praetorio Orientis and the destruction of the Allat temple in Palmyra'. *Archeologia: rocznik Instytutu historii kultury materialnej Polskiej akademii nauk* 22, 107–123.

Gatier, P.-L. 1995. 'Un moine sur la frontière, Alexandre l'Acémète en Syrie'. In A. Rousselle (ed.). *Frontières terrestres, frontières célestes dans l'antiquité*. Paris: Presses Universitaires de Perpignan, 435–457.

Gawlikowski, M. 1968. 'Die Polnischen Ausgrabungen in Palmyra 1959–1967'. *Archäologishe Anzeiger* 2, 289–307.

Gawlikowski, M. 1969. 'Wykopaliska w Palmyrze ostatnich lat'. *Studia Palmireńskie* 3, 105–109.

Gawlikowski, M. 1970. *Les monuments funéraires de Palmyre*. Warsaw: PWN, Editions Scientifiques de Pologne.

Gawlikowski, M. 1973. *Palmyre (VI). Le temple palmyrénien. Étude d'épigraphie et de topographie historique*. Warsaw: PWN-Éditions scientifiques de Pologne.

Gawlikowski, M. 1974. *Recueil d'inscriptions palmyréniennes provenant de fouilles syriennes et polonaises récentes à Palmyre*. Paris: Imprimerie Nationale, C. Klincksieck.

Gawlikowski, M. 1975a. 'Remarks on the ramparts of Palmyra'. *Studia Palmireńskie* 6, 45–46.

Gawlikowski, M. 1975b. 'Palmyre 1972 (chantier remparts)'. *Études et Travaux* 8, 377–78.

Gawlikowski, M. 1976a. 'Palmyre 1973'. *Études et Travaux* 9, 273–282.

Gawlikowski, M. 1976b. 'Le Camp de Dioclétien: bilan préliminaire'. In E. Frezouls (ed.). *Palmyre. Bilan et perspectives. Colloque de Strasbourg, 18–20 Octobre 1973, à la mémoire de Daniel Schlumberger et de Henri Seyrig*. Strasbourg: Université des Sciences Humaines de Strasbourg, 153–163.

Gawlikowski, M. 1977. 'Le temple d'Allat à Palmyre'. *Revue Archéologique* 2, 253–274.

Gawlikowski, M. 1978. 'Palmyre 1974'. *Études et Travaux* 10, 421–422.

Gawlikowski, M. 1979a. 'Palmyre 1975'. *Études et Travaux* 11, 267–270.

Gawlikowski, M. 1979b. 'Palmyre 1976'. *Études et Travaux* 11, 271–274.

Gawlikowski, M. 1983a. 'Réflexions sur la chronologie du sanctuaire d'Allat à Palmyre'. *Damaszener Mitteilungen* 1, 59–67.

Gawlikowski, M. 1983b. 'Palmyre (mission polonaise)'. *Syria* 60, 297.

Gawlikowski, M. 1983c. 'Le sanctuaire d'Allat à Palmyre, aperçu préliminaire'. *Annales Archéologiques Arabes Syriennes* 33, 179–195.

Gawlikowski, M. 1983d. 'Palmyre et l'Euphrate'. *Syria* 60, 53–68.

Gawlikowski, M. 1984 (ed.). *Palmyre (VIII). Les principia de Dioclétien. "Temple des Enseignes"*. Warsaw: PWN, Editions Scientifiques de Pologne.

Gawlikowski, M. 1985. 'Świątynia Allat w palmyrze. Wstępny raport z wykopalisk 1974–1976'. *Studia Palmireńskie* 7, 5–25.

Gawlikowski, M. 1986a. 'Residential area by the south decumanus'. In F. Zayadine (ed.). *Jerash Archaeological Project, 1981–1983, I*. Amman: Department of Antiquities, 107–136.

Gawlikowski, M. 1986b. 'Palmyre (mission Polonaise)'. *Syria* 63, 397–399.

Gawlikowski, M. 1987a. 'Polnische Ausgrabungen in Palmyra: Das Diokletianslager'. In E. M. Ruprechtsberger (ed.). *Palmyra, Geschichte, Kunst und Kultur der syrischen Oasenstadt; Einführende Beiträge und Katalog zur Ausstellung*. Linz: Verlagsanstalt Gutenberg, 249–252.

Gawlikowski, M. 1987b. 'Das Horreum-Gebäude in Diokletianslager. Vorbericht über die 28. Ausgrabungskampagne (September–Oktober 1985)'. In E. M. Ruprechtsberger (ed.). *Palmyra, Geschichte, Kunst und Kultur der syrischen Oasenstadt; Einführende Beiträge und Katalog zur Ausstellung*. Linz: Verlagsanstalt Gutenberg, 253–254.

Gawlikowski, M. 1990a. 'Palmyra'. *Polish Archaeology in the Mediterranean* 1, 38–44.

Gawlikowski, M. 1990b. 'Les dieux de Palmyre'. In W. Haase (ed.). *Aufstieg und Niedergang der Römischen Welt*, 2.18.4. Berlin, New York: de Gruyter, 2605–2658.

Gawlikowski, M. 1991a. 'Palmyra'. *Polish Archaeology in the Mediterranean* 2, 85–90.

Gawlikowski, M. 1991b. 'Fouilles récentes à Palmyre'. *Comptes rendus/Académie des inscriptions et belles-lettres* 135, 399–410.

Gawlikowski, M. 1992a 'Palmyra 1991'. *Polish Archaeology in the Mediterranean* 3, 68–76.

Gawlikowski, M. 1992b. 'Palmyre 1981–1987'. *Études et Travaux* 16, 325–335.

Gawlikowski, M. 1993. 'Eine neuentdeckte frühchristliche Kirche in Palmyra'. In E. M. Ruprechtsberger (ed.). *Syrien: Von den Aposteln zu den Kalifen*. Mainz, Linz: P. von Zabern, Stadtmuseum Nordico, 150–157.

Gawlikowski, M. 1994. 'Palmyra'. *Polish Archaeology in the Mediterranean* 5, 133–143.

Gawlikowski, M. 1995. 'Tempel, Gräber und Kasernen. Die polnische Ausgrabungen im Diokletianslager'. In A. Schmidt-Colinet (ed.). *Palmyra. Kulturbegegnung im Grenzbereich*. Maiz: P. von Zabern, 21–27.

Gawlikowski, M. 1996. 'Palmyra. Excavations 1995'. *Polish Archaeology in the Mediterranean* 7, 139–146.

Gawlikowski, M. 1997a. 'L'habitat à Palmyre de l'antiquité au Moyen-Age'. In C. Castel, M. al-Maqdissi and F. Villeneuve (eds). *Les maisons dans la Syrie antique du IIIe millénaire aux débuts de l'Islam: pratique et représentations de l'espace domestique. Actes du Colloque International, Damas, 27–30 juin 1992.* Beirut: Institut Français d'Archéologie du Proche-Orient, 161–166.

Gawlikowski, M. 1997b. 'Palmyra, excavations 1996'. *Polish Archaeology in the Mediterranean* 8, 191–197.

Gawlikowski, M. 1997c. 'The oriental city and the advent of Islam'. In W. Gernot (ed.). *Die orientalische Stadt: Kontinuität, Wandel, Bruch.* Saarbrücken: Saarbrücker Druckerei und Verlag, 339–350.

Gawlikowski, M. 1998. 'Palmyra, excavations 1997'. *Polish Archaeology in the Mediterranean* 9, 197–211.

Gawlikowski, M. 1999. 'Palmyra, excavations 1998'. *Polish Archaeology in the Mediterranean* 10, 189–196.

Gawlikowski, M. 2000. 'Palmyra, season 1999'. *Polish Archaeology in the Mediterranean* 11, 249–260.

Gawlikowski, M. 2001. '*Le groupe épiscopal de Palmyre*'. In C. Evers and A. Tsingarida (eds). *Rome et ses province: genèse et diffusion d'une image du pouvoir: hommages à Jean-Charles Balty.* Bruxelles: Le Livre Timperman, 119–127.

Gawlikowski, M. 2002. 'Palmyra, season 2001'. *Polish Archaeology in the Mediterranean* 13, 257–269.

Gawlikowski, M. 2003. 'Palmyra, season 2002'. *Polish Archaeology in the Mediterranean* 14, 279–290.

Gawlikowski, M. 2004. 'Palmyra. Season 2003. Preliminary report'. *Polish Archaeology in the Mediterranean* 15, 313–324.

Gawlikowski, M. 2005 'Palmyra 2004'. *Polish Archaeology in the Mediterranean* 16, 461–465.

Gawlikowski, M. 2007. 'Beyond the colonnades: domestic architecture in Palmyra'. In K. Galor and T. Waliszewski (eds). *From Antioch to Alexandria: recent studies in domestic architecture.* Warsaw: University of Warsaw, 79–94.

Gawlikowski, M. 2009. 'Palmyra in the early Islamic time'. In K. Bartl and A. R. Moaz (eds). *Residences, Castles, Settlements. Transformation Processes from Late Antiquity to Early Islam in Bilad al-Sham. Proceedings of the International Conference held at Damascus, 5–9 November 2006.* Rahden, Westf.: Verlag Marie Leidorf, 89–96.

Gawlikowski, M. 2014. 'Le trésor Sasanide'. In A. Krzyżanowska and M. Gawlikowski (eds). *Monnaies des fouilles Polonaises à Palmyre* (= *Studia Palmireńskie* 13). Warsaw: Warsaw University Press, Polish Centre of Mediterranean Archaeology, 61–120.

Genequand, D. 2002, 'Project "Implantations umayyades de Syrie et de Jordanie". Rapport sur une campagne de prospection et reconnaissance (2001)'. *SLSA – Jahresbericht* 2001, 3–33.

Genequand, D. 2003a. 'Project "Implantations umayyades de Syrie et de Jordanie". Rapport de la champagne de prospection (Juin–Juillet 2002)'. *SLSA – Jahresbericht* 2002, 31–68.

Genequand, D. 2003b. 'Rapport préliminaire de la campagne de fouille 2002 à Qasr al-Hayr al-Sharqi (Syrie)'. *SLSA – Jahresbericht* 2002, Zürich, 69–96.

Genequand, D. 2004a. 'Al-Bakhra᾽ (Avatha), from the Tetrarchic fort to the Umayad castle'. *Levant* 36, 225–242.

Genequand, D. 2004b. 'Rapport préliminaire de la campagne de fouille 2003 à Qasr al-Hayr al-Sharqi et al-Bakhra᾽ (Syrie)'. *SLSA – Jahresbericht* 2003, Zürich, 69–98.

Genequand, D. 2004c. 'Châteaux omeyyades de Palmyrène'. *Annales Islamologiques* 38, 3–44.

Genequand, D. 2004–2005 [2008]. 'Nouvelles recherches à Qasr al-Hayr al-Sharqi. La mosque Ayyoubide et la nécropole'. *Annales Archéologiques Arabes Syriennes* 47–48, 271–293.

Genequand, D. 2005a. 'From "desert castle" to medieval town: Qasr al-Hayr al-Sharqi (Syria)'. *Antiquity* 79, 350–361.

Genequand, D. 2005b. 'Rapport préliminaire de la campagne de fouille 2004 à Qasr al-Hayr al-Sharqi (Syrie)'. *SLSA – Jahresbericht* 2004, 143–166.

Genequand, D. 2005c, 'The Early Islamic Settlement in the Syrian Steppe: a New Look at Umayyad and Medieval Qasr al-Hayr al-Sharqi (Syria)'. *Al-'Usur al-Wusta* 17(2), 21–28.

Genequand, D. 2006a. 'Umayyad castles: the shift from Late Antique military architecture to early Islamic palatial building'. In H. N. Kennedy (ed.). *Muslim Military Architecture in Greater Syria. From the Coming of Islam to the Ottoman Period.* Leiden: Brill, 3–25.

Genequand, D. 2006b. 'Some thoughts on Qasr al-Hayr al Gharbi, its dam, its monastery and the Ghassanids'. *Levant* 38, 63–84.

Genequand, D. 2006c. 'Qasr al-Hayr al-Sharqi: une ville neuve des débuts de l'Islam dans la steppe syrienne'. *Archäologie* 29, 22–29.

Genequand, D. 2008a. 'An early Islamic mosque in Palmyra'. *Levant* 60, 3–15.

Genequand, D. 2008b. 'The new urban settlement at Qasr al-Hayr al-Sharqi: components and development in the early Islamic period'. In K. Bartl and M. A. al-Razzaq (eds). *Residences, Castles, Settlements. Transformation Processes from Late Antiquity to Early Islam in Bilad al-Sham. Proceedings of the International Conference Held at Damascus, 5–9 November 2006.* Rahden, Westf.: Verlag Marie Leidorf, 261–286.

Genequand, D. 2009a. 'Activités de la mission archéologique Syro-Suisse à Qasr al-Hayr al-Sharqi et à Palmyre en 2008'. *SLSA – Jahresbericht* 2008, 185–190.

Genequand, D. 2009b. 'Économie de production, affirmation du pouvoir et dolce vita: aspects de la politique de l'eau sous les Omeyyades au Bilad al-Sham'. In M. al-Dbiyat and M. Mouton (eds). *Stratégies d'acquisition de l'eau et société au Moyen-Orient depuis l'Antiquité.* Beirut: Presses de l'IFPO, 157–177.

Genequand, D. 2010. 'Rapport préliminaire des campagne 2008 et 2009 de la mission archéologique Syro-Suisse de Palmyre'. *SLSA – Jahresbericht* 2009, 221–232.

Genequand, D. 2011. 'Rapport préliminaire des travaux de la mission archéologique Syro-Suisse de Palmyre en 2010'. *SLSA – Jahresbericht* 2010, 81–86.

Genequand, D. 2012. *Les établissements des élites omeyyades en Palmyène et au Proche-Orient.* Beirut: Institut Français du Proche-Orient.

Genequand, D. 2013. 'Between Rome and Islam: recent research on the so-called Caesareum of Palmyra'. *Studia Palmireńskie* 12, 97–114.

Genequand, D. and al-As'ad, W. 2006–2007. 'Qasr al-Hayr al-Sharqi, travaux de la mission archéologique Syro-Suisse 2003–2007'. *Annales Archéologiques Arabes Syriennes* 49–50, 177–194.

Genequand, D. and Studer. J. 2011. 'Rapport préliminaire des travaux de la mission archéologique Syro-Suisse à Qasr al-Hayr al-Sharqi en 2010'. *SLSA – Jahresbericht* 2010, 55–80.

Genequand, D., Kühn, M. and de Reynier, C. 2006. 'Rapport préliminaire des travaux de la mission archéologique Syro-Suisse à Qasr al-Hayr al-Sharqi (Syrie) en 2005'. *SLSA – Jahresbericht* 2005, 161–203.

Genequand, D., Hull, D. and Studer, J. 2007. 'Rapport préliminaire des travaux de la mission archéologique Syro-Suisse à Qasr al-Hayr al-Sharqi en 2006'. *SLSA – Jahresbericht* 2006, 123–156.

Genequand, D., Ali, R., Haldemann, M., Studer, J. and Vokaer, A. 2010. 'Rapport préliminaire des campagne 2008 et 2009 de la mission archéologique Syro-Suisse de Qasr al-Hayr al-Sharqi'. *SLSA – Jahresbericht* 2009, 177–219.

Genequand, D., Amoroso, H., Haldemann, M., Hull, D., Kühn, M. and Studer, J. 2008. 'Rapport préliminaire des travaux de la mission archéologique Syro-Suisse à Qasr al-Hayr al-Sharqi en 2007'. *SLSA – Jahresbericht* 2007, 141–178.

Geyer, B. 2000. 'Des fermes Byzantines aux palais omayyades ou l'ingénieuse mise en valeur des plaines steppiques de Chalcidique'. In L. Nordiguian and J.-F. Salles (ed.). *Aux origins de l'archéologie aérienne. A. Poidebard (1878–1955).* Beyrut: PUSJ, 109–122.

Geyer, B. and Rousset, M.-O. 2001. 'Les steppes arides de la Syrie du Nord à l'époque Byzantine ou "la ruée vers l'est"'. In B. Geyer, (ed.). *Conquête de la steppe et appropriation des terres sur les marges arides du Croissant fertile.* Lyon: Maison de l'Orient Méditerranéen, 55–67.

Gibbon, E. 1831. *The History of the Decline and Fall of the Roman Empire. A New Edition, in One Volume, with Some Account of the Life and Writings of the Author by Alexander Chalmers.* London: Longman-Brown and Co.

Gichon, M. 2002. '45 years of research on the Limes Palaestinae – the findings and their assessment in the light of the criticism raised (C1st–C4th)'. In P. Freeman, J. Bennett, Z. T. Fiema and B. Hoffmann (eds). *Limes XVIII. Proceedings of the XVIIIth International Congress Of Roman Frontier Studies, Held in Amman, Jordan (September 2000).* British Archaeological Report S1084. Oxford: Archaeopress, 185–206.

Gisler, J. R. and Huwiler, M. 1984. 'La maison aux pilastres'. In J. Balty (ed.). *Apamée de Syrie. Bilan des recherches archéologiques 1973–1979. Aspects de l'architecture domestique d'Apamée. Actes du colloque tenu á Bruxelles les 29, 30 et 31 Mai 1980.* Bruxelles: Centre Belge de Recherches Archéologiques á Apamée de Syrie, 79–94.

Goodchild, R. G. 1960. 'A Byzantine palace at Apollonia. *Antiquity* 34, 246–258.

Goubert, P. 1951. *Byzance avant l'Islam, I. Byzance et l'Orient sous les successeurs de Justinien. L'emperor Maurice.* Paris: Picard.

Grabar, O., Holod, R., James, K. and Trousdale, K. 1978. *City in the Desert : Qasr al-Hayr East: an account of the excavations carried out at Qasr al-Hayr East on behalf of the Kelsey Museum of Archaeology at the University of Michigan, with the help of Harvard University and the Oriental Institute, the University of Chicago.* Cambridge, MA: Harvard University Press.

Graf, D. F. 1989. 'Zenobia and the Arabs'. In D. H. French and C. S. Lightfoot (eds). *The Eastern Frontier of the Roman Empire, vol. 1.* British Archaeological Report S553. Oxford: Archaeopress, 143–167.

Grahame, M. 2000. *Reading Space: social interaction and identity in the houses of the Roman Pompeii. A syntactical approach to the analysis and interpretation of built space.* British Archaeological Report S886. Oxford: Archaeopress.

Grassi, M. T. 2009a. 'Il "progetto Palmira" (Siria)'. *LANX. Rivista della scuola di specializzazione in archeologia, Università degli Studi di Milano* 2, 194–205.

Grassi, M. T. 2009b. 'Nuovi scavi e ricerche nella Siria Romana: il "progetto Palmira" dell'Università degli Studi di Milano'. In A. Coralini (ed.). *Vesuviana. Archeologie a confronto, Atti del convegno internazionale (Bologna, 14–16 gennaio 2008).* Bologna: Ante Quem, 339–349.

Grassi, M. T. 2010 'Il "progetto Palmira". I nuovi scavi dell'Università nell'Oriente romano (campagne 2007–2008)'. In G. Zanetto and M. Ornaghi (eds). *Documenta Antiquitatis, Atti dei Seminari di Dipartimento 2009.* Milano: Cisalpino, 1–25.

Grassi, M. T. 2011. 'Une nouvelle Mission conjointe syro-italienne à Palmyre (Pal.M.A.I.S.): observations prèliminaires sur les campagnes 2007–2009 dans le quartier sud-ouest'. *Chronique Archéologique en Syrie: publication spéciale consacrée aux rapports annuels de l'archéologie en Syrie* 5, 189–196.

Grassi, M. T. 2012. 'Un nuovo scavo urbano della Statale di Milano: il quartiere sud-ovest di Palmira'. In C. Chiaramonte Treré, G. Bagnasco Gianni and F. Chiesa (eds). *Interpretando l'antico. Scritti di archeologia offerti a Maria Bonghi Jovino, Quaderni di Acme 134.* Milano: Cisalpino, 889–907.

Grassi, M. T. and al-As'ad, W. 2013. '*Pal.M.A.I.S. Recherches et fouilles d'une nouvelle Mission conjointe syro-italienne dans le quartier sud-ouest de Palmyre*'. *Studia Palmireńskie* 12, 115–128.

Grassi, M. T., Rocca, G. and Piacentini, D. 2015. 'Les nouveautés épigraphiques de la Mission Archéologique Italo-Syrienne de Palmyre'. *LANX. Rivista della scuola di specializzazione in archeologia, Università degli Studi di Milano* 20, 1–48.

Grassi, M. T., Zenoni, G. and Rossi, G. 2012. 'Tecniche e materiali dell'architettura palmirena: il caso dell'Edificio con Peristilio del quartiere Sud-Ovest (PAL.M.A.I.S. scavi 2008–2010)'. In M. P. Bologna and M. Ornaghi (eds). *Novissima Studia. Dieci anni di antichistica milanese, Atti dei Seminari di Dipartimento 2011, Quaderni di Acme 129.* Milano: Cisalpino, 53–82.

Greatrex, G. 2007. 'Dukes of the eastern frontier'. In J. Drinkwater and B. Salway (eds). *Wolf Liebeschuetz Reflected. Essays Presented by Colleagues, Friends, and Pupils.* London: Institute of Classical Studies, 87–99.

Greatrex, G. and Lieu, S. N. C 2002. *The Roman Eastern Frontier and the Persian Wars. Part II, AD 363–630. A Narrative Sourcebook.* London, New York: Routledge.

Gregory, S. 1995–1997. *Roman Military Architecture on the Eastern Frontier.* Amsterdam: Adolf M. Hakkert.

Griffith, S. H. 1992. 'Images, Islam and christian icons. A moment in the Christian/Muslim encounter in early Islamic times'. In P. Canivetand and J.-P. Rey-Coquais (eds). *La Syrie de Byzance à l'Islam. VIIe–VIIIe siècles: actes du colloque international Lyon – Maison de l'Orient Méditerranéen, Paris – Institut du monde arabe, 11–15 Septembre 1990.* Damascus: Institut Français de Damas, 121–138.

Grimme, H. 1886. *Palmyrae sive Tadmur urbis fata quae fuerint tempore muslimico.* Munich: Ex Typographia Coppenrathiana.

Groot, J. C., Jones, J. E. and Parker, S. T. 2006. 'The barracks at el-Lejjūn (Areas K, L, R, and B.6)'. In S. T. Parker (ed.). *The Roman Frontier in Central Jordan. Final Report on the Limes Arabicus Project, 1980–1989*. Harvard, NJ: Harvard University Press, 161–186.

Grossmann, P. 1973. *S. Michele in Africisco zu Ravenna; baugeschichtliche Untersuchungen*. Mainz: P.von Zabern.

Guidetti, M. 2009. 'The Byzantine heritage in the Dār al-Islām: churches and mosques in al-Ruha between the sixth and twelfth centuries'. *Muqarnas* 26, 1–36.

Guidobaldi, F. 1994. 'Spazio urbano e organizzazione ecclesiastica a Roma nel VI e VII secolo'. In N. Cambi and E. Marin (eds). *Acta congressus internationalis archaeologiae christianae. Split-Porec (25–9.–1.10.1994)*. Split-Città del Vaticano: Arheološki Muzej-Pontificio Istituto di Archeologia Cristiana, 29–54.

Gussone, M. and Müller-Wiener, M. 2012. 'Resafa-Rusafat Hisham, Syria. "Long term survival" of an Umayyad residence; first results of the extended surface survey'. In R. Matthews and J. Curtis (eds). *Proceedings of the 7th International Congress on the Archaeology of the Ancient Near East, 12–16 April 2010, the British Museum and UCL, London. Volume II, Ancient and Modern Issues in Cultural Heritage, Colour and Light in Architecture, Art and Material Culture, Islamic Archaeology*. Wiesbaden: Harrassowitz, 569–584.

Haldon, J. F. 1999. 'The idea of the town in the Byzantine empire'. In G. P. Brogiolo and B.Ward-Perkins, (eds). *The Idea and Ideal of the Town between Late Antiquity and the Early Middle Ages*. Leiden: Brill, 1–24.

Haldon, J. F. 2000. *Byzantium, a History*. Stroud: Tempus.

Halley, E. 1695. 'Some account of the ancient state of the city of Palmyra, with short remarks upon the inscriptions found there'. *Philosophical Transaction of the Royal Society* 19, 160–175.

Hammad, M. 2010. *Palmyre: transformations urbaines: développement d'une ville antique de la marge aride syrienne*. Paris: P. Geuthner.

Hanfmann, G. M. A. 1959. 'Excavations at Sardis 1958'. *Bulletin of the American Schools of Oriental Reserarch* 154, 8–43.

Hanson, R. P. C. 1978. 'The transformation of pagan temples into churches in the early Christian centuries'. *Journal of Semitic Studies* 23, 257–267.

Harding, G. L. 1951. 'Excavations on the Citadel, Amman'. *Annual of the Department of Antiquities of Jordan* 1, 7–16.

Harper, R. P., 1975. 'Excavations at Dibsi Faraj, northern Syria, 1972–1974: a preliminary note on the site and its monuments with an appendix'. *Dumbarton Oaks Papers* 29, 319–338.

Hartmann, U. 2011. *Das Palmyrenische Teilreich*. Stuttgart: Franz Steiner Verlag.

Hartmann, U. 2016. 'What was it like to be a Palmyrene in the age of crisis?'. In A. Kropp and R. Raja (eds). *The World of Palmyra: Palmyrene Studies Vol. 1*. Copenhagen: Royal Danish Academy of Science and Letters, 53–69.

Hauser, S. R. 2012. 'Wasser als Ressource: Palmyra als Territorialmacht'. In F. Klimscha, R. Eichmann, C. Schuler and H. Fahlbusch (eds). *Wasserwirtschaftliche Innovationen im archäologischen Kontext: von den prähistorischen Anfängen bis zu den Metropolen der Antike*. Rahden, Westf: VML, 211–224.

Hirschfeld, J. 1995. *The Palestinian Dwellings in the Roman-Byzantine Period*. Jerusalem: Franciscan Printing Press-Israel Exploration Society.

Hof, C. 2009. 'Masonry techniques of the early sixth century city wall of Resafa, Syria'. In K. E. Kurrer, W. Lorenz and V. Wetzk (eds). *Proceedings of the Third International Congress on Construction History: Brandenburg University of Technology Cottbus, Germany, 20th–24th May 2009*. Cottbus: Brandenburg University of Technology, 813–820.

Honigmann, E. 1925. 'Studien zur Notitia Antiochena'. *Byzantinische Zeitschrift* 25, 60–88.

Honigmann, E. 1951. *Évêques et évêchés monophysites d' Asie antérieure au VIe siècle*. Leuven: Imprimerie Orientaliste L. Durbecq.

Hoyland, R., 2009. 'Late Roman provincia Arabia, monks and Arab tribes: a problem of centre and periphery'. *Semitica et Classica* 2, 117–139.

Hoyland, R. 2011. *Theophilus of Edessa's Chronicle and the Circulation of Historical Knowledge in Late Antiquity and Early Islam*. Liverpool: Liverpool University Press.

Huart, C. I. 1929. 'Inscriptions Arabes de Palmyre'. *Revue des Études Islamiques* 3, 237–244.

Humbert, J.-B. and Desmeraux, A. 1990. 'Huit campagnes de fouilles au Khirbet es-Samra (1981–1989)'. *Revue Biblique* 97, 252–269.

Humpreys, R. S. 2010. 'Christian communities in early Islamic Syria and northern Jazira: the dynamics of adaptation'. In J. F. Haldon (ed.). *Money, Power and Politics in Early Islamic Syria. A Review of Current Debates*. Farnham: Ashgate, 45–56.

Iacobini, I. 2012. 'La Sapienza Bizantina. Il contributo della storia dell'arte (1896–1970)'. In A. A. Longo, G. Cavallo, A. Guiglia and A. Iacobini (eds). *La Sapienza Bizantina. Un secolo di ricerche sulla civiltà di Bisanzio all'Università di Roma* (Milion 8). Rome: Campisano, 9–38.

Ingholt, H. 1932. 'Quelques fresques récentemment découvert à Palmyre'. *Annales Archéologiques Arabes Syriennes* 3, 1–20.

Ingholt, H. 1935. 'Five dated tombs from Palmyra'. *Berytus* 2, 57–120.

Intagliata, E. E. 2014. 'The white ware from Palmyra (Syria): preliminary data from the new excavation in the southwest quarter'. In N. Poulou-Papadimitriou, E. Nodarou, V. and Kilikoglou (eds). *LRCW 4: late Roman coarse wares, cooking wares and amphorae in the Mediterranean. Archaeology and archaeometry. The Mediterranean: a market without frontiers*. British Archaeological Report S2616. Oxford: Archaeopress, 649–655.

Intagliata, E. E. 2017a. 'The post-Roman occupation of the northern courtyard of the Sanctuary of Baalshamin in Palmyra; A reassessment of the evidence based on the documents in the Fonds d'Archives Paul Collart, Université de Lausanne'. *Zeitschrift für Orientarchäologie* 9, 180–199.

Intagliata, E. E. 2017b. 'Palmyra and its ramparts during the Tetrarchy'. In E. Rizos (ed.). *New Cities in Late Antiquity. Documents and Archaeology* (Bibliothéque de l'Antiquité Tardive). Turnhout: Brepols, 71–83.

Isaac, B. 1990. *The Limits of Empire: The Roman army in the East*. Oxford: Oxford University Press.

Isaac, B.1997. 'The eastern frontier'. In A. Cameron and P. Garnsey (eds). *The Cambridge Ancient History Vol. 13: the late empire, AD 337–425*. Cambridge: Cambridge University Press, 437–460.

Jacobs, I. 2009. 'Encroachment in the eastern Mediterranean from the fourth to the seventh century AD'. *Ancient Society* 39, 203–244.

Jacobs, I. 2013. *Aesthetic Maintenance of Civic Space. The 'Classical City' From the 4th to the 7th C. AD*. Leuven: Peeters.

Jacobs, I. 2014. 'Ecclesiastical dominance and urban setting. Colonnaded streets as back-drop for Christian display'. *Antiquité Tardive* 22, 281–304.

Janniard, S. 2006. 'Armée et "acculturation" dans l'Orient Romain tardif: l'exemple des confins syro-mésopotamiens (V^{e}–VIe s. aps. J.-C.)'. *Mélanges de l'École française de Rome. Antiquité* 118, 133–149.

Jastrzębowska, E. 2013. 'La christianisation de Palmyre: l'exemple du temple de Bel'. *Studia Palmireńskie* 12, 177–192.

Jones, A. H. M., Martindale, J. R. and Morris, J. 1971. *The Prosopography of the Later Roman Empire, Vol. 1*. Cambridge: Cambridge University Press.

Juchniewicz, K. 2013. 'Late Roman fortifications in Palmyra'. *Studia Palmireńskie* 12, 193–202.

Juchniewicz, K. and Żuchowska, M. 2012. 'Water supply in Palmyra, a chronological approach'. In M. Żuchowska (ed.). *The Archaeology of Water Supply*. British Archaeological Report S2414. Oxford: Archaeopress, 61–73.

Juchniewicz, K. and Żuchowska, M. 2013. 'Remarks on water supply in Palmyra. Results of a survey in 2010'. *Polish Archaeology in the Mediterranean* 22, 341–350.

Juchniewicz, K., al-As'ad, K. and al-Hariri, K. 2010. 'The defense wall in Palmyra after recent Syrian excavations'. *Studia Palmireńskie* 11, 55–73.

Kaizer, T. 2002. *The Religious Life of Palmyra. A Study of the Social Patterns of Worship in the Roman Period*. Stuttgart: Franz Steiner Verlag.

Kaizer, T. 2010. 'From Zenobia to Alexander the Sleepless: paganism, Judaism and Christianity at late Roman Palmyra'. In B. Bastl, V. Gassner and U. Muss 2010 (eds). *Zeitreisen. Syrien-Palmyra-Rom. Festsschrift für Andreas Schmidt-Colinet zum 65. Geburtstag*. Vienna: Phoibos-Verlag, 113–123.

Karnapp, W. 1976. *Die Stadtmauer von Resafa in Syrien*. Berlin: de Gruyter.

Kennedy, D. L. 1992. 'The Roman frontier in Arabia (Jordan)'. *Journal of Roman Archaeology* 5, 437–489.

Kennedy, D. L. and Falahat, H. 2008. '*Castra Legionis VI Ferratae*: a building inscription for the legionary fortress at Udruh near Petra'. *Journal of Roman Archaeology* 21, 121–169.

Kennedy, D. L. and Riley, D. N. 1990. *Rome's Desert Frontier from the Air*. Austin: University of Texas Press.

Kennedy, H. N. 1985. 'From polis to madina: urban change in Late Antique and early Islamic Syria'. *Past and Present* 106, 3–27.

Kennedy, H. 1992. 'Antioch: from Byzantium to Islam and back again'. In J. Rich (ed.). *The City in Late Antiquity. London,* New York: Routledge, 181–198.

Khatchatrian, A. 1962. *Les baptisteries paléochrétiens: plans, notices et bibliographie*. Paris: École Pratique des Hautes Études, Section des Sciences Religieuses.

Khoury, W. 2005. 'Hawarine: premiers résultats, campagnes 2003–2004'. In J.-P. Sodini, F. Baratte, V. Déroche, C. Jolivet-Lévy and B. Pitarakis (eds). *Travaux et Mémoires 15. Mélanges Jean-Pierre Sodini*. Paris: Association des amis du centre d'histoire et civilisation de Byzance, 299–316.

King, G. R. D. 1985. 'Islam, iconoclasm and the declaration of doctrine'. *Bulletin of the School of Oriental and African Studies* 48, 267–277.

Kleinbauer, W.G. 1973.'The origin and functions of the aisled *tetraconch* churches in Syria and northern Mesopotamia'. *Dumbarton Oaks Papers* 27, 89–114.

Kołątaj, W. 1975. 'Wstępny project konsolidacji tzw. Świątyni sztandarów obozu Diokecjana w Palmyrze'. *Studia Palmireńskie* 4, 79–85.

Kollwitz, J. 1959. 'Die Grabungen in Resafa'. In N. Bochringer, (ed.). *Neue Deutsche Ausgrabungen im Mittelmeergebiet und im Vorderen Orient*. Berlin: Mann, 45–70.

Kollwitz, J., Wirth, J. and Karnapp, W. 1958–1959. 'Die grabungen in Resafa: Herbst 1954 und 1956'. *Annales Archéologiques Arabes Syriennes* 8–9, 21–54.

Konrad, M. 1999. 'Research on the Roman and early Byzantine frontier in north Syria'. *Journal of Roman Archaeology* 12, 392–410.

Konrad, M. 2001. *Der spätrömische Limes in Syrien: archäologische Untersuchungen an den Grenzkastellen von Sura, Tetrapyrgium, Cholle und in Resafa*. Mainz: P. von Zabern.

Korn, L. 2007. 'La mosquée d'Omar (al-Jâmi' al-'Umarî, grande mosquée, mosquée du Vendredi)'. In J. Dentzer-Feydy, M. Vallerin, T. Fournet, R. Mukdad and A. Mukdad (eds). *Bosra. Aux portes de l'Arabie*. Beirut: Presses de l'IFPO, 283–286.

Kowalski, S. P. 1994. 'The praetorium of the camp of Diocletian in Palmyra'. *Studia Palmireńskie* 9, 39–70.

Kowalski, S. P. 1995. 'The prefect's house in the late Roman legionary fortress in Palmyra'. *Études et Travaux* 17, 73–78.

Kowalski, S. P. 1996. 'Doubtful Christian reutilization of the Baalshamin temple in Palmyra'. *Damaszener Mitteilungen* 9, 217–226.

Kowalski, S. P. 1997. 'Late Roman Palmyra in literature and epigraphy'. *Studia Palmireńskie* 10, 39–62.

Kowalski, S. P. 1998. 'The camp of the Legio I Illyricorum in Palmyra'. *Novaensia: Badania ekspedycji archeologicznej Uniwersytetu Warszawskiego w Novae: studia i materialy* 10, 189–209.

Kowalski, S. P. 1999. 'The prefect's house in the late Roman legionary fortress in Palmyra'. *Études et Travaux* 18, 161–172.

Kraelig, C. H., 1938. 'The history of Gerasa'. In C. H. Kraelig (ed.). *Gerasa, City of the Decapolis. An Account Embodying the Record of a Joint Excavation Conducted by Yale University and the British School of Archaeology in Jerusalem (1928–1930), and Yale University and the American Schools of Oriental Research (1930–1931, 1933–1934)*. New Haven, CO: American Schools of Oriental Research, 27–69.

Krautheimer, R. 1981. *Early Christian and Byzantine Architecture*. Harmondsworth: Penguin.

Krencker, D. 1932. 'Das Diocletianslager'. In T. Wiegand (ed.). *Palmyra: Ergebnisse der Expeditionen von 1902 und 1917*. Berlin: Verlag Heinrich Keller, 85–105.

Krogulska, M. 1983. 'Une lampe à symboles juifs du temple d'Allath à Palmyre'. *Études et Travaux* 13, 209–214.

Krogulska, M. 1984. 'Le Forum'. In M. Gawlikowski (ed.). *Palmyre (VIII). Les principia de Dioclétien. 'Temple des Enseignes'*. Warsaw: PWN, Editions Scientifiques de Pologne, 70–91.

Krogulska, M. 1985. 'A ceramic workshop in the western quarter of Palmyra'. *Studia Palmireńskie* 8, 43–68.

Krogulska, M. 1997. 'Second and third century A.D. pottery from Palmyra'. In A. Bounni (ed.). *Special Issue Documenting the Activities of the International Colloquium on Palmyra and the Silk Road. Annales Archéologiques Arabes Syriennes* 42. Damascus: DGAM, 339–354.

Krogulska, M. 2005. 'A lamp from the cella of the temple of Allat in Palmyra'. In P. Bieliński and F. Stępniowski (eds). *Aux pays d'Allat: mélanges offerts à Michał Gawlikowski.* Warsaw: Warsaw University, Institute of Archaeology, 123–129.

Krzyżanowska, A. 1981. 'A hoard dating the destruction of a temple at Palmyra'. In L. Casson and M. Price (eds). *Coins, Culture and History in the Ancient World: Numismatic and Other Studies in Honor of Bluma L. Trell.* Detroit, MI: Wayne State University Press, 39–41.

Krzyżanowska, A. 2014. 'Monnaies Grecques et Romaines'. In A. Krzyżanowska and M. Gawlikowski (eds). *Monnaies des fouilles Polonaises à Palmyre. Studia Palmireńskie* 13. Warsaw: Warsaw University Press, Polish Centre of Mediterranean Archaeology, 13–70.

Lain, A. and Parker, S. T. 2006. 'The principia of el-Lejjun (Area A)'. In S. T. Parker (ed.). *The Roman Frontier in Central Jordan. Final Report on the Limes Arabicus Project, 1980–1989.* Cambridge, MA: Harvard University Press, 123–160.

Lander, J. K. 1984. *Roman Stone Fortifications: Variation and Change from the First Century A.D. to the Fourth.* British Archaeological Report S206. Oxford: British Archaeological Report.

Lassus, J. 1947. *Sanctuaire chrétiens de Syrie. Essai sur la gènese, la forme et l'usage liturgiques des édifices du culte Chrétien, en Syrie, du IIIe siècle à la conquête Musulmane.* Paris: P. Geuthner.

Lassus, J. 1972. Les Portiques d'Antioche (Antioch-on-the-Orontes, V). Princeton, NJ: Princeton University Press.

Lassus, J. 1984. 'Sur les maisons d'Antioche'. In J. Balty (ed.). *Apamée de Syrie: bilan des recherches archéologiques, 1973–1979: aspects de l'architecture domestique d'Apamée: actes du colloque tenu à Bruxelles les 29, 30 et 31 mai 1980.* Bruxelles: Centre belge de recherches archéologiques à Apamée de Syrie, 361–372.

Lauffray, J. 1983. *Ḥalabiyya-Zenobia, place forte du limes oriental et la Haute-Mésopotamie au VIe siècle, I: les duchés frontaliers de Mésopotamie et les fortifications de Zenobia.* Paris: P. Geuthner.

Lauffray, J. 1991. *Ḥalabiyya-Zenobia, place forte du limes oriental et la Haute-Mésopotamie au VIe siècle, II: l' architecture publique, religieuse, privée et funéraire.* Paris: P. Geuthner.

Lavan, L. 1999. 'The residences of Late Antique governors: a gazeteer'. *Antiquité Tardive* 7, 135–164.

Le Quien, M. 1740. *Oriens christianus, in quatuor patriarchatus digestus quo exhibentur ecclesiae, patriarchae, caeterique praesules totius orientis.* Paris: Ex Typographia Regia.

Lehner, H. 1932. 'Zur Bauinschrift des Diocletianslagers'. In T. Wiegand (ed.). *Palmyra: Ergebnisse der Expeditionen von 1902 und 1917.* Berlin: Verlag Heinrich Keller, 106–107.

Lenoir, M. 2011. *Le camp Romaine: Proche-Orient et Afrique du nord.* Rome, Paris: École Française de Rome, de Boccard.

Leroy, J. 1964. *Les manuscrits syriaques à peintures conservés dans la bibliothèques d'Europe et du Proche-Orient.* Paris: P. Geuthner.

Levi, D. 1947. *Antioch mosaic pavements.* London: Princeton University Press.

Levy-Rubin, M. 2011. *Non-Muslim in the Early Islamic Empire. From Surrender to Coexistence.* Cambridge: Cambridge University Press.

Lewin, A. S. 1991. *Studi sulla città imperiale Romana nell'Oriente tardoantico.* Como: New Press.

Lewin, A. S. 2001. 'Urban public building from Constantine to Julian: the epigraphic evidence'. In L. Lavan (ed.). *Recent Research in Late Antique Urbanism.* Portsmouth: *Journal of Roman Archaeology* Supplement 42, 27–37.

Lewin, A. S. 2002. 'Diocletian: politics and limites in the Near East'. In P. Freeman, J. Bennett, Z. T. Fiema and B. Hoffmann (eds). *Limes XVIII. Proceedings of the 18th International Congress of Roman Frontier Studies Held in Amman, Jordan (September 2000), Vol. 1.* British Archaeological Report S1084. Oxford: Archaeopress, 91–101.

Lewin, A. S. 2007. "Amr ibn 'Adi, Mavia, the phylarchs and the late Roman army: peace and war in the Near East'. In A. S. Lewin and P. Pellegrini (eds). *The Late Roman Army in the Near East from Diocletian to the Arab Conquest: proceedings of a colloquium held at Potenza, Acerenza and Matera, Italy (May 2005).* British Archaeological Report S1717. Oxford: Archaeopress, 243–262.

Lewin, A. S. 2011. 'The new frontiers of Late Antiquityin the Near East from Diocletian to Justinian'. In O. Hekster and T. Kaizer (eds). *Frontiers in the Roman World. Proceedings of the Ninth Workshop of the International Network Impact of Empire (Durham, 16–19 April 2009).* Leiden, Boston: Brill, 233–263.

Liebeschuetz, J. H. W. G. 1977. 'The defences of Syria in the sixth century'. In C. B. Rüger (ed.). *Studien zu den Militärgrenzen Roms II. Vorträge des 10. internationalen Limeskongresses in der Germania Inferior.* Cologne: Rheinland, 487–499.

Liebeschuetz, J. H. W. G.1992. 'The end of the ancient city'. In J. Rich (ed.). *The City in Late Antiquity.* London, New York: Routledge, 1–49.

Liebeschuetz, J. H. W. G. 2001a. *The Decline and Fall of the Roman City.* Oxford: Oxford University Press.

Liebeschuetz, J. H. W. G. 2001b. 'The uses and abuses of the concept of "decline" in later Roman history, or was Gibbon politically incorrect?' (responses by A. Cameron, B. Ward-Perkins, M. Whittow and L. Lavan). In L. Lavan (ed.). *Recent Research in Late Antique Urbanism.* Portsmouth: *Journal of Roman Archaeology* Supplement 42, 233–245.

Loosley, E., 2012. *The Architecture and Liturgy of the "Bema" in Fourth to Sixth Century Syrian Churches.* Leiden, Boston: Brill.

Lucchesi, G., 1967. 'Olibia (Libia), Eutropia e Leonide'. *Bibliotheca Sanctorum* 9, 1152–1154.

Mackensen, M. 2009. 'The tetrarchic fort at Nag el-Hagar in the province of Thebaïs: preliminary report (2005–08)'. *Journal of Roman Archaeology* 22, 286–312.

MacMullen, R. 1963. *Soldiers and Civilians in the Late Roman Empire.* Cambridge, MA: Harvard University Press.

MacNicoll, A. W., Smith, R. H. and Hennessy, B. 1982. *Pella in Jordan. 1. An Interim Report on the Joint University of Sydney and College of Wooster Excavations at Pella 1979–1981*. Canberra: Australian National Gallery.

MacNicoll, A., Smith, R. H. and Watson, P. 1992. 'The Byzantine period'. In A. W. McNicoll, P. C. Edwards, J. Hanbury-Tenison, B. Hennessy, T. F. Potts, R. H. Smith, A. Walmsley and P. Watson 1992. *Pella in Jordan 2. The Second Interim Report of the Joint University of Sydney and College of Wooster Excavation at Pella 1982–1985*. Sydney: Meditarch, 145–181.

Majcherek, G. 2005. 'More churches from Palmyra – an inkling of the Late Antique city'. In P. Bieliński and F. M. Stępniowski (eds). *Aux pays d'Allat. Mélanges offerts à Michal Gawlikowski*. Warsaw: Warsaw University, Institute of Archaeology, 141–150.

Majcherek, G. 2008. 'Palmyra (Syria), 46th season of excavations, Basilica IV'. *Newsletter of the Polish Centre of Mediterranean Archaeology of the University of Warsaw* 2008. [available at <http://www.pcma.uw.edu.pl/en/pcma-newsletter/2008/hellenistic-and-graeco-roman-period/palmyra-syria>; accessed 18/08/2013].

Majcherek, G. 2009. 'Palmyra (Syria), 47th season of excavations, Basilica IV'. *Newsletter of the Polish Centre of Mediterranean Archaeology of the University of Warsaw* 2009. [available at <http://www.pcma.uw.edu.pl/en/pcma-newsletter/2009/hellenistic-and-graeco-roman-period/palmyra-syria>; accessed 18/08/2013].

Majcherek, G. 2012. 'Polish archaeological mission to Palmyra. Seasons 2008 and 2009'. *Polish Archaeology in the Mediterranean* 21, 459–479.

Majcherek, G. 2013. 'Excavating the basilicas'. *Studia Palmireńskie* 12, 251–268.

Majcherek, G. and Taha, A. 'Roman and Byzantine layers at Umm el-Tlel: ceramics and other finds'. *Syria* 81, 229–248.

Mango, M. 2002. 'Excavations and survey at Androna, Syria: the Oxford team 1999'. *Dumbarton Oaks Papers* 56, 307–315.

Mango, M. 2003. 'Excavations and survey at Androna, Syria: the Oxford team 2000. *Dumbarton Oaks Papers* 57, 293–297.

Mango, M. 2008. 'Baths, reservoirs and water use at Androna in Late Antiquity and the early Islamic period'. In K. Bartl and A. Moaz (eds). *Residences, Castles, Settlements: transformation processes from late antiquity to early Islam in Bilad al-Sham: proceedings of the international conference held at Damascus, 5–9 November, 2006*. Rahden, Westf.: Verlag Marie Leidorf, 73–96.

Mango, M. 2011, 'Byzantine settlement expansion in north central Syria: the case of Androna/Andarin'. In A.Borrut, M. Debié, A. Papacosantinou, D. Pieri and J.-P. Sodini, (eds). *Le Proche-Orient e Justinien aux Abbasides. Peuplement et dynamiques spatiales. Actes du colloque 'continuités de l'occupation entre les périodes Byzantine et Abbaside au Proche-Orient, VIIe–IXe siècles', Paris, 18–20 Octobre 2007*. Turnhout: Brepols, 93–122.

Mansi, J. D. 1759–1798. *Sacrorum conciliorum nova et amplissima collectio*. Florence-Venice: Apud Antonii Zatta.

Maoz, Z.U. 1993. 'Kanaf, Ḥorvat'. In E. Stern (ed.). *The New Encyclopedia of Archaeological Excavations in the Holy Land, Vol. 3*. New York: Simon and Schuster, 847–850.

Marsden, E. W. 1969. *Greek and Roman Artillery; historical development*. Oxford: Clarendon Press.

Marsden, E. W. 1971. *Greek and Roman Artillery: technical treatises*. Oxford: Clarendon Press.

Matthews, J. F. 1984. 'The tax law of Palmyra: evidence for economic history in a city of the Roman east'. *Journal of Roman Studies* 74, 157–180.

Maudrel, H. and Shaw, T. 1758. *A Compendium of a Journey from Aleppo to Jerusalem by Mr. Henry Maundrel, Chaplain to the English Factory at Aleppo. The Travels of Dr. Thomas Shaw, F.R.S. and a Journey to Palmyra*. Dublin: printed for J. Smith, on the Blind Quay.

Meyer, J. C. 2008. 'Surface survey between Palmyra and Isriye. April 2008. Joint Syrian-Norwegian Project. Preliminary Report' [available at <http://www.org.uib.no/palmyrena/documents/Survey2008.pdf>; accessed 12/15/2016]

Meyer, J. C. 2009. 'Palmyrena. Palmyra and the surrounding territory. Joint Syrian-Norwegian project. Surface survey north of Palmyra. April and May 2009. Preliminary report, Historical period' [available at <http://www.org.uib.no/palmyrena/documents/2009_I.pdf>; accessed 12/15/2016]

Meyer, J. C. 2011. 'Palmyrena. Palmyra and the surrounding territory. Joint Syrian-Norwegian project. Surface survey north of Palmyra. Jebel Merah. April and May 2009. Report – historical period' [available at <http://www.org.uib.no/palmyrena/documents/Report2011x.pdf>; accessed 12/15/2016]

Meyer, J. C. 2013. 'City and hinterland. Villages and estates north of Palmyra. New perspectives'. *Studia Palmireńskie* 12, 269–286.

Meyer, J. C. 2016. 'Palmyrena. Settlements, forts and nomadic networks'. In A. Kropp and R. Raja (eds), *The World of Palmyra: Palmyrene Studies Vol. 1*. Copenhagen: The Royal Danish Academy of Science and Letters, 86–102.

Meyza, H. 1985. 'Remarks on the western aqueduct of Palmyra'. *Studia Palmireńskie* 8, 27–33.

Michałowski, K. 1960a. *Palmyre (I). Fouilles Polonaises 1959*. Warsaw, La Haye, Paris: PWN, Editions Scientifiques de Pologne, Mounton.

Michałowski, K. 1960b. 'Fouilles Polonaises à Palmyre 1959'. *Annales Archéologiques Arabes Syriennes* 10, 3–20.

Michałowski, K.1960c. 'Fouilles Polonaises à Palmyre 1960'. *Annales Archéologiques Arabes Syriennes* 10, 93–110.

Michałowski, K. 1961–1962. 'Fouilles Polonaises à Palmyre 1961'. *Annales Archéologiques Arabes Syriennes* 11–12, 63–82.

Michałowski, K. 1962. *Palmyre (II). Fouilles Polonaises 1960*. Warsaw, La Haye, Paris: PWN, Editions Scientifiques de Pologne, Mounton.

Michałowski, K., 1963a. *Palmyre (III). Fouilles Polonaises 1961*. Warsaw, 'S-Gravenhage: PWN, Editions Scientifiques de Pologne, Mouton.

Michałowski, K. 1963b. 'Fouilles Polonaises à Palmyre 1962'. *Annales Archéologiques Arabes Syriennes* 13, 79–96.

Michałowski, K. 1964a. *Palmyre (IV). Fouilles Polonaises 1962*. Warsaw-'S-Gravenhage: Państwowe Wydawnictwo Naukowe-Mouton.

Michałowski, K. 1964b. 'Fouilles Polonaises à Palmyre 1963'. *Annales Archéologiques Arabes Syriennes* 14, 23–38.

Michałowski, K. 1966. *Palmyre (V). Fouilles Polonaises 1963 et 1964*. Warsaw, 'S-Gravenhage: PWN, Editions Scientifiques de Pologne, Mouton.

Michałowski, K. 967. 'Rapport préliminaire de la septième champagne des fouilles Polonaises à Palmyre en 1965'. *Annales Archéologiques Arabes Syriennes* 17, 9–16.

Michałowski, K. 1969. 'Fouilles Polonaises à Palmyre 1967'. *Annales Archéologiques Arabes Syriennes* 19, 71–76.

Michałowski, K. 1970. *Palmyra*. London: Pall Mall Press.

Michałowski, K. 1971. 'Les fouilles Polonaises à Palmyre'. *Annales Archéologiques Arabes Syriennes* 21, 137–142.

Milik, J. T. 1967. 'Inscription Araméenneen caractères grecs de Doura-Europos et une dédicace grecque de Cordoue'. *Syria* 44, 289–306.

Millar, F. 2008. 'Community, religion and language in the middle-Euphrates zone in Late Antiquity'. *Scripta Classica Israelica* 27, 67–93.

Millar, F. 2013. 'A Syriac codex from near Palmyra and the "Ghassanid" Abokarib'. *Hugoye* 16, 15–35.

Mouterde, R. 1930. 'Nouvelles archéologiques: l'aménagement des ruines de Palmyre'. *Syria* 11, 203–205.

Mouterde, R. 1942–1943. 'Inscription syriaque du Gebel Bil'ās'. *Mélanges de l'Université Saint-Joseph* 25, 83–86.

Mouterde, R. and Poidebard, A. 1945. *Le limes de Chalcis. Organisation de la steppe en haute Syrie Romaine*. Paris: P. Geuthner.

Musil, A. 1928. *Palmyrena: a topographical itinerary*. New York: American Geographical Society.

Naumann, R. 1979, *Der Zeustempel zu Aizanoi. Nach den Ausgrabungen von Daniel Krencker und Martin Schede bearbeitet und herausgegeben*. Berlin: de Gruyter.

Nava, S. 2015. 'The marble decoration of the Peristyle Building in the SW quarter of Palmyra (Pal.M.A.I.S mission)'. In P. Pensabene and E. Gasparini (eds). *ASMOSIA X. Proceedings of the Tenth International Conference. Interdisciplinary Studies on Ancient Stones, Rome, 21–26 May 2012*. Rome: L'Erma di Bretchneider, 241–252.

Netzer, E. and Weiss, Z. 1995. 'New evidence for late-Roman and Byzantine Sepphoris'. In J. H. Humphrey, (ed.). *The Roman and Byzantine Near East: some recent archaeological research*. Portsmouth, RI: *Journal of Roman Archaeology Supplement* 14, 164–176.

Niepokólczycki, M. 1969. 'Pomiary Geodezyjne terenu 'Świątyni Sztandarów' w Palmyrze'. *Studia Palmireńskie* 3, 77–83.

Northedge, A. 1992. *Studies on Roman and Islamic 'Amman. Volume 1: history, site and architecture*. Oxford: Oxford University Press.

Northedge, A. 1994. 'Archaeology and new urban settlement in early Islamic Syria and Iraq'. In G. R. D. King and A. Cameron (eds). *The Byzantine and Early Islamic Near East, II, Land Use and Settlement Patterns*. Princeton, NJ: Darwin Press, 231–265.

Notebook 1956a. *Notebook (Excavation Diary)*. Unpublished. Fond d'Archives Paul Collart, University of Lausanne.

Notebook 1966a. *Notebook (Excavation Diary)*. Unpublished. Fond d'Archives Paul Collart, University of Lausanne.

Notebook 1966b. *Notebook (Monnaies)*. Unpublished. Fond d'Archives Paul Collart, University of Lausanne.

Noth, A. 1987. 'Abgrenzungsprobleme zwischen Muslimen und Nicht-Muslimen. Die "Bedingungen 'Umar (aš-Šurūṭ al-'umayya)" unter einem anderen Aspekt gelesen'. *Jerusalem Studies in Arabic and Islam* 9, 290–315.

Oates, D. 1968. *Studies in the Ancient History of Northern Iraq*. London: Oxford University Press.

Ostratz, A. 1969. 'Note sur le plan de la partie médiane de la rue principale à Palmyre'. *Annales Archéologiques Arabes Syriennes* 19, 109–120.

Özgenel, L. 2007. 'Public use and privacy in Late Antique houses in Asia Minor: the architecture of spatial control'. In L. Lavan, L. Özgenel and A. Sarantis (eds). *Housing in Late Antiquity, From Palaces to Shops*. Leiden: Brill, 240–281.

Paridaens, N. and Vannesse, M. 2014. 'Des bains au quartier Nord-Est d'Apamée. Résultats préliminaires'. In M.-F. Boussac, S. Denoix, T. Fournet and B. Redon (eds). *25 siècles de bain collectif en Orient (Proche-Orient, Égypte et péninsule Arabique). Actes du colloque de Damas*. Cairo: Presses de l'IFPO, 335–359.

Palmieri, L. 2010. *'Étude préliminaire sur les stucs trouvés dans le "Bâtiment à Péristyle" du quartier sud-ouest de Palmyre (Pal.M.A.I.S., Fouilles 2008–2009)'. Rivista della scuola di specializzazione in archeologia,* Università degli Studi di Milano 6. Milan: Università degli Studi di Milano, 175–186.

Parker, S. T. 1986. *Romans and Saracens: a history of the Arabian frontier*. Winona Lake, IN: Eisenbrauns.

Parker, S. T. 2006. 'The legionary fort of el-Lejjūn'. In S. T. Parker (ed.). *The Roman Frontier in Central Jordan. Final Report on the Limes Arabicus Project, 1980–1989*. Cambridge, MA: Harvard University Press, 111–122.

Paribeni, A. 2012. 'Le missioni di studio in Oriente e il Centro di Documentazione di Storia dell'Arte Bizantina (1966–2006)'. In A. A. Longo, G. Cavallo, A. Guiglia and A. Iacobini (eds). *La Sapienza Bizantina. Un secolo di ricerche sulla civiltà di Bisanzio all'Università di Roma* (Milion 8). Rome: Campisano, 39–54.

Parlasca, K. 1996. 'Funde figürlicher Stuckdekorationen auf dem Gelände des Hotel Meridien in Palmyra'. In A. Bounni (ed.). *Special Issue Documenting the Activities of the International Colloquium on Palmyra and the Silk Road. Annales Archéologiques Arabes Syriennes* 42. Damascus: DGAM, 291–296.

Paschoud, F., 1996. *Historie Auguste, tome V, 1ere partie. Vies d'Aurélien et de Tacite*. Paris: Collection des Universités de France.

Petruccioli, A. 2006. 'The courtyard house: typological variations over space and time'. In B. Edwards, M. Sibley, M. Hakmi and P. Land (eds). *Courtyard Housing: past, present and future*. New York: Taylor and Francis, 3–20.

Petruccioli, A. 2007. *After Amnesia: learning from the Islamic Mediterranean urban fabric*. Bari: ICAR.

Piccirillo, M. 1981. *Chiese e mosaici della Giordania settentrionale*. Jerusalem: Franciscan Printing Press.

Piraud-Fournet, P. 2003. 'Le "Palais de Trajan" à Bosra'. *Syria* 80, 5–40.

Piraud-Fournet, P. 2007. 'Le palais dit "de Trajan"'. In J. Dentzer-Feydy, M. Vallerin, T. Fournet, R. Mukdad and A. Mukdad (eds). *Bosra. Aux portes de l'Arabie*. Beyrouth: Presses de l'IFPO, 147–153.

Poccardi, G. 1994. 'Antioche de Syrie. Pour un nouveau plan urbain de l'île de l'Oronte (Ville Neuve) du IIIe au Ve siècle'. *Mélanges de l'École française de Rome. Antiquité* 106, 993–1023.

Poidebard, A. 1934. *La trace de Rome dans le désert de Syrie; le limes de Trajan à la conquête Arabe; recherches aériennes (1925–1932)*. Paris: P. Geuthner.

Polci, B. 2003. 'Some aspects of the transformation of the Roman domusbetween Late Antiquity and the early Middle Ages'. In

L. Lavan and W. Bowden (eds). *Theory and Practice in the Late Antique Archaeology*. Leiden: Brill, 79–109.

Popović, V. 1984. 'Donjii Milanovac – Veliki Gradac (Taliata)'. *Starinar* 33–34, 265–280.

Pringle, D. 1981. *The Defence of Byzantine Africa from Justinian to the Arab Conquest: an account of the military history and archaeology of the African provinces in the sixth and seventh centuries*. British Achaeological Report S99. Oxford: British Achaeological Reports.

Puchstein, O. 1932. 'Grundplan der Stadt, Strassen und Plätze, Basilika und Wohnbauten'. In T. Wiegand (ed.). *Palmyra: Ergebnisse der Expeditionen von 1902 und 1917*. Berlin: Verlag Heinrich Keller, 17–35.

Raepsaet, G. and Raepsaet-Charlier M.-T. 1984, 'La maison aux colonnes trilobées'. In J. Balty (ed.). *Apamée de Syrie. Bilan des recherches archéologiques 1973–1979. Aspects de l'architecture domestique d'Apamée. Actes du colloque tenu á Bruxelles les 29, 30 et 31 Mai 1980*. Bruxelles: Centre Belge de Recherches Archéologiques á Apamée de Syrie, 181–201.

Rapp, C. 2004. 'Bishops in Late Antiquity: a new social and urban élite?'. In J. F. Haldon and L. I. Conrad (eds). *Late Antiquity and Early Islam, Vol. 6*. Princeton, NJ: Darwin Press, 144–173.

Reekmans, L. 1969. 'Fresques des portiques de la grande colonnade'. In J. Balty (ed.). *Apamée de Syrie: Bilan des recherches archéologiques 1965–1968: Actes du colloque tenu à Bruxelles les 29 et 30 avril 1969*. Bruxelles: Centre belge de recherches archéologiques à Apamée de Syrie, 117–123.

Rheidt, K. 2003. 'Archäologie und Spätantike in Anatolien. Methoden, Ergebnisse und problem der ausgrabungen in Aizanoi'. In G. Brands and H.-G. Severin (eds). *Die Spätantike Stadt und ihre Christianisierung*. Wiesbaden: Reichert, 239–247.

Richardson, P. 2004. 'Towards a typology of Levantine/Palestinian houses'. *Journal for the Study of the New Testament* 27, 47–68.

Ritterling, E. 1925. 'Legio'. In *Paulys Realencyclopädie der classischen Altertumswissenschaft: neue Bearbeitung* 24. Stuttgart: J. B. Metzler, 1329–1837.

Rizos, E. 2013. 'Centres of the late Roman military supply network in the Balkans: a survey of horrea'. *Jahrbuch des Römisch-Germanischen Zentralmuseums Mainz* 60, 659–696.

Rocco, M. 2010. 'The reasons behind *Constitutio Antoniniana* and its effects on the Roman military'. *Acta Classica Universitatis Scientiarum Debreceniensis* 46, 131–155.

Romagnolo, M. 2012. 'Dati preliminari sui vetri dell'edficio con peristilio di Palmira (Siria)'. In A. Coscarella (ed.). *Il vetro in Italia: testimonianze, produzioni, commerci in età basso medievale. Il vetro in Calabria: vecchie scoperte, nuove acquisizioni. Atti XV Giornate Nazionali di Studio sul Vetro A.I.H.V.* Cosenza: Università della Calabria, 599–604.

Roques, D. 2011. *Procope de Césarée, Constructions de Justinen Ier (Περίκτισμάσων/De aedificiis)*. Alessandria: Edizioni dell'Orso.

Rostovtzeff, M. I. 1934. *The Excavations at Dura Europos: preliminary report of the fifth season, October 1931–March 1932*. New Haven, CO: Yale University Press.

Rousseau, J.-B. L. J. 1899. *Voyage de Baghdad à Alep, 1808*. Paris: J. André.

Rousset, M.-O. 2012. 'Chalcis/Qinnasrin: from Hellenistic city to the jund capital of North Syria'. In R. Matthews and J. Curtis (eds). *7ICAANE. Proceedings of the 7th International Congress on the Archaeology of the Ancient Near East, 12–16 April 2010, the British Museum and UCL, London. Volume 2 Ancient & Modern Issues in Cultural Heritage, Colour & Light in Architecture, Art & Material Culture in Islamic Archaeology*. Wiesbaden: Harrassowitz, 551–567.

Sack, D. 1996. *Resafa IV. Die Grosse Moschee von Resafa-Rusāfat Hishām*. Mainz: P. von Zabern.

Sack, D. and Becker, H. 1999. 'Zur städtebaulichen und baulichen Konzeptin frühilsamischer Residenzen in Nordmesopotamien mit ersten Ergebnissen einer Testmessung zur geophysikalischen prospection in Resafa-Rusafat Hisham'. In E.-L. Schwandner and K. Rheidt (eds). *Stadt und umland: Neue Ergebnisse der archäologischen Bau- und Siedlungsforschung. Bauforschungskolloquium in Berlin vom 7. Bis 10. Mai 1997 veranstaltet vom Architektur-Refereat des DAI*. Mainz: P. von Zabern, 270–286.

Sadurska, A. 1972. 'Rapport préliminaire de la huitieme campagne de fouilles Polonaises à Palmyre en 1966'. *Annales Archéologiques Arabes Syriennes* 22, 117–128.

Sadurska, A. 1973a. 'Palmyre'. *Études et Travaux* 7, 273–284.

Sadurska, A. 1973b. 'Rapport préliminaire de la douzieme campagne de fouilles Polonaises à Palmyre en 1970'. *Annales Archéologiques Arabes Syriennes* 23, 111–120.

Sadurska, A. 1975. 'Wykopaliska polskie w Palmyrze 1970. "Świątynia Sztandarów"'. *Studia Palmireńskie* 5–6, 111–119.

Sadurska, A. 1977. *Palmyre (VII). Le tombeau de famille de 'Alainê*. Warsaw: PWN, Editions Scientifiques de Pologne.

al-Saghir, M., Golvin, J.-C., Reddé, M., al-Sayed, H. and Wagner, G. 1986. *Le camp Romain de Louqsor: (avec une étude des graffites gréco-romains du temple d'Amon)*. Cairo: Institut Français du Proche-Orient.

Salame-Sarkis, H. 1989. 'Syria grammata kai agalmata'. *Syria* 61, 313–330.

Saliby, N. 1996.'Maisons palmyréniennes à l'est du temple de Nabu'.In A. Bounni (ed.). *Special Issue Documenting the Activities of the International Colloquium on Palmyra and the Silk Road. Annales Archéologiques Arabes Syriennes* 42. Damascus: DGAM, 289–290, 233–240 (Arabic).

Saliou, C. 1994. *Les lois des bâtiments: voisinage et habitat urbain dans l'empire Romain: recherches sur les rapports entre le droit et la construction privée du siècle d'Auguste au siècle de Justinien*. Beirut: Institut Français d'Archéologie du Proche-Orient.

Saliou, C. 1996. 'Du portique à la rue à portiques: Les rues à colonnades de Palmyre dans le cadre de l'urbanisme Romain impérial, originalité et conformisme'. In A. Bounni (ed.). *Special Issue Documenting the Activities of the International Colloquium on Palmyra and the Silk Road. Annales Archéologiques Arabes Syriennes* 42. Damascus: DGAM, 319–330.

Saliou, C. 2014. 'Bains et histoire urbaine. L'exemple d'Antioche sur l'Oronte dans l'Antiquité'. In M.-F. Boussac, S. Denoix, T. Fournet and B. Redon (eds). *25 siècles de bain collectif en Orient (Proche-Orient, Égypte et péninsule Arabique). Actes du colloque de Damas*. Cairo: Presses de l'IFPO, 657–685.

Sanlaville, P. and Traboulsi, M. 1996. 'Palmyre et la steppe syrienne'. In A. Bounni (ed.). *Special Issue Documenting the*

Activities of the International Colloquium on Palmyra and the Silk Road. Annales Archéologiques Arabes Syriennes 42. Damascus: DGAM, 29–40.

Saradi, H. 1997. 'The use of ancient spolia in Byzantine monuments: the archaeological and literary evidence'. *International Journal of the Classical Tradition* 3, 395–423.

Saradi, H. 1998. 'Privatization and subdivision of urban properties in the early Byzantine centuries: social and cultural implications'. *Bulletin of the American Society of Papyrologists* 35, 17–43.

Saradi, H. 2006. *The Byzantine City in the Sixth Century. Literary Images and Historical Reality*. Athens: Society of Messenian Archaeological Studies.

Saradi, H. 2008. 'Towns and cities'. In E. Jeffreys, J. F. Haldon and R. Cormack (eds). *The Oxford Handbook of Byzantine Studies*. Oxford: Oxford University Press, 317–327.

Saradi, H. 2011. 'Late Antique paganism and christianisation in Greece'. In L. Lavan and M. Mulryan (eds). *The Archaeology of Late Antique 'Paganism'*. Leiden: Brill, 263–309.

Sarris, P. 2011. *Empires of Faith. The Fall of Rome to the Rise of Islam, 500–700*. Oxford: Oxford University Press.

Sartre, M. and Sartre-Fauriat, A. 2008. *Palmyre. La cité des caravanes*. Paris: Gallimard.

Sauer, E. 2003. *The Archaeology of Religious Hatred: in the Roman and early medieval world*. Stroud: Tempus.

Sauvaget, J. 1931. 'Inscriptions Arabes du temple de Bel à Palmyre'. *Syria* 11, 143–153.

Sauvaget, J. 1934. 'Le plan de Laodicée-sur-mer'. *Bulletin d'Études Orientales* 4, 81–116.

Sauvaget, J. 1941. *Alep: Essai sur le développement d'une grande ville Syrienne des origines au milieu du XIXe siècle*. Paris: P. Geuthner.

Sauvaget, J. 1967. 'Châteaux umayyades de Syrie. Contribution à l'étude de la colonization arabe aux Ier et IIe siècles de l'Hégire'. *Revue des Études Islamiques* 35, 1–52.

Savino, E. 1999. '*Palmira*'. In E. Savino (ed.). *Città di frontiera nell'impero Romano. Forme della romanizzazione da Augusto ai Severi*. Bari: Edipuglia, 47–93.

Schaefer, J. and Falkner, R.K. 1986. 'An Umayyad potters' complex in the north theatre, Jerash'. In F. Zayadine (ed.). *Jerash Archaeological project, 1981–1983, I*. Amman: Department of Antiquities, Hashemite Kingdom of Jordan, 411–460.

Schlumberger, D. 1935. 'Études sur Palmyre: I, le développement urbain de Palmyre'. *Berytus* 2, 149–162.

Schlumberger, D. 1939a. 'Bornes frontières de la Palmyrène'. *Syria* 20, 43–73.

Schlumberger, D. 1939b. 'Les fouilles de Qasr el-Heir el-Gharbi (1936–1938): rapport préliminaire'. *Syria* 20, 197–238, 325–373.

Schlumberger, D. 1951. *La palmyréne du Nord-Ouest, Villages et lieux de culte de l'époque imperial. Recherches archéologiques sur la mise en valeur d'une region du desert par les Palmyréniens*. Paris: P. Geuthner.

Schlumberger, D. 1962. 'Le prétendu camp de Dioclétien à Palmyre'. *Mélanges de l'Université Saint-Joseph* 38(3), 79–87.

Schlumberger, D. 1986. *Qasr el-Heir el Gharbi*. Paris: P. Geuthner.

Schmidt-Colinet, A., al-As'ad, K. and al-As'ad, W. 2013. 'Thirty years of Syro-German/Austrian archaeological research at Palmyra'. *Studia Palmireńskie* 12, 299–318.

Seigne, J. 1992. 'Jerash Romaine et Byzantine: développement urbain d'une ville provinciale orientale'. *Studies in the History and Archaeology of Jordan* 4, 331–341.

Seller, A. 1705. *The Antiquities of Palmyra. Containing the History of the City, and its Emperors, from its Foundation to the Present Time. With an Appendix of Critical Observations on the Names, Religion, and Government of the Country. And a Commentary on the Inscriptions Lately Found There*. London: Smith and Walford.

Sellers, R. V. 1953. *The Council of Chalcedon. A Historical and Doctrinal Survey*. London: SPCK.

Seyrig, H. 1931. 'Antiquités syriennes. 1. Les Jardins de Kasr el-Heir, 2. Note épigraphiques. 3. Numismatique suppose de Chalcis au Liban'. *Syria* 12, 316–325.

Seyrig, H. 1940. 'Rapport sommaire sur le fouilles de l'agora de Palmyre'. *Comptes rendus/Académie des inscriptions et belles-lettres* 84, 237–249.

Seyrig, H. 1950. 'Antiquités Syriennes'. *Syria* 27, 229–252.

Seyrig, H. 1959. 'Antiquités Syriennes'. *Syria* 36, 184–192.

Shahīd, I. 1984a. *Rome and the Arabs: a prolegomenon to the study of Byzantium and the Arabs*. Washington, DC: Dumbarton Oaks Research Library and Collection.

Shahīd, I. 1984b. *Byzantium and the Arabs in the Fourth Century*. Washington, DC: Dumbarton Oaks Research Library and Collection.

Shahīd, I. 1995. *Byzantium and the Arabs in the Sixth Century. Vol. I, Part I. Political and Military History*. Washington, DC: Dumbarton Oaks Research Library and Collection.

Simpson, I. 2008. 'Market buildings at Jarash: commercial transformations at the tetrakonion in the 6th to 9th C. CE'. In K. Bartl and A.-R. Moaz (eds). *Residences, Castles, Settlements. Transformation processes between Late Antiquity and early Islam in Bilad al-Sham. Proceedings of the international conference held at Damascus, 5–9 November 2006*. Rahden, Westf.: Verlag Marie Leidorf, 115–124.

Smith, A. M. 2013. *Roman Palmyra. Identity, Community and State Formation*. Oxford: Oxford University Press.

Sodini, J.-P. 1997. 'Habitat de l'antiquite tardive (2)'. *Topoi (Lyon)* 7, 435–524.

Southern, P. and Dixon, K. R. 1996. *The Late Roman Army*. London: Batsford.

Spieser, J.-M. 1986. 'La christianisation de la ville dans l'antiquité tardive'. *Ktèma* 11, 49–55.

Stanchev, D. 1999. 'Das Prätorium des Kastells Iatrus. Vorläufiger Bericht'. In G. Von Bülow and A. Milcheva (eds). *Der Limes an der unteren Donau von Diokletian bis Heraklios: Vorträge der internationalen Konferenz, Svištov, Bulgarien (1.–5. September 1998)*. Sofia: Nous, 151–154.

Starcky, J. 1941. *Palmyre. Guide archéologique*. Beirut: Imprimerie Catholique.

Starcky, J. 1949. 'Autour d'une dédicace palmyrénienne à Sadrafa et à Du'anat'. *Syria* 26, 43–85.

Starcky, J. 1952. *Palmyre*. Paris: A. Maisonneuve.

Starcky, J. 1981. 'Allath, (B.): Allath sous les traits d'Athéna'. *Lexicon Iconographicum Mythologiae Classicae* I(1), 564–570.

Starcky, J. and Gawlikowski, M. 1985. *Palmyre*. Paris: Librairie d'Amérique et d'Orient Adrien Maisonneuve.

Stępniowski, F. M. (ed.). *Aux pays d'Allat. Mélanges offerts à Michal Gawlikowski*. Warsaw: Warsaw University, Institute of Archaeology, 141–150.

Stern, H. 1977. *Les mosaïques des maisons d'Achille et de Cassiopée à Palmyre*. Paris: P. Geuthner.

Stillwell, R. 1961. 'Houses of Antioch'. *Dumbarton Oaks Papers* 15, 45–57.

Stoll, O. 2007. 'The religions of the armies: a complex "system"'. In P. Erdkamp (ed.). *A companion to the Roman Army*. London: Wiley-Blackwell, 452–476.

Strube, C. 2003. 'Androna/al Andarin. Vorbericht über die Grabungskampagnen der Jahre 1993–2001'. *Archäologischer Anzeiger* 2003, 25–115.

Strube, C. 2008. 'Al-Andarin/Androna: site and setting'. In K. Bartl and A. Moaz (eds). *Residences, Castles, Settlements: transformation processes from late antiquity to early Islam in Bilad al-Sham: proceedings of the international conference held at Damascus, 5–9 November, 2006*. Rahden, Westf.: Verlag Marie Leidorf, 57–71.

Tabaczek, M. 2001. *Zwischen Stoa und Suq. Die Säulenstraßen im Vorderen Orient in römischer Zeit unter besonderer Berücksichtigung von Palmyra*. Unpublished Ph.D. thesis, Universität zu Köln.

Talbert, R. J. A. 2010. *Rome's World: the Peutinger map reconsidered*. Cambridge, New York: Cambridge University Press.

Tardieu, M. 1992. 'L'arrivee des manicheens à al-Hira'. In P. Canivet and J.-P. Rey-Coquais (eds). *La Syrie de Byzance à l'Islam, VIIe–VIIIe siècles actes du colloque international 'de Byzance à l'Islam', Lyon, Maison de l'Orient Méditerranéen, Paris, Institut du Monde Arabe, 11–15 Septembre 1990*. Damascus: Institut Français de Damas, 15–24.

Tate, G. 1996. 'Le problème de la défense et du peuplement de la steppe au Syrie du nord entre la chute de Palmyre et le règne de Justinien'. In A. Bounni (ed.). *Special Issue Documenting the Activities of the International Colloquium on Palmyra and the Silk Road. Annales Archéologiques Arabes Syriennes* 42). Damascus: DGAM, 33–37.

Tchalenko, G. 1953. *Villages antiques de Syrie du nord, Vol. 1*. Paris: P. Geuthner.

Tchalenko, G. 1974. 'La basilique de Qalbloze'. *Annales Archéologiques Arabes Syriennes* 24, 9–15.

Tchalenko, G. 1990. *Eglises Syriennes à bêma: texte*. Paris: P. Geuthner.

Tchalenko, G. and Baccache, E. 1979. *Eglises de village de la Syrie du nord. Planches*. Paris: P. Geuthner.

Teixidor, J. 1979. *The pantheon of Palmyra*. Leiden: Brill.

Teixidor, J. 1984. *Un port Romain du desert: Palmyre et son commerce d'Auguste a Caracalla*. Paris: Librairie d'Amérique et d'Orient.

Thomsen, P. 'Die römischen Meilensteine der Provinzen Syria, Arabia und Palastina.' *Zeitschrift des Deutschen Palästina–Vereins* 40, 1–103.

Todd, M. 1983. 'The Aurelianic wall of Rome and its analogues'. In B. Hobley and J. Maloney (eds). *Roman Urban Defences in the West: a review of current research on urban defences in the Roman empire with special reference to the northern provinces, based on papers presented to the conference on Roman urban defences, held at the Museum of London on 21–23 March 1980*. Council for British Archaeology Research Report 51. London: Council for British Archaeology, 58–67.

Tourtechot 1735. 'Les ruines de Palmyre en 1753'. Published by B. Chabot in *Journal Asiatique* 1987, 335–355.

Trimingham, J. S. 1979. *Christianity Among the Arabs in pre-Islamic Times*. London, New York: Longman.

Trombley, F. R. 1993. *Hellenic Religion and Christinisation c. 370–529, Vol. 1*. Leiden: Brill.

Trombley, F. R. 1995. *Hellenic Religion and Christinisation c. 370–529, Vol. 2*. Leiden: Brill.

Tsafrir, Y. and Foerster G. 1997. 'Urbanism at Scythopolis-Bet Shean in the fourth to seventh centuries'. *Dumbarton Oaks Papers* 51, 85–146.

Turner, C. M. 1899. *Ecclesia occidentalis. Monumenta iuris antiquissima, Vol. 1*. Oxford: Ex Typographeo Calendoniano.

Ulbert, T. 1986. *Die Basilika des Heiligen Kreuzes in Resafa-Sergiupolis*. Mainz: P. von Zabern.

Ulbert, T. 1989. 'Villes et fortifications de l'Euphrate à l'époque paléochrétienne (IVe–VIe s.)'. In J.-M. Dentzerand and W. Orthmann (eds). *Archéologie et histoire de la Syrie. II. La Syrie de l'époque Achéménide à l'avènement de l'Islam*. Saarbrücken: Saarbrücker Druckerei und Verlag, 283–296.

Ulbert, T. 1992. 'Beobachtungen im Westhofbereich der Großen Basilika von Resafa'. *Damaszener Mitteilungen* 6, 403–416.

Vaes, J. 1989. '"*Nova construere sed amplius vetusta servare*". La reutilisation chrétienne d'édifices antiques (en Italie)'. In N. Duval, F. Baritel and P. Pergola (eds). *Actes du XIe Congrès International d'archéologie Chrétienne: Lyon, Vienne, Grenoble, Genève et Aoste (21–28 Septembre 1986)*. Rome, Vatican City: École Française de Rome, Pontificio Istituto di Archeologia Cristiana, 299–321.

Vailhé, S. 1907. 'La "Notitia Episcopatuum" d'Antioche du patriarche Anastase, VIe siècle'. *Échos d'Orient* 10, 139–145, 363–368.

Van Berchem, D. 1954. 'Recherches sur la chronologie des enceintes de Syrie et de Mesopotamie'. *Syria* 31, 254–270.

Villeneuve, F. 1997. 'Les salles à alcove dans les maisons d'époque Romaine et Byzantine en Syrie, particulièrement dans le Hauran'. In C. Castel, M. al-Maqdissi and F. Villeneuve (eds). *Les maisons dans la Syrie antique du IIIe millénaire aux débuts de l'Islam. Pratiques et représentations de l'espace domestique. Actes du colloque international, Damas, du 27 au 30 Juin 1992*. Beirut: Institut Français du Proche-Orient, 269–281.

Von Bülow, G. 2007. 'The fort of Iatrus in Moesia Secunda: observations on the late Roman defensive system of the lower Danube (4th–6th C. AD)'. In A. Poulter (ed.). *The Transition to Late Antiquity in the Danube and Beyond*. Oxford: Oxford University Press, 459–478.

Von Gerkan, A. 1935. 'Die Stadtmauer von Palmyra'. *Berytus* 2, 25–33.

Walmsley, A. 1992. 'Early Islamic occupation in Area IV'. In A. W. McNicoll, P. C. Edwards, J. Hanbury-Tenison, B. Hennessy, T. F. Potts, R. H. Smith, A. Walmsley and P. Watson (eds). *Pella in Jordan 2. The Second Interim Report of the Joint University of Sydney and College of Wooster Excavation at Pella 1982–1985.* Sydney: Meditarch, 183–186.

Walmsley, A. 1996. 'Byzantine Palestine and Arabia: urban prosperity in Late Antiquity'. In N. J. Christie and S. T. Loseby (eds). *Towns in Transition: urban evolution in Late Antiquity and the early Middle Ages.* Aldershot: Scholar Press, 126–158.

Walmsley, A. 2003. 'The Friday mosque of early Islamic Jarash in Jordan'. *Journal of the David Collection* 1, 110–131.

Walmsley, A. 2007a. *Early Islamic Syria. An Archaeological and Historical Assessment.* London: Duckworth.

Walmsley, A. 2007b. 'The excavations of an Umayyad period house at Pella in Jordan'. In L. Lavan, L. Özgenel and A.Sarantis (eds). *Housing in Late Antiquity, from Palaces to Shops.* Leiden: Brill, 515–521.

Walmsley, A. and Damgaard, K., 2005. 'The Umayyad congregational mosque of Jarash in Jordan and its relationship to early mosques'. *Antiquity* 79, 362–378.

Ward-Perkins, B. 1996. 'Urban continuity?'. In N. Christie and S. T. Loseby (eds). *Towns in Transition. urban evolution in Late Antiquity and the early Middle Ages.* Aldershot Scolar Press.

Ward-Perkins, B. 2001. 'Land, labour and settlement'. In A. Cameron (ed.). *The Cambridge Ancient History. Vol. 14. Late Antiquity. Empire and Successors A.D. 425–600.* Cambridge: Cambridge University Press, 315–345.

Ward-Perkins, B. 2005. *The Fall of Rome and the End of Civilization.* Oxford, New York: Oxford University Press.

Ward-Perkins, B., Little, J. H. and Mattingly, D. J. 1986. 'Two houses at Ptolemais, Cyrenaica'. *Libyan Studies* 17, 109–153.

Wareth, U. and Zignani P. 1992. 'Nag al-Hagar. A fortress with a palace of the late Roman Empire. Second preliminary report'. *Bulletin de l'Institut Français d'Archéologie Orientale* 92, 185–210.

Watson, G. R. 1969. *The Roman Soldier.* London: Thames and Hudson.

Wellhausen, J. 1963. *The Arab Kingdom and its Fall.* Translated by Margaret Graham Weir. Beirut: Khayats.

Westphalen, S. 2006. 'Resafa. Untersuchungen zum Strassennetz in byzantinischer Zeit'. In R. Harreither (ed.). *Acta Congressus internationalis XIV archaeologiae christianae Vindobonae 19–26.9.1999: Frühes Christentum zwischen Rom und Konstantinopel.* Roma, Vienna: Pontificio Istituto di Archeologia Cristiana, Österreichische Akademie der Wissenschaften, 783–793.

Westphalen, S. 2009. 'Die byzantinischen Malereien im Beltempel und der Kirchenbau Palmyras: ein Resümee'. In C. Strube, I. Eichner and V. Tsamakda (eds). *Syrien und seine Nachbarn von der Spätantike bis in die islamische Zeit.* Wiesbaden: Reichert, 155–165.

Whitby, M. 1986. 'Procopius' description of Dara (Building II.1–3)'. In P. Freeman and D. Kennedy (eds). *The Defence of the Roman and Byzantine East.* British Archaeological Report S297 Oxford: Archaeopress, 737–783.

Whittaker, C. R. 1994. *Frontiers of the Roman Empire. A Social and Economic Study.* Baltimore, MD: Johns Hopkins University Press.

Whittow, W. 1990. 'Ruling the late Roman and early Byzantine city: a continous history'. *Past and Present* 129, 3–29.

Wiegand, T. 1932a (ed.). *Palmyra: Ergebnisse der Expeditionen von 1902 und 1917.* Berlin: Verlag Heinrich Keller.

Wiegand, T. 1932b. 'Die befestigten Gutshöfe von Hâzîme und Bâzūrīje'. In T. Wiegand (ed.). *Palmyra: Ergebnisse der Expeditionen von 1902 und 1917.* Berlin: Verlag Heinrich Keller, 10–12.

Wiegand, T., Wulzinger, K. and Schulz, B. 1932. 'Der Korinthische Tempel östlich des Theaters'. In T. Wiegand (ed.). *Palmyra: Ergebnisse der Expeditionen von 1902 und 1917.* Berlin: Verlag Heinrich Keller, 108–121.

Wielgosz, D. 2013. 'Coepimus et lapide pingere: marble decoration from the so-called baths of Diocletian in Palmyra'. *Studia Palmireńskie* 12, 319–332.

Will, E. 1963. 'Nouvelles archéologiques. Les fouilles Polonaises et le "camp de Dioclétien" à Palmyre'. *Syria* 40, 385–393.

Will, E. 1966. '*Le sac de Palmyre'.* In R. Chevallier (ed.). *Mélanges d'archéologie et d'histoire offerts á André Piganiol.* Paris: S. E.V.P.E.N., 1409–1416.

Will, E. 1983. 'Le développement urbain de Palmyre: témoignages épigraphiques anciens et nouveaux'. *Syria* 60, 69–81.

Wood, R. 1753. *The Ruins of Palmyra; otherwise Tedmor in the desart.* London: [n. p.].

Wright, W. 1872. *Catalogue of the Syriac Manuscripts in the British Museum.* London: Trustees of the British Museum.

Wright, W. 1895. *An Account of Palmyra and Zenobia, with Travels and Adventures in Bashan and the Desert.* London, Edinburgh, New York: Thomas Nelson and Sons.

Yon, J.-B. 2001. 'Evergetism and urbanism in Palmyra'. In L. Lavan, (ed.). *Recent Research in Late Antique Urbanism.* Portsmouth, RI: Journal of Roman Archaeology Supplement 42, 173–181.

Yon, J.-B. 2009. '*La gestion de l'eau à Palmyre: l'exemple de la source Efqa'.* In M. al-Dbiyat and M. Mouton (eds). *Stratégies d'acquisition de l'eau et société au Moyen-Orient depuis l'antiquité.* Beirut: Presses de l'IFPO, 97–106.

Young, G. K. 2001. *Rome's Eastern Trade. International Commerce and Imperial Policy 31 BC–AD 305.* London, New York: Routledge.

Zanini, E. 1995. 'Il restauro Giustinianeo delle mura di Palmira'. In A. Iacobini and E. Zanini (eds). *Arte profana e arte sacra a Bisanzio.* Rome: Argos, 65–103.

Zanini, E. 1996. 'Ricognizione archaeologica in Siria. Il sito di Hawarine'. In C. Barsanti (ed.). *Bisanzio e l'Occidente, arte, archeologia, storia. Studi in onore di Fernanda de' Maffei.* Roma: Viella, 147–157.

Zanini, E. 2003. 'The urban ideal and urban planning in Byzantine new cities of the sixth century A.D.'. In L. Lavan and W. Bowen (ed.). *Theory and Practice in Late Antique Archaeology.* Leiden, Boston: Brill, 196–223.

Zanini, E. 2012. 'Storici dell'arte, esploratori, antropologi, archeologi: le missioni lungo il limes orientale (1982–1992)'. In A. A. Longo, G. Cavallo, A. Guiglia and A. Iacobini (eds). *La Sapienza Bizantina. Un secolo di ricerche sulla civiltà di Bisanzio all'Università di Roma* (Milion 8). Rome: Campisano, 99–118.

Zenoni, G. 2014. *Uno sguardo sulle ricerche della Missione Archeologica Italo-Siriana a Palmira (PAL.M.A.I.S.).* Rivista della scuola di specializzazione in archeologia, Università degli Studi di Milano 17. Milan: Università degli Studi di Milano, 85–92.

Żuchowska, M. 2000. 'Quelques remarques sur la grande colonnade á Palmyre'. *Bulletin d'Études Orientale* 52, 187–193.

Żuchowska, M. 2003. 'Palmyra: Test trench in the street of the great colonnade'. *Polish Archaeology in the Mediterranean* 14, 291–294.

Żuchowska, M. 2006. 'Palmyra. Excavations 2002–2005 (insula E by the Great Colonnade). Preliminary report'. *Polish Archaeology in the Mediterranean* 17, 439–450.

Żuchowska, M. 2011. Space organization and house planning at Hellenistic and Roman Palmyra. *Światowit* 9, 141–153.

Cartographic material

Bureau Topographique des Troupes Française du Levant 1931, *Palmyre* (echelle 1:10.000).

Schnädelbach, K. 2010. *Topographia Palmyrena. 1-Topography*. Bonn: Rudolf Habelt.

Websites

UNESCO [n.d.] *Site of Palmyra* [http://whc.unesco.org/en/list/23; accessed: 15/06/16].

Appendix: Written sources

This appendix gathers a selection of the written sources mentioned in the book. It deliberately omits poetry, which often provides little information on the history of the city and it is, therefore, not pertinent with the aim of this work. For the sake of convenience, texts are given a consecutive number. They are arranged diachronically based on the events accounted in the text until n. 65. Texts n. 66–72 are general descriptions of the city in the Islamic period.

1. Late Antiquity (273–633)

3rd century

1. *HA Aurelianus*, 31.5–9
'From Aurelian Augustus to Cerronius Bassus. The sword of the soldiers should not proceed further. Already enough Palmyrenes have been killed and slaughtered. We have not spared the women, we have slain the children, we have butchered the old men, we have destroyed the peasants. To whom, at this rate, shall we leave the land and the city? Those who still remain must be spared. For it is our belief that the few have been chastened by the punishment of the many. Now as the Temple of the Sun at Palmyra, which has been pillaged by the eagle-bearers of the Third Legion, along with the standard-bearers, the dragon-bearer, and the buglers and trumpeters, I wish it restored to the condition in which it formerly was. You have three hundred pounds of gold from Zenobia's coffer, you have eighteen hundred pounds of silver from the property of the Palmyrenes, and you have the royal jewels. Use all these to embellish the temple; thus both to me and to the immortals gods you will do a most pleasing service. I will write to the Senate and request it to send one of the pontiffs to dedicate the temple' (tr. Dodgeon and Lieu 1991, 102).

2. Zos., *Hist. Nov.*, 1.60–61
But Aurelian kept on his way to Europe, and as he went a message caught up with him to his effect, that some of those left in Palmyra had associated with themselves Apsaeus, who had been responsible for their actions in the past as well, and they were working on Marcellinus, whom the emperor had made prefect of Mesopotamia and entrusted with the administration of the East, if perchance he might allow himself to be invested with the imperial regalia. However, he kept putting them off, in order that he might deliberate as to what should be done. Although they troubled him in similar fashion again and again and again, he kept making ambiguous replies until he could inform Aurelian of his decision himself. But now the Palmyrenes had placed the purple robe around Antiochus, and were staying put at Palmyra.

Having heard these things Aurelian at once, just as he was, set off for the East. He reached Antioch as a horse race was being run off and, appearing before the populace unexpectedly, terrified everybody. Then he marched to Palmyra. He took the city without a struggle and razed it to the ground, but let Antiochus go, considering him because of his meanness to be unworthy even of retribution … At this period also he constructed the sumptuous temple of Sol, embellishing it with ornaments from Palmyra, and consecrated therein statues to both Sol and Belus. (tr. Buchanan and Davis 1967, 36–7).

4th century

3. Le Quien 1740, 2, 845
44. Marinus of Palmyra

4. Mich. Syr., *Chr.*, 7.2
Names of the bishops that gathered at the council which took place at Nicea:
[…]
49. Marinos of Palmyra

5. *Not. Dig., Or.*, 22.30
(Headquarters of the) Prefect of *Legio I Illyricorum*, at Palmyra (tr. Dodgeon and Lieu 1991, 341)

6. *Not. Dig., Or.*, 7.34
Cuneus equitum secundorum clibanariorum Palmirenorum

7. *Not. Dig., Or.*, 31.49
Ala octava Palmyrenorum

5th century

8. *Pall., Dial. John Chris.*, 20.35–38
A deacon who had travelled with them told us on his way back that Cyriacus was in Palmyra, the fort on the Persian frontier, eight milestones from Emesa (tr. rev. Kowalski 1997, 47).

9. *Alex. Akoim.*, 35
The Blessed, while passing through the whole desert among the brethren who were singing continuously, came to the city of Solomon, which is mentioned in the Book of the King, and which he erected in the desert and is called Palmyra. The citizens, having seen from a distance a mass of brethren (and thus being Jews who call themselves Christians) approaching them, closed the gates of the city saying to each other, 'Who is capable of feeding all these; if they only entered our city we would all starve' (tr. Kowalski 1997, 48).

10. Le Quien 1740, 2, 845
John of the city of Palmyra

11. Mich. Syr., *Chr.*, 9.13
(20) John of Tadmur

12. *Chr. Zuq.*, 3.19
The names of the holy bishops who were chased out of their sees: ... from Syria: ... John of Palmyra who died in exile [... (tr. Witakowski 1995, 19)

6th century

13. Proc., *Aed.*, 2.11, 10–12
And there is a city in *Phoenicia* by Lebanon. Palmyra by name, built in a neighbourless region by men of former times, but well situated across the track of the hostile Saracens. Indeed it was for this very reason that they had originally built this city, in order, namely, that these barbarians might not be unobserved make sudden inroads into Roman territory. This city, which through lapse of time had come to be almost completely deserted, the emperor Justinian strengthened with defences which defy description, and he also provided it with abundant water and a garrison of troops, and thus put a stop to the raids of the Saracens (tr. Dewing 1961, 177).

14. Proc., *Aed.*, 5.1.1
All the fortifications of cities and the fortresses, as well as the other buildings which he erected throught the East, from the boundary of Persia as far as the city of Palmyra, which chances to be in *Phoenicia* by Lebanon – these, I think, have been sufficiently described by me above (tr. Dewing 1954, 317).

15. Mal., *Chr.*, 17.2
In the month of October of the 6th indiction the emperor appointed an Armenian named Patrikios as *comes Orientis* in Antioch. He gave him a large sum of money with instructions to go and reconstruct the city in *Phoenice* on the *limes*, known as Palmyra, and its churches and public baths. He ordered a *numerus* of soldiers to be stationed there with the *limitanei*, and also the *dux* of Emesa, to protect the Roman territories and Jerusalem (tr. Jeffreys *et al.* 1986, 245).

16. Theoph., *Chr.*, 1.174
AM 6020
In this year Justinian the elder became sole emperor. He appointed Patricius the Armenian as *comes Orientis*, provided him with money and ordered him to go out and restore Palmyra, as it is called, a city in *Phoenicia Libanensis*, situated on the inner *limes*. He also gave orders that the *dux* be stationed there *the Holy Places ... (tr. Mango and Scott 1997, 266).

17. *Mansi 1762*, 921
Julianus, deacon and *hospitalarius*/ξενοδόχος of the Church of Palmyra signed.

18. Hier., *Synec.*, 717.1–8
Phoenicia by Lebanon: Emesa, Laodicea, Damascus, Eliopolis, Abila, Palmyra.

19. Georg. Cypr., *Descr. Orb. Rom.*, 984–996
Phoenicia by Lebanon: Emesa, Laodicea, Eliopolis, Abila, Damascus, Yabrud, Huwwarin, Burqus, that is Justinianopolis, Palmyra, Klima Magludon, Salton Gonaitikon, Selemye, Klima Anatolikon.

20. Honigmann 1925, 75
[Metropolis] of Damascus, to which 11 bishops are subjected: [bishop] of Eliopolis, Abila, Palmyra, Laodicea, Evaria, Khonokhora, Iabroud, Danaba, Kora, Arlane and the Saracens.

21. *Wright* 1872,2. 468, n. 585
This book belongs to the holy monastery of NṬP DZGL which is near Tadmur. By the grace of God the Archimandrite Symeon took pains and made it, along with the remainder of the brothers who are with him, in the days of the holy and devout bishops, Mar Jacob and Mar Theodore, so that by their prayers Our Lord might show his compassion to King Abokarib and to all their Christian brothers, and that as regards their errors the Lord might lead them back to true knowledge. And as for anyone who participated in (the writing of) this book, may our Lord grant him a precious recompense. Amen. And that whoever hides it away, let him know that before the fearsome judgment seat of God he

will give a reckoning for it, unless he returns it to its place unharmed. Our Lord is near. (tr. Millar 2013, 23).

22. Steph. Byz., *Ethnika*, Π 6
Palmyra, fort in Syria …

Early 7th century

23. Ḥamza al-Iṣfahānī, *Tā'rīkh,* 121
al-Ayham b. Jabala b. al-Ḥārith b. Abū Shamr [ruled] 27 years and two months: he was the ruler of Tadmur, Qaṣr Barka and Dhāt Anmār.

24. Abū al-Fidā', *Taqwīm al-Buldān,* 128–130
al-Ḥārith b. Ḥajar [ruled], then his son Jabala b. al-Ḥārith, then his son al-Ḥārith b. Jabala, then his son al-Nu'mān b. al-Ḥārith, whose teknonym was Abū Karb and whose epithet was Qaṭām. Then al-Ayham b. Jabala b. al-Ḥārith ruled after him, who was the ruler of Tadmur.

25. Mich. Syr., *Chr.*, 11.3
The King having removed to Mabbūgh patriarch Athanasius entered his presence with 12 bishops: Thomas of Palmyra, Basil of Emesa, Sergius of 'Urd, John of Cyrrhus, Thomas of Mabbūgh, Daniel of Harrān, Isaiah of Edessa, Severus of Qenneshrīn, Athanasius of Arabīssus, Cosmas of Cilician Epiphania and Severus of Samosata. They remained in his presence for twelve days, debating (tr. Palmer 1993, 142–3, n. 332).

26. *Anas. Per.,* 1.102–104
Therefore, after having venerated the relic of the martyr appropriately and after having left the brother in the hand of the phylarch of the Saracens, they sent him away in peace with personal letters for the person who had sent him. The phylarch led the brother, who had been staying long with them in their camps, across the desert to Palmyra. From there, he left to *Arados*, embarked on a ship and reached Tyre.

27. *Anas. Per.*, 1.129–130
At Palmyra
The monk, then, the one we spoke about, took the holy relic and praying on the road to the holy city of Christ our God, reached the city of Palmyra. The inhabitants of the city went out to adore the holy relic. Among them was a young man whose eyes were swollen and who implored the martyr that God would be merciful to him through him and that he would heal his infirmity. When the monk asked the cause of the disease and how long he had been sick, the people of the city replied: 'he has not been able to see for four years, after having spent all his fortune on medicines, in the end he became blind'. The monk asked him 'if you believe that God can heal you, you will see his glory through Saint Anastasius'. And he replied crying: 'yes, I believe!'. He then told him: 'then it is necessary that you fast and that you wait the grace of God'. And he said: 'I will abstain myself from anything you say; but I am not able to keep myself from wine for many days'. The monk asked him: 'not even for at least seven days?'. He replied: 'yes'. The monk had, besides the precious box, a small parcel that he opened and having taken a balm, he gave it to him, with instructions to open his eyes and scrub it on his pupils. He then left, doing what he was told and after seven days he was healed, praising and glorifying God and his martyr Anastasius.

2. Early Islamic period (634–750)

28. al-Ṭabarī, *Tā'rīkh*, 4.2109
He [Khālid b. al-Walīd] also came to Tadmur, whose people had fortified themselves but then made a peace agreement with him (tr. Blankinship 1993, 109).

29. *al-Balādhurī, Futūḥ*, 111–112
… then he [Khālid b. al-Walīd] came to Tadmur, whose inhabitants held out [against him] and took to their fortifications. Then they sought a guarantee of safety. He granted it to them on condition that they would be *dhimma* people, accept Muslims's authority, and be subordinate to them.

30. al-Ya'qūbī, *Tā'rīkh,* 2.134
He [Khālid b. al-Walīd] passed by Tadmur, where its people took to their fortifications. He surrounded them and, therefore, they opened the gates for him. He made a peace treaty with them and then he continued to Ḥawrān.

31. Ibn al-Faqīh, *Mukhtaṣar*, 125
… and what they [the people of al-Kūfa] conquered with Khālid b. al-Walīd on their way to Syria: al-Muḍayyaḥ, Ḥuṣayd, Bishr, Qurāqir, Suwā, Arāk, and Tadmur.

32. Ibn 'Asākir, *Tā'rīkh,* 2.80
Abū Bakr wrote to Khālid b. al-Walīd, who then went to Syria and attacked the tribes of Ghassān in Marj Rāhiṭ. Then, he continued his expedition and camped at the Buṣrā canal. He met Yazīd b. Abī Sufyān, Abū 'Ubayda b. al-Jarrāḥ, and Shuraḥbīl b. Ḥasana there. Then, the people of Buṣrā made a peace treaty with him. It was the first conquered city of Syria. In his way, Khālid made a peace treaty with the people of Tadmur and passed by Ḥuwwārīn, [where] he killed and took prisoners.

33. Yāqūt, *Mu'jam*, 1.832
Tadmur was conquered by treaty. That happened as follow: Khālid b. al-Walīd, may God be pleased with him, passed by them on his way from Iraq to Syria. They took to their fortifications. He surrounded them from all sides but he

could not overcome them. When this frustrated him and time was short for his departure, he said, 'O people of Tadmur, I swear by God, even if you were in the clouds, we would still bring you down so that God would defeat you. If you do not make a treaty [with us], I will come back to you when I have finished my current objective and I shall, indeed, conquer and enter your city, to the extent that I will kill your soldiers and take your offspring as prisoners'. Then, when he left, the people of Tadmur sent him [someone] and stipulated a peace treaty conditioned by what they offered him, and he accepted it.

34. al-ʿUṣfurī, *Tāʾrīkh*, 1.103
In his way [to Syria], Khālid b. al-Walīd agreed a peace treaty with the people of Tadmur. He [then] passed by Ḥuwwārīn, where he killed and took prisoners and raided the villages of Ghassān in Marj Rāhiṭ, where he [also] killed and took prisoners.

35. al-Wāqidī, *al-Maghāzī*, 1.44
... the people of Arāk came to Khālid and spoke with him about a peace treaty. Khālid responded positively to their demand, was affable towards them in his speech, and met them friendly. [He did this] in order that others from the people of al-Sakhna, Ḥawrān, Tadmur, and al-Qaryatayn would hear and make a peace treaty too. Khālid said, 'I make peace with you on condition that we move away from you; we will accept whoever embraces our religion and we will be content with a tribute from whoever keeps his own religion.

Al-Wāqidī, may God bless him, said, 'I have heard that he made a peace treaty with the people of Arāk on condition of two thousand *dirhams* of white silver and one thousand *dinars*. He wrote the treaty document for them and did not leave his place until the people of al-Sakhna and Tadmur made peace with him. The news reached the people of Tadmur, where its governor was a Roman commander whose name was al-Karkar. He gathered his people around him and said, "It has reached me that these Arabs have conquered Arāk and al-Sakhna by peace treaty and that our people speak about their righteousness, their justice, their good reputation, and that they do not seek corruption. Our fortification is impregnable; there is no way through it for anyone. However, we are afraid about our palm trees and crops [outside the city]. It will not be harmful to us if we make a peace treaty with those people. Then, if our people achieve a victory, we can break this peace treaty; if [victory is] with the Arabs, we are safe with respect to them". His people were happy at that [speech] and they prepared the matter of animal feed and hospitality until Khālid camped near them. They went out to him with services, and he accepted that from them and made a peace treaty with them on condition of three hundred *ūqiyya* of gold and silver. Then, he wrote the peace treaty document for them, bought food and fodder from them, and departed from them heading to the territory of Ḥawrān'.

36. Ibn Aʿtham al-Kūfī, *Kitāb*, 1.140–2
[Al-Kūfī] said, 'Khālid led his army out and, when he approached the land of Syria, he noticed one of the Romans' cities called Tadmur where a great number of Romans were residing. He approached it and surrounded it from all sides'. He [al-Kūfī] said, 'The Romans came out and approached Khālid b. al-Walīd like fierce lions. The people fought a hard battle; among the Muslims, four people, who were brothers, were killed, Saʿīd, Qays, al-Ḥajjāj, and Sāʾib b. al-Ḥārith al-Sadūsī. The fifth person was ʿAbd Allāh b. ʿAbd Shams, the brother of Jarīr b. ʿAbd Allāh al-Bajilī'.

He [al-Kūfī] said, 'Then Khālid shouted out at the top of his voice, "O people of Islam! Courage! Courage! Because if you fight them desiring what is with God, I hope that you will defeat them and they will not be able to resist your strength anymore, God willing"'. He said, 'Then Khālid launched an attack, and the army launched an attack with him against all the people of Tadmur. Khālid met one of their commanders. He struck him a blow with his sword that sent the top half of his skull into the air. The people [of Tadmur] fled, entered the city of Tadmur, and closed the city gate. Khālid kept following them until he camped that day opposite to their city'.

'When the next day came, he rode out leading some of his companions and moved around the city [trying to find a weak point]. However, Khālid could not find any strategem against them, owing to the strength of the [city] walls. Then he resolved to leave and called his companions to depart from them. He approached the city wall until he stopped opposite them and said, "I swear by God, O people of Tadmur! Even if you were in the clouds, we will bring you down by permission of God, mighty and powerful is He! We will overcome you, but I want to travel to my companions residing in Syria, because I have written to them and informed them about my approach, and they are waiting for me and I must hurry to them. By God, if you will not make a peace treaty with me this time, I will come back to you when I have finished my current objective and I shall indeed conquer and enter your city, kill your soldiers and take captive your women and children. I have alerted you and I have warned you. I am Khālid b. al-Walīd, and perhaps you have already heard my name"'

'Then he left them, but they shouted out to him, "Come back and we will make a peace treaty with you on the conditions you want!"'. He said, 'Then Khālid b. al-Walīd returned to them and made a peace treaty with them on condition of wealth that he took from them and distributed among his companions. Then Khālid set out from Tadmur until he arrived to the point of Thaniyat al-ʿAqāb, because Khālid's banner was black'.

37. al-Ṭabarī, *Tā'rīkh*, 4.2154–5
After Damascus had been captured, Yazīd sent Diḥya b. Khalīfa al-Kalbī with cavalry to Tadmur and Abū al-Zahrā' al-Qushayrī to al-Bathaniyya and Hawrān. The inhabitants made peace agreements with both of them according to the peace agreement of Damascus and they both appointed deputies over [the conquest] on which he had sent them (tr. rev. Blankinship 1993, 168–9).

38. Ibn 'Asākir, *Tā'rīkh*, 2.132
Yazīd b. Ābī Sufyān sent Diḥya b. Khalīfa al-Kalbī with an army to Tadmur after the conquest of Damascus, and [he sent] Abū al-Zahrā' al-Qushayrī to al-Bathaniyya and Ḥawrān. They made a peace treaty with them according to the peace agreement of Damascus and they both appointed deputies over [the conquest] on which he had sent them.

39. *Chron. 1234*, 248–9
Khālid b. al-Walīd set out with an Arab army from Damascus for Jordan, the Balqa' and the land of Hawran. The Arabs wanted to take captives and to loot, but Abu 'Ubayda, at the command of King 'Umar, prevented them and made the people tributaties instead. From there they went to Baalbek, Palmyra and Hims (tr. Hoyland 2011, 98).

40. al-Ṭabarī, *Tā'rīkh*, 6.3447
In this year too, Mu'āwiya dispatched al-Ḍaḥḥāk b. Qays telling him to traverse the region below Wāqiṣa and attack every Bedouin whom he came upon who recognised the authority of 'Alī. With him he sent 3000 men. As he proceeded, he seized the property of the people and killed those Bedouins whom he met. He passed by al-Tha'labiyya and attacked the garrisons of 'Alī and seized their goods. When he had got as far as al-Quṭquṭāna, 'Amr b. 'Umays b. Mas'ūd came with some horsemen of 'Alī, and his family going in front, intending to make the annual pilgrimage. Al-Ḍaḥḥāk attached those who were with him and prevented him from going on. When 'Alī heard that, he dispatched Ḥujr b. 'Adī al-Kindī with 4000 men, giving them fifthy *dirhams* each. He caught up with al-Ḍaḥḥāk at Tadmur and killed nineteen of his men. Two of his own men were killed. Night prevented any further fighting and al-Ḍaḥḥāk and his men fled, while Ḥujr and his went back (tr. Hawting 1996, 201–2).

41. Ibn al-Athīr, *al-Kāmil*, 3.317
Mu'āwiya dispatched al-Ḍaḥḥāk b. Qays and ordered him to traverse the region below Wāqiṣa, and attack everyone who passed by him among those of the nomads who were in obedience to 'Alī. [Mu'āwiya] sent 3000 men with him. Then, the army set out, seized wealth, and proceeded until al-Tha'labiyya. The army attacked and killed 'Alī's forces and went as far as al-Quṭquṭāna. When 'Alī received this news, he dispatched Ḥujr b. 'Adī with 4000 soldiers to reach him and gave them fifty *dirhams*. He met al-Ḍaḥḥāk at Tadmur and he killed nineteen of his men while [only] two of Ḥujr's men were killed. When night separated them, al-Ḍaḥḥāk fled with his companions, and Ḥujr went back with his soldiers.

42. al-Ṭabarī, *Tā'rīkh*, 7.482
It is said that when 'Ubayd Allāh b. Ziyād came from Iraq to Syria, he found the Banū Umayyah at Palmyra. B. al-Zubayr had driven them out of Medina and Mecca and the Ḥijāz as a whole and they had settled in Palmyra, finding al-Ḍaḥḥāk b. Qays governing Syria for b. al-Zubayr. When b. Ziyād came, Marwān wanted to ride to b. al-Zubayr, give him the oath of allegiance as caliph and obtain a pledge of security for the Banū Umayyah for him. But b. Ziyād said to him, 'I implore you by God not to do so! It is not a good idea that you, the shaykh of Quraysh, should rush to Abū Khubayb to give him the caliphate. Rather, summon the people of Palmyra, take the oath of allegiance from them and then go against al-Ḍaḥḥāk b. Qays with them and those of the Banū Umayyah who are with you and drive him out of Syria'. 'Amr b. Sa'id b. al-'Ās then said, 'By God, 'Ubayd Allāh b. Ziyād has spoken right! I say again that you are the *sayyid* of Quraysh and its branch, and of all the people you have the most right to stand in this matter. Only the claims of this lad (he meant Khālid b. Yazīd b. Mu'āwiyah) are under consideration, but you marry his mother and then you will be his guardian'. Marwān therefore did that and married the mother of Khālid b. Yazīd, Fākhitah, the daughter of Abū Hāshim b. 'Utbah b. Rabī'ah b. 'Abd Shams. Afterward, he gathered together the Banū Umayyah and they gave him the oath of allegiance as the one with authority over them and the people of Palmyra also gave him the oath of allegiance. Then he set off with a great host against al-Ḍaḥḥāk b. Qays, who, at that time was in Damascus. When al-Ḍaḥḥāk b. Qays heard that the Banū Umayyah had done and of their coming against him, he set off with those of the people of Damascus and others who followed him, including Zufar b. al-Ḥārith. The forces met at Marj Rājiṭ, where they fought a great battle. Al-Ḍaḥḥāk b. Qays al-Fihrī and most of his men were killed, while survivors fled and scattered (tr. Hawting 1989, 64–5).

43. Ibn al-Athīr, *al-Kāmil*, 4.125
It is said that 'Ubayd Allāh b. Ziyād came to the Banū Umayya while they were at Tadmur. Marwān was preparing to go to Ibn al-Zubayr to pledge allegiance to him and ask for a guarantee of safety for Banū Umayya. But ['Ubayd Allāh] persuaded him not to do that and told him to travel with the people of Tadmur to al-Ḍaḥḥāk and fight him.

[...]

The people of Tadmur pledged allegiance to him [Marwān], and he set out to fight al-Ḍaḥḥāk leading a large army. Al-Ḍaḥḥāk then came out to confront him. They fought, and al-Ḍaḥḥāk and those with him were defeated; al-Ḍaḥḥāk was killed.

44. Ibn ʿAsākir, *Tāʾrīkh*, 55.261
ʿUbayd Allāh b. Ziyād said, duping him [al-Ḍaḥḥāk], 'Whoever wants what we want does not stay in cities and fortresses, he goes out in the open and gathers around him the army. So, leave Damascus and gather troops around you'. So al-Ḍaḥḥāk left and camped at Marj. ʿUbayd Allāh remained in Damascus, while Marwān and the Banū Umayya were at Tadmur. Khālid and ʿAbd Allāh, the sons of Yazīd b. Muʿāwiya were at al-Jābiya, the place of their maternal uncle, Hassān b. Mālik b. Baḥdal.

45. al-Iṣfahānī, *al-Aghānī*, 17.112–13
ʿUmayr began approaching quickly. He left Qarqisīyā and approached an edge of the Wādī Kalb. He attacked it and anyone he met of the people of Quḍāʿa and the people of al-Yaman. He provoked the people of Kalb and Taghlib before the war between Qays and Taghlib had started. So, he made the Bedouins take vengeance on all the people of the villages. Thus, when the people of Kalb saw what happened to their companions and that they were not able to resist the horsemen of the city, they gathered under the leadership of Ḥumayd b. Ḥurayth b. Baḥdal. He set out with them until they camped at Tadmur, where Banū Numayr resides. There was an agreement [still valid] between the Banū Numayr, in particular, and the people of Kalb who were in Tadmur together with Ibn Baḥdal b. Baʿāj al-Kalbī. The people of Numayr sent messengers to Ḥumayd imploring him concerning its sanctity, but Ibn Baʿāj al-Kalbī attacked and slaughtered them, and then they sent a message to them: 'We have broken the treaty that was between us and you. Thus, try to go wherever you can'. So, they met and he [Ḥumayd b. Ḥurayth b. Baḥdal] killed Ibn Baʿāj and defeated the people of Numayr and they killed extensively and took captives.

46. al-Iṣfahānī, *al-Aghānī*, 20.120–1
When Ḥumayd b. Ḥurayth b. Baḥdal came to know of what had befallen his folk, he proceeded to Tadmur to gather his men and launch a raid on Qays. When the bloodshed ensued, the Banū Numayr advanced from the valley where they were stationed near their waters towards Ḥumayd b. Ḥurayth b. Baḥdal until they approached the latter who was preparing for the raid. The tribe of Kalb unanimously gathered to support him. The Banū Numayr told him: "Only if you intend to free us from blame and ensure our safety will we stay. If you threaten us with your folk, we shall return to our people." Thereupon he replied: "Do you wish to become their ushers until this conflict is resolved?" Saying this, he detained them. His deputy in Tadmur was a man from Kalb called Maṭar b. ʿAwṣ. He was a ruthless warrior. When Ḥumayd decided to kill them, Maṭar refused since he did not prefer bloodshed. When Ḥumayd mobilised his men to contain Zufar who had returned seeking more raids, he stationed his men in a friendly village. There he was informed of Zufar's return whereupon he was enraged and began to prepare for a counterattack. Maṭar, who had accompanied Ḥumayd in order to kill the captured Numayrīs, approached Ḥumayd and asked: "What should I do with these prisoners now that the people of Muṣayyakh have been killed?" Overcome with grief and no longer in control of his faculties, he replied: "Go and kill them." Maṭar quickly returned to Tadmur so as to not frighten them. Upon reaching Tadmur, he killed them. When Ḥumayd regained his senses, he said: "Where is Maṭar, I wish to give him instructions?" Those present replied: "He returned (to Tadmur)." Thereupon he exclaimed: "Rush to stop him, that enemy of God, I fear the fate of the Numayrīs I have entrusted him with!"

Ḥumayd sent a horseman in pursuit of Maṭar with instructions to not kill the captives. When the messenger reached him, Maṭar had already killed all of them except two. They were sixty men in total.

47. al-Ṭabarī, *Tāʾrīkh*, 9.1796
Then al-Abrash Saʿīd b. al-Walīd al-Kalbī said to (Yazīd) b. al-Walīd, 'O commander of the faithful, Tadmur is well fortified and my people there will defend you'. Al-Walīd replied: 'I don't think it is wise for us to go to Tadmur, since the people there are the Banū ʿAmir, who are the ones who have rebelled against me. But suggest another fortified place to me' (tr. Hillenbrand, 1989, 149).

48. Ibn ʿAsākir, *Tāʾrīkh*, 63.337
Yazīd b. Khālid b. Yazīd b. Muʿāwiya said to him [Walīd b. Yazīd], 'O Commander of the Faithful! Set out to camp at Homs, for it is fortified, and send your troops against Yazīd; he will be killed or taken as a prisoner'. But ʿAbd Allāh b. ʿAnbasa b. Saʿīd b. al-ʿĀs replied, 'The Caliph ought not leave his army and women without fighting and finding an excuse for himself. May God help the Commander of the Faithful and grant him victory!'.

[...]

al-Abrash Saʿīd b. al-Walīd al-Kalbī said to him, 'O Commander of the Faithful, Tadmur is impregnable. And there resides my people who will resist you. He [the Caliph] replied, 'I do not think we should go to Tadmur; its people are the Banū ʿĀmir who rebelled against me. Rather, suggest to me [another] fortified place'.

49. Ibn ʿAsākir, *Tāʾrīkh*, 63.338
Then he passed by al-Ḍaḥḥāk b. Qays al-Fihrī's [land], where his sons, and grandsons were – forty men. They went with him, and they said, 'We are unarmed, so would you ask for weapons for us'. But he did not give them a spear nor a sword. Then, Bayhas b. Zumayl said to him, 'If you refused to go either to Homs or Tadmur, then go to this

fortress of al-Bakhrāʾ. It is impregnable and it is of non-Arab construction'. He replied, 'I am afraid of the plague' and the other, 'What is intended for you is even worse than plague'. So, he accepted and went to the fortress of al-Bakhrāʾ.

50. Ibn ʿAsākir, *Tāʾrīkh*, 63.345
al-Walīd was killed at al-Bakhrāʾ on a Thursday, two days before the end of Jumādā al-Ākhira, in the year one hundred twenty six, when he was 35 to 36 years old.

51. Agapius, *Kitāb*, 511–12
Walid b. Yazid was killed at Palmyra. The reason for his killing was that Yazid, known as the Deficient, was from the Qariyya and he had travelled to Damascus in secret, gathered the like-minded men of the Qariyya, seized the city, destroyed the royal treasuries and dispatched a large army with ʿAbd al-ʿAziz b. Hajjaj to Walid to kill him. Walid had gone out to raid an Arab tribe and had reached Palmyra. When Walid b. Yazid had been killed, Yazid the Deficient took the two sons of Walid b. Yazid, ʿUthman and Yazid and imprisoned them. When ʿAbd al-ʿAziz b. al-Hajjaj returned with the head of Walid, he (Yazid) ordered it to be put on a lance, to have wine spinkled on it and to be pared around the city, to know of the killing of Walid, they were troubled and divided and their opinion was split. Sedition, trials and brigandage occurred, alarm prevailed in every place and the people were sorely afflicted (tr. Hoyland 2011, 244–5).

52. al-ʿUṣfurī, *Tāʾrīkh*, 2.548
In this year [AH 126] al-Walīd b. Yazīd b. ʿAbd al-Malik b. Marwān was killed. Al-Walīd b. Hishām reported to me from his father [who reported from] his grandfather. Also, ʿAbd Allāh b. Mughīra reported to me from his father and also Abū al-Yaqḍān and others. They said, ʿal-Walīd was killed at al-Bakhrāʾ, near Tadmur'.

53. al-Ṭabarī, *Tāʾrīkh*, 9.1892
Abū Jaʿfar reported than when order had been restored in Syria (*al-Shām*) on behalf of Marwān b. Muḥammad and he had gone off to his residence in Ḥarrān, Ibrāhīm b. al-Walīd and Sulaymān b. Hishām asked for a guarantee of security and Marwān granted it. Sulaymān, when was at Tadmur, came to Marwān with his brothers, the members of his family and his *mawlās*, the *Dhakwāniyyah*, who were there, and they swore allegiance to Marwān (tr. Williams 1985, 4).

54. Ibn ʿAsākir, *Tāʾrīkh*, 15.83
When *al-Shām* was under Marwān's control and he [Marwān] went back to his residence near Ḥarrān, Ibrāhīm b. al-Walīd and Sulaymān b. Hishām sought a guarantee of safety from him, and he granted it to them. Sulaymān, who was then at Tadmur, came to him; among those with him were his brothers, his household and his clients, the *Dhakwāniyya*. They all gave the pledge of allegiance to Marwān.

55. Agapius, *Kitāb*, 514–15
Marwan marched to Damascus and its people opened the gates to him. He entered it and the Arabs gathered and pledged alliagence to him. He camped at a place three miles from Damascus called al-ʿAliya. He ordered that Yazid the Deficient be disinterred from his grave and crucified on a wooden stake. He ordered the Qariyya to be assembled before him and made an example of them. He cut off the arms and legs of some and others he had crucified; he ordered the killing of some and the banishment of others. Marwan ordered the royal treasuries to be carried to Harran and that was done. Ibrahim came to him and took from him a guarantee of safety. As for Sulayman, he went off to the desert of *Phoenicia* and sought to hide out there for a time. An Arab people in the desert called the Kalbites united with Sulayman and they journeyed to Palmyra, which is in their desert, east of Rusafa (tr. Hoyland 2011, 252–3).

56. al-Ṭabarī, *Tāʾrīkh*, 9.1892–3
When Marwān left for his residence in Ḥarrān after settling with the Syrian army, he had not been there more than three months before they openly opposed him and rebelled against him. The one who incited them to that was Thābit b. Nuʿaym, who sent them messengers and wrote them letters. Information about them reached Marwān, and he marched against them himself. The army of Ḥomṣ sent word to the Kalb who were at Tadmur, whereupon al-Aṣbagh b. Dhuʾālah al-Kalbī set off toward them accompanied by three of his sons, full grown men, Ḥamzah, Dhuʾālah and Furāfiṣah. Also accompanying him were Muʿāwiyah al-Saksakī, one of the Syrian cavalry, and ʿIṣmah b. al-Muqshaʿirr, Hishām b. Maṣād, Ṭufayl b. Ḥārithah and about a thousand horsemen of their tribe. They entered the city of Ḥomṣ on the night of the ʿId al-Fiṭr in 127 (tr. Williams 1985, 4–5).

57. Ibn ʿAsākir, *Tāʾrīkh*, 17.326
Dhuʾāla b. al-Aṣbagh b. Dhuʾāla al-Kalbī – One of the famous horsemen of Kalb. His father was among those who supported Yazīd b. al-Walīd al-Nāqiṣ ('The Deficient'). Then Dhuʾāla, Ḥamza, and Furāfiṣa, the sons of al-Aṣbagh, threw off allegiance to Marwān b. Muḥammad following a group from *al-Shām*, and went from Tadmur to Homs and took to their fortifications. Marwān approached and besieged them until he took [the city] by force. He killed Dhuʾāla, and crucified him on the gate of Homs.

58. al-Hamadānī, *al-Iklīl*, 124
Hishām b. Muḥammad al-Kalbī reported from al-Sharqī from Muḥammad b. Khālid b. ʿAbd Allāh al-Qasrī. He said, 'I was with Marwān b. Muḥammad'. He said, 'He demolished a side part of Tadmur. And behold, there, at the base of the walls, there was a long stone trough made of marble. A group of people gathered around it and raked

through the soil. Marwān thought there was a treasure there, but, instead, there was a woman lying on her back and upon her were 90 robes weaved with gold with one collar. She had long tresses of hair running from her head to her foot. Her foot was measured and it was a cubit in length. There was a sheet of gold among some of her tresses on which was written, "I am Tadmur b. Ḥassān b. Udhayna al-Malik. May God ruin the life of whoever destroys my home"'.

59. al-Ṭabarī, *Tā'rīkh*, 9.1895–6
He [Marwān] mobilised the army of Syria, strengthened it and placed one of the Syrian officers over each corps. He then ordered them to join Yazīd b. ʿUmar b. Hubayrah, whom he had sent ahead before his Syrian campaign with twenty thousand men of Qinnasrīn and the Jazīrah. He had ordered Yazid b. ʿUmar b. Hubayrah to camp at Dūrayn until he should come, thus establishing this force as his vanguard. Marwān left Dayr Ayyūb for Damascus when all of Syria except for Tadmur had been pacified. He ordered that Thābit b. Nuʿaym, his sons, and the group he had mutilated be brought forward. They were put to death and crucified on the gates of Damascus. Abū Hāshim reports, 'I saw them at the time they were slain and gibbeted'. He adds, 'Marwān spared one man among them, called ʿAmr b. al-Ḥārith al-Kalbī; it is claimed he had knowledge of the wealth which Thābit had deposited with certain kinsmen'. Then Marwān moved on with his men to camp at Qasṭal, in the territory of Ḥomṣ adjacent to that of Tadmur, the distance between them being three days march. Word reached him there that the enemy [i.e. the Kalb] had spoiled all the wells lying between him and Tadmur, filling them in with stones so he prepared waterskins, canteens, fodder, and camels to transport the provisions for him and his men. Al-Abrash b. al-Walīd, Sulaymān and other Umayyads interceded with him and asked that they (the Kalb) be excused, and that they make representations to them. He agreed to this and al-Abrash sent them his brother ʿAmr b. al-Walīd. Al-Abrash wrote them a letter urging caution and informing them that he feared they would be the death of him and all their kinsmen. They drove ʿAmr away, however, and did not comply. Al-Abrash now asked Marwān to let him go to them himself, and to give him a few days. This, Marwān did. Al-Abrash went to them, spoke to them, and put fear into them. He told them that they were stupid and that they could not withstand Marwān and his troops. Most of them agreed with this, while those who did not trust him fled into the desert lands of the Kalb. These were al Saksakī, ʿIṣmah b. al-Muqshaʿirr, Ṭufayl b. al-Ḥārithah, and Muʿāwiyah b. Abī Sufyān b. Yazīd b. Muʿāwiyah, who was the son in law of al-Abrash. Al-Abrash wrote to Marwān informing him of this, and Marwān wrote back to him, 'Tear down the walls of their city and come back to me with those who have given you their allegiance'. He therefore went back to Marwān with their chief men, al-Aṣbagh b. Dhuʿālah and his son Ḥamzah, and a number of others (tr. Williams 1985, 7–8).

60. Ibn al-Faqīh, *Mukhtaṣar*, 110
And when Marwān b. Muḥammad razed the walls of Tadmur, he reached a locked chamber with plastered walls. He opened it and there was woman lying on her back. Among some of her hair tresses, was a sheet of copper on which was written, "In your name, o God! I am Tadmur b. Ḥassān. May God impose humiliation upon whoever enter my home". Then he said, 'By God! Marwān only ruled for a few days after that before ʿAbd Allāh b. ʿAlī approached. He killed Marwān b. Muḥammad, routed his cavalry, and destroyed his army, so it was said that her prayer became true'. It is said that Sulaymān b. Dāwūd built the city of Tadmur. It was of marvellous construction, with many statues. It is said that he [Sulaymān] built there a palace in which there were wings, colonnades, chambers, arched hallways and other things. The roof of these chambers and enclosures and other [spaces] was a single stone by a single cut, and it is still standing until the present time. There is also a sculpture of two maidens, remaining of other statues that were there'.

61. Yāqūt, *Muʿjam*, 1.829
From Ismāʿīl b. Muḥammad b. Khālid b. ʿAbd Allāh al-Qasrī. He said, 'I was with Marwān b. Muḥammad, last of the caliphs of the Banū Umayya when he razed Tadmur's city wall after they rebelled against him. He killed them and scattered the cavalry among them to trample them when they were [already] dead. Their flesh and bones rose and were smashed among the hooves of the horses. Then he razed the city wall. The destruction revealed a great trench. They removed a boulder from it. A new plastered chamber was found there, which was as if a hand had just left it that moment. And there, in it, a couch was found. On this couch was a woman lying on her back. Upon her were 70 robes. She had seven taut hair tresses attached to her anklet'. He said, 'I measured her foot, and it was one cubit long without the toes. And there, among some of her hair tresses was a sheet of gold on which was written, "In your name, o God. I am Tadmur b. Ḥassān. May God bring humiliation upon anybody who enters my chamber". Then Marwān ordered to restore the trench. So the escarpment was put back as it was. He did not take anything from the adorments she was wearing'. He said: 'I swear to God that we did not stay but a few days before ʿAbd Allāh b. ʿAlī came and killed Marwān, scattered and destroyed his army, and put an end to his rule and that of his clan.

62. Theop., *Chr.*, 1.422
Sulayman gathered his armies and, after engaging Marwan once again, was defeated with the loss of 7000 men and escaped first to Palmyra then to Persia. Marwan killed

all the relatives and freedmen of Hisham (tr. Hoyland 2011, 258).

63. Agapius, *Kitāb*, 517–18
Then Sulaymān caught up with him [Marwān] and they engaged in battle; Sulaymān was defeated and 7000 of his men were killed. Sulaymān escaped and reached the desert of *Phoenicia* and went to Tadmur. Then, Marwān ordered the destruction of the estates of Hishām that were on the Euphrates and in other places.

64. Ibn ʿAsākir, *Tāʾrīkh*, 22.395
Sulaymān b. Hishām b. ʿAbd al-Malik b. Marwān b. al-Ḥakam b. Abī al-ʿĀṣ b. Umayya Abū Ayyūb [...]

His mother is Umm Ḥakīm b. Yaḥyā b. Abī al-ʿĀṣ. He consulted ʿAṭāʾ, al-Zuhrī, and Qatāda, and had some fine poetry. Al-Walīd b. Yazīd had imprisoned him at Amman after his father's death. When al-Walīd was killed, he left prison and joined Yazīd b. al-Walīd, who made him commander of some of his armies up until Marwān b. Muḥammad routed him at ʿAyn al-Jarr. Then he fled to Tadmur, sought a guarantee of safety from Marwān b. Muḥammad and pledged allegiance to him. Later, he threw off allegiance to him and about 70.000 men gathered to him, which made him covet the Caliphate. But Marwān sent an army against him. He defeated Sulaymān and went back to Homs.

65. *Chron. 1234*, 321–2
When Marwan heard that Dahhak the Harurite was besieging Nisibis and contending with his son ʿAbdallah, he set off to oppose him. Dahhak, hearing of the approach of Marwan, set off, leaving Nisibis, and marched towards Marwan. Sulayman b. Hisham was with him, for he had left Palmyra with many men of his household a few days before and come to Dahhak. So Dahhak came with Sulayman and pitched camp in the village of Tabiata, between the city of Dara and Kafartuta. Marwan arrived at both sides met nearby and joined the battle. On the first day of the battle many were killed on both sides, including Dahhak the Harurite (tr. Hoyland 2011, 262).

66. al-Muqaddasī, *Aḥsan*, 158–160
The district of Ḥomṣ. Its capital bears the same name. Among its cities are: Salamiyya, Tadmur, al-Khunāsira, Kafartāb, al-Lādhiqiyya, Jabala, Antarsūs, Bulunyās, Hisn al-Khawābī.

[...]

The other towns here [district of Ḥomṣ] are also going to ruin. Prices are moderate all over, and those towns on the coast are well fortified. Tadmur is in similar condition and it is, as it were, built on an elevated throne. It is one of the cities of Solomon, the son of David (tr. Collins 1994, 141, 144).

67. al-Masʿūdī, *Murūj*, 1.190
... the city of Tadmur, which is located in the steppe between Iraq and Syria ...

68. al-Masʿūdī, *Murūj*, 4.77–8
The city of Tadmur is in the steppe between Iraq, Damascus and Homs of Syria. It is located roughly five or six days march from Syria. The city is of marvellous construction, made using stone and so is the vast open space in it. Some bedouins from Qaḥṭān, lives there.

69. al-*Dimashqī, Kitāb*, 39
One of the ancient marvelous constructions is that of Tadmur, with its columns and walls, its monuments and mounds, which has no parallels in length, height and quantity and also the absence of the quarry from which it was built. In its built up area is the mosque, which is sheltered by five stones and four walls. Its width is 12 cubits, and so is the length. The height of the walls is seven cubits.

70. Ṣafī al-Dīn, *Marāṣid*, 1.200
Tadmur (with a *fataḥ*, then a *sukūn*, and a *ḍam* following the letter *mīm*) is a famous ancient city in the Syrian desert. It is situated five days march from Aleppo, and it is close to Homs. One of its marvellous buildings was built on columns of marble. The people of Tadmur claim that it was built even before Sulaymān b. Dāwūd. At present, its people live in its fortress, which has a stone wall. Its gate has two stone door panels. It also has towers that remains to the present. They have a river that irrigates their palm trees and gardens.

71. Yāqūt, *Muʿjam*, 1.828–9
Tadmur (with a *fataḥ*, then a *sukūn* and a *ḍam* following the letter *mīm*) is a famous ancient city in the Syrian desert. It is situated five days march from Aleppo. Ptolemy said that the city of Tadmur's longitude is 71° and 30' in the fourth 'clime' ... It is said that it was named after Tadmur b. Ḥassān b. Udhayna b. al-Summaydaʿ b. Mazyad b. ʿAmlīq b. Laūdh b. Sām b. Nūḥ, may peace be upon her! It was among the marvelous and wonder cities [lit. buildings]; [its buildings] were built on marble columns. It is alleged that it was among the construtions of the *jinns* made for Sulaymān, may peace be upon him!

[...]

The people of Tadmur claim that [its] construction was even before Sulaymān b. Dāwud, may peace be upon him, in a period longer than that between Sulaymān and us. However, when the people see an extraordinary building and ignore who built it, they used to ascribe it to Sulaymān and to the *jinns*.

72. Yāqūt, *Muʿjam*, 1.829
And among the statues [lit. images] found in Tadmur was a stone relief of two maidens, remaining of other statues that were there.

Index